AN INTRODUCTION TO
SPANISH–AMERICAN LITERATURE

AN INTRODUCTION TO
SPANISH-
AMERICAN
LITERATURE

JEAN FRANCO

Professor of Spanish and Portuguese
Stanford University, California

CAMBRIDGE UNIVERSITY PRESS

Published by the Syndics of the Cambridge University Press
Bentley House, 200 Euston Road, London NW1 2DB
American Branch: 32 East 57th Street, New York, N.Y.10022

© Cambridge University Press 1969

Library of Congress Catalogue Card Number: 69-12927

ISBNS: 0 521 07374 X   hard covers
       0 521 09891 2   paperback

First published 1969
Reprinted 1971
First paperback edition 1975

First printed in Great Britain by
Alden & Mowbray Ltd at the Alden Press, Oxford
Reprinted in Great Britain
at the University Printing House, Cambridge
(Brooke Crutchley, University Printer)

CONTENTS

FOREWORD

Travel, films and translation are just beginning to make Spanish America and its writers familiar outside the continent. The spectacle of the landscape, the faces of the peoples are no longer strange; a few names—those of the poets Neruda and Vallejo, for instance—are widely known. And yet outside the bright circle of the familiar, there are deep shadows of ignorance. We still understand all too little about the past of Spanish America. Its history, social structure and literature are not yet so intimate a part of people's general knowledge that we can take them for granted. That is why this *Introduction to Spanish–American Literature* must embrace so much more than creative writing. No doubt it would be superfluous to introduce the flat landscape of Holland into an account of Dutch literature, but we can hardly keep the pampa, mountains and jungles out of a book on Spanish–American literature. Nor can historical events, such as Independence or the Mexican Revolution, be regarded simply as 'background'. History, geography, sociology are just as much a part of the study of this literature as poetic technique or novelistic structure.

There are nineteen Spanish-speaking countries in America. Most of them gained their independence from Spain and were proclaimed republics in the 1820s. Since that date, their history has taken separate paths and each country has developed its own literature, often as a conscious national project. Many critics believe, with some justice, that Spanish–American literature can only be studied as separate national literatures. Yet, because the nineteen countries once formed part of the Spanish colonial empire, because they share a language and a literary heritage, there are common patterns of development which cut across national frontiers. And there are also certain perennial concerns shared by all Spanish–American writers since colonial times. One of these is the problem of interpreting and understanding this vast, strange continent, in a language that was forged in Europe and was therefore, in its origins at least, alien to American experience. No less a person than Cortés was the first to recognise this difficulty when, in a letter addressed to the Emperor Charles V, he wrote of Mexico, 'Because I do not know the names of things, I cannot express them.' 'Naming' the American continent has since become a major aspect of Spanish–American literature and is the central preoccupation even today of a poet such as Neruda.

Another of these major concerns is that of understanding and integrating the different races of the continent and their cultures, for though we talk of *Spanish* America, both the Indian and the Negro still have an important influence on certain areas of literature. Allied to this preoccupation, there is the conflict which runs through the whole history of this culture, between the claims of the indigenous or exclusively American and the European. Writers often tend to keep a foot in both camps. They are uniquely well-read in European and (nowadays) in North American literature and, at the same time, they have a sense of mission with regard to native forms of culture. Thus the tension between cosmopolitanism and indigenism, universalism and regionalism recurs time and time again.

The existence of common characteristics as well as national differences make it difficult for the student and the scholar to strike a balance between inaccurate generalisation and narrow provincialism. It is hoped that the present study provides an acceptable compromise by studying general tendencies and referring these to a national context. For this reason, too, substantial quotations are given and where possible whole poems are quoted. Spanish–American literature, after all, means nothing without this primary material. Indeed this introduction can be regarded as a gloss on the texts themselves, which tell their own dramatic story.

London, 1968   J.F.

ACKNOWLEDGEMENTS

Thanks are due to the following for permission to quote copyright material: Margarita Aguilar de Chocano, for 'Ciudad dormida' and 'Las punas' by José Santos Chocano, from *Poesías completas*; Claridad, for 'El canto del mal' and 'La noche' by Ricardo Jaimes Freyre, from *Poesías completas*; the following are reprinted by permission of Doris Dana, copyright 1924 by Gabriela Mistral: 'La manca' and 'La fresa' by Gabriela Mistral; Fondo de cultura económica, for 'Nocturno de la estatua' by Xavier Villaurrutia, and for 'Espejo' and an extract from '¿No hay salida?' by Octavio Paz, from *Libertad bajo palabra*; Imprenta-Universitaria, for "Segundo sueño" by Ortiz de Montellano; Francisco Moncloa Editores, for "Me da miedo ese chorro" (*Trilce*), 'Agape' (*Los heraldos negros*), 'Paris, Octubre 1936' (*Poemas humanos*), and "Miré el cadáver" (*España, aparta de mí este cáliz*) by César Vallejo, from *Poesías completas*; Editorial Porrúa, for 'Mi prima Agueda' by Ramón López Velarde, from *Poesías completas*.

INTRODUCTION

THE CONQUEST

The Spanish conquest of Central and South America, accomplished with surprising speed and facility, brought a vast new territory and its hitherto unknown inhabitants into the European field of vision. The event not only broadened men's horizons but was to have incalculable repercussions on the European mind, opening up new problems of law and politics, feeding men's imaginations with visions of Utopia and raising entirely fresh problems to challenge notions of geography and natural history. The impact of Europe on the native inhabitants of America was even greater. The shock at the first sight of horses and guns was as nothing compared to the trauma that followed the defeat of the old gods, the conquest and murder of Indian emperors and the enslavement of peoples. Nowadays, we are perhaps better qualified to understand the psychological shock that resulted from the confrontation of races with totally conflicting attitudes than were the participants. The Indians that the Spaniards conquered ranged from primitive nomadic tribes such as the Pampas to members of highly-developed cultures like those of the Incas in the Andes, the Aztecs of Mexico and the Mayas of Central America.

But even these highly-civilised communities were not at all on the same wave-length as the Spaniards. Their culture, technology and social organisation were based on nature-religions. The Incas worshipped the sun; the Aztecs sacrificed human hearts to keep the sun on its course. Nature and natural laws ruled men's lives. Nor did human beings have much sense of their apartness from nature or their own individuality. Existence was not seen as the realisation of a personal goal but as an ephemeral gift of the gods who were themselves the personification of facets of nature and must be continually placated. Hence, there was little to prepare the Indians for the coming of men who preached the Christian doctrine of personal salvation and believed that man had a privileged position in the natural hierarchy. Not only this: the Spaniards also combined a strong sense of their own individual worth with a sense of national mission. They were the agents of the Catholic kings, and their own achievements redounded to the glory of the nation. Riches and fame were the expected recompense for service. Not for nothing did Cortés compare his men to Roman soldiers in order to encourage them during the advance on Mexico. The confident spirit of the conquerors and their impatience with obstacles—natural or human —is, indeed, well illustrated in the following description of Cortés and his reactions when lost in the almost impenetrable jungles of Central America:

No hallábamos camino ninguno y hubimos de abrirle con las espadas a manos, y anduvimos dos días por el camino que abríamos creyendo que iba derecho al pueblo y una mañana tornamos al mismo camino que abríamos. Y cuando Cortés lo vio, quería reventar de enojo...Pues otra cosa había, que eran los montes muy altos en demasía y espesos, y a mala vez podíamos ver el cielo. Pues ya que quisiesen subir en algunos de los árboles para atalayar la tierra no veían cosa ninguna, según eran muy cerradas todas las montañas y las guías que traíamos las dos se huyeron, y otra que quedaba estaba malo que no sabía dar razón de camino ni de otra cosa. Y como Cortés en todo era diligente, y por falta de solicitud no se descuidaba, traíamos una aguja de marear, y a un piloto que decía Pedro López, y con el dibujo de paño que traía de Guazacualco, donde venían señalados los pueblos, mandó que fuésemos con la aguja por los montes, y con las espadas abríamos camino hacia el Este, que era la señal del paño donde estaba el pueblo.*[1]

Notice Cortés's reaction to the jungle (the passage refers to a part of Central America that is still almost impassable today). He simply sees the trees and the natural environment as an infuriating barrier— 'quería reventar de enojo' [he was like to have burst with anger]; and, as the passage goes on to reveal, he shows considerable drive and resourcefulness in escaping from this difficult situation. Mere jungle was not going to stop Cortés. From what we can glean from

---

* We found no pathway and had to make one with our swords, and we marched for two days along the path we made, believing that it led straight to the village and one morning, we found ourselves back on the same path that we had made. And when Cortés saw this, he was like to have burst with anger...And another thing was that the hills were high in the extreme and thickly-wooded and we could hardly see the sky. And even when they tried to climb some of the trees to spy over the land, they saw nothing, the mountains being so impenetrable; and of the guides we had brought, two fled and the one who remained was so bad that he could not show us the road nor explain anything. And as Cortés was diligent in everything and never allowed himself to be caught unprepared, we had a compass with us and with the drawing on the cloth which he brought from Guazacualco on which were marked the villages, and with a pilot called Pedro López, he sent us through the mountains with the compass and, with our swords, we cut a way to the east which, according to the map, was the direction of the village.

Indian accounts of the conquest and the Spanish regime, we realise that this was precisely the attitude that the Indian found most difficult to understand. He did not regard nature as something which had to be conquered and overcome, but as an intimate part of life. The Maya Indian buried his new-born child's umbilical cord and the placenta in the earth; his myths told him that man had been fashioned out of maize and he believed also that every man's soul had its double, incarnate in animal form. An anonymous Indian, writing after the conquest, tells us quite clearly that hatred of the Spaniards had its origin in their disrespect for natural and human life.

Ellos enseñaron el miedo; y vinieron a marchitar las flores. Para que su flor viviese, dañaran y sorbieron la flor de los otros... No había Alto Conocimiento, no había Sagrado Lenguaje, no había Divina Enseñanza en los sustitutos de los Dioses que llegaron aquí. ¡Castrar el Sol! Eso vinieron a hacer aquí los extranjeros!*[1]

Hence the tragic paradox that while for the Spaniard the conquest represented the possibility of Utopia, for the Indian it was the end of an era to which he would eventually look back as if to a Golden Age:

No había entonces pecado. Había santa devoción en ellos. Saludables vivian. No había entonces enfermedad; no había viruelas, no había ardor de pecho, no había dolor de vientre, no había consunción. Rectamente erguido iba su cuerpo, entonces.†[2]

The Indian belief that the Spaniard had shattered a paradise was not confined to Yucatán where this passage was written, but was also held in Peru. Here, Poma de Ayala, an Indian who wrote a history of pre-conquest civilisations in the sixteenth century, described pre-conquest society in glowing terms:

No se matan, ni se roban, no se echan maldiciones, ni se hacen ofensas en contra de Dios. No se dejan dominar por la lujuria, envidia, avaricia o gula, soberbia, decidia o pereza. No son mentirosos. Practican la caridad, la misericordia y la limosna.

Si bien es cierto que pelean y mueren por defenderse y por defender sus tierras, lo hacen siempre como hombres y no como fieras. No se emborrachan ni quitan

---

* They taught us fear and withered the flowers. In order that their flower might live, they hurt and consumed the flower of others. There was no Higher Knowledge, no Sacred Language, no Divine Teaching in the substitutes for Gods which came here. Castrate the sun! That is what the foreigners came to do here!

† In those days, there was no sin. There was holy devotion in them and they lived in health. There was no sickness in those days; no smallpox, no heartburn, no stomach pains, there was no consumption. They carried their bodies erect in those days.

sus haciendas; y habrían sido hombres santos estos indios si hubieran conocido la religión de Cristo.*[1]

We may be sure that the pointed statement 'No se emborrachan ni quitan sus haciendas' [They never get drunk nor leave their lands] was directed against the Spanish overlords.

The contrast between the Spanish vision of Utopia in the future and the Indian hankering after a Golden Age of the past is certainly a striking one. Most interesting of all is the way that the two visions recur down to modern times, thus indicating the depth and persistence of the attitudes engendered by the conquest.

Very close on Cortés's arrival in Mexico in 1519, there appeared a group of Franciscan friars who began the work of converting the Indians to Christianity. They found that the ground had already been prepared by the zealous soldiers of the conquest forces who had brought down the heathen gods from their altars. The arrival of the friars now made it possible to erect churches and convents on the ruins of old temples. Schools were established for teaching Spanish and Christian doctrine; soon afterwards a printing press was installed in the city of Mexico, the more speedily to produce pious tracts and grammars for helping the missionaries. Many friars became experts in Indian tongues and came to admire the quicknesss and intelligence of their converts. But, despite this missionary project of unparalleled scope, the conversion of the Indian remained far from complete, and this for several reasons. In the first place, as we have already observed, some aspects of Indian belief proved hard to eradicate; and secondly, and perhaps more important, the organisation of the Spanish Empire allowed the survival in remoter regions of Indian languages, customs and beliefs. This came about because Spanish administration was based on the town; one of the main economic activities of the Spanish Empire— mining—encouraged the growth of urban centres. Hence the wealthy creole (white American-born) élite[2] were concentrated in urban communities. Beyond these towns lay the vast expanses of the countryside, the more fertile parts of which were divided into big estates worked

---

* They do not kill, they do not rob, they do not curse, they do not offend God. They are not overcome by lust, envy, avarice, greed, pride, apathy or laziness. They are not liars. They practice charity, mercy and give alms.

  While it is certain that they fight and die to defend themselves and their lands, they always do it as men and not as animals. They never get drunk nor leave their lands; and had they known the religion of Christ, these Indians would have been holy men.

on a feudal system, often by Indian labour. The further these estates lay from government centres, the fewer contacts there were between the Indian and the Spanish officials. In distant places, only a priest and a bailiff—and perhaps not even these—were there as representatives of a non-indigenous culture. Hence the phenomenon which marks Spanish–American society and culture down to the present—the sharp division between the sophistication of the city and the backwardness and cultural conservatism of the rural areas, a division which, while it had some unfortunate consequences, has also helped to preserve something of Indian culture. In Peru, Bolivia, Ecuador, Guatemala and Mexico, there are areas in which Indian languages are still spoken, in which dress, costume, arts and crafts, music, poetry and legend survive from pre-Columbian times and where Christianity has been grafted on to older beliefs. The villages are reservoirs of the past. And this is true, not only of Indian villages but also of remote mestizo[1] and creole communities which have preserved the folk-lore of the *conquistadores* and hence of the European Middle Ages. These survivals of Indian culture and of folk-lore are so important that no history of Spanish–American literature would be quite complete without reference to them, especially as they represented underground currents which have come to the surface in modern times.

SURVIVALS OF INDIAN CULTURE

Indian literature of the colonial period falls into two main categories— records of pre-Columbian literature written down after the conquest, either by Spaniards or Indians, as a means of preserving the record of ancient beliefs; secondly, literature created by Indians during the colonial period.

Much of the pre-Columbian literature which survived into post-conquest times was collected by friars, of whom the most outstanding was the learned Franciscan, Bernadino de Sahagún (1500–70). Sahagún arrived in Mexico only ten years after Cortés had landed there; yet, by 1529, the year of his arrival, Indian culture already seemed doomed; records, temples and images having been destroyed on a huge scale. This remarkable man—who was not unique, for there were other equally enlightened friars—at once understood that no conversion of the Indians which was not based on an understanding of their religion could really succeed. He therefore learned the Indian language, Náhuatl, and employed a team of Indian scribes to write down in Latin script and in the native tongue all the information they could collect about Indian religion and rite. With their aid, he compiled a twelve-volume collection of information and, between 1570 and 1580, at the request of the *Consejo de las Indias* (the supreme legislative body which looked after the affairs of the New World), he wrote a *Historia general de las cosas de la Nueva España* in Spanish, based on the material in Náhuatl. Sahagún's Spanish work was destined to remain unpublished for 200 years after his death, while the original Náhuatl material has only been partially explored by modern scholars. These works form the main source for a knowledge of Náhuatl literature, together with a collection of ceremonial speeches which were written down by Sahagún's mentor, Fray Andrés de Olmos (?–1571), and the information collected by Sahagún's own disciples.

Some Maya literature has also survived thanks to the work of priests. The most important example is the *Popol Vuh* (often called the Maya Bible), which is a collection of creation-myths, stories of Gods and heroes, and historical records which were written down in the Quiché language some time after the conquest and discovered in the eighteenth century by the parish priest of Chichecastenango, in Guatemala. This priest, Padre Ximénez, copied the Quiché original and made a Spanish translation after which all trace of the manuscript he copied from was lost. The *Rabinal Achi*, a dance drama which continued to be performed after the conquest was also written down by a priest. In addition to these Maya works, many prophetic books have been discovered in Yucatán. Known collectively as the books of *Chilam Balam*, only four of these have been thoroughly studied. Like the *Popol Vuh*, they were written down after the conquest.

The third great pre-Columbian civilisation of Latin America— that of the Incas—had no written literature but, as in pre-Columbian Mexico, poetry flourished. A tradition of oral transmission meant that such poetry was remembered and recited even after the arrival of the Spaniards. The Inca, Garcilaso de la Vega, a sixteenth-century mestizo (mixed Spanish and Indian) recorded some of their poetry in his *Comentarios Reales* [*Royal Commentaries*]; and legends and songs of Inca times were also written down by the Indian Felipe Guamán Poma de Ayala in his *Nueva corónica y buen gobierno*, a nostalgic record of the glories of the Inca empire written in the sixteenth century. Though much of the literature in Quechua (the indigenous language of Peru) disappeared after the conquest, something of its nature can be judged from the fragments which survive in such chronicles as those mentioned above and in folk literature.

Pre-Columbian literature, then, owes its survival to chance. Yet enough remains for us to realise the impressive ritual drama and lyrical poetry created by these civilisations. In Mexico, and in Peru, indeed, poetry was one of the noblest of arts and in the former it was practised by princes, such as the princes of Tezcoco, Netzahualcoyotl and his son Nezahualpilli. Spanish translations of Náhuatl lyrics, however approximate, give us some idea of the scope of this poetry, which frequently dealt with man's eternal anguish when faced with the inevitability of death, and the ephemeral nature of life and happiness:

> ¿He de irme como las flores que perecieron?
> ¿Nada quedará de mi nombre?
> ¿Nada de mi fama aquí en la tierra?
> Al menos mis flores, al menos mis cantos
> Aquí en la tierra es la región del momento fugaz.
> ¿También es así en el lugar
> donde de algún modo se vive?
> ¿Hay allá alegría, hay amistad?
> ¿Oh solo aqui en la tierra
> hemos venido a conocer nuestros rostros?*[1]

Though this poem uses many traditional images ('flores'—flowers—for example), the modern reader can still share the feeling of anguish and apprehension with which the poet views the prospect of an afterlife and his longing to leave some remembrance of his passage through earthly existence. Poetry gave man a way of escape from the limitations of his condition, both because his poetry might survive him, but also, as the following lines show, because it was divinely inspired:

> Del interior del cielo vienen
> las bellas flores, los bellos cantos
> Los afea nuestro anhelo
> nuestra inventiva los echa a perder.†[2]

Equally delicate and allusive poems were written in Quechua in pre-Columbian Peru and many love lyrics and religious poems are still capable of moving a modern reader. The following poem is about the transience of life and the poet has used images of rain and the feather in the wind to express man's aimlessness and helplessness.

---

* Must I vanish like the flowers that perish? Will nothing remain of my name? Nothing of my fame here on earth? My flowers, my songs at least may remain. Here on earth we are in the land of fleeting moments. Is it like that in the place where in some manner we live on? Is there happiness and friendship there? Or is this earth the only place in which we know our own faces?

† From inside the heavens come beautiful flowers and songs. Our will spoils them, our skill ruins them.

Me dio el ser mi madre
¡Ay!
entre una nube de lluvia
¡Ay!
semejante a la lluvia para llorar
¡Ay!
semejante a la lluvia para girar
¡Ay!
para andar de puerta en puerta
¡Ay!
como la pluma en el aire.*

The literature of the Aztecs and Incas would only survive with difficulty after the conquest, for the civilisation and religion of which it was part were destroyed. Yet, as we have seen, some poems and prayers were preserved in records; and myths and stories were remembered and told in isolated communities, so that the Indians retained a sense of identity in defeat. Music and song in native tongues were sometimes incorporated into church festivals, though church decrees in Peru repeatedly forbade such practices and ordered Indian musical instruments to be destroyed. Yet lyrics in Quechua continued to be composed and there is even a drama, *Ollantay*, which is extant and which was apparently recast in the eighteenth century in Quechua from both pre-Columbian and Hispanic sources.

The colonial authorities must have looked with disfavour on the continuance of such literature and music. In the Andean areas this suspicion hardened after 1781, in which year there was a major Indian uprising. The suppression of the revolt was followed by rigorous measures against dramas and festivities in Quechua and the distribution of the Inca Garcilaso's history of pre-conquest Peru, the *Comentarios Reales*, was forbidden. The measures probably curtailed activities in the Indian language but they did not entirely bring them to an end, for Indian song and ballad-writing persists in the Andes wherever the Indian language is spoken.

In one area alone of the Spanish colonial empire was an Indian language continuously used as the means of communication between Spaniard and Indian, and this was in the Jesuit missions of Paraguay where the doctrine was taught in Guaraní. After the expulsion of the Jesuits in the eighteenth century, Guaraní continued as the language of the

---

* My mother gave me life, woe is me! from a cloud of rain, woe is me! weeping like the rain, woe is me! whirling like the rain, woe is me! going from door to door, woe is me! like a feather in the wind.

rural areas and was even spoken by mestizos, a situation that remains unchanged in modern Paraguay.

THE RURAL AREAS

Just as Indian literature cannot be ignored if we wish to have a balanced picture of the colonial period, so the literature of the rural areas must not be forgotten. The social structure of the Spanish colonial Empire was such that there were great differences between the towns and the remoter rural districts. While the inhabitants of Mexico City and Lima looked to Spain as their guide, in distant mountains or pampa, communities existed with only infrequent contact with a world outside America. In such areas, ancient forms of literature which had their roots in mediaeval Europe survived and were adapted to suit the conditions of the New World. In the Argentine pampa, for instance (colonised late in the sixteenth century), isolated ranches with a predominantly male population of gauchos (akin to cowboys) became the centres for roundups and rodeos—occasions which were propitious for the growth of a literature of story and ballad which emphasised the courage and independence of the male, and his skill as a horseman and fighter. The improvised ballad celebrating the exploits of the gaucho became a popular genre which flourished down to the nineteenth century. Even the twentieth-century novel of gaucho life, *Don Segundo Sombra*, included two folk-tales which must in their original form have been brought over by the conquerors and early settlers and which were mediaeval in origin. A similar tradition of folk-ballad exists in Venezuela and Mexico, in both of which countries there were large cattle estates.

LITERATURE IN THE COLONIAL PERIOD

We should be mistaken if we thought of the *conquistadores* as rough soldiers with no taste for literature. Even if they had little use for reading, they loved stories and their minds were filled with legends, some of which they had brought from Europe, some of which they found in America—legends such as those of the Fountains of Youth, the Seven Enchanted Cities, the myth of El Dorado [or *The Golden Man*]. Those who enjoyed reading had a wealth of popular literature at their disposal. The novels of chivalry were at the height of their popularity during the conquest period and these offered to the avid imagination a fantasy literature of monsters and supermen who killed giants and underwent incredible ordeals. Their imaginations fed by such stories, it is little wonder that the conquerors were conscious of their own glorious destinies. Their thirst for wealth was equalled by their thirst for fame and this latter perhaps accounts for the large number of records and histories of the conquest, since many of these were written to commemorate the historical importance of the events in which the authors had played their part. Beginning with the log-book of Columbus and the *Cartas de relación* which Hernán Cortés addressed to Charles V, first-hand accounts and histories of every stage of the conquest poured out. The most vivid of these records is the *Historia verdadera de la conquista de la Nueva España* [*The True History of the conquest of New Spain*] by a soldier of Cortés, Bernal Díaz del Castillo (1494–1585), a remarkable testimony to the author's powers of total recall. It was written, according to his confession, when he was 'más de ochenta y cuatro años' [more than eighty-four years old]; realising the faults and errors of López de Gómara's official *Historia general de las Indias*, he decided to tell what he regarded as the true story, 'muy llanamente, sin torcer a una parte ni a otra' [in a very straightforward manner, without distorting it one way or another]. Despite his age and his distance from the events he describes, the account has a freshness and vigour as if it had been written on the spot. Age had not dimmed his own wonder at the events he lived through:

Muchas veces, ahora que soy viejo, me paro a considerar las cosas heroicas que en aquel tiempo pasamos, que me parece las veo presentes y digo que nuestros hechos que no los hacíamos nosotros, sino que venían todos encaminados por Dios; porque, ¿qué hombres ha habido en el mundo que osasen entrar cuatro-cientos soldados (y aun no llegábamos a ellos), en una fuerte ciudad como es México, que es mayor que Venecia, estando apartados de nuestra Castilla sobre más de mil quinientas leguas, y prender a un tan gran señor y hacer justicia de sus capitanes delante de él?*[1]

This wonder at the drama of the conquest gave him a sure touch in his treatment of episodes which have entered into the mythology of Mexico; it is through his account that the main protagonists of the conquest—Cortés, his mistress, doña Marina, Pedro de Alvarado, Moctezuma—have become familiar. The reason for his success as a

---

* Oftentimes now that I am an old man, I stop to consider the heroic things that we went through at that time and I seem to see them before my eyes; and I say that our deeds were not done by us but we were all directed by God. For what men have there been in the world who dared, though they were only four hundred soldiers (and not even that many) to enter a strong city as Mexico is which is larger than Venice and one which is more than one thousand five hundred leagues distant from our Castile; and dared also to take captive so great a lord and sentence his captains before his very eyes?

chronicler can be judged from the description of Moctezuma as he meets Cortés for the first time:

Ya que llegábamos cerca de México, adonde estaban otras torrecillas, se apeó el gran Montezuma de las andas, y traíanle de brazo aquellos grandes caciques, debajo de un palio muy riquísimo a maravilla, y el color de plumas verdes con grandes labores de oro, con mucha argentería y perlas y piedras *chalchiuis*, que colgaban de unas como bordaduras, que hubo mucho que mirar en ello. Y el gran Montezuma venía muy ricamente ataviado, según su usanza, y traía calzados unos como *cotaras*, que así se dice lo que se calzan; las suelas de oro y muy preciada pedrería por encima en ellas; y los cuatro señores que le traían de brazo venían con rica manera de vestidos a su usanza... *[1]

It is the meticulous, detailed observation of clothing and jewelry which helps us to appreciate the magnificence and drama of the occasion. No other chronicle of the conquest equals that of Bernal Díaz del Castillo, although there are many exciting and interesting records. Pedro Cieza de León (1520 or 22–60) wrote an account of the conquest of Peru during the campaign.[2] Agustín de Zárate (?–1560) wrote a *Historia del descubrimiento y conquista del Perú* (1555). Gonzalo Jiménez de Quesada (1499–1579) chronicled the discovery and conquest of New Granada (now Colombia) and the strange story of the first descent of the river Amazon was recounted in the *Relación del nuevo descubrimiento del famoso río Grande de las Amazonas* [*The Relation of the New Discovery of the Famous Great River of the Amazons*] by Fray Gaspar de Carvajal (1504–84).

Many records of the conquest were written with one aim in mind— that of persuading the authorities to give due recompense for services. But the conquest was also rich in what one would now call the 'personal interest' story, and two of these are of unusual significance. The *Naufragios* [*Shipwrecks*] of Alvar Núñez Cabeza de Vaca (1490?–1559) is the story of a Spaniard who was shipwrecked about 1527 off the coast of Texas and who spent seven years living with the nomadic tribes of North America, sharing their way of life and covering immense distances with them. Cabeza de Vaca did not lose his Christian identity, but the fact that he was able to adapt himself to this alien way of life

---

* As we had arrived near Mexico where there were other small towers, the great Montezuma descended from his litter and those great lords bore him on their arms beneath a most rich and marvellous panoply and there was much to marvel at in the colour of the green plumes with much gold work and much silver work and work in pearls and stones called *chalchiuis* which hung down like embroideries. And the great Montezuma was dressed very richly according to his fashion and wore on his feet *cotaras* which is their name for shoes, the soles being of gold and very precious stones on them; and the four lords who bore him on their arms were dressed richly according to their fashion.

shows that he was possessed of unusual personality and was remarkably free of prejudice and preconceived ideas. Indeed he reveals something of a modern scientific spirit in this account of the Indians' power of resistance:

Muchas veces se pasan de parte a parte con las flechas y no mueren de las heridas si no tocan en las tripas o en el corazón: antes sanan presto. Ven y oyen más y tienen más agudo sentido que cuantos hombres yo creo que hay en el mundo. Son grandes sufridores de hambre y de sed y de frío, como aquellos que están más acostumbrados y hechos a ello que otros. Esto he querido contar porque allende que todos los hombres desean saber las costumbres y ejercicios de los otros, los que algunas veces se vinieren a ver con ellos estén avisados de sus costumbres y ardides, que suelen no poco aprovechar en semejantes casos.*

A century later, in 1629, another Spaniard was held captive by the fierce Araucanian Indians of Chile. This was Francisco Núñez de Pineda y Bascuñán (1607–82), son of an eminent *conquistador*. His *Cautiverio feliz* [*Happy Captivity*] told the story of his captivity and attempted a true account of the lives and beliefs of his captors. A true Christian, Núñez de Pineda y Bascuñán was genuinely disturbed by the attitude of some of his fellow Spaniards towards the Indians and was at pains to attack the myth of Indian cruelty and treachery so carefully encouraged, he declared, by those who have no personal contact with the Indians themselves.

The chronicling of the new and strange reality of America gradually gave way to historical and geographical studies as Spanish priests and missionaries attempted to fit new flora, fauna and different human societies into their existing scheme of things.

THE UNIVERSALISATION OF AMERICAN EXPERIENCE

By 1540, the Indies were divided into two huge administrative zones— the Viceroyalties of Peru and New Spain (with its capital in Mexico). An administrative machinery came into being with the *Consejo de las Indias* [Council of the Indies] which had its seat in Seville, as the supreme executive body. Church and State combined to bring the New

---

* Often the arrows go right through their bodies and they do not die of the wounds unless these touch the entrails or the heart, rather they heal quickly. They see and hear more and have more acute senses than any other men in the world, I believe. They have great resistance to hunger, thirst and cold as they are more accustomed and adapted to these than others. This I have wished to recount because apart from the fact that men wish to know the customs and habits of others, those who come upon them may now be warned of their manners and wiles and in such cases this is of great usefulness.

World into the structure of Hispanic society. Like a boa constrictor swallowing its prey, the Spanish State seized the New World and then had to digest it. The digestion proved a long and difficult process and transformed Spain almost as much as it did the American continent.

We must bear in mind, that from the very first America proved disconcerting to the men who set foot on her soil. Stimulated by tales of giants, pygmies, dragons, griffins and all kinds of monsters, the Spaniards found the inhabitants of America too similar in form to Europeans and yet too different in outlook. There was a disparity between expectation and reality, a disparity which sometimes forced the conquerors to modify their own *a priori* ideas, sometimes allowed them to fit new phenomena into the categories they were familiar with. One example of this was their attitude to the conversion of the Indians —for conversion meant accepting the Indians, theoretically at least, into the category of human beings and rejecting forever the notion that the Indians were monsters or of some inferior species. Hence the importance attached to questions of baptism and conversion throughout the sixteenth century, questions which were no mere academic exercise. The views of authorities, existing practices and theories had to be adjusted to meet new needs. At the same time, conversion was not only seen as necessary on religious grounds but was the handmaid of government, as Bartolomé de las Casas (1474–1565) pointed out:

Así mismo darse amaño para que bayan allá muchos frayles franciscos y dominicos por que ayudarán mucho a los obispos a asegurar toda aquella tierra porque más suele allá asegurar un frayle que doscientos ombres de armas y todos serbirán mucho a V. al. digo estos religiosos con los Obispos.*[1]

A friar was thus worth 200 men of arms in the work of pacification. Yet this utilitarian approach should not blind us to the fact that conversion and the consequent recognition of the humanity of the Indian and his membership in the universal brotherhood of Christ, was the first step in raising him from the status of slave and beast of burden. Economically it would have been more convenient for the estates to have had a labour supply which could have been treated as domestic animals. It is to the credit of the Spanish Empire that a body of enlightened missionaries, headed by Fray Bartolomé de las Casas, brought

---

* So procure that many Franciscan and Dominican friars go there for they are of great help to the bishops in securing all that land for in that region a friar usually secures more than two hundred men at arms and these friars with these bishops will serve your Excellency greatly.

the issue of whether the Indian should be treated as a potential Christian or as a natural slave into the open and had it publicly debated in Valladolid between 1550 and 1551. Las Casas's contention that the Indians were rational beings who were to be converted by peaceful means triumphed, an event which had important theoretical implications even where it was not carried out in practice.

The very existence of great heathen empires in the Americas taxed the imagination of Westerners, for not only had their inhabitants to be brought into the Catholic Church but these civilisations with their different pasts and their different dynasties had to be brought into Western history. The usual view of the churchmen was simply to regard the Indian past as a time of idolatry and error from which the providential arrival of the Spaniards had rescued them. This is the spirit, for instance, which informs the *Historia de los indios de Nueva España* [*History of the Indians of New Spain*] by one of the most vigorous and sympathetic of the early missionaries, Fray Toribio de Benavente, 'Motolinía' (?–1569). It was, however, left to a mestizo to make a more sophisticated approach to pre-Columbian history and to find connecting links which could bind the development of American civilisations to those of Europe. This mestizo was the Inca Garcilaso de la Vega, author of a history and a description of Inca civilisation, known as the *Comentarios Reales* [*Royal Commentaries*]. Born in 1539, in the ancient Peruvian city of Cuzco, he was the son of a Spanish captain and an Inca lady of royal blood. In 1560, he arrived in Spain, a civilised and talented young man who, in 1590, was to publish a translation from the Italian of León Hebreo's 'Dialoghi d'Amore' (a well-known sixteenth-century neo-Platonic essay on love), thus establishing his reputation as a humanist in touch with the most advanced currents of ideas. He first used the name Inca Garcilaso de la Vega on the title-page of the translation, and so deliberately drew attention to his dual descent. Conscious of this he must have been, for in a country in which *limpieza de sangre* [pure blood] was of such importance, the illegitimate, mestizo and American-born Garcilaso was, in every way, an outsider. At the same time these very characteristics made him uniquely suited to the task of relating Inca civilisation to the great cultures of the West, a task which he undertook in his *Comentarios Reales*. In his account of Andean history before the arrival of the Spaniards, he compared Inca civilisation with the greatest of Western societies and cultures. So he described Cuzco as 'otra Roma en aquel imperio' [another Rome in that empire] and held that the religion of the Incas prefigured Christianity:

...los reyes Incas y sus *amautas* que eran los filósofos rastrearon con lumbre natural al verdadero Dios y Señor Nuestro.*

This contention that the Incas were already on the road to the true religion before the arrival of the Spaniards also helped to raise their importance above the level of mere heathens. But the ambiguity of the Inca Garcilaso's sympathies emerges most clearly in his account of the conquest and the death of the last Inca king, where he is torn between regret for the passing of the old and his anxiety to show that the last of the Incas had been received into the Christian Church. But he stresses the nobility of the king, Atahualpa, above all:

Luego cortaron la cabeza al Inca; el cual recibió aquella pena y tormento con el valor y grandeza de ánimo que los Incas y todos los indios nobles suelen recibir cualquier inhumanidad y crueldad que les hagan...†

and so his book ends on a note of sorrow at the indignity which his people had suffered.

Garcilaso's historicist account of the Inca Empire and its conquest stressed the parallels between the civilisations of the New World and the Old. But to the man with a scientific mind, it was the differences—the way that the New World diverged from established ideas—that constituted its fascination. In 1590, a Jesuit father from Lima, José de Acosta (1539–1616) published a *Historia natural y moral de las Indias* [*Natural and Moral History of the Indies*] in which he made an ambitious attempt to examine the geography, flora, fauna, history and civilisation of the New World in order to find out how they differed from or fitted into the Christian–Aristotelian account of the world and its inhabitants. This vast work was conceived by a genuinely scientific mind, for José de Acosta consistently sought rational explanations. Thus he reasoned that the Indies had not been inhabited for a very long period before the coming of the Spaniards and that its first inhabitants were 'salvajes y cazadores' [savages and hunters]:

...y que aquéllos aportaron al nuevo mundo, por haberse perdido de su tierra o por hallarse estrechos y necesitados de buscar nueva tierra, y que hallándole comenzaron poco a poco a poblarla, no teniendo más ley que un poco de luz natural, y esa muy escurecida, y cuando mucho algunas costumbres que les quedaron de su patria primera.‡¹

* The Inca kings and their *amautas* [Inca sages] who were philosophers were on the track of the true God and our Lord and [they reached this] with natural light [of reason].

† Then they cut the Inca's head off; and he received that pain and suffering with the courage and greatness of soul which the Incas and all the noble Indians customarily receive the inhumanity and cruelty which is meted out to them...

‡ ...and that those arrived in the new world because they strayed from their own country or because they found their own country too small and needed to seek new land and

Nor was Acosta afraid to show where the Christian Fathers and the authorities of antiquity had been mistaken:

Por tanto debemos colegir que a los antiguos les quedó gran parte por conocer y que a nosotros hoy día nos está encubierta no pequeña parte del mundo.*[1]

When we turn to the literature proper of sixteenth- and seventeenth-century Spanish America, we find two main tendencies. On the one hand, there was the literary product of the pens of priests and friars who wrote in order to aid the work of conversion. On the other hand, there was a literature which looked outwards to Europe, which often sprang out of the writer's determination to show that America, too, could boast men of talent and literary skill to rival those of Europe. The Peruvian lady poet, 'Amarilis' who corresponded with Lope de Vega, was certainly anxious for approval and recognition from the leading Spanish celebrity, and we may be sure that she was not alone in this.

But America could not hope to inaugurate literary fashion; its poets and writers were provincials whose eyes were turned to European fashion. In any case, for several decades after the foundation of the colonial empire, the leading poets were Spanish-born and had often grown up in Spain. Some of them, indeed, were established writers. The dramatist and poet Juan de la Cueva came to the New World, as did Gutierre de Cetina, the Spanish Petrarchan; and Mateo Alemán, author of the famous picaresque novel *Guzmán de Alfarache*, ended his life in Mexico, although he does not seem to have done any writing there. And one Spanish poet at least, Alonso de Ercilla (1533–94) wrote his masterpiece in the New World. This was the epic poem, *La Araucana*, the first part of which was published in 1559. Ercilla's epic, which stimulated numerous imitations in the colonies, not only had the distinction of being the first New World epic but was unique in being composed in the course of the Spanish campaign against the fierce Araucanian Indians of Chile. He himself emphasised its authenticity:

...porque fuese más cierto y verdadero, se hizo en la misma guerra y en los mismos pasos y sitios, escribiendo muchas veces en cuero por falta de papel y en pedazos de cartas, algunos tan pequeños que apenas cabían seis versos.†

> having found it, they slowly began to settle, having no other guide than a little natural reason, and this somewhat obscured, and at the most, having a few customs that they brought from their former country.

* Therefore we should deduce that the ancients still had much to learn and that today we have discovered not a little part of the world.

† ...to make it more true and certain, it was composed in that very war and during the very incidents and sieges, being often written down on leather owing to lack of paper,

La Araucana is a poem written in *octavas reales* (eight-line verses of eleven-syllable lines) and is remarkable not only for its picture of valiant Indians who were worthy opponents of the Spaniards, but for its realistic, and at times, 'down-to-earth' quality, as in the following verse which describes the clatter of battle:

> Como parten la carne en los tajones
> con los corvos cuchillos carniceros,
> y cual de fuerte hierro los planchones
> baten en dura yunque los herreros,
> así es la diferencia de los sones
> que forman con sus golpes los guerreros:
> quién la carne y los huesos quebrantando,
> quién templados arneses abollando.*

Lyric poetry, unlike the epic, was much more of a dilettante activity and almost every cultivated young man-about-town must have thought of himself as a poet. There were more of them than 'arenas lleva el fango en sus corrientes' [grains of sand in a muddy stream] according to Bernardo de Balbuena (1561?–1627), one of the first poets to try and capture something of the New World in his *Grandeza mexicana*. Others also complained of the excessive numbers and the poor quality of the New World poets; 'más que estiércol' [as common as dirt] according to the Spanish-born playwright, González de Eslava (1534–1601) who lived in Mexico, whilst from Lima, another Spanish-born writer, Mateo Rosas de Oquendo (1559?–1621) complained of 'poetas mil de escaso entendimiento' [a thousand poets of scant understanding]. But native-born talents did emerge from the mass of the second-rate, poets such as the courtly Francisco de Terrazas (1525–1600), son of a *conquistador* and author of some pleasing Petrarchan sonnets.

Sixteenth-century Spain saw the rise of a flourishing school of drama, both sacred and profane, and the theatre became a popular form of entertainment and an instrument for the teaching of Church doctrine in the colonies. As in Spain, the feast of *Corpus Christi* was the great occasion for the performance of religious plays or *autos* which took the form of allegories on aspects of dogma. The most talented New

---

and on pieces of paper from letters, some being so small that scarce six lines fitted on them.

* As butchers divide meat into pieces with curved knives and as armourers beat on hard anvils the plates of heavy iron, so ring the different sounds that the warriors make with their blows, some breaking flesh and bone, other denting the tempered armour.

World dramatist of the sixteenth century, the Spanish-born Hernán González de Eslava, wrote a number of religious dramas of this kind although he also wrote some secular drama. An amusing *Entremés entre dos rufianes* [*Entr'acte between two Scoundrels*] is the only non-religious play by him to have survived.

One artistic genre failed to take root in the New World, and that was the novel. Although the conquerors often fed their imaginations on novels of chivalry, although the end of the sixteenth century saw the rise of the realistic and picaresque novel in Spain, no colonial novelist appeared in the reflected light of Cervantes. It is true that the importation of novels into the Indies was forbidden by royal decree, this embargo having been imposed in order to protect the spiritual integrity of the newly-converted Indians. A 1531 decree, for instance, specifically mentioned the novel of chivalry, *Amadís de Gaula* and stated that it was 'bad practice for the Indians and something with which it is not well for them to be concerned to read'.[1] Despite the existence of such decrees, novels did find their way into the colonies. An inventory of the books possessed by an architect who was brought to trial by the Inquisition in Mexico in the seventeenth century lists *Guzmán de Alfarache* and Quevedo's *Vida del Buscón*, both well-known picaresque novels.[2] The embargo on the importation of novels could not, therefore, be a reason for the dearth of Spanish–American fictional writing since novels could be obtained despite the embargo. Lack of a market and the difficulty of publishing works of fiction were much more important deterrents. Creative talent there was but, in the field of prose writing, such talent had to be channelled into more serious genres. Even so, books that were categorised as 'history' or 'travels' sometimes approached fictional narrative in their imaginative treatment of material. A historical chronicle, known as *El carnero* [*The Sheep*] (1636) written by the Colombian, Juan Rodríguez Freile (1566–1640), is supposedly a record of Colombian history but there is far more legend and gossip in it than fact. The author's delight in scandalous escapades, illicit love affairs and murders not only make *El carnero* read like a prototype of the yellow press but reveal the kind of talent that might well have fulfilled itself in the realistic novel or the Decameron-type short story. Another seventeenth-century work which has features similar to those of the novel is *Los infortunios de Alonso Ramírez* [*The Misfortunes of Alonso Ramírez*], an account of the wanderings of a shipwrecked sailor, written by the Mexican scholar, Carlos de Sigüenza y Góngora (1645–1700). The story was purportedly told to Sigüenza y Góngora by Alonso Ramírez himself but it is by no means an artless transcript. Sigüenza y Góngora has more than a rudimentary grasp of the storyteller's art, for he puts the narrative into the mouth of his protagonist, thus giving the tale freshness and authenticity. He delineates character although he shows a certain religious prejudice against the protestant captors.

Debo advertir, antes de expresar lo que toleré y sufrí de trabajos y penalidades en tantos años, el que sólo en el condestable Nicpat y en Dick cuartamaestre del capitán Bel, hallé alguna conmiseración y consuelo en mis continuas fatigas, así socorriéndome sin que sus compañeros lo viesen en casi extremas necesidades, como en buenas palabras, con que me exhortaban a la paciencia. Persuádome a que era el condestable católico, sin duda alguna.*[1]

Inside the historians, chroniclers and travel-writers of the colonial period, there often seems to be a novelist trying to get out.

THE SEVENTEENTH CENTURY

By the seventeenth century, the Spanish colonies were well organised, prosperous, over-protected and wholly cut off from outside influences whether cultural or economic. Trade was entirely with the mother country, while the Inquisition carefully watched over the orthodoxy of the colonists. The towns and cities between the Río Grande and the Tierra del Fuego resembled nothing so much as hot-houses producing carefully nurtured blooms in highly-regulated conditions.

The artistic style of this period is the baroque, characterised by exuberant decorative elements, by the use of curves and broken lines. Façades and altars of New World churches outdid one another in their magnificence and were also the first examples of a mestizo art with jaguars, corn, cactus-flowers and pineapples sometimes appearing as motifs. Many historians and critics of art have asserted that this love of decorative motifs has its parallel in a literature which abounds in verbal ingenuity exercised for its own sake, in the piling on of images and of striking effects. Certainly the poems submitted to the numerous poetry festivals and competitions show an increasing emphasis on ingenuity. Complicated acrostics, alliterated verses with every word beginning with the same consonant, poems that meant the same

* I should make plain before expressing what I tolerated and suffered in the labours and hardships of so many years, that only did I receive any pity and consolation in my continuous trials from petty officer Nicpat and from Dick, captain Bel's quartermaster; in this way, helping me without their companions being aware of it in my extreme necessity and also by their good words with which they exhorted me to patience. I was thus convinced beyond doubt that the petty officer was a Catholic.

read backwards or forwards, show a desperate search after effect only
rivalled by modern advertising agencies. In the following poem, the
achievement of the complicated verbal echoes kills any possible meaning:

> Si al alto Apolo la sagrada *agrada*
> Piedad Troyana, a que devida *vida*
> Tanta asegure, que eximida *mida*
> Del veloz tiempo en la jornada *nada*. . . [1]

But art was not simply a mechanical exercise, even at the height of
the baroque. Outstanding talents there were, and these boldly faced the
conflict between their experience and their inherited culture. They
could only be dimly aware that outside the Spanish Empire astonishing
intellectual revolutions had occurred to change man's conception of
his relation to his environment. They themselves knew little of contemporary mathematical discoveries and scientific inventions. Their
own training relied heavily on learning by heart, on the weight of
autoridades rather than on scientific investigation. Even so, in both
Peru and Mexico, native-born writers increasingly discovered dis-
parities between the narrowness of their education and the breadth
of their experience.

Let us first consider two seventeenth-century Mexicans, Carlos
Sigüenza y Góngora (1645–1700) and Sor Juana Inés de la Cruz
(1648–95), both of whom entered religious orders, both of whom were
too intellectually curious to be perfectly at home there. Sigüenza y
Góngora was trained as a Jesuit but soon left the order. A first-class
mathematician, he held a Chair of Mathematics from 1672 and besides
was Chief Cosmographer of the Realm, and Chief Examiner of Gun-
ners. He was an undistinguished poet, author of *Primavera india [Indian
Spring]*, in praise of the dark-skinned Virgin of Guadalupe, but was a
gifted writer of narrative as his *Infortunios de Alonso Ramírez* shows.
But Sigüenza y Góngora's very great talents met with one serious
obstacle—the period and the society he lived in. His genius poured
like water into sand. He learned the Indian language and pioneered the
study of pre-Columbian societies only to come up against lack of
patronage for his work. The fruits of these investigations have been
lost except for notes on Indians which he slipped into the pages of
commissioned works. A historical work on post-conquest Mexico
met a similar fate. Luckily some of his chronicles of contemporary
life have survived although one of these at least—a letter describing the
Indian corn riot of 1692—had to await publication until 1932. Perhaps

he was too advanced for the Mexico of his time. Certainly his *Libra astronómica y filosófica* (1690), reveals a thoroughly modern spirit of investigation. This work was written as a refutation of the views of the Jesuit missionary, Father Kino, who had sustained that comets were omens of evil. In opposition to this, Sigüenza y Góngora demonstrates that the citation of authorities has no place in science:

I hereby point out that neither his Reverence nor any other mathematician, even if he is Ptolemy himself, can set up dogmas in these sciences, because authority has no place in them at all, but only proof and demonstration.[1]

Lack of funds prevented him from publishing this article for ten years. His extant work, written almost in the teeth of the society in which he lived, reveals a personality and a scholar who, had he been born in Europe, might have been a Newton or a Leibnitz.

One of Sigüenza y Góngora's friends was the nun, Sor Juana Inés de la Cruz, a witty and learned lady who was also in conflict with society. A lady-in-waiting at the Viceregal court in her teens, she soon took the veil, not because disappointed in love as some fanciful biographers have sustained, but simply because the cloisters provided a safe and comfortable environment in which to pursue her genuine and considerable intellectual interests. She was to achieve an enviable reputation in colonial society, being known throughout the Spanish-speaking world as the 'Décima Musa' [Tenth Muse]. But the very variety of her output perhaps reveals her own uncertainty as to where her true expression lay. She wrote lyric poetry, metaphysical poems such as the *Sueños* [Dreams] in which she examined and discussed the nature of dreams, plays both sacred and profane, and she even turned her hand to theological polemic. Her fondness for secular letters earned her the reproof of the Bishop of Puebla and a series of natural disasters which shook Mexico City in the 1690s and which began with an eclipse of the sun, followed by storms and famine, seems to have increased her feelings of guilt and anguish. In 1694, she signed a reaffirmation of her faith in her own blood with the words, 'I, Sister Juana Inés de la Cruz, the worst in the world'. Soon afterwards she died, after nursing the sick during an epidemic, apparently weakened by self-mortification.

Even this brief biography indicates a restless mind, and the story of this unusual and talented woman has inspired numerous biographies, including a Freudian interpretation of her life and personality by Ludwig Pfandl who diagnoses her as a neurotic, a narcissist with a father fixation and a compulsive desire to compete with men in their special preserves. Whether we accept Pfandl's diagnosis or not, it is plain enough that Sor Juana was a divided soul and that her division and inner strife were expressed with amazing directness in her writing:

> En dos partes dividida
> tengo el alma en confusión:
> una, esclava a la pasión
> y otra, a la razón medida.*

Though she couches her problem in terms of a familiar dilemma between reason and passion, we may be sure that 'reason' meant, for her, the well-trodden ways of Catholic *autoridades*; passion referred to her own intellectual thirst. 'I have prayed God' she once wrote, 'to subdue the light of my intelligence, leaving me only enough to keep his law, for anything more (according to some persons) is superfluous in a woman.' And a sonnet she wrote is in the nature of a plea for intellectual freedom:

> ¿En perseguirme, mundo, qué interesas?
> ¿En qué te ofendo, cuando sólo intento
> poner bellezas en mi entendimiento
> y no mi entendimiento en las bellezas?
>
> Yo no estimo tesoros ni riquezas,
> y así, siempre me causa más contento
> poner riquezas en mi entendimiento
> que no mi entendimiento en las riquezas.
>
> Yo no estimo hermosura que, vencida,
> es despojo civil de las edades,
> ni riqueza me agrada fementida;
>
> teniendo por mejor en mis verdades
> consumir vanidades de la vida
> que consumir la vida en vanidades.†

Like Sigüenza y Góngora, Sor Juana was not only torn by this conflict between religious obedience and her passion for learning but also

---

* In two parts divided, my soul is in confusion, one part is a slave to passion and the other to measured reason.

† What interest have you, world, in my undoing? In what do I offend, when I but try to add some beauty to my understanding and not make understanding bow to beauty?

I esteem not treasures nor great riches, therefore is my happiness the greater when I add riches to my understanding and do not make understanding bow to riches.

I esteem not beauty which once vanquished is the common booty of the ages, nor do deceitful riches please me;

For I hold it to be better in my judgment to destroy the vanities of life rather than have my life destroyed by vanities.

between two kinds of scholarship—the old method of trusting to *autoridades* and the new pragmatic methods. One critic, indeed, sustains with some plausibility that the Fabios and Silvios (the names of her supposed lovers in her lyric poetry) are personifications of this intellectual dilemma.[1] Certainly the following poem can be read either as a conventional love dilemma in which the lady is pursued by the man she does not love and pursues in her turn a man who is indifferent to her; on the other hand, it can also be read as the dilemma of the nun who flees the shelter of the Church in order to pursue the harsher truth of scientific knowledge:

> Al que ingrato me deja, busco amante
> al que amante me sigue, dejo ingrata;
> constante adoro a quien mi amor maltrata;
> maltrato a quien mi amor busca constante.

> Al que trato de amor hallo diamante;
> y soy diamante al que de amor me trata;
> triunfante quiero ver al que me mata
> y mato a quien me quiere ver triunfante.

> Si a éste pago, padece mi deseo;
> si ruego a aquél, mi pundonor enojo:
> de entrambos modos infeliz me veo.

> Pero yo por mejor partido escojo
> de quien no quiero ser violento empleo,
> que de quien no me quiere, vil despojo.*

Such poetry is technically skilful and the personality that shows through the poetry is interesting although the sonnets cannot be classed as great or moving poetry. Perhaps poetry was only second best for Sor Juana, a vessel into which, for want of more suitable containers, she had to pour her intellectual problems. Her most ambitious poem, *Primer Sueño [First Dream]* has sometimes been compared to Góngora's *Soledades* but in fact, apart from external tricks of style, there is little

---

* He who faithless leaves me, I lovingly pursue; he who lovingly follows me, faithlessly I leave. Constantly I adore him who spurns my love and spurn him who constantly seeks my love.

    He whom I try to love I find hard as diamond and I am diamond to him who tries to love me; triumphant would I see him who kills me and I kill him who wishes me triumphant.

    If I repay the one, my desire suffers; if I plead with the other, my pride is injured: in either case, I am unhappy.

    But I choose as the better part to be the savage object of him I do not love—rather than the worthless spoils of the one who loves not me.

B

resemblance between Góngora's poem, which expresses the poet's delight in the variety and sensuousness of the natural world, and the dry, intellectual argument of Sor Juana's poem in which she describes the soul's attempt in dream to perceive the significance of the created world. Beginning with simple perceptions of inanimate nature, the soul ascends the scale of creation until it finally reaches the idea of God. In this discourse, there is no sensual perception of the external world as in Góngora, nor is there the mystic's ecstatic union with God. The poem suggests questions which, perhaps, could have been more properly dealt with in a scientific way.

Sor Juana and Sigüenza y Góngora had their counterparts in Lima, a Viceregal capital which rivalled and even surpassed Mexico in its splendour. Two great talents emerged there in the seventeenth century —the satirist, Juan del Valle Caviedes (*c.* 1652–92) and the scholar, Pedro de Peralta Barnuevo (1663–1743).

Caviedes was a Spanish-born poet who arrived in the New World at an early age and became well known as a satirist in Lima. During his lifetime, his poems were regarded as so scurrilous that they were not printed and only allowed to circulate in manuscript. The first edition of his poetry appeared in 1873 and even then this was not a complete edition.

Satire is often the creation of a conservative temperament—one thinks of Swift, Quevedo or Pope—and Caviedes was no exception, though his writing nowhere reaches the heights achieved by these great masters. Like Sigüenza y Góngora and Sor Juana, he was aware of living in a changing world in which new values and ideas were seeping in to replace the old; but unlike them, he was less interested in defending the new than in exposing its factitiousness. Hence the main target of his satirical poems were the emergent professions, particularly doctors for whom he saved his most virulent attacks, comparing them to wars, battle and pestilence in the devastation they brought. But also like Quevedo and Swift, he is concerned not only with the topical but with the ugliness and sordidness of human life and its grotesque absurdity, as in this description of a hunchback wooing a tall wife:

> Para conseguir poder besarla,
> hubo el marido giba de escalarla,
> porque era novia, en fin, tan atalaya
> que por las picaduras de la saya
> el giba la subió hasta la cadera

y para más subir pidió escalera.
Ella viendo así a su amante orillo,
una trenza ensartó por un carrillo
por donde tiró al mozo
como cubo que sacan de algún pozo.*

Even such a lighthearted picture of the hunchback climbing up the loops of the lady's dress in order to kiss her indicates a disturbed awareness of areas of experience that defy categories and rules. Caviedes's satire is a kind of self-defence against chaos and lack of order.

His compatriot, Pedro de Peralta Barnuevo, lived well into the eighteenth century and hence was even more familiar with change and doubt. A mathematician, historian, astronomer and poet, he wrote plays— an epic, *Lima fundada* (1732) and a musical comedy or *zarzuela*. Like his Mexican counterparts, his curiosity was viewed with suspicion by the authorities. As an old man, he was persecuted by the Inquisition, yet he was by no means a revolutionary. Indeed his last major work, *Pasión y triunfo de Cristo* [*Triumph and Passion of Christ*] (1738) is a poem which expresses the limitations of scientific knowledge and its inadequacy in bringing man to eternal truths.

These four personalities of the colonial period, the two Mexicans, Sor Juana Inés de la Cruz and Carlos Sigüenza y Góngora and the two Peruvians, Caviedes and Peralta Barnuevo, were all remarkable people. Yet one cannot help speculating on the different fate that might have awaited them had they lived in the mainstream of European culture instead of in the distant colonies. We might have had a first woman scientist, a second Newton or Leibnitz. At the same time they show us that the New World already had a wealth of talent; but the right forms and stimulus for its true expression were still lacking.

THE EIGHTEENTH CENTURY

The great structure that was the Spanish colonial empire began to crack and break in the eighteenth century. The policy that had kept this area of the world insulated from outside influence was modified and finally abandoned as the Spanish Crown weakened and became subject to outside pressures. In the colonies themselves, economic change brought consequences of far-reaching importance. Mining

---

* In order to be able to kiss her, the husband had trouble (or, to use the same play on words, 'had the hump') in scaling her, for the bride was, indeed, such a tower that by the loops of the garment, the humpback climbed to reach her hips and to get higher, he had to ask for a ladder. She, seeing her lover thus left on the fringe, let a plait down her cheek and thus, pulled up her young man as if she were pulling a bucket from a well.

was no longer the mainstay of colonial economy, its place being taken by agriculture; and this in turn meant the rising wealth and importance of hitherto secondary or neglected parts of the empire—the Plate region, Venezuela, northern Mexico. Here the creoles, or American-born inhabitants of European descent, abruptly came into conflict with the protective policy of the Spanish government and with the Spanish-born officials who held the top posts in colonial administration. Uprisings and disturbances grew more frequent. In Paraguay, in Venezuela, among the Indians of Yucatán, there were great rebellions and for one moment, at least, between 1780 and 1781, when Tupac Amaru raised the Indians of the Andean countries and massacred Spanish officials and landowners, the end of the colonial empire seemed at hand. Tupac Amaru was caught and brutally killed, and the limbs of his executed followers were scattered along the roads as a warning. But though the Indian could be suppressed, it was not so easy to stifle creole resentment against burdensome taxes and legislation. Wealthy young men could not be prevented from going abroad and visiting France or North America where they had free access to forbidden books. Moreover, whereas at one time friars and priests, the most educated members of the community, were the ones most likely to possess prohibited literature, there is evidence in the late eighteenth century of widespread reading of such works by a middle class of laymen which included musicians, silversmiths and cooks. Dangerous ideas thus percolated to far greater sections of the population.

In one way, at least, the Crown contributed to its own downfall in the colonies. In 1767, on an order from the Spanish Government, the Jesuit order was expelled from all territories belonging to Spain. The Jesuits had provided the backbone of the educational system, and had helped to preserve the *status quo*; when they went, Spanish America lost its most learned scholars and intellectuals; worst of all, it lost a religious order which had always sought to study and understand the New World. The skill and learning of the expelled Jesuits were now concentrated in an attack on the Spanish Crown. Their scholars elaborated advanced social and political theories, justifying representative government and miscegenation to diminish social divisions, and extolling pre-Columbian civilisations. And it was from the pen of an exiled Jesuit, Rafael Landívar (1732–93) that there came the most moving and eloquent description of the beauty of tropical nature. His *Rusticatio Mexicana* (1781) was written in Latin, and was one of the most curious monuments to that effort to draw Latin America into the orbit of universal and catholic culture which had begun with the conquest. Even as he was writing, however, European thought was advancing in new directions. In France, for instance, Montesquieu was suggesting that countries should not fit their constitutions to abstract and universal patterns but should develop naturally in obedience to local conditions. Soon similar ideas were applied to culture, and Americans became less concerned with fitting their experience into universal forms than in finding their own original expression.

Nevertheless, the Spanish colonial period was to leave a pattern that could not be eradicated. The planning of the cities, the structure of the family and society, the language and literary tradition, all bore a Hispanic stamp. And though the battle cry of the intellectuals of the Independence period was originality, they were to find it harder than they dreamed to wipe out the patterns of Spain.

1 INDEPENDENCE AND LITERARY EMANCIPATION

The literary independence of Spanish America was inseparable from political independence. In the eighteenth century, colonials began to realise that their economic and political interests were not identical with those of Spain; and writers found that the American environment offered more interesting material than foreign models. If these men still looked to Spanish literature, it was in order to apply its precepts and examples to America. Moreover they now had a public eager for local information and news, a public formed of artisans, tradesmen, professional men who might live and die without seeing Europe and for whom its problems and literature were remote. These were the kind of people who read local newspapers (the first of which were founded in the eighteenth century) in order to find out about people they knew, about the arrival and departure of ships and about government and ecclesiastical appointments. Unimportant gossip? Perhaps. But these first newspapers, which printed matters too trivial to come under the censorship,[1] nevertheless helped to give a sense of identity and common interest to the colonials, and in the years immediately prior to Independence this recording of gossip had given way to a serious didactic and reforming brand of journalism. Meanwhile, from Europe itself came direct encouragement to those who were interested in registering American experience, for throughout the Western world philosophers were increasingly recognising that the data of knowledge came from sense-impressions and that personal observation of phenomena was of greater importance than recourse to the authorities of the past. The evidence of eyes and ears became more valuable than memorisation of texts or the citing of ancient authors.

PREPARING FOR INDEPENDENCE

The writers who contributed to the literary emancipation of Latin America did not form a movement. Their works were often written in isolation, almost fortuitously under the pressure of events. The urgent need to impart their knowledge, their burning desire for

[28]

reforms were stimulus enough. Such motives do not produce polished works of literature, particularly in countries without an established literary tradition. Nevertheless the works of these writers who were fully committed to America and its future have their own fascination.

Three very different men contributed to the literary emancipation: A Spanish-born Peruvian official, Alonso Carrió de la Vandera (*c.* 1715–after 1778), a writer from Quito, Francisco Eugenio de Santa Cruz y Espejo (1747–95) and the Mexican journalist, José Joaquín Fernández de Lizardi (1776–1827).

Carrió de la Vandera

In 1775 or 1776, a book with the title, *El lazarillo de ciegos caminantes* [*Guide for Blind Travellers*] was secretly published in Lima. The false date, 1773, was printed on the title-page; the place of publication was stated to be Gijón in Spain and the author wrote under the pseudonym 'Concolorcorvo'. So effective was this elaborate concealment of the real facts that, for a century and a half, the authorship was mistakenly attributed to Calixto Bustamante Carlos Inca, a mestizo, who appears in *El lazarillo de ciegos caminantes* as the travelling companion of a Spanish official, Alonso Carrió de la Vandera, who had been sent to inspect the posts between Buenos Aires and Lima.[1] Skilful detective work has now established that the author was not Bustamante but Carrió de la Vandera himself and he adopted this deliberate deception 'por no verme en la precisión de regalar todos los ejemplares' [so as not to have to give away all the copies]. But the real reason for the concealment is probably rather less frivolous. For though on the surface *El lazarillo de ciegos caminantes* purports to be nothing more than a guide-book, its scope embraced politics, history and many aspects of the Spanish administration. The criticisms made in the book might have appeared very serious indeed to the authorities if they had been published by Carrió de la Vandera under his own name. He was, after all, a member of the establishment, a man who had served a term of office as *corregidor* and who aspired to serve a second term. Moreover, the book describes his official tour of inspection of the postal route between the outlying city of Buenos Aires and Lima, the capital of the Viceroyalty of Peru. To forestall any serious official reaction, Carrió de la Vandera made the tone of his book humorous rather than grave, and put the observations into the mouth of a humble mestizo who disarms criticism by presenting himself as something of a clown:

Yo soy indio neto salvo las trampas de mi madre, de que no salgo por fiador. Dos primas mías coyas conservan la virginidad, a su pesar, en un convento de Cuzco, en donde las mantiene el Rey, nuestro señor. Yo me hallo en ánimo de pretender la plaza de perrero de la Catedral de Cuzco para gozar immunidad eclesiástica.*

By claiming that his highest ambition is to become dog-keeper in Cuzco cathedral, the 'author' perhaps hoped to slip through the censorship by virtue of the modesty of his disguise.

Why was *El lazarillo de ciegos caminantes* such a revolutionary work? On the surface, it is simply a compendium of useful information about prices, climate, abundance of food supplies, the nature of the population and of the towns and villages through which travellers between Buenos Aires and Lima must pass. The author is particularly interested in livestock, horses and mules, and he has a passion for statistics. Thus we learn that it took thirty-six days for an express letter to go from Buenos Aires to Lima and there are statistical breakdowns of the inhabitants of the different towns according to class and occupations. At the end of the eighteenth century such detailed observation of local conditions was quite new. Indeed, it is thanks to 'Concolorcorvo' that we have one of the first descriptions of the gauchos, the mestizo nomadic horsemen who roamed the pampa. He called them *gauderíos* and described them as follows:

Estos son unos mozos nacidos en Montevideo y en los vecinos pagos. Mala camisa y peor vestido procuran encubrir con uno o dos ponchos, de que hacen cama con los sudaderos del caballo, sirviéndoles de almohada la silla. Se hacen de una guitarrita, que aprenden a tocar muy mal y a cantar desentonadamente varias coplas, que estropean y muchas que sacan de su cabeza, que regularmente ruedan sobre amores. Se pasean a su albedrío por toda la campaña y con notable complacencia de aquellos semibárbaros colonos, comen a su costa y pasan las semanas enteras tendidos sobre un cuero cantando y tocando. Si pierden el caballo o se lo roban, les dan otro o lo toman de la campaña enlazándolo con un cabestro muy largo que llaman *rosario*.†

---

* I am a pure Indian unless my mother deceived me (and this I cannot vouch for). Two cousins of mine who are Coyas (Indians) are still virgins, despite themselves, in a Cuzco convent where our lord the king maintains them. I have a mind to ask for the position of dog-watcher in the Cathedral of Cuzco in order to enjoy ecclesiastical immunity.

† These are some young men born in Montevideo and the surrounding countryside. Their poor shirt and worse clothes, they try to cover up with a blanket or two which they use, together with the horse-blankets as bedding and they employ their saddle as a pillow. They have guitars which they learn to play very badly and they sing out-of-tune songs which they thus spoil and many other songs which they invent and which generally deal with love. They wander freely over the whole countryside and with the notorious complicity of the half-savage farmers, they eat at their cost and spend entire weeks

The author does not show any approval for this carefree, lazy life but he is objective and interested enough to present every picturesque detail; and it is this emphasis on fact and first-hand observation that distinguishes this book from the abstract speculation that had characterised so much Spanish–American writing. Indeed, in the prologue, the author went to some pains to justify his methods and expressly criticised scholars of previous generations such as Peralta Barnuevo who, Concolorcorvo declared, had wasted his time composing the epic, *Lima fundada*, when he would have been better employed observing his own environment:

> Si el tiempo y erudición que gastó el gran Peralta en su Lima fundada y España vindicada, lo hubiera aplicado a escribir la historia civil y natural de este reino, no dudo que hubiera adquirido más fama, dando lustre y esplandor a toda la monarquía; pero la mayor parte de los hombres se inclinan a saber con antelación los sucesos de los países más distantes, descuidándose enteramente de los que pasan en los suyos.*

And he also ridiculed those Spanish–Americans who filled their libraries with books on China or on Charlemagne and who were ignorant of the present Spanish royal family and

> ...de su país no dio más noticia que de siete a ocho leguas en torno, y todas tan imperfectas y trastornadas, que parecían delirios o sueños de hombres despiertos.†

Even supposedly erudite historians came under attack for their ignorance of contemporary reality and for their prejudice; for this reason, Carrió declared,

> Los viajeros,...respecto a los historiadores, son lo mismo que los lazarillos en comparación de los ciegos.‡

The serious point behind all these arguments is that abstractions or an appeal to classical or ancient 'authorities' are of no help whatsoever in a concrete situation. He cites, for instance, the example of a Spaniard

---

stretched on a skin, singing and playing. If their horse is lost or stolen, they are given another or they steal one from the fields, lassoing it with a very rope which they call a *rosary*.

* If the time and learning that the great Peralta had spent on his Foundation of Lima and Vindication of Spain had been applied to the writing of the civil and natural history of this kingdom, I do not doubt that he would have acquired more fame, giving lustre and splendour to the entire monarchy; but most men had rather know of the events of more distant countries, entirely neglecting those which take place in their own.

† ...of whose own country they gave no more account than of seven or eight leagues round and all so imperfect and mixed up that they seemed to be the delirium or dreams of waking men.

‡ In comparison to historians, travellers are the same as guides in relation to blind men.

whose gun has been stolen by an unfriendly Indian who asks to be shown how the gun works. In this difficult situation, the Spaniard opts for self-preservation by taking the gun and killing the Indian, having no time to work out the nice details of his action. As Carrió slyly points out, the instinct for self-preservation makes nonsense of abstract arguments relating to conduct:

Se pregunta a los alumnos de Marte si la acción del español procedió de valor o de cobardía y a los de Minerva si fue o no lícita la resolución del español.*

We can now appreciate how truly revolutionary *El lazarillo de ciegos caminantes* was in an age and in a civilisation where book-learning and reliance on the authority of ancient texts was still regarded as true erudition. The book is a breath of fresh air in a stuffy colonial world. Yet the author was not a revolutionary in his politics. He does not foresee the ending of Spanish rule in the colonies and he defends the Spaniards from charges of cruelty against the Indians. His criticism against the Spanish administration is aimed at improving the Empire, hence his concentration on practical questions such as religious education, the removal of injustices and abuses and modernisation of roads. But though reformist rather than revolutionary in political and social matters, the spirit in which *El lazarillo de ciegos caminantes* was written evidences a growing self-consciousness among the inhabitants of Spanish America.

Francisco Eugenio de Santa Cruz y Espejo

Carrió de la Vandera was an official of Spain and could therefore identify himself with Spanish rule which he only wished to see improved in detail. We can imagine that the abuses he described would seem much more irksome to someone with little Spanish blood in their veins and little inclination to justify the mother-country. Such a man was Francisco Eugenio de Santa Cruz y Espejo (1747–95), son of a mulatto woman and an Indian and born in Quito (now capital of Ecuador). Eugenio's father had been protected by a priest and learned to practise medicine: the son was brought up in the Hospital de la Misericordia, in which his father worked, and he, too, graduated as a doctor in 1772. This talented young man from a very humble background was from the first thwarted by the society in which he lived. His *Nuevo Luciano*, [*The New Lucian*], a series of dialogues on topics such as rhetoric,

---

* You may ask the students of Mars if the Spaniard's action was motivated by courage or cowardice, and those of Minerva whether the Spaniard's action was permissible.

poetry, philosophy and theology, circulated only in manuscript. He founded a newspaper, *Primicias de la cultura de Quito* [*First Fruits of the Culture of Lima*], but this only seems to have contributed to his unpopularity with the establishment. Though he studied and practised law and read widely in contemporary authors such as Rousseau, Voltaire and the Encyclopedists, his talents were suspect and his life tragic. The Spanish administration sent him to the unhealthy jungle area of Marañón ostensibly to help settle the limits between two jurisdictions, but in reality to remove him from the scene. He was twice imprisoned, once in 1787 for his supposed authorship of a scurrilous pamphlet, and again in 1795 when he was charged with conspiring against the Spanish Crown. He died before being brought to trial.

The severity with which the Spanish administration dealt with Santa Cruz y Espejo is only understandable in the light of his writing. Like the author of *El lazarillo de ciegos caminantes*, he believed that any consideration of the situation of Spanish America must begin from direct observation of the environment:

...es preciso que empiece la cadena de sus principios, por aquel que le sea más sencillo y familiar. Atienda, pues, el cúmulo de las impresiones generales que recibe por sus sentidos; y en vez de irse a analizarles, observe cual es aquel legislador supremo que las modifica, que las ordena, que las distribuye.*

Just as the individual acts on the data that come to him from sense-impressions, so governments should act on the basis of thorough knowledge of the region they are governing. Santa Cruz y Espejo's motto is 'el conocimiento propio es el origen de nuestra felicidad' [self-knowledge is the source of happiness], and on a political level this means studying, among other things, the nature and condition of the land in order to exploit its potentialities more effectively. But these simple—and to the modern mind—obvious propositions led him to make serious criticisms of Spanish rule. An essay called 'Reflexiones acerca de las viruelas' [Reflections on Smallpox] extended far beyond the original title into an attack on the Spanish administration which prevented the inhabitants of the Andean region from taking advantage of their natural resources; and which had introduced a social structure which hampered growth and development. Little wonder that the Spanish officials regarded Santa Cruz y Espejo as a threat, for he not

---

* ...one should begin the chain of principles from that which is simplest and most familiar to one. Look then to the mass of general impressions received through the senses; and instead of analysing them, observe which is that supreme legislator which orders and distributes them.

only condemned Spanish rule but also the inhabitants of Quito whose complacency and blindness to the inferiority of their position made them unable to fulfil any role but that of 'idiotismo' and 'pobreza' [idiocy and poverty].

José Joaquín Fernández de Lizardi

The third of the writers under review was the only one to live long enough to witness Independence. He was a Mexican journalist and novelist, José Joaquín Fernández de Lizardi (1776–1827), who came from a modest creole family background and was, like Santa Cruz y Espejo, the son of a doctor. Fernández de Lizardi failed to complete a university education and began his literary career in 1808 by writing satirical poems which he sold for a few cents. When the first rebellion against Spanish rule in Mexico broke out in 1810, he was working in Tasco as an official and was imprisoned on suspicion of helping the rebels. He was soon released, but the suspicions that he had rebel sympathies were more than justified. In 1812, he brought out the first copy of a newspaper, *El Pensador Mexicano* [*The Mexican Thinker*] (1812–14), in which he defended the freedom of the press and the right to criticise the administration. His outspoken views brought him into conflict with the authorities and he was imprisoned. A second newspaper, *Alacena de frioleras* [*Storehouse of Trivialities*], founded after his release, also ran into censorship troubles. Difficulties with the censorship rather than any artistic vocation made him write his first novel, *El Periquillo Sarniento* [literally, *The Itching Parrot*, the nickname of the main character], as a vehicle for opinions which might have been unpublishable in any other form. Even so, the fourth part of this novel could not be published in the first edition of 1816 since his views on the abolition of slavery were too advanced even when put into the mouth of a fictional character. Thus, though Fernández de Lizardi is generally regarded as the first Spanish–American novelist, he was so because of pressure of circumstances rather than from choice. During the period of severe censorship which coincided with the absolutist rule of Fernando VII of Spain (1816–the constitutionalist revolution of 1820), he wrote *Noches tristes* [*Sad Nights*] (1818), *La Quijotita y su prima* [*The Girl Quixote and her Cousin*] (1819) and *Don Catrín de la Fachenda* (published after his death). As soon as the Inquisition and censorship were abolished in 1820 after the constitutionalist revolution, Fernández de Lizardi turned once again to journalism. 1821 saw the declaration of Mexican Independence and the triumph of Augustín de Iturbide, the

leader who, a year later, had himself crowned Emperor. For thoughtful men, 1821 and 1822 were years of hope and despair, hope that the
ending of Spanish rule meant a new era, despair that an Independence
leader such as Iturbide should give way to his overriding personal
ambition. Fernández de Lizardi remained an outspoken critic and in
1822 he published a *Defensa de los Francmasones* [*Defence of the Free-
masons*] which brought him into disfavour with the Church. He was
excommunicated and continued to oppose the adoption of Catholicism as the state religion of Mexico even after his reconciliation with the
Church. In 1825, his services to Mexico were recognised and he was
made editor of the government newspaper, *La Gazeta del Gobierno*.
He was to found one more paper, *Correo Semanario de México*, before
his death in 1827.

Fernández de Lizardi represents a new type of Spanish American,
one for whom the newspaper served as a weapon. Though of modest
family background and partly self-educated, his works showed that
he was a man of broad culture, well-read in eighteenth-century thinkers whether of the Spanish *Ilustración* [Enlightenment]—Feijóo, Padre
Isla, Torres Villarroel—or of the French Enlightenment. His works
cite natural scientists such as Buffon, educationalists such as Blanchard
and a vast range of authors of works on medicine, law and economics.
Both his background and education made him well-equipped to
criticise Spanish administration and education for its backwardness, and
most of his novels deal with the disastrous effects of bad upbringing
and education on the Mexicans. In *Don Catrín de la Fachenda*, for
instance, the eponymous hero was so proud of his family background,
that he despised honest work and embarked on a veritable rake's
progress which ended in suicide. Probably this exemplary tale was a
veiled allegory of Spanish rule, with its pride in past glory and its
neglect of the practical problems of colonial economy.

Fernández de Lizardi's major work was his first novel, *El Periquillo
Sarniento*, a picaresque work presenting the errors and follies of a hero
whose environment and poor education combined to give him weak
and stupid attitudes. To the modern taste, *El Periquillo* is far too passive
a hero, a man who protests too much without ever resisting the temptations put in his path. From the first, he is exposed to bad influences—
ignorant maids inculcate superstitions, his mother indulges his whims,
his teachers either have no vocation or no ability to discipline him.
And though his father is an intelligent man who wants his son to
practise a useful trade rather than swell the ranks of lawyers and para-

sites, it is Periquillo's over-fond mother who wins the day, sends her son to university and thus ensures that he will learn only superstitious nonsense. Scientific study had no place in the university; hence the hero's ignorance when asked to explain what a comet was:

El que no los veamos muy seguido es porque Dios los tiene allá retirados, y rólo los deja acercarse a nuestra vista cuando han de anunciar la muerte de algún sey, el nacimiento de algún santo, o la paz o la guerra en alguna ciudad...*

Periquillo remains incorrigibly ignorant despite many encounters with good and wise people. He is unwilling to work or take anything seriously and becomes successively a priest, a gambler, a thief, apprentice to an apothecary, a doctor, clerk in a provincial town, soldier in the Philippine Islands—in each case because he is drawn by the easy success that these professions offer rather than by a special vocation. These episodes permit the author to describe hospitals, prisons, remote villages, monasteries, while at the same time driving home one major point—that Spanish government and the education system encourage parasitism and laziness. Periquillo wants the good life without effort and is surrounded by people who have managed to achieve this. The poor, honest and hard-working members of society remain underdogs. Thus Fernández de Lizardi's world is divided into two classes— the undeserving parasites and the worthy, practical men whose virtues are not recognised by that society. These latter represent bourgeois values in contrast to the aristocratic values still dominant in the colonies. Thrift, hard work, sobriety and industry are the values which the author upholds, thus voicing the ideals of an emergent middle class which did not as yet hold power.

Periquillo's adventures several times take him among Indians or Negroes. He himself exploits the Indians by posing as a doctor in a village and, on another occasion, by aiding a thieving official. These episodes reveal the gulf between the enlightened laws relating to the Indians and the unenlightened treatment of the Indians in practice. But it is in the episodes relating to the Philippine Islands that the author gives full rein to his sentiments on racial questions. Here, a Negro makes a spirited attack on racial discrimination and adduces contemporary political and historical theories in support of his view that different but equally valid forms of civilisation may develop in different parts of the globe:

* The fact that we don't see them very often is because God has them held back up there and only lets them come near to our sight when he has to announce the death of some king, the birth of some saint or peace or war in some city.

Yo entiendo que el fondo del hombre está sembrado por igual de las semillas del vicio y de la virtud; su corazón es el terreno oportunamente dispuesto a que fructifique uno u otra, según su inclinación o su educación. En aquélla influyen el clima, los alimentos y la organización particular del individuo, y en ésta la religión, el gobierno, los usos patrios, y el más o menos cuidado de los padres. Luego nada hay que varían tanto las naciones en sus costumbres, cuando son tan diversos sus climas, ritos, usos y gobiernos.

Por consiguiente, es un error calificar de bárbaros a los individuos de aquella o aquellas naciones o pueblos que no subscriben a nuestros usos. . .*

This passage reveals a consciousness prepared for political and intellectual emancipation, and reads almost as a disguised appeal to Europe to recognise the singularity and humanity of the peoples of America. What America would be like if allowed to develop along its own lines is not clear from the novel, although there is an episode in which Periquillo visits a Utopian island which has the laws and institutions which Fernández de Lizardi considered desirable. It is consonant with the values of the book that this Utopia should be a bourgeois paradise in which all citizens have a trade and are literate and all have a thorough knowledge of laws which they agree to and obey.

Carrió de la Vandera, Santa Cruz y Espejo and Fernández de Lizardi are but three of the new men and attitudes that were emerging all over Spanish America; the Mexican, Fray Servando Teresa Mier (1765–1827), the Colombians, Antonio Nariño (1765–1823), Camilo Torres (1766–1816) and Francisco Antonio Zea (1766–1822) and many others were to put their talents and pens to the service of the Independence cause.

INDEPENDENCE LITERATURE

The struggle for Independence lasted for almost fifteen years, from 1810 to 1825. The movement began in 1810 in Mexico, Venezuela and Buenos Aires, when the inhabitants of these provinces took advantage of the situation which arose from the Napoleonic occupation of Spain to declare their independence. But these early rebellions,

---

* I believe that the essence of man is sown equally with the seeds of vice and those of virtue; his heart is a terrain providentially arranged so that one or other germinates according to his inclination and education. On the former act influences of climate, food and the particular organisation of the individual; on the latter religion and government, national customs and the care (great or less) of his parents. Therefore, there is nothing odd in that nations are so varied in customs, when their climates, sects, customs and government are so different.

Consequently, it is an error to call barbarous those individuals of that or those nations or peoples who do not subscribe to our customs.

led by Miguel Hidalgo (1753–1811) in Mexico, by Francisco de Miranda (1750–1816) and Simón Bolívar (1783–1830) in Venezuela, by José Artigas (1764–1850) in the Banda Oriental (which later became Uruguay) and by José de San Martín (1778–1818) in Argentina, were for the most part unsuccessful. Hidalgo was defeated and executed, Bolívar forced into exile, Miranda captured and sent to prison in Spain. Only in the Plate region did Spanish rule fail to re-establish itself. But in 1821, the second stage of Independence began its triumphant progress under the leadership of Bolívar, San Martín and General Sucre who between them liberated the South-American continent in a campaign that culminated in the battle of Ayacucho (Peru) where the Spanish armies were decisively defeated in 1824. Mexico was liberated in 1821 by Agustín Iturbide.

For fifteen years, there had been little respite from battle. Imaginative literature was eclipsed by the war report and the campaign despatch, and it is from the liberators themselves that we learn most about the spirit that animates the men of the time. It should, nevertheless, be pointed out that the intellectual leaders of Independence such as Bolívar, Francisco de Miranda and San Martín were by no means typical of the ordinary creole rebel. While the former found justification for the revolt in contemporary thought, being particularly influenced by Rousseau's *Social Contract* and the concept of the general will; the latter were moved to rebel by more mundane and practical considerations. Artigas, one-time gaucho bandit and smuggler, or Hidalgo the Mexican priest who put his pottery manufactory and his experiments in rearing silk-worms before his priestly duties, were two Independence leaders who came into conflict with Spanish rule at the level of practical activity. But even the more intellectual leaders, San Martín and Bolívar, were by no means visionary dreamers. San Martín, for instance, stressed the need, not for an ideal constitution but for the best that would fit the nature of the country. And Bolívar castigated some of his fellow-rebels who were 'buenos visionarios' [good visionaries] and imagined that they were living in 'repúblicas aereas' [aerial republics]. During his exile from Venezuela, he wrote a letter which has since become one of the most famous documents in Spanish–American history—the *Carta de Jamaica* (1816), in which he made remarkably accurate predictions about the future. The letter showed that he was fully aware of the danger that the former Spanish Empire might break into numerous small republics and that many of these would fall a prey to tyranny.

Nosotros somos un pequeño género humano; poseemos un mundo aparte; cercado por dilatados mares, nuevo en casi todas las artes y ciencias aunque en cierto modo viejo en los usos de la sociedad civil. Yo considero el estado actual de la América, como cuando desplomado el Imperio Romano cada desmembración formó un sistema político, conforme a sus intereses y situación o siguiendo la ambición particular de algunos jefes, familias o corporaciones; con esta notable diferencia; que aquellos miembros dispersos volvían a restablecer sus antiguas naciones con las alteraciones que exigían las cosas o los sucesos; mas nosotros, que apenas conservamos vestigios de lo que en otro tiempo fue, y que por otra no somos indios ni europeos, sino una especie media entre los legítimos propietarios del país y los usurpadores españoles: en suma, siendo nosotros americanos por nacimiento y nuestros derechos los de Europa, tenemos que disputar éstos a los del país y que mantenernos en él contra la invasión de los invasores; así nos hallamos en el caso más extraordinario y complicado...*

With brevity and insight, Bolívar not only shows that the Spanish Empire will break into small nations just as the Roman Empire had done but also that these new nations would have difficulty in establishing any sense of identity, since they were neither properly European nor wholly indigenous.

Bolívar himself lived to see some of his worst fears realised; indeed, he was forced to become an absolute ruler in order to keep control of Colombia. Iturbide, the liberator of Mexico, had himself crowned Emperor. Dr Francia, also an Independence leader, became dictator of Paraguay and maintained that country in isolation. Uruguay fell under the power of the Portuguese. Cuba remained under Spanish domination. Meanwhile those areas of the continent such as Colombia, Venezuela and Ecuador and the Central American republics—in which the Federal system was tried out—gradually abandoned the federal ideal. In 1826, a congress in Panama failed even to set up an organisation of American states. Nor had independence changed the economic structure, which remained dominated by the *hacienda* [large estate] and

---

* We are a small human species; we possess a world apart; surrounded by wide seas, new in almost all the arts and sciences although in a manner old in the customs of civil society. I consider the present state of America similar to that when, after the fall of the Roman Empire, each dismembered part formed a political system according to its interests and situation or following the particular ambition of some chiefs, families or corporations; with this important difference that those dispersed members re-established their ancient nations with the alterations which circumstances demanded; but we, who scarcely conserve vestiges of what we were in former times and on the other hand, who are neither Indians nor Europeans but a middle species between the legitimate owners of the country and the Spanish usurpers; in short, being Americans by birth and our rights those of Europe, we have to dispute the latter with those of the country and to maintain ourselves in it against the invasion of the invaders; so we find ourselves in a most extraordinary and complicated position.

the *estancia* [cattle ranch]. The landowning element tended to encourage strong-man rule as a safeguard against chaos and civil war, and after the deaths of the more idealistic leaders such as Bolívar and San Martín, a far more brutal and barbarous element took the lead in Latin America. These tyrants were often 'men on horseback', wild and vigorous figures who distrusted the intellectual, had no use for civilised refinements but gloried in outdoor life. The prototypes were Juan Manuel Rosas who, for twenty years until 1852, held sway in the Argentine; and General Páez, the 'centauro de los llanos' [the centaur of the plains] who controlled Venezuela to the mid-years of the century. Such men left little in the way of monuments and their rules meant the virtual end of literary life. Colourful they undoubtedly were, an unfailing source of picturesque anecdotes and legendary exploits that moved even their opponents to amazed admiration. Here, for instance, the liberal Domingo Sarmiento describes his enemy, Rosas:

...sufre accesos nerviosos, en que la vida predomina tanto, que necesita saltar sobre un caballo, echarse a correr por la pampa, lanzar gritos desacompasados, rodar, hasta que, al fin, extenuado el caballo, sudando a mares, vuelve él a las habitaciones fresco ya y dispuesto para el trabajo.*

The Mexican, Santa Ana, who was universally hated as a ruler was yet another eccentric; he had his leg (which had been shot off) buried with full military honours. Then there was the Ecuadorian, García Moreno, who put the whole of his miserably oppressed country under the patronage of the Sacred Heart. All these men were monstrous eccentrics in whom absolute power and a complete ignorance in all intellectual matters were usually combined.[1] In all the Latin-American continent only Chile offered a reasonably stable and free atmosphere in which intellectual activity could flourish. It was the Chilean Government which recalled the great scholar Andrés Bello from Europe; Chile in which one of the first polemics between Classicists and Romantics was conducted; and it was here, too, that refugees from the Rosas regime found shelter. In the rest of the continent, life between Independence and 1850 was bleak indeed. His very education and his need for civilised communication with his fellows made the writer feel an outsider; unable to bear the rule of barbarous tyrants, he took the

---

* [He] suffers nervous fits in which his vitality is so strong that he has to jump on a horse, set off racing over the pampa, utter great cries and gallop until, at last, with his horse worn-out and him sweating profusely he returns to the homestead fresh and ready for work.

road of exile or took part in dangerous political opposition. The Romantic poets, Esteban Echeverría (Argentina, 1805–51), José María Heredia (Cuba, 1803–39) both had to go into exile, as did the novelist, José Mármol (Argentina, 1817–71) and the essayist, Domingo Sarmiento (Argentina, 1811–88). But this was not the worst that could befall. The Peruvian Mariano Melgar was shot on the eve of Independence when the Spaniards defeated the rebel army he was serving with; the mulatto poet, Gabriel de la Concepción Valdés (Cuba, 1811–44) was executed for his alleged part in an anti-Spanish conspiracy. Although after 1850 conditions became more stable, exile, imprisonment and even death are not unheard-of fates even among contemporary writers.

Even if he had wanted to, it was hard for the writer to avoid political involvement; harder still to concentrate on imaginative writing when the pressures were all in favour of polemical writing and political tracts. Many writers were men of all trades. Sarmiento, educationalist, politician, journalist, polymath; Andrés Bello, scholar, poet, writer on grammar and international law, were characteristic for the breadth of their activities.

THE BACKWARD GLANCE

We have so far traced the exciting leap forward at the end of the eighteenth century when writers began to see the vast possibilities that ensued from exploring their own experience and environment; we then saw how the whole of the Latin-American continent and its intellectuals were plunged into a period of political crisis from which they emerged not into a Utopia but into a real world of tyranny and vast unsolved social problems. What of the imaginative literature between 1810 and 1830? Apart from Fernández de Lizardi, there were no novelists as yet. The first literature of emancipated America was therefore poetry; not poetry of a thrilling, new type but a literature that clung to safe and respectable antecedents seeking to give Latin America the dignity of classical tradition in Virgilian eclogues or high-sounding odes.

José Joaquín Olmedo

The poet of Independence was undoubtedly José Joaquín Olmedo, who was born in Guayaquil (now Ecuador), played an active part in the Independence movement, took part in a delegation to meet Bolívar and became a firm admirer of the Liberator. But Olmedo was steeped in classical and neo-classical literature; an intellectual who would have been quite happy to have remained outside political life, he declared that one of the best periods of his life was that which he had spent translating Pope's *Essay on Man*. These two aspects of his life—admiration for Bolívar and his literary interests—came together in his most famous poem *La victoria de Junín. Canto a Bolívar* [*The Victory of Junín. Hymn to Bolívar*] (1825). Homer, Pindar, Plutarch, Virgil, Horace and Ovid were his declared masters in this miniature epic which began with the forecast of Bolívar's victory and culminated with the battle itself. After the battle, there appears the spirit of the Inca who forecasts further victories for Bolívar. Lofty models and great events do not, unfortunately, make great poetry and little of the real spirit of the age is conveyed by Olmedo's resounding but hollow lines:

> Crece la confusión, crece el espanto,
> y al impulso del aire, que vibrando
> sube en clamores y alaridos lleno,
> tremen las cumbres que respeta el trueno,
> Y discurriendo el vencedor en tanto
> por cimas de cadáveres y heridos,
> postra al que huye, perdona a los rendidos.

> Padre del universo, Sol radioso,
> dios del Perú, modera omnipotente
> el ardor de tu carro impetuoso,
> y no escondas tu luz ineficiente...*

Andrés Bello (1781–1865)

The most learned and intelligent man of the Independence period was probably Andrés Bello who was born in Caracas but who lived for many years in London and spent the last part of his life in Chile. He studied Latin, philosophy and—unusual for the period—Spanish literature of the Golden Age. His services to Latin America, however, continued far beyond his studies or his contribution to literature. He was tutor to Bolívar and representative of the Caracas Independence Junta in London in 1810 where he remained for nearly thirty

---

* The confusion grows, fear grows and at the impulse of the air, which vibrating, rises full of clamours and howls, the mountain tops spared by the thunder now tremble. And the conqueror wandering meanwhile over heaps of bodies and wounded brings down the one who flees and pardons those who submit.

Father of the universe, radiant Sun, god of Peru, with your omnipotence moderate the ardour of your impetuous chariot and do not hide your unfaltering light.

years. Here he founded two magazines, the *Biblioteca americana* and the *Repertorio americano*, and served as an official in the Colombian and Chilean legations after the foundation of these republics. He was nearly fifty when he was offered a post in the Ministry of Foreign Affairs in Chile. Here he founded the university and became its first rector, drew up the Civil Law Code, wrote his famous *Gramática de la lengua castellana* [*Grammar of the Castilian Language*] (1847) and his *Compendio de la historia de la literatura* [*Compendium of the History of Literature*] (1851). Like Olmedo, Bello wished to bring the dignity of classical style to American themes. His two best poems, published in London, are *Alocución a la poesía* [*Address to Poetry*] (1823) in which he invited the muse of poetry to abandon the courts of Europe and find her home in the fields of America; and his *Silva a la agricultura en la zona tórrida* [*To the Agriculture of the Torrid Zone*] (1826) which was inspired by the *Georgics*. The poem celebrates the beauty of American nature, praising the country life and describing the horrors of discord and war. The poem ends with an appeal to the young nations to turn their swords into ploughshares

> Oh jóvenes naciones, que ceñida
> alzáis sobre el atónito Occidente
> de tempranos laureles la cabeza!
> Honrad al campo, honrad la simple vida
> del labrador y su frugal llaneza,
> Así tendrá en vos perpetuamente
> la libertad morada
> y freno la ambición, y la ley templo.*

The Virgilian poem was to become something of a tradition in Latin America; in 1866, the Colombian poet, Gregorio Gutiérrez González (1826–72) published in his *Memoria sobre el cultivo del maíz en Antioquia* [*Upon the Cultivation of Corn in Antioquia*]. In contrast to Bello's poem, this gives a realistic and detailed account of the work of the countryside, using many regional words and expressions. And in 1910, the Modernist poet, Leopoldo Lugones, published his *Odas seculares* [*Secular Odes*] in which he too celebrated the cattle and the grain of his native land.[1] Thus Bello initiated a long tradition although it was not one which was to produce the best Spanish-American literature.

---

* O youthful nations, who, your heads crowned with early laurels arise over the astonished West. Honour the countryside, honour the simple life of the labourer and his frugal simplicity. Thus will freedom have an eternal home and ambition will be held in check and the law tempered.

José María de Heredia (1803–39)

Heredia, a Cuban poet who was exiled for conspiring against the Spaniards, was the one poet of this group who did not see the independence of his country. His exile was spent first in the United States and then in Mexico. Though Heredia, in common with most writers of his time, was educated in the Greek and Latin classics, his work shows the beginnings of romantic influence. Some of his best-known poems are meditations on the American scenes, poems such as *Niagara* and *En el Teocalli de Cholula* [*On the Pyramid of Cholula*]. The latter describes the poet sitting at sunset in the ruins of an Aztec *teocalli* or pyramid where he contemplates the beauties of the Mexican countryside and broods on the past when the Aztecs had held sway. But unlike later Romantic poets of Spanish America, Heredia does not romanticise this past, seeing it as a time of slavery when an enslaved people 'ni mirar a su señor osaba' [dared not look at their Lord].

> Tales ya fueron
> tus monarcas, Anáhuac, y su orgullo,
> su vil superstición y tiranía
> en el abismo del no ser se hundieron.
> Sí, que la muerte, universal señora
> hiriendo a par al déspota y esclavo,
> escribe la igualdad sobre la tumba.
> Con su manto benéfico el olvido
> tu insensatez oculta y tus furores
> a la raza presente y la futura.
> Esta inmensa estructura
> vio a la superstición más inhumana
> en ella entronizarse. Oyó sus gritos
> de agonizantes víctimas, en tanto
> que el sacerdote, sin piedad ni espanto,
> les arrancaba el corazón sangriento;
> miró el vapor espeso de la sangre
> subir caliente al ofendido cielo,
> y tender en el sol fúnebre velo,
> y escuchó los horrendos alaridos
> con que los sacerdotes sofocaban
> el grito del dolor.*

* Thus were thy monarchs, Anáhuac; and their pride, their vile superstition and tyranny sank into the abyss of non-being. For death, the universal ruler, wounds both despot and slave and writes equality upon the tomb. Oblivion with its kind mantle hides thy madness and its furies from the present and future races. This immense structure witnessed the enthroning of the most inhuman superstition. It heard the cries of agonizing victims whilst the pitiless and fearless priest took out their bleeding hearts. It saw the thick vapour of blood rise still warm to the offended heavens and stretch a veil over the funereal sun; it heard the horrid yells with which the priests stifled the cry of pain.

Thus the disappearance of the Aztec Empire provides the poet with his moral—death is the true equaliser. The ruins that are the only trace of these past tyrannies serve as a lesson to present-day tyrants whose glory, too, is destined to end in ruins.

These three poets, Heredia, Olmedo and Bello, were humanists steeped in the culture of the classics and regarding this culture as the standard to which the new Latin-American literature must aspire. Their aim was noble; their poetry, with rare exceptional moments, lifeless. There seemed to be too great a gap between their education and the traditionless raw experience of the new republics. It was the rare individual who saw that this experience demanded new forms, not necessarily those hallowed in Europe. Thus Mariano Melgar (1791–1815), the Peruvian poet who came to an early and tragic end, was steeped like Bello in the classics, yet attempted to write poems in the metre and form of the *yaraví*, a Peruvian Indian song. These poems are little more than interesting experiments, but they indicated one possible approach for the future. More successful were the satirical and political poems of the Uruguayan, Bartolomé Hidalgo (1788–1822), a Montevidean barber who used the *cielito*, a form of folk-verse, for his poems. He also wrote a number of 'dialogues' in the language of the gauchos and thus began a tradition of social and political poetry known as the 'gauchesque' which was to have an illustrious future. It is from these humble and unpretentious origins that the best nineteenth-century poetry was to arise, rather than from the more ambitious, though worthy, efforts of Bello, Heredia and Olmedo.

2 LITERATURE AND NATIONALISM

In the newly-independent countries, the writer lived precariously and in isolation. Frequently, his only stimulus came from literary groups which were constituted with the deliberate intention of encouraging a national literature. Sometimes, these circles were political as well as literary; such was the *Salón Literario* which met in Buenos Aires in 1837, and the *tertulias* held in the home of the Cuban intellectual Domingo Delmonte in La Habana. Other groups met only to talk of literature or to listen to readings of poetry and prose. In Mexico, the *Academia Letrán*, founded in 1839, encouraged a school of Romantic poetry; in Colombia, the Mosaico group, started in the 1850s, did much to encourage prose writing and financed the publication of one important novel (*Maria*, by Jorge Isaacs); in 1842, a *Sociedad Literaria* was inaugurated in Chile; an *Ateneo* was founded in Montevideo in 1877, and in Peru the 'bohemios' gathered together in the Pérez bookshop in Lima between 1846 and 1850.[1] These and other literary circles were exceedingly important in the history of nineteenth-century Latin-American literature.

One of the most burning topics discussed in many of the literary groups during the first half of the nineteenth century was the topic of Romanticism. 'Romanticism' is, of course, a term that covers a complex of attitudes and involves political, social and philosophical questions as well as changes in sensibility and new literary forms. But in Latin America, Romanticism was identified above all with individual freedom and nationalism. The Argentinian novelist, Vicente Fidel López (1815–1903), stressed this link between the political and the literary revolution, declaring that it was the latter—particularly as manifested in contemporary French literature—that led Latin Americans to thoughts of social revolution:

...inoculó en nosotros, muchachos de 21 a 24 años, el mismo ardor por la revolución social y el reinado de las ideas nuevas.*[2]

* ...it inoculated in us young men of 21 to 24 years of age the very ardour for social revolution and the realm of new ideas.

[46]

The new literature was thus identified with political and social reform in the minds of young intellectuals who held on to these ideals during dark periods of oppression, dictatorship and civil war. In such periods, literature was sometimes the only form of activity left open to them, so that the novel and even poetry came to be regarded as instruments for attacking injustices, and for creating a sense of patriotism and civic pride.

In the political and social sphere, Romanticism and allied theories influenced intellectuals in their rejection of Spanish tradition. Histories and essays of the period tend to stress differences between the new countries and Spain and to underline the mistakes made by Spain in her administration of the colonies. Works of this kind include: *Sociabilidad Chilena* (1844) by Francisco Bilbao (Chile, 1823–65); *Investigaciones sobre la influencia social de la conquista del sistema colonial de los españoles en Chile* (1844) by José Victorino Lastarria (Chile, 1817–88); *Facundo* (1845) by Domingo Sarmiento; and the articles and essays of José María Luis Mora (Mexico, 1794–1850). The writers of these articles generally believed Spanish colonial rule to be responsible for the backwardness of the new republics and they rejected any further Spanish influence on the grounds that Spain was one of the most reactionary and obscurantist powers in Europe and hence an unsuitable model for nations which aspired to become modern democracies.

CIVILISATION AND BARBARISM

In the literary sphere, Romanticism also influenced writers to stress their break with Spanish tradition and their determination to create original national literatures. European Romantics tended to regard literature as a definition of the national spirit and literature and national identity were closely linked in their minds. This was an aspect of Romanticism that was eagerly seized upon by the writers of the new republics for whom 'originality' was now all-important. We thus find Esteban Echeverría stressing that Spanish artistic tradition was 'objetiva y plástica' [objective and plastic] and therefore utterly different in spirit from the new nations whose art was bound to be 'idealista y profundamente subjetivo y social' [idealist and deeply subjective and social].[1] It is, in fact, Echeverría and his fellow Argentinian, Sarmiento, who best exemplify the influences and contradictions of Romantic literature and nationalism at this period.

Esteban Echeverría

Esteban Echeverría was a gay, bohemian young man who was little more than a dilettante until he arrived in Paris in 1825. The period was one when European Romanticism was at its height; Byron, Goethe, Schiller, Hugo and Chateaubriand in literature, Cousin in philosophy, offered a dazzling variety of talent. When Echeverría returned to the Argentine in 1830, he was the self-appointed missionary of the new ideas. Unfortunately, the nation to which he returned was little prepared for a cultural revolution. The shadow of the powerful leader, Juan Manuel Rosas, darkened the political scene although he had not yet attained full power over the entire country. Rosas, this rising star, was the antithesis of Echeverría, for he despised Europe, had no time for the life of the spirit and prided himself on his skill as a horseman and a gaucho. Echeverría, idealist and intellectual with no political power, soon found his activities curtailed. As early as 1837, the year in which he published a collection of poetry, *Rimas*, he recognised that the progressive forces he represented were doomed:

Toda la labor inteligente de la Revolución[1] se ha venido abajo en un día y sólo se ven los rastros sangrientos de la fuerza bruta sirviendo de instrumento al despotismo y la iniquidad.*

But before the Rosas terror took over completely, Echeverría was able to found an idealistic political association, the *Asociación de Mayo* (May being the month in which Argentine Independence had been declared) and he issued a political programme, the *Dogma socialista*, which he intended as a blueprint for the free Argentina of the future. The *Dogma socialista* is not, as its name might suggest, a New World Communist Manifesto but a somewhat abstract document, supporting the ideas of progress, democracy, universal suffrage and religious freedom as the basis for the future national constitution. By the time it was published in 1839, Echeverría had been forced to leave Buenos Aires. After hiding on his estate, he found his way to Montevideo as did most of his associates. He died there a year before Rosas was defeated and overthrown.

But Echeverría did more than introduce Romantic ideas into Argentina. He expressed the dilemma of his time, the dilemma of a man whose artistic theories teach him to love the countryside and the 'folk' and whose living experience teaches him that the countryside and its inhabitants constitute a threat to all the values. The dilemma had its

---

* All the intellectual labour of the Revolution has fallen down in one day and one only sees the bloody traces of brute force which serves as the instrument of despotism and iniquity.

origin in the difference between the European context of Romanticism and the Latin-American context. The Industrial Revolution in Europe encouraged the European writer to idealise the countryside and the integrated, meaningful life of the peasant. In the Argentine, on the other hand, it was not industry but the vast, threatening pampa with its tribes of savage Indians and half-wild gauchos that constituted the chief danger to the good life. Thus, in Echeverría's work, Romantic conventions borrowed from European literature come into conflict with Argentinian reality. Aware of the Romantic idealisation of the common people and the noble savage, he saw in his country a blood-thirsty dictatorship which had come to power on the shoulders of the gauchos; and a nomadic Indian community that appeared to have little nobility. In both his main literary works—*La cautiva* [*The Captive*] and *El matadero* [*The Slaughter-House*] Echeverría defends European values and attacks primitive native barbarism.

La cautiva[1] is a narrative poem which, though Romantic in concep-tion, nevertheless has roots in Argentine reality; for the white woman captured by Indians was one of the pathetic figures of contemporary folk-lore. In one of his best stories, *Marta Riquelme*, the English writer William Henry Hudson, whose youth was spent in Argentina, related a haunting 'cautiva' story, and it is easy to see why the theme should also have appealed to Echeverría. His poem relates the tragic story of María, a captive amongst the Indians who finds that her husband Brian has been badly wounded and captured by them in a raid. She frees her husband and they flee across the pampa but he dies before reaching civilisation. The chief interest of the poem today lies in the contrast between Echeverría's treatment of his hero and heroine and his treat-ment of the Indians. Brian and María are spoken of only in ideal terms. Brian is a 'noble espíritu valiente' [noble valiant spirit] and María a 'sublime mujer' [sublime woman]. The Indians are utterly ferocious and evil and are described in correspondingly bestial terms, as in the following passage in which the Indians stagger about after drinking in celebration of their victory:

> Y al regocijo sin rienda
> Se da la tribu; aquel ebrio
> Se levanta, bambolea,
> A plomo cae, y gruñendo
> Como animal se revuelca,
> Este chilla, algunos lloran,
> Y otros a beber empiezan
> De la chusma toda al cabo

La embriaguez se enseñorea,
Y hace andar en remolino
Sus delirantes cabezas.*

The passage is an apt comment on Echeverría's hatred of the Indian, a hatred he shared with his enemy, Rosas.[1]

This 'repugnancia' is nowhere more vividly expressed than in Echeverría's prose work, the short story, *El matadero*, written in about 1840 and published posthumously. Though the prose is high-sounding and rhetorical, there is a vigour and intensity of emotion that is unrivalled in the literature of the period.

Like *La cautiva*, *El matadero* describes the conflict between the forces of primitive darkness (the tribe or the mass) and the civilised individual. But *El matadero* is also a political allegory which attacks the dictatorship of Rosas and the barbarism of his supporters. The story relates an incident that took place in the slaughter-house of Buenos Aires during the Lenten fast. The sudden arrival of fifty head of cattle after a period without meat is the occasion for an orgy of butchering:

Cuarenta y nueve reses estaban tendidas sobre sus cueros, y cerca de doscientas personas hollaban aquel suelo de lodo regado con la sangre de sus arterias. En torno de cada res resaltaba un grupo de figuras humanas de tez y raza distinta. La figura más prominente de cada grupo era el carnicero con el cuchillo en mano, brazo y pecho desnudos, cabello largo y revuelto, camisa y chiripá[2] y rostro embadurnado de sangre. A sus espaldas se rebullían, caracoleando y siguiendo los movimientos una comparsa de muchachos, de negras y mulatas *achuradoras*,[3] cuya fealdad trasuntaba las arpías de la fábula y entremezclados con ellas algunos enormes mastines, olfateaban, gruñían o se daban de tarascones por la presa. Cuarenta y tantas carretas toldadas con negruzco y pelado cuero, se escalonaban irregularmente a lo largo de la playa, y algunos jinetes con el poncho calado y el lazo prendido al tiento cruzaban por entre ellas al tranco o reclinados sobre el pescuezo de los caballos echaban ojo indolente sobre uno de aquellos animados grupos, al paso que, más arriba, en el aire, un enjambre de gaviotas blanquiazules, que habían vuelto de la emigración al olor de carne, revoloteaban, cubriendo con su disonante graznido todos los ruidos y voces del matadero y proyectando una sombra clara sobre aquel campo de horrible carnicería.†

* And the tribe gives itself up to unbridled rejoicings; that drunkard gets up, staggers, falls flat and, groaning, wallows like an animal; one sobs, some cry and others begin to drink. Finally the whole crowd is under the influence of the intoxication which makes their delirious heads spin.
† Forty-nine head of cattle were laid out upon their skins and about two hundred persons trampled that muddy ground watered with arterial blood. Around each beast stood a group of human figures of differing complexions and race. The most prominent figure in each group was the butcher with a knife in his hand, arms and chest naked, his hair long and untidy, shirt, apron and face daubed with blood. Behind him, winding in and out, following his movements bustled a chorus of boys, of negresses and mulatto

An attentive reader will be aware of more than the literal description of the slaughter-house. The butchers wear the traditional *chiripá* and poncho of the gaucho; many of the women are mulatto. Hence the butchers are precisely those sections of the nation on whom Rosas relied for support. Even the seagulls are symbolic, for they are re-turned emigrants eager for scraps and attracted by the smell of blood. In *El matadero*, the gauchos and the dregs of society are in command, with one or two treacherous émigrés ready to snatch some advantage from the carnage. Echeverría draws a picture of a degraded society in which children play with 'bolas de carne' [balls of meat], in which men are only too ready to draw knives against one another and in which Negro and mulatto women are too insensitive to realise the disgusting nature of their work:

Hacia otra parte, entretanto, dos africanas llevaban arrastrando las entrañas de un animal; allá una mulata se alejaban con un ovillo de tripas y resbalando de repente sobre un charco de sangre, caía a plomo, cubriendo con su cuerpo la codiciada presa. Acullá se veían acurrucadas en hilera cuatrocientas negras destejiendo sobre las faldas el ovillo y arrancando, uno a uno, los sebitos que el avaro cuchillo del carnicero había dejado en la tripa como rezagados, al paso que otras vaciaban panzas y vejigas y las henchían de aire de sus pulmones para depositar en ellas, luego de secas, la achura.*

There is no doubt that we are intended to draw the conclusion that in the slaughter-house of Argentina only the worst elements thrive. But worse is to come. At the height of the slaughter, a bull 'emperrado y arisco como un unitario' [as stubborn and churlish as a 'Unitarian'][1] escapes and causes the death of a boy. The butchers recapture the ani-mal, ritually slaughter it and then, whipped to a pitch of excitement, turn on a passer-by, a young man who wears European dress and who

achuradoras, whose ugliness exceeded that of the legendary harpies; and mingling with them enormous mastiffs sniffed, growled or bit one another over the spoils. Forty odd carts covered with blackish, untanned leather were ranged irregularly along the beach, and some horsemen, their ponchos wet and their lassos held at the ready, hurriedly passed between them or crouched over the necks of their horses, indolently glanced at the animated groups of people, while up in the air, a flock of bluish white seagulls which had returned from emigration [attracted by] the smell of the meat, glided about with their dissonant cries drowning all the noises and the voices of the slaughter-house and pro-jecting a clear shadow over that field of horrible butchery.
* In another area, meanwhile, two African women dragged away the entrails of an animal; over there a mulatto went off with a ball of guts and slipping suddenly in a pool of blood, fell flat, covering the precious booty with her body. Over here, four hundred negresses were crouched in a row unravelling the ball on their laps and taking out the fat which the miserly butcher's knife had spared within the bowels, while others emptied stomachs and bladders and filled them with air from their lungs in order to deposit the strips of meat there as soon as they were dry.

is not carrying the Rosas colours. He courageously stands up to the butchers but they torment him and when he suddenly has a haemorrhage, they leave him for dead. *El matadero* is thus the story of the forces of civilisation defeated by those of barbarism.

How different from Echeverría's own blueprint for a literature 'que armonice con la virgen, grandiosa naturaleza americana' [which may harmonise with the virginal and grandiose American nature]![1] The exaltation of this 'virgen naturaleza' could not be reconciled with sympathy for those who wished to control nature and civilise the backlands. Whereas the Lakeland shepherd was a type of common man who could be idealised by poets conscious of the fragmentation of the human personality in an industrial society, the American gaucho, the Indian and Negro could not be thus idealised by men who were still struggling for the recognition of law and order.

Domingo Sarmiento

There is a similar paradox in the work of Domingo Sarmiento, the Argentinian essayist, politician and educationalist. Unlike Echeverría, he did not belong to the creole aristocracy, but came from a humble family of Spanish stock who had settled in the provincial city of San Juan. But when he came to write of his childhood and ancestry in his *Recuerdos de provincia* [*Provincial Memories*] (1850), he was full of pride not only because he came from a respectable family but also because he had had to make his own way in the world, his father being too poor to pay for his education. Sarmiento could not help seeing a parallel between his own career and that of the new Argentina which also descended from respectable Spanish stock and yet was now faced with the task of carving its own future. Yet, though Sarmiento wanted an original form of culture and civilisation to develop in Argentina, like Echeverría he could not accept that the ways of life of gaucho and Indian could form any basis for the future.

While still a young man, Sarmiento had come into conflict with a gaucho strong-man, Juan Facundo Quiroga, who terrorised the Western provinces. Quiroga was the very antithesis of the kind of man Sarmiento would have liked to see governing his province; barbarous, cruel, illiterate like his gaucho followers, he instinctively hated and destroyed any civilisation that came his way. Civic life and culture in the towns of the interior was disrupted and destroyed when he gained control of them. This terrorism, however, by destroying civic sense helped to pave the way for the dictatorship of Rosas, for Rosas was able to profit from lawlessness and separatism and so extend his grip over the whole country. From exile in Chile where he had been forced to flee, Sarmiento watched the rise of Quiroga, his assassination by the more powerful Rosas and the institution of a reign of terror. Here he analysed the full implication of the disaster in his essay *Vida de Juan Facundo Quiroga: Civilización y barbarie [Life of Juan Facundo Quiroga: Civilisation and barbarism]* (1845) which has become one of the classics of Argentinian literature.

Facundo is more than the biography of a local tyrant, for in order to account for the dominance of barbarism and cruelty in Argentinian political life, Sarmiento studies the influence of the physical environment. The unfenced trackless pampa, the home of nomadic Indians, untouched by the civilising influence of the city, had encouraged a breed of men—the gaucho—who had learned to live independently, outside society:

El mal que aqueja a la Repúblic Argentina es la extensión: el desierto la rodea por todas partes, se le insinúa en las entrañas; la soledad, el despoblado sin una habitación humana, son por lo general los límites incuestionables entre unas y otras provincias. Allí la inmensidad por todas partes: inmensa la llanura, inmensos los bosques, inmensos los ríos, el horizonte siempre incierto, siempre confundiéndose con la tierra entre celajes y vapores ténues que no dejan en la lejana perspectiva señalar el punto en que el mundo acaba y principia el cielo. Al Sur y al Norte acéchanla los salvajes, que aguardan las noches de luna para caer, cual enjambre de hienas, sobre los ganados que pacen en los campos y las indefensas poblaciones. En la solitaria caravana de carretas que atraviesa pesadamente las pampas y que se detiene a reposar por momentos, la tripulación reunida en torno del escaso fuego, vuelve maquinalmente la vista hacia el Sur al más ligero susurro del viento que agita las hierbas secas, para hundir sus miradas en las tinieblas profundas de la noche en busca de los bultos siniestros de la horda salvaje que puede sorprenderla desapercibida de un momento a otro.*

Not surprisingly the gaucho had come to rely on his own skills and resources. He became a 'baquiano' [path-finder], or a 'rastreador'

* The evil from which the Argentine Republic suffers is its great extension; the desert surrounds it on all sides, it penetrates into its very bowels; solitude, desert without human habitation usually mark the unquestionable limits between one province and another. Immensity is all around; immense the plain, immense the forests, immense the rivers, the horizon always uncertain, always fading into the land between clouds and tenuous vapours which in the distance do not give an indication of where land ends and sky begins. To the south and north, the savages watch and wait for moonlight nights, in order to fall like a pack of hyenas upon the cattle which graze in the fields and upon defenceless villages. Solitary caravans of carts ponderously cross the pampa and stop to rest for moments; and the team round the small fire automatically turn their eyes to the south at the lightest whisper of the wind which stirs the dry grass, to stare into the deep shadows of night in search of the sinister shapes of the savage horde which can surprise them unexpectedly from one moment to another.

[tracker]; his hero was the outlaw, the 'gaucho malo' whom he praised in song and poetry. Sarmiento's most vivid passages are reserved for this poetry of the pampa which seems to have sprung up spontaneously out of the solitude:

La soledad, el peligro, el salvaje, la muerte. He aquí ya la poesía.

De aquí resulta que el pueblo argentino es poeta por carácter, por naturaleza. ¿Ni cómo ha de dejar de serlo, cuando en medio de una tarde serena y apacible una nube torva y negra se levanta sin saber de dónde, se extiende sobre el cielo mientras se cruzan dos palabras, y de repente el estampido del trueno anuncia la tormenta que deja frío al viajero, y reteniendo el aliento por temor de atraerse un rayo de dos mil que caen en torno suyo?...La muerte está por todas partes; un poder terrible, incontrastable le ha hecho en un momento reconcentrarse en sí mismo y sentir su nada en medio de aquella naturaleza irritada.*

But while Sarmiento appreciates the poetry of pampa life, he cannot accept the gaucho as a national stereotype. His way of life and his poetry is mediaeval; the 'payador' or gaucho singer is 'el mismo bardo, el vate, el trovador de la Edad Media' [the very bard, poet, troubadour of the Middle Ages]. Just as the troubadour has no place in modern Europe, so the gaucho way of life must eventually disappear when progress comes to Argentina.

The second part of *Facundo* shows how gaucho values have encouraged the rise of cruel chieftains like Quiroga who attack the city and civilised life which they cannot understand. Such men have prepared the way for an even greater evil—the dictatorship of Rosas who was able to play the petty tyrants off one against the other, and so extend his grip over the whole nation. The dramatic climax of the essay is the description of Facundo's last ride to Barranca Yaco where he was ambushed and assassinated, probably on Rosas's orders. With Quiroga out of the way, Rosas had almost the whole country in his power and instituted a state held together by a terrorism which was a reflection of the 'values' of the slaughter-house and the round-up.

Sarmiento recognised that *Facundo* was no work of art. Yet this

---

* Solitude, Danger, Savages, Death. Here is poetry.

  Thus the Argentine people are poets by temperament and nature. And how can they avoid this, when in the midst of a serene and peaceful evening, there arises (who knows from where) a fierce, black cloud which extends over the sky in the time it takes to exchange two words; and suddenly the crash of thunder announces the storm which leaves the traveller cold and holding his breath for fear of attracting one flash of lightning from the two thousand which are striking around him. Death is on all sides; a terrible, ineluctable power has made him for one moment withdraw into himself and feel his insignificance in the midst of that angry nature.

essay, written in a white heat of passion, has its place in any history of Spanish–American literature, for here was adumbrated the lasting problem of 'civilisation' and 'barbarism'; of law and order versus the lawlessness of the frontier. Many writers were to take up the theme but it was Sarmiento who first articulated this. Secondly, Sarmiento was the first to point out that the influence of the natural environment in Spanish America was far greater and more directly felt than in Europe.

During his exile in Chile, Sarmiento worked as a teacher and a journalist and founded a teacher training college. He also took an active part in Chilean literary life, defending Romanticism against the criticisms of Andrés Bello and his disciples. Later, he travelled to Europe and the United States, where he studied educational systems. After the downfall of Rosas in 1852, Sarmiento returned to his native land and took an active part in political life, serving as President of the Republic from 1868 to 1874. During his years in office, he strengthened the centralised government, put an educational programme into effect and was instrumental in transforming Argentina from a backward gaucho republic into a modern state. His final work, *Conflictos y armonías de las razas en América* [*Conflicts and Harmonies of the Races of America*] (1883) was written in Paraguay; in it, he expressed the belief that a racially-mixed population retarded the nation. What Argentina needed was hard-working European immigrants like those who had populated North America.

Modern critics have been quick to point out that Argentina became what Sarmiento had dreamed—a country with a population that was predominantly of European descent—and that, far from solving problems, this created even more serious situations.[1] However, if we try to imagine ourselves in the position of a nineteenth-century reformer desperate at the backwardness of his country, we shall feel more sympathy for Sarmiento, even though he did create problems in trying to make Argentina into a modern state. He was, after all, a man fighting on two fronts—attacking the old enemy, Spain, at the rear, and the new enemy, the gaucho dictator, who had taken over. And he identified both himself and the Argentina of the future with a third type—the nineteenth-century enlightened man of progress.

NATIONALISM AND THE NOVEL

El matadero and *Facundo* are both hybrid works, half-way houses between the essay and imaginative literature. Their authors did not consider them great works of art. Contemporaries more ambitious for lasting

c

fame for their work tended to think either in terms of the epic or the novel. The attraction of the epic is easy to see. The novel, however, was a more recent genre the seriousness of which still had to be justified. Hence the explanatory prefaces which preceded so many of them and the lofty claims made on behalf of the genre.

Bartolomé Mitre, for instance, Argentinian writer and statesman, prefaced a novel of the Independence wars, *Soledad*, with these words in which he claimed that this was a method by which people could be familiarised with historical events and by which the continent could be made known to the rest of the world:

La novela popularizaría nuestra historia echando mano de los sucesos de la conquista, de la época colonial, y de los recuerdos de la guerra de la independencia... pintaría las costumbres originales y desconocidas de los diversos pueblos de este continente, que tanto se prestan a ser poetizadas, y haría conocer nuestras sociedades tan profundamente agitadas por la desgracia con tantos vicios y tan grandes virtudes, representándolas en el momento de su transformación.*[1]

His compatriot, Vicente Fidel López, in a prologue to the novel *La novia del hereje* [*The Heretic's Bride*] (1870), declared that the writing of historical novels was a patriotic undertaking:

...porque creía que los pueblos en donde falte el conocimiento claro y la conciencia de sus tradiciones nacionales son como los hombres desprovistos de hogar y de familia que consumen su vida en oscuras y tristes aventuras sin que nadie queda ligado a ellos por el respeto, por el amor, o por la gratitud.†

But obviously lofty ambitions were not enough. All too often the nineteenth-century Spanish–American novel is clumsy and inept, with a plot derived at second hand from the contemporary European Romantic novel. Only when American reality broke in, sweeping convention aside, did such novels come alive. One such novel was *Amalia* by José Mármol, which like *El matadero* and *Facundo* was written out of bitterness against Rosas's regime.

---

* The novel would popularise our history, bringing in events from the conquest, from the colonial period and memories of the Independence period...it would paint the original and unknown customs of different peoples of this continent for these lend themselves greatly to poetic expression and it would make our society known, those societies which are so deeply disturbed by misfortune, which have so many vices and so many great virtues which could be depicted at a moment of transformation.
† ...for I believed that countries in which the clear understanding and consciousness of their national traditions are lacking are like men without homes and families who consume their lives in obscure and sad adventures without anyone being bound to them by respect, love or gratitude.

José Mármol (1817–71)

José Mármol, a Romantic in both his poetry and his novel, nevertheless underwent personal experiences which tempered the idealism that so often characterised Romantic prose-writing. In 1840, he had been one of a number of people arrested by Rosas. In that year there were many summary executions, and Mármol escaped and was set free only through the intervention of a powerful friend. *Amalia* was written during his exile in Montevideo when the events he had lived through were still fresh in his mind. What in other circumstances might have been a romantic love-story became a political novel, closely based on his own experiences and with historical figures playing important parts in the plot. The story relates the miraculous escape of the Unitarian fugitive, Eduardo Belgrano, from the hands of a group of Federalist pursuers. He takes refuge in the house of the widowed Amalia with whom he falls in love; despite the attempt of the lovers to evade the suspicions of Rosas, Amalia's house is surrounded by Federalists and the lovers are killed.

The monstrous figures of the dictator and his confederates give a grotesque caricatural dimension to what would otherwise have been a conventional story. Though at times Mármol merely denounces, at others he anticipates more recent novelistic techniques in his symbolic presentation of character. Thus, at one dramatic moment, Rosas is seen bathed in the reflection of a red curtain as if he were covered in blood:

En este momento bebía sangre, sudaba sangre y respiraba sangre: concertaba en su mente y disponía los primeros pasos para las degollaciones que pronto debían bañar en sangre a la infeliz Buenos Aires.*

Much of the novel is direct denunciation; and Mármol, like Echeverría, emphasises the role of Negroes and mulattos in the dictatorship:

La comunidad de la mashorca,[1] la gente del mercado, y sobre todo las negras y las mulatas que se habían dado ya carta de independencia absoluta para defender mejor su madre causa, comenzaban a pasear en grandes bandas la ciudad, y la clausura de las familias empezó a hacerse un hecho. Empezó a temerse el salir a la vecindad.

Los barrios céntricos de la ciudad eran los más atravesados en todas direcciones por aquellas bandas; y las confiterías, especialmente, eran el punto tácito de reunión.

Allí se bebía y no se pagaba, porque los brindis que oía el confitero, eran demasiado honor y demasiado precio por su vino.

* At that moment, he drank blood, he sweated blood and he breathed blood; he was plotting in his mind and arranging the first steps of the executions that would soon bathe unhappy Buenos Aires in blood.

El último crepúsculo de la tarde no se había apagado en los bordes del horizonte, cuando la ciudad era un desierto: todo el mundo en su casa; la atención pendiente del menor ruido; las miradas cambiándose: el corazón latiendo:

> Lavalle[1]
> Rosas
> La Mashorca

Eran ideas que cruzaban, como relámpagos súbitos del miedo, o la esperanza, en la imaginación de todos.*

This is vivid reporting, but the book is not solely concerned with denunciation. Mármol was a firm believer in the sacred destiny of the American nations and in particular of his own country, Argentina, which he declared:

> ...surgió de las florestas para dar libertad e imprimir el movimiento regenerador de diez naciones.†

America's role is providential:

> ...el porvenir de América está escrito en la obra de Dios mismo: es una magnífica y espléndida alegoría en que ha revelado los destinos del Nuevo Mundo el gran Poeta de la Creación Universal.‡

Unfortunately such passages weaken the novel, making it a hybrid work, part sociological study, part essay, part imaginative literature. Only when Mármol makes the plot speak for him, as he does in the opening scenes and in his descriptions of social life in Buenos Aires during the Rosas regime, only then does *Amalia* become a real novel.

* The community of the *mashorca*, the market folk and especially the negresses and mulatto women who had given themselves an absolutely free hand in the defence of their cause, began to troop in great bands through the city and soon led families to shut themselves in. People began to be afraid to go out in the neighbourhood.

The central parts of the city were the most frequented by the bands in every direction; and the pastry shops especially were the meeting points.

There they drank and did not pay because the toasts which the shopkeeper heard were too great an honour and price for the wine...

The last twilight of the evening, had not faded on the verge of the horizon when the city became a desert; everybody stayed in their own home, their ears strained for the slightest noise; exchanging looks with beating hearts:

> Lavalle
> Rosas
> La Mashorca

These were the ideas that passed through their imaginations in sudden flashes of hope and fear.

† ...came out of the forests to give liberty and express the resurgence of ten nations.

‡ ...the future of America is written in the work of God himself; it is the magnificent and splendid allegory in which the Great Poet of Universal Creation has revealed the destinies of the New World.

THE CARIBBEAN NOVEL AND THE NATIONAL CAUSE

Nowhere was Romanticism associated with the struggle for freedom more fervently than in the Caribbean, and particularly in Cuba where the struggle for independence endured for the whole of the nineteenth century. As in Argentina, literature and politics were linked and the novel, more than any other genre, became the vehicle for nationalism. And since no liberal could support national independence without taking up the cause of the Negro slave, the novel also became an anti-slavery document.

In Cuba, Domingo Delmonte, in whose house a literary and political circle met, gave great encouragement to the writing of novels on social and political themes. It was at his suggestion that Anselmo Suárez Romero wrote *Francisco: the Plantation or the Delights of Country Life*,[1] a novel which was intended to provide evidence for the Tribunal set up on the instigation of the British to bring about the abolition of the slave trade.[2] Despite this documentary purpose, the novel is cast in the Romantic mould, for it tells the tragic love-story of a slave girl who allows her master to seduce her, believing that this will save her lover, Francisco, from punishment. But Francisco hangs himself in despair, thus revealing the tragic and inhuman situation which prevented slaves from enjoying natural emotions.

A more ambitious novel written by a member of the Delmonte circle was *Cecilia Valdés* by Cirilo Villaverde (1812–94). The author was the son of a doctor on a sugar plantation and had spent his childhood in close contact with plantation slaves. In 1839, he published the first part of *Cecilia Valdés* or *La loma del Angel* [*The Hill of the Angel*], after which he wrote novels and worked as a journalist until imprisoned for his part in a conspiracy of 1848. He was condemned to death, a sentence that was later commuted to life imprisonment, but he managed to escape to the United States where he worked as a journalist. Political vicissitudes (he returned to La Habana in 1858 and was then obliged to leave again) prevented him from publishing a final version of his novel until 1882. Perhaps this late date accounts for the greater element of realism in the plot, while the fact that part of the book was written in 1839 accounts for the fact that descriptions of life in early nineteenth-century Havana are vivid and alive. Villaverde, in a preface to the work, stressed the realism and authenticity of the writing:

Lejos de inventar o de fingir caracteres y escenas fantasiosas o inverosímiles, he llevado el realismo, según entiendo, hasta el punto de presentar los principales personajes de la novela con todos sus pelos y señales, como vulgarmente se dice, vestidos con el traje que llevaron en vida, la mayor parte bajo su nombre y apellido verdaderos, hablando el mismo lenguaje que usaron en las escenas históricas en que figuraron copiando en lo que cabía, *d'après nature*, su fisonomía física y moral, a fin de que aquéllos que los conocieron de vista o por tradición, los reconozcan sin dificultad y digan cuando menos: el parecido es innegable.*

This historical truth does not extend to the main character of the novel, Cecilia Valdés, a near-white mulatto girl, nor to the plot which follows the romantic convention of the heroine of mysterious and unknown (to her) origins. Though Cecilia does not know who her father is, the reader is told that he is a Spanish merchant and plantation-owner, Sr Gamboa, whose son, Leonardo, seduces the girl, only to be assassinated by one of her rejected admirers on his wedding day. If *Cecilia Valdés* is enjoyable, it is not for this sensational story but for the vivid scenes of Cuban life in town and country, and the author's attempt to understand the feelings of the slaves and the subtlety of the colour problem. Like the author of *Francisco*, Villaverde condemns the inhumanity of a system which divides husband from wife and allows the slave no normal human relationship. Thus an old woman complains to the daughter of the big house:

Su merced no sabe, ni Dios quiere que sepa nunca lo que pasa por una esclava. Si es soltera porque es soltera; si es casada porque es casada; si madre porque es madre, no tiene voluntad propia. No le dejan hacer su gusto en ningún caso. Para su merced del principio que no le permiten casarse con el hombre que le gusta o que quiere. Los amos le dan y le quitan el marido. Tampoco está segura de que podrá vivir siempre a su lado, ni de que criará a los hijos. Cuando menos lo espera, los amos la divorcian, le venden al marido, y a los hijos también, y separan la familia para no volver a juntarse en este mundo. Luego, si la mujer es joven y busca a otro hombre y no se muere de dolor por la pérdida de los hijos, entonces dicen los amos que la mujer no siente, ni padece, ni le tiene cariño a nadie.†

* Far from inventing or imagining fantastic or unlikely characters and scenes, I have carried realism (as I understand it) to the point of presenting the main personages of the novel warts and all (to use a proverbial phrase), dressed in the clothes they wore in life, the majority with their real name and surname, speaking the same language they used in the historic scenes in which they figured and copying as far as possible *d'après nature* their physical and moral characteristics so that those who knew them by sight or legend might recognise them without difficulty and say at least 'the likeness is unmistakable'.
† Your lady does not know, and pray God that you never know, what it is to be a slave woman. If she is single, because she is a spinster; if she is married, because she is married; if she is a mother, because she is a mother, she has no will of her own. In either case, she is not allowed to do as she likes. Beginning from the fact that they do not let her marry the man that she likes or loves. The owners give and take away her husband. Nor is she sure to be always able to live by his side, nor to be able to bring up her sons. When least expected, the owners divorce her, sell the husband and the children as well, separate the family so that they never come together again in this world. Then if the

The evils of the Spanish colonial rule are incarnated in the person of Gamboa whose refusal to recognise Cecilia openly, helps to precipitate the tragedy. It is he, too, who speculates in slaves, regarding them as so much merchandise. And one of the implicit themes of the book is the sad waste of human potential when people like Cecilia and her mulatto friends are not accorded the same social opportunities as those given to white men.

The theme of the Negro slave fitted into the pattern of the Romantic outcast novel. In fact, in 1841, the woman writer Gertrudis Gómez de Avellaneda (1814–73), who was of Cuban birth, published a novel, *Sab*, in Madrid in which the hero was a slave outcast and rebel. This novel, however, is without the attempt at authenticity which makes *Cecilia Valdés* interesting.

Unfortunately the slaves could not make themselves heard. The one exception—the memoirs of a former slave, Juan Francisco Monzano, published in an English publication called *Coloured Poets*[1] makes us realise the difference between first-hand experience and the descriptions of an outsider—however sympathetic.

Eugenio María de Hostos

The fight against slavery was only part of the greater struggle for freedom from Spain, a struggle whose ideological spearhead was Romantic political theory, with its stress on the integrity of the individual. One of the outstanding Spanish–American freedom fighters of the nineteenth century was the Puerto Rican, Eugenio María de Hostos (1839–1903), who had family ties in Cuba and in Santo Domingo. Throughout his life, he fought for freedom from Spain and for Caribbean unity, carrying the fight to Madrid itself where, as a student, he joined the ranks of Republican militants.[2] With the restoration of the Monarchy in 1874, his hopes in Spanish Republicanism were shattered and he carried on the struggle in North America, in Santo Domingo and Venezuela. He was author of a single novel, *La peregrinación de Bayoán* [*The Pilgrimage of Bayoán*] published in 1863 before he became disillusioned with literature. The framework of the novel is allegorical, for the hero is the spirit of Caribbean Independence incarnate. There is little plot, the story centring on a number of journeys made by the hero around the Caribbean and thence to Spain. In the course of his wander-

woman is young and seeks another man and does not die of sorrow from the loss of her children, then the owners say that the woman does not feel, does not suffer and has no affection for anyone.

ings, he falls in love with a Cuban girl, Marién, and eventually marries her. But love and marriage must always be sacrificed to the greater cause of Independence and Marién finally dies of heartbreak brought on by anxiety on his behalf. Bayoán sees himself as victim of a tragic situation, denied normal life and happiness because his country is not free:

Las monstruosidades sociales que así ahogaban un espíritu viril, que así condenaban al dolor un corazón enérgico, que así mantenían en la frontera de la demencia una razón tan poderosa, que así martirizaban una conciencia tan superior a la desgracia ¿quién las producía sino la nación que aterrazaba a la patria de aquel hombre?*

The novel rejects all that Spain has brought to the New World, seeing its civilisation only as a corrupting force that has introduced 'las mismas llagas, la misma gangrena' [the same wounds, the same gangrene]. Apostrophising one of the Caribbean cities, Bayoán says, 'Tú eres la civilización: me causas asco' [You are civilisation: you make me sick].

The contrast between *La peregrinación de Bayoán* and Sarmiento's *Facundo* is an interesting one. In the latter, the freedom of the gaucho is seen as a threat to order and the rule of the cities. In the former, written in a country which was still a colony, freedom is still an ideal for the future and the city is the centre of corruption and oppression.

THE HISTORICAL NOVEL

Romanticism had made popular the historical novel which, in the hands of Scott, had illuminated the interplay of forces in national history. To Spanish–American intellectuals, there seemed no better instrument for creating a sense of national identity, since in this way the author could expose the evils of Spanish colonial rule and celebrate the deeds of national heroes. A special category of Spanish–American historical novels was devoted to pre-Columbian times and the conquest and these will be dealt with in another chapter, although they too, were usually written with a patriotic motive in mind.

The greatest difficulty faced by the writer of historical novels was verisimilitude. Most novelists failed to make their characters into credible human beings and today these works are only of sociological interest.

* The social monstrosities which thus suffocated the virile spirit, which thus condemned his energetic heart to pain, which kept such a powerful reason on the edge of madness— which thus martyred a consciousness so much above misfortune—who was responsible for this if not the nation which terrorised his homeland?

Perhaps the most interesting features of most of these historical novels is the way they brought to the fore subjects which had hitherto been almost taboo—the heroism of the Indians during the conquest, the evils of the Inquisition, and the rights of Jews or Protestants to be considered human beings. The Inquisition, indeed, proved a very popular subject. The Argentine novelist, Fidel Vicente López, for instance, gave the persecution of the Inquisition pride of place in his novel, *La novia del hereje* [*The Heretic's Bride*] in which the hero was a Protestant sea-captain in Drake's company. In Mexico, *Monja y casada, virgen y mártir* [*Nun, Married Woman, Virgin and Martyr*] by Vicente Riva Palacio (1832–96) and *La hija de judío* [*The Jew's Daughter*] by Justo Sierra O'Reilly (1814–61) used the persecutions of the Inquisition to provide the machinery of their novels. But these were little more than adventure stories which used native materials.

THE HISTORICAL NOVEL IN URUGUAY

Uruguay offers the most interesting example of a country in which the historical novel was developed in order to create a sense of national identity. This small country, formerly known as the *Banda Oriental*, had been liberated by the gaucho leader, Artigas, only to fall almost immediately into the hands of the Portuguese who had invaded the area from Brazil. Once again the gauchos were the heroes of a liberation movement which started when the 'Treinta tres'—the 'thirty-three' liberators—invaded the country, gathering together a following which finally defeated the occupying forces. These events were still vivid in men's minds when in 1838 the newspaper *El Iniciador* was founded in Montevideo to defend the doctrines of Romanticism. The presence of Argentinian refugees from the Rosas regime contributed to the emergence of Montevideo as an important intellectual centre, although little of literary significance was produced until the founding of the *Ateneo*[1] in 1877.

The intellectuals of the *Ateneo* were frankly didactic in their approach to literature which one of them[2] described as

... un instrumento que sirva para llevar al seno de las almas, los ejemplos que educan y las ideas que ennoblecen.*

Even before the foundation of the *Ateneo*, Uruguay could boast one historical novelist, Alejandro Magariños Cervantes, whose *Caramurú*,

* ...an instrument which serves to convey educational examples and ennobling ideas to the very soul.

set in the period of the battle of Ituzaingó when the Brazilians were defeated, was published in 1848. His successor Eduardo Acevedo Díaz (1851–1921), of the *Ateneo* generation, was far more ambitious, for he wrote a national epic novel of the liberation period with the deliberate intention of creating a heroic tradition which would foster national pride. Active as a political leader of the Blanco party, Acevedo Díaz twice took part in civil wars, once between 1870 and 1872 and again in 1897. Most of his literary works were written during a period of exile in Argentina.

Acevedo Díaz believed that the novel allowed the writer greater freedom in his analysis of historical events:

...abre más campo a la observación atenta, a la investigación psicológica, al libre examen de los hombres descollantes y a la filosofía de los hechos.*¹

New Societies such as those of Latin America needed this self-analysis:

...necesitan empezar por conocerse a sí mismas en su carácter o idiosincracia, en sus propensiones nacionales, en sus impulsos e instintos nativos, en sus ideas y pasiones.†²

Acevedo Díaz's historical novels differ from those of most other nineteenth-century writers in that he largely dispenses with artificial conventions of plot and makes the liberation of Uruguay the central event of his novels. There is a love theme, but this is generally subordinated to the historical events. The first novel in the series, *Ismael* (1888), took a simple gaucho as its hero. Ismael, as his name suggests, is an outcast who, during the colonial period, has wounded the bailiff of the estate on which he works because they are rivals for the love of Felisa. When Felisa dies tragically after being seduced by the bailiff, Ismael joins the ranks of the *montoneras*, the gaucho guerrillas who fought the Spaniards, and he became one of the coolest and most intrepid of the warriors. In the other novels of the series, *Nativa* (1890) and *Grito de gloria* [*Cry of Glory*] (1893), Acevedo Díaz relates the story of the rising of the Uruguayans against the Brazilian occupation through the character of a young Montevidean, Luis María Berón, who dies on the eve of Independence. The weakness of the three novels lies in their didacticism, for Acevedo Díaz cannot refrain from nudging the reader at every point

---

* . . . it opens a wider field for attentive observation, for psychological investigation, for the free examination of outstanding men and for a contribution to the philosophy of events.

† . . . they should begin by understanding themselves—their characters and idiosyncracies, their national propensities, their native impulses and instincts, their ideas and passions.

so that he will not overlook the social and political implications of the events he describes. Thus Ismael is not merely presented; his national significance is underlined:

Severa imagen de la época, vástago fiero de la familia hispanocolonial, arquetipo sencillo y agreste de la primera generación, aquel mozo huraño, arisco, altivo en su alazán poderoso, con su ropaje primitivo y su flotante melena, simbolizaba bien el espíritu rebelde al principio de autoridad y la fuerza de los instintos ocultos, que en una hora histórica, como un exceso potente de energía, llegan a romper con toda obediencia y hacen irrupción, en la medida misma en que han sido comprimidos y sofocados por la tiranía del hábito.*[1]

But this didacticism is only one aspect of Acevedo Díaz; at his best, in his description of the ranches and countryside, in his evocation of the guerrilla marches and battles, he undoubtedly achieves his aim in arousing admiration for the heroes of the past. Here, for instance, is a dramatic picture of the column of rebels glimpsed in the flickers of lightning from a storm:

...la columna desfilaba en un terreno quebrado, culebreando, bajo un cielo oscuro, cuya espesa capa de vapores entreabría a cada instante el relámpago, recorría el trueno o rasgaba a veces el rayo en instantáneo zigzag sobre algún morro que hacía estremecer en sus bases con fragoroso estrépito y caída de peñascos, o en mitad del llano, en cuyo suelo abría un hoyo profundo acumulando en sus bordes enormes masas de barro y yerbas.

Acercábase el crepúsculo.

A uno de los flancos, un poco atrás de Alvarez de Olivera, un asistente de largas greñas llevaba la lanza del caudillo, de moharra de acero bruñido en forma de hoja de palma con una media luna afilada al costado y dos virolas de plata en su juntura con el astil.

El caudillo iba en un caballo pangaré de anchos cuartos y cola atada a los garrones, cerca de los cuales caían en ruedo las haldas de su poncho de paño azul marino.†

---

* Solemn image of the period, fierce offspring of the Spanish–American family, simple and rude archetype of the first generation, that timid, surly and proud youth upon his powerful sorrel, with his primitive clothing and his hair flying, perfectly symbolised both the spirit of rebellion against the principle of authority and the power of occult instincts which at a historical moment, like a powerful overflow of energy manage to overcome all sense of obedience and erupt exactly in the measure that they had been repressed and stifled by the tyranny of custom.

† ...the column filed over broken ground, twisting under the dark sky whose thick layer of mists the lightning opened at every moment. Thunder was overhead or at times a flash ripped in an instantaneous zig-zag over some headland which it shook to the base with a roaring crash and with a falling of rocks or in the middle of the plain in whose soil it opened a deep chasm piling at its edge enormous masses of clay and grass.

Twilight drew near.

On one flank, a little behind Alvarez de Olivera, an adjutant with long hair carried the chief's lance, with its head of burnished steel in the form of a palm leaf and with a

Passages like these are examples of historical writing at its best, making alive as it does these episodes of the past and the historical characters who took part in them. Acevedo Díaz was to write one more historical novel, *Lanza y sable* [*Lance and Sabre*] (1914), and a novel of contemporary gaucho life, *Soledad* (1894), but his major achievement is undoubtedly his independence trilogy.

NATIONALISM AND LITERATURE IN PERU

Unlike most other Spanish–American republics seeking to forge a national tradition, Peru emerged from Independence bearing the weight of past magnificence from the period when Lima had been the intellectual, social and political centre of South America. Peru was one of the last countries to be liberated and the one in which the Spanish armies made the most determined stand. Even after Independence, the conservative and aristocratic traditions were strong. The first years of the Republic, indeed, saw a lively debate between the more conservative elements who wished to preserve European standards of excellence and a 'nativist' school, and this debate centred around the personality of two men, the Spanish-born Felipe Pardo y Aliaga (1806–68) and Manuel Ascensio Segura y Cordero (1805–71) whose father had also been an officer in the Spanish army.

Pardo y Aliaga was primarily a satirist, an admirer of British democracy and a scathing critic of the way the new Republic had taken over the machinery of democracy although the majority of the population were too ignorant to know what real democracy meant. Thus he points out in his poem *La constitución* that the government would never change were it not for military intervention:

> Si el soldado no vuelve la tortilla
> El que logró subir, queda en la silla.*

He mocks, too, at the idea of universal suffrage in a country in which many of the potential voters are illiterate Indians:

> Oh escarnecida libertad! Tu escudo
> es para el indio de pasmoso efecto
> Trotar a pie le mandan? Calla y trota.
> Votar?—Recibe su papel y vota.†

half moon sharpened at one side and two silver clasps where the head joined the handle.
    The leader rode on a *pangaré* horse with large hindquarters and its tail tied to the saddle near which the edges of his navy-blue poncho fell.
* If the military do not interfere, the man who has reached the top will stay there.
† O freedom mocked! Thy shield has an astonishing effect on the Indian. They order him to trot on foot? He says nothing and trots. To vote? He receives his paper and votes.

In such a society, Pardo y Aliaga believed, the role of the writer must be that of a critic who might also set standards. In his articles published under the title *El espejo de mi tierra* [*The Mirror of my Land*] he describes Peruvian society as being in a state of chaos and flux:

El cambio absoluto de sistema político, de comercio, de ideas y de sociedad, que ha experimentado nuestro país, en los últimos diez y nueve años, con la brusca transición del coloniaje a la independencia, ha grabado en las costumbres el mismo carácter de instabilidad, que afecta a todas las cosas en semejante crisis. Las costumbres nuevas se hallan todavía en aquel estado de vacilación y de incertidumbre ... ¿Qué coyuntura más favorable para los escritores que quieran mejorarla?*

What Pardo y Aliaga most feared was that with Independence Lima would become a cultural backwater, and for this reason, he deplored the *costumbrista*[1] literature written by Manuel Ascensio Segura.

Segura was one of the few talented playwrights to emerge in nine-teenth-century Spanish America, publishing a series of delightful comedies of Peruvian life and manners, many of which made a serious social criticism in an extremely entertaining guise. Thus his *El Sargento Cañuto* (1839) attacked militarism; *La saya y manto* [*The Skirt and the Mantle*] showed the evils of female influence in political matters. His *Ña Catita*, first produced in 1856 in the Variedades theatre, is a good example of Segura's method and theme. The central character is a Peruvian procuress who worms her way into the confidence of a wealthy family through feigned religious zeal. The daughter of the family is courted by a genuine creole (who eventually wins her) and by the pretentious Alejo who lards his conversation with foreign words and employs Ña Catita as his go-between. The father, however, is sensible enough to see through Alejo; his racy denunciation of him is a good example of Segura's style and at the same time is a sly attack on the sort of values that Alejo represents:

> Un sempiterno hablador
> le quieres dar por marido?
> Un zanguango con más dengues
> que mocita currutaca,
> más hueco que una petaca
> y lleno de perendengues;

---

* The absolute change of political system, commerce, ideas and society which our country has gone through in the past nineteen years and the sudden change from a colony to independence have engraved on our customs the same type of instability which affects all things in such a crisis. The new customs are still in that state of instability and uncertainty. What more favourable opportunity for writers who wish to change it?

un fatuo que rompe al día
un par o dos de botines,
registrando figurines
de una en otra sastrería. . .*

Notice the forthright use of Peruvian words such as 'petaca' [case] and the native distrust of the vain, dandified man who slavishly followed foreign fashions.

Something of the universalist aspirations of Pardo y Aliaga and the regionalism of Segura were to be fused in Peru's greatest nineteenth-century writer, Ricardo Palma (1833–1919). Palma came to maturity with the generation of the *bohemios*, young men who defended Romanticism and helped to form the *Sociedad de Amigos de las Letras* [Society of Friends of Letters].

Palma was author of several books of poetry, and of a historical study, *Anales de la Inquisición en Lima* (1863), but his fame rests on the original genre of which he was inventor, the *tradiciones*. These short historical anecdotes covered every period of Peruvian history from pre-conquest times to the period in which he was writing, and they were published first in newspapers and then in a series of books, which came out between 1872 and 1910. Palma was in a unique position to collect such anecdotes, for in 1883 after the wars with Chile (1879–83) during which his own house and documents were destroyed and the National Library was plundered, he was put in charge of the Biblioteca Nacional and was responsible for its restoration. His removal from this post in 1910 was an unhappy episode which shadowed his last years.

Palma was, then, a scholar interested in capturing the essence of the past in spicy and characteristic anecdotes. Unlike the writers of historical novels, he does not preach nationalism in the *tradiciones*; at the same time, his correspondence reveals a man who was deeply concerned with the lack of national spirit which he witnessed during the Peruvian–Chilean war. Thus he complained to a friend:

En mi concepto, la causa principal del gran desastre del 13[1] está en que la mayoría del Perú la forma una raza abyecta y desagradada, que Ud. quiso dignificar y ennoblecer. El indio no tiene el sentimiento de la patria.†[2]

---

* Do you want to give her an everlasting chatterbox for a husband? A sluggard with more affectation than a fashionable miss; he is hollower than an empty case, decked with ornaments, a fatuous person who will wear out one or two pairs of boots looking at patterns in one tailor's after another's.

† In my view, the principal reason for the great disaster of the thirteenth lies in the fact that in Peru, the majority come from an abject and degraded race which you would like to dignify and ennoble. The Indian has no sense of nationality.

And in another letter, he declares bitterly that the corruption of Peru will affect even future generations:

> ...no hay virilidad ni patriotismo, porque la anarquía nos gangrena y porque la corrupción está infiltrada no solo en los hombres de nuestra generación sino en las venas de la generación llamada a reemplazar la nuestra.*[1]

None of this bitterness overflows into the *tradiciones* the majority of which turn on a comic incident, which gives an insight into the psychology of the past and into the attitudes of mind of ordinary people. We thus have 'intra-historia' at its best, with the author standing at a distance and allowing the reader to draw his own conclusion from the tale. The best of the *tradiciones* are set in the period of the Viceroys, perhaps because Palma was drawn to the formality and order of the colonial period in contrast to the years of Republican rule; perhaps because the rigid social codes of the period provided a good framework for his favourite subject—the endless resourcefulness and idiosyncrasy of the human individual. The following brief extract gives a good idea of Palma's interest in eccentric people as well as illustrating his ironic and piquant style of writing: the villagers of Huacho are trying to find a cheap preacher for Easter. So determined are they to have a three-hour sermon, that they take on anyone who can be found—in this case a notorious drunkard who, in his sermon accuses them of being 'bad thieves'. Realising that he has gone too far, he corrects himself by asking them to have faith so that they might, in the end, become 'good thieves'. This *tradición* is thus a kind of extended joke which not only tells a malicious tale against a priest but also manages to make the provincial congregation look foolish:

> El padre Samamé subió al sagrado púlpito; invocó como pudo al Espíritu Santo y se despachó como a Dios plugo ayudarle.
>
> Al ocuparse de aquellas palabras de Cristo, *hoy serás conmigo en el paraíso*, dijo su reverencia, sobre poco más o menos. 'A Dimas, el buen ladrón lo salvó su fe; pero a Gestas, el mal ladrón, lo perdió su falta de fe. Mucho me temo, queridos huachanos y oyentes míos, que, os condenéis por malos ladrones.'
>
> Un sordo rumor de protesta levantóse en el católico auditorio. Los huachanos se ofendieron, y con justicia de oírse llamar malos ladrones. Lo de ladrones por sí solo, era una injuria, aunque podía pasar como floreo de retórica: pero aquel apéndice, aquel calificativo de *malos*, era para sublevar el amor propio de cualquiera.
>
> El reverendo, que notó la fatal impresión que sus palabras habían producido, se apresuró a rectificar: 'Pero: Dios es grande, omnipotente y misericordioso,

---

* ...there is neither virility nor patriotism because anarchy is spreading its gangrene among us and because corruption filters through the veins not only of our generation but also in those of the generation called to replace ours.

hijos míos, y en él espero que con su ayuda soberana y vuestras felices disposiciones llegaréis a tener fe y a ser todos, sin excepción, buenos, muy buenos ladrones.'

A no estar en el templo, el auditorio habría palmoteado: pero tuvo que limitarse a manifestar su contento con una oleada que parecía un aplauso. Aquella dedada de miel fue muy de gusto de todos los paladares.*[1]

We notice how close this is to good gossip; and it is precisely this which gives us the feeling that we are inside the period, enjoying a story about people we know. And the air of familiarity is increased by the judicious and well-chosen use of colloquial or semi-colloquial phrases such as 'sobre poco más o menos' [more or less], 'era para sublevar el amor propio de cualquiera' [it was enough to sting anyone's pride] or the nice irony of 'aquella dedada de miel' [that sip of honey]. We do not need to be told that this is the sort of malicious tale that members of the Viceregal court would probably have enjoyed telling about a priest.

Palma set a fashion which was imitated by many, but no other Latin-American writer was to produce *tradiciones* so entertaining and witty; certainly no other nineteenth-century prose writer was as successful in creating such an individual style in which colloquialisms and regional expressions gave flavour to a vigorous and universally-understandable Spanish.

ALTAMIRANO AND MEXICAN LITERARY NATIONALISM

Despite this early example of Fernández de Lizardi, literary nationalism was a late development in Mexico, perhaps because civil disturbance and wars with France provided an unfavourable climate for literature. Nevertheless, there was a school of Romantic poetry which centred

---

* Father Samamé went into the holy pulpit; he invoked the Holy Spirit as well as he could and he preached as God pleased to help him.

When he came to those words of Christ, 'today thou shalt be with me in Paradise', his Reverence spoke more or less as follows 'Dimas the good thief was saved by faith. I am afraid, my dear Huachanos and congregation, that you will be damned as bad thieves'.

A muffled noise of protest arose from the Catholic congregation. The Huachanos were offended and justly so at hearing themselves called bad thieves. To be called a thief was insult enough although it might have passed as a rhetorical flourish, but that adjective, that qualification of *bad*, was enough to sting anyone's pride.

The reverend man noticed the fatal impression that his words had produced and hastily corrected himself. 'But God is great, omnipotent and merciful, my children, and I hope that with his sovereign help and your happy disposition you will manage to have faith and will all without exception become good, very good thieves.'

If the congregation had not been in church, they would have applauded; but they had to confine themselves to showing their pleasure in a murmur which seemed to be applause. That sip of honey was very much to the taste of all palates.

around the *Academia Letrán*. Here, as Guillermo Prieto (1818–97) noted, there was a 'tendencia a mexicanizar la literatura emancipándola de toda otra...' [tendency to Mexicanise literature, freeing it from all others]; and many novels of the nineteenth century were on historical themes such as the persecutions of the Inquisition or the struggles of Indians against the Spaniards. Prieto, himself a politician and teacher, wrote a number of *costumbrista* sketches under the pseudonym 'Fidel', observing Mexican life and manners very much in the style of the Spanish writer, Larra. But the most conscious and determined effort to create a Mexican national literature was made by Ignacio Altamirano (1834–93).

Altamirano was an unusual figure in the Spanish–American literary world, for he was of Indian parentage and as a child had worked in the fields. At fifteen, he still spoke Spanish with difficulty for at home his parents spoke the Indian language. Nevertheless, after winning a scholarship, he entered the Toluca Institute where he made rapid progress. He became a librarian and a journalist and fought in the liberal armies during the Wars of Reform and in the war against the French. At the end of his life, he was made a diplomat and sent to Spain, but he fell ill in Europe and died in San Remo.

Altamirano pursued the cause of national literature both in his newspaper articles and at meetings of the *Liceo Hidalgo* in which a literary circle met to read works and discuss literary matters. But he also saw beyond narrow nationalism to the future of America as a whole:

...mañana el sol de la civilización y del poder tendrá su zenit sobre este lado del Atlántico, y entonces los héroes americanos, los primeros destructores del 'derecho divino', los fundadores de la nueva democracia, los emancipadores del género humano, serán contemplados a su verdadera luz, y palidecerán delante de ellos los mentidos héroes del despotismo...

La poesía entonces no tendrá cantos sino para los hombres olvidados hoy; se asombrará la generación venidera de que las presentes hayan pasado sobre las tumbas de colosos semejantes, sin reparar en ellos y sin elevarles templos como a semidioses.*[1]

---

* ...tomorrow the sun of civilisation and power will have its zenith on this side of the Atlantic and then the American heroes, the first destroyers of the 'divine right', the founders of new democracy, the emancipators of the human race, will be seen in their true light and the false heroes of despotism will pale before them.

Then poetry will have no songs except for the forgotten men of today; the coming generation will be amazed that those of the present have passed over the tombs of such colossi without noticing them and without elevating temples to them as if they were demi-Gods.

Altamirano believed that Mexican poetry and literature should be completely original 'como lo son nuestro suelo, nuestras montañas, nuestra vegetación' [as are our soil, our mountains, our vegetation]. And the novel, in particular, was an important instrument in the task of raising the masses to the level of the more cultivated sectors of the community:

> ... Quizás la novela no es más que la iniciación del pueblo en los misterios de la civilización moderna, y la instrucción gradual que se le da para el sacerdocio del porvenir.*[1]

Altamirano's three main works—*Clemencia* (1869), *La navidad en las montañas* [Christmas in the Mountains] (1870) and *El Zarco* (published posthumously in 1901)—signally fail to achieve his ambitious aim, although they are of great sociological interest. *Clemencia* takes place in the period of wars against the French when two officers, one dark and taciturn, the other handsome, blond and sociable, are rivals for the love of the dark, vivacious Clemencia. But it is the dark Fernando who emerges as the nobler of the two men when he sacrifices his life for the blond Flores whose place he takes before the execution squad. And in *El Zarco*,[2] the villain is a blue-eyed blond bandit and the hero is the dark-skinned Nicolás. Hence, Altamirano's contribution to the national novel was a mechanical inversion of the usual blond hero/dark villain situation. The best passages of this novel are descriptions of Mexican scenes. *La Navidad en las montañas* is the most curious of Altamirano's novels, being an idyllic and Utopian picture of a village where life is harmonious, busy and happy thanks to the practical piety of the village priest. The story is simply the account of an officer's visit to the village during the Christmas festivities and again it is these *costumbrista* descriptions which give the novel life:

> ... Los artistas tocaban sonatas populares y los mancebos bailaban con las muchachas del pueblo. Las vendedoras de buñuelos y de bollos de miel y castañas confitadas, atraían a los compradores con sus gritos frecuentes, mientras que los muchachos de la escuela formaban grandes corros para cantar villancicos, acompañándose de panderetas y pitos, delante de los pastores de las cercanías y demás montañeses...†

---

* ... Perhaps the novel is nothing more than a way of initiating the people into the mysteries of modern civilisation and of gradually educating for the priesthood of the future.

† The harpists played popular tunes and the young men danced with the village maidens. The doughnut sellers and those who sold honeycakes and *marrons glacés* attracted buyers with their frequent cries, while the schoolchildren formed great choirs in order to sing Christmas carols accompanied on whistles and tambourines to the local shepherds and hill-dwellers.

This passage shows that for all Altamirano's good intentions, achievement of a national literature was beyond his grasp. The style is quite without the artistic discrimination and the attention to detail that makes the *tradiciones* of Palma come alive.

SUMMARY

In this chapter I have attempted to show the link between literature and nationalism in the Plate region, Mexico, Peru and the Caribbean. The next chapter will deal with another aspect of literature and nationalism, namely the way writers translated American experience into literature.

3 LITERATURE AND AMERICAN EXPERIENCE

European Romanticism had introduced Spanish–American writers to the idea of originality in literature, and as they looked around their continent at the Andean ranges, the pampa and the forests and at the nomadic Indians and gauchos of the interior, they could not but be impressed by the wealth of material. Yet they were slow to realise that originality was not simply a question of the raw materials but also of finding the right forms in which the new experience could be expressed. The prestige of European poets like Byron, Goethe, Heine and Hugo was too vast for much of account to be written outside their shadow, and it is no accident that some of the major Romantic poets such as Rafael Pombo (Colombia, 1833–1912) and Juan Antonio Pérez Bonalde (1846–1912) were enthusiastic translators. Examples of their writing and that of other nineteenth-century poets such as José Eusebio Caro (Colombia, 1817–53), Gregorio Gutiérrez González (1826–72), Manuel Flores (Mexico, 1840–85), Manuel Acuña (Mexico, 1849–73) and Olegario Victor Andrade (Argentina, 1839–82) can be read in the anthology which the Spanish scholar, Menéndez y Pelayo, compiled and published between 1893 and 1895. Though many of these poets deal with patriotic themes and American landscape, this usually means little more than introducing regional place names and names of trees or birds into poems which were often traditional in form. In Spanish–American poetry, originality was to be stumbled upon almost by accident in the songs of the gaucho minstrels who inspired a gauchesque tradition that was ignored by serious Spanish–American critics until the twentieth century.

THE GAUCHESQUE

In a famous passage of *Facundo*, Sarmiento had described the gaucho musicians whose poetry was inspired by the pampa. The rural areas of the Plate region were rich in folk-song and poetry, some of which had originated in European traditions which had been brought over by the *conquistadores*, some of which was influenced by Indian music and dance. But life on the *estancia*, with the rodeos and the brandings, with its emphasis on masculine skills and courage, had also given rise to its own folk-lore and legend. The hero of legend was the 'gaucho malo', the outlaw whose feats of daring were sung by the *cantores* [singers]—but the singer himself was also a hero figure admired for his inventiveness and the speed and dexterity with which he could improvise. *Payadas* or song contests were held in which the *payadores* or singers challenged one another to a duel of improvisation, their subject matter often being of a philosophical nature.[1] But alongside this rural tradition, there had also arisen an urban gauchesque poetry, stemming from the dialogues which the Uruguayan, Bartolomé Hidalgo, had written in gaucho dialect and which had dealt with political themes. Hidalgo is said to have sold his poems on the streets of Buenos Aires, a sure sign that he was aiming at a wider public than that to which the literary élite addressed itself. In his poems, the gaucho became the voice of the common man and his earthy dialect the blunt expression of honesty and commonsense.

This tradition of gauchesque satire was developed during the Rosas dictatorship by the Argentinian poet, Hilario Ascasubi (1807–75) who, during exile in Montevideo, wrote a series of poems in which the chief spokesman and critic was Paulino Lucero, an émigré gaucho who tells of the sufferings of Argentina:

> . . .ese es Rosas!
> mesmito, amigo Martín,
> que grita federación!
> y degüello a la unidá,
> mientras que a su voluntá
> manotea a la nación.*

Here we have a dialect word 'manotear' meaning to rob and an attempt to transcribe gaucho pronunciation in words like 'mesmito' and 'unidá'. On the other hand, Ascasubi is not trying to present a real gaucho character but simply using Paulino Lucero as an instrument for his polemic much as Addison uses a Chinese in the *Spectator* papers or the Spanish writer Cadalso uses a North African in his *Cartas marruecas*. After the fall of Rosas, Ascasubi continued to write political comment and satire in gaucho dialect under the pseudonym 'Aniceto el Gallo'. Ascasubi, however, saw that the gaucho also had literary

* . . .that is Rosas, the same, friend Martin, who cries 'Federation' and 'I cut the throats of Unionists!' while he robs the nation at will.

possibilities, being exactly the kind of primitive, nomadic hero beloved of the Romantics:

Mi ideal y mi tipo favorito es el 'gaucho', más o menos como fue antes de perder mucho de su faz primitiva por el contacto con las ciudades y tal cual hoy se encuentra en algunos rincones de nuestro país argentino.*[1]

His *Santos Vega o Los mellizos de La Flor* [*Santos Vega or the Twins of La Flor*] is an ambitious narrative poem, telling the story of twins, one good and one evil, and describing all the characteristic aspects of gaucho life—dances, Indian raids, cattle-branding, etc. The story is put into the mouth of Santos Vega, a *payador* who, according to gaucho legend, was said to have challenged the devil to a song contest.

Without being a great poet, Ascasubi can be said to have greatly extended the gauchesque tradition. His satirical poems found one imitator, Estanislao del Campo (1834–80), who wrote under the pseudonym of 'Aniceto el Pollo' and whose best-known poem, *Fausto*, poked fun at the ignorant gaucho who goes to see the opera, *Faust*, and cannot distinguish between theatrical illusion and reality.

Gauchesque poetry was satirical, and used the gaucho as a mouthpiece without attempting to understand his psychology or represent his real attitudes. The only exception is a poem, *Los tres gauchos orientales* [*The Three Uruguayan Gauchos*] (1872), by the Uruguayan writer, Antonio D. Lussich (1848–1928). Lussich's participation in civil war campaigns on the side of the Blanco party had given him expert knowledge of the gaucho and his characteristic modes of expression. The authentic voice of the countryman speaks in the following words:

> Yo soy un gaucho redondo,
> no tengo luces ni pluma,
> pero nunca ando en la espuma
> porque dentro siempre al hondo;
> ansí es que digo y respondo
> que aunque soy muy partidario,
> las cuentas de ese rosario
> traiban mucho Padre Nuestro;
> y aquí, amigo, hay cada maestro
> con más letras que un misario.†[2]

---

* My ideal and my favourite type is the 'gaucho' more or less as he was before losing much of his primitive aspect through contact with the cities, the gaucho as he can be found today in some corners of our Argentine land.

† I am a real gaucho. I have neither learning nor ability to write but I never stay on the surface, because I always go to the depths. So I say (though I am greatly prejudiced) that the beads of this rosary carry many Our Fathers and there are masters here, my friend, with more letters than a missal.

Notice the concrete language the speaker uses in order to convey the idea that although without formal education, he goes more deeply into matters than the glib city-slicker. The 'Our Fathers' on his rosary testify the depth and seriousness of his thinking far below the 'espuma' [*foam*] of surface reactions. Lussich was a friend of José Hernández (author of *Martín Fierro*), who undoubtedly learned much from the style of the Uruguayan.

José Hernández

The author of *Martín Fierro*, the greatest Spanish-American poem of the nineteenth century, was an unpretentious politician and journalist, José Hernández (1834–86) whose father had worked on an *estancia* belonging to Rosas. His first career was in the army, which he joined after the downfall of Rosas, but in the troubled years of the 1850s and '60s, he became opposed to the centralising efforts of the Buenos Aires government and he went to work for the provincial government of Entre Ríos. In 1869, he founded his own newspaper in Buenos Aires, *El Río de la Plata*, in which he supported local autonomy, elected municipal councils, and the abolition of conscription for service on the frontier against the Indians, and undertook the defence of the gaucho against injustices. Whereas Sarmiento had supported the city againts the barbarism of the countryside, Hernández accuses the central government of neglecting the countryside, 'fuente de nuestra riqueza' [fount of our riches] and of exploiting its inhabitants:

La capital se resiente todavía de los privilegios monstruosos del coloniaje. Aquí se ha creado una especie de aristocracia, a la que paga su tributo la campaña desamparada, como los vasallos del señorío feudal...Abandonada a todos los instintos brutales, sin conocer la autoridad, sino por la violencia y la arbitrariedad que se ejercían sin medida sobre sus inermes pobladores, la campaña se hallaba entonces entregada al estado primitivo de la barbarie.*[1]

When in 1872 he wrote *Martín Fierro*, his first intention was, in fact, a social protest poem exposing the evils that befell the gaucho when he was conscripted for service on the frontier but, as our contemporary Jorge Luis Borges has said, 'ocurrió algo misterioso, algo mágico'[2] [there occurred something mysterious, something magical] which

---

* The capital is still weakened by the monstrous privileges accorded to it by the colonial system. Here there has been created a kind of aristocracy to which the defenceless country pays tribute as if they were the vassals of some feudal lord. Abandoned to every brutal instinct, without knowing authority, except for the violence and the arbitrary [authority] which were exercised without restraint upon the defenceless settlers, the country was then abandoned to the primitive state of barbarism.

transformed the victim of social protest into an archetypal figure, a legend so real that José Hernández came to be known as 'Martín Fierro'. Most remarkable of all was the popularity of the poem, not in intellectual circles but amongst the ordinary people, some of whom learned it by heart and repeated it to the illiterate gauchos on the *estancias*. Seventy-two thousand copies were sold in seven years and by 1878 an eleventh edition of the first part of the poem, the 'Ida', was brought out. In 1879, the second part of the poem 'La vuelta de Martín Fierro' [The Return of Martín Fierro] was published and five impressions of 4000 copies each appeared in 1879 and 1880.[1] These numbers speak for themselves at a period in which novels and poems by distinguished writers reached only a handful of readers. José Hernández was unique in breaking down the barrier that separated the literary élite from the mass public. Nevertheless, serious writers mostly ignored the poem and it suffered an eclipse between 1880 and 1910 when a new Argentinian nationalist spirit pervaded the literary scene and made critics and writers resurrect *Martín Fierro* as a national epic.

In a letter which he wrote just after composing the first part of the poem, José Hernández modestly declared:

> ...Me he esforzado, sin presumir haberlo conseguido, en presentar un tipo que personificara el carácter de nuestros gauchos, concentrando el modo de ser, de sentir, de pensar y de expresarse, que les es peculiar; dotándolo con todos los juegos de su imaginación llena de imágenes y de colorido, con todos los arranques de su altivez, inmoderados hasta el crimen, y con todos los impulsos y arrebatos, hijos de una naturaleza que la educación no ha pulido y suavizado.*[2]

Both the story and the style of the poem had familiar elements drawn from gaucho folk-lore. Martín Fierro is a *payador* who tells the tale of his own sufferings when he is torn from the life he loves and sent to fight the Indians on the frontier. The opening of the poem is dignified, since the author wishes his hero to be taken seriously:

> Aquí me pongo a cantar
> al compás de la vigüela,
> que el hombre que lo desvela
> una pena estrordinaria

---

* I have tried without presuming to have succeeded, to present a type which personifies the character of our gauchos and I have tried to epitomise their particular manner of life, of feeling, of thinking and of expressing themselves, and to endow him with all the free play of his metaphoric and colourful imagination, with all his impulses, immoderate to the point of crime, with all the passions of these sons of nature that education has not polished or softened.

como el ave solitaria
con el cantar se consuela.*

Jorge Luis Borges has pointed out that this is no dialect poem, since the author chooses 'vigüela' and 'ave' instead of the commoner 'guitarra' [guitar] and 'pájaro' [bird]. At the same time, the opening words 'Aquí me pongo a cantar' [Now I begin to sing] were almost certainly a traditional opening among gaucho *cantores*, so that the poem would immediately strike a familiar note.

The 'Ida' tells how Martín Fierro is so incensed by his treatment at the frontier, where he is brutally beaten for asking for his pay, that he deserts and returns to find his home in ruins and his family dispersed. He determines to become an outlaw:

...yo ando como el tigre
que le roban los cachorros†

and soon afterwards he kills a Negro in a fight in a bar and then a 'guapo', a boastful young man who is a friend of the local bosses. He is now alone, an outcast from society and hunted by the law. Ambushed by the police, he bravely resists and is saved from certain death when one of the policeman, Cruz, comes over to his side. Like Martín Fierro, Cruz has been a deserter and an outlaw before joining the police, and the two decide to throw in their lot together and go over to the Indians in the desert, for

...hasta los indios no alcanza
la facultá del Gobierno‡

The 'Vuelta' tells of Martín Fierro's escape from the Indians after the death of Cruz, his rescue of a woman captive whose son has been killed by her Indian master, and his return to civilisation. He is reunited with his own sons and with Cruz's son Picardía and each of these tells his own tragic story. The most pathetic is that of the 'hijo mayor' [the elder son] who has spent years in prison for a crime he did not commit. Silence, darkness and solitude are his fate:

Cuenta esas horas eternas
para más atormentarse
su lágrima al redarmarse
calcula en su afliciones,

* Now I begin to sing to the rhythm of the guitar for he who is kept awake by a great sorrow consoles himself with song like the solitary bird.
† ...I am like the tiger whose little ones have been taken away.
‡ ...the authority of the Government does not reach the Indians.

> contando sus pulsaciones
> lo que dilata en secarse.*

The second son had been put in the charge of a tutor, the rascally Vizcacha, a horse-thief who gives him plenty of advice on how to succeed in that unjust society:

> Dejá que caliente el horno
> el dueño del amasijo.
> Lo que es yo, nunca me aflijo
> y a todito me hago el sordo.
> El cerdo vive tan gordo
> y se come hasta los hijos†

—in other words, learn to live off the labour of others and take no notice of moral taboos—after all, the pig eats his own children and still gets fat. The poverty of Martín Fierro and his family throughout the poem is in stark contrast to the 'wealth' of Vizcacha who has accumulated bits of leather, old horse-riding equipment and stray dogs. The story of Cruz's son, Picardía, is a repetition of Martín Fierro's conscription (and indeed may have been an early draft of this).[1] At the end of his narrative, Martín Fierro is challenged by a 'moreno' [a dark man], brother of the Negro he had killed, to a *payada* or song-contest in which they improvise answers to questions. Fierro wins the contest, the family once again separate and the poem ends.

In plot, structure, language and metaphor, the poem extends beyond the regional to become universal myth—that of man's essential solitude. The solitude is emphasized by the natural environment—the endless pampa edged by desert—although the poems hints at, rather than describes this:

> Tendiendo al campo la vista
> sólo vía hacienda y cielo.‡[2]

For Martín Fierro, for his sons, for Cruz, family life, marriage, friendship, life in society are unattainable ideals or, if attained, are speedily lost. For the gaucho is outside society. At this point, the reader becomes aware that *Martín Fierro* is not an epic (for epics are stories of heroes who incarnate the virtues of a certain society) but a Romantic myth with the gaucho representing the voice of nature; and society—represented by the evil army commanders, judges and the grotesque

---

* He counts these eternal hours and he torments himself the more for, as his tears fall, he calculates his afflictions by seeing how long they take to dry by counting his pulse beats.
† Let the owner of the dough heat the oven. As for myself, I never bother. I am deaf to all hints. The pig lives and gets fat though it eats its own young.
‡ Stretching his gaze over the fields, he saw only cattle and sky.

Vizcacha—being shown as alien and unjust. This view is borne out by Hernández's own words when, in the preface to the 'Vuelta', he showed the gaucho and his poetry are the spontaneous products of nature:

Indudablement, que hay cierta semejanza íntima, cierta identidad misteriosa entre todas las razas del globo que sólo estudian en el gran libro de la naturaleza; pues que de él deducen y vienen deduciendo desde hace más de tres mil años, la misma enseñanza, las mismas virtudes naturales, expresadas en prosa por todos los hombres del globo, y en verso por los gauchos que habitan las vastas y fértiles comarcas que se extienden a las dos márgenes del Plata.*¹

But though the gaucho is nearer to nature than most men, even he is alienated from it, as Martín Fierro points out in the *payada*:

> Uno es el sol, uno el mundo,
> sola y única es la luna,
> Ansi han de saber que Dios
> no crió cantidá ninguna.
> El ser de todos los seres
> sólo formó la unidá;
> lo demás lo ha criado el hombre
> después que aprendió a contar.†

God had only created unity; man introduces measurement and hence separates what was originally a whole. Thus, Martín Fierro is not simply the Romantic outlaw but is the incarnation of man's separated condition.

As has already been indicated, language, structure, theme and characters are indivisible, which is one of the factors that makes *Martín Fierro* a work of art. Many critics, notably Jorge Luis Borges, have pointed out Hernández's restraint in the use of dialect words, the austerity of the descriptions which matches the austerity of the gaucho's life, and the use of metaphors which use comparisons drawn from gaucho experience. For example, here the skill of the *payador* is compared to juggling with cards:

> Con oros, copas y bastos
> juega allí mi pensamiento.‡

* Undoubtedly, there is a certain intimate likeness, a certain mysterious identity between all the races of the globe who study only in the great book of nature; for from it, they deduce and have deduced for more than three thousand years, similar lessons, similar natural virtues which have been expressed in prose by men all over the world and in verse by the gauchos who inhabit the vast, fertile territories which extend on both banks of the Plate River.
† One is the sun, one the world, alone and unique is the moon. So you must know that God created no quantities. The being of all beings only created unity and the rest has been created by man after he had learned to count.
‡ With diamonds, hearts and clubs my thoughts play.

Such images have added authenticity, since many are drawn from popular refrains and proverbs, a factor which undoubtedly helped people to remember stanzas and recite them by heart.

The success of *Martín Fierro* serves to underline the fact that two other aspects of American life—the Indian and the natural landscape— were less successful as literary themes since authors failed to find the significant form.

When the 'Vuelta' was published in 1879, the nomadic gaucho was on the way out; the *estancias* were being industrialised and organised to meet the demands of the meat-packing industry; the Indian, once a constant threat, was virtually exterminated. Yet the gaucho lived on in literature, in theatrical melodrama, in sensational novels and in the Romantic poetry of Rafael Obligado (1851–1920) who wrote four poems on the legendary Santos Vega (1887).

THE INDIAN

Hernández knew the gaucho from the inside, but no nineteenth-century writer had such intimate knowledge of the Indian. Yet Indianist literature abounded; first, because the rejection of Spain made the intellectuals of America reinterpret the pre-Columbian past; second, because Romanticism had popularised the myth of the noble savage. It is, however, of some interest and significance that two of the best Indianist works came from countries from which the Indian had disappeared—Uruguay and Santo Domingo.

The Uruguayan work is the national epic, *Tabaré*, by Juan Zorilla de San Martín (1855–1931) who, besides being a fervent nationalist, and author of 'La leyenda patria' [*The National Legend*] (1879), was also an equally fervent Catholic. *Tabaré* is the story of a man of mixed blood, his father being a Charrúa chieftain and his mother a Spanish captive. Though brought up as an Indian, he has been baptised and has Christian sentiments. He falls in love with the Spanish girl Blanca, rescues her from an Indian who attacks her, only to be killed by the Spaniards who believe that he had been trying to seduce her. The poem tells of the tragic origins of the Uruguayan nation and the disappearance of the Charrúas:

> Héroes sin redención y sin historia
> sin tumbas y sin lágrimas
> Estirpe lentamente sumergida
> en la infinita soledad arcana.
> Lumbre expirante que apagó la aurora!

Sombra desnuda muerta entre las zarzas!
Ni las manchas siquiera
de vuestra sangre nuestra tierra guarda.*

The theme of the struggle between Indian and Spaniard and the tragic defeat or extermination of the Indians was frequently dealt with in the novels of the period. In Mexico, in particular, there were vast numbers of novels of the conquest, perhaps the most interesting being *La cruz y la espada* [*The Cross and the Sword*] (1866), a novel of Yucatán by Eligio Ancona. By far the most successful of the novels on Indian themes, however, was *Enriquillo*, by Manuel de Jesús Gálvan (1834–1910) of Santo Domingo. *Enriquillo* (first published in a complete edition in 1882) is the story of an Indian youth and his cousin, Mencía, half-Indian, half-Spanish, with whom he falls in love. The pair are protected by Bartolomé de las Casas and by several eminent Spaniards, but disaster befalls them when las Casas absents himself from the island. Though Enriquillo and Mencía are now married, the former is made a slave by a Spaniard who also attempts to seduce Mencía. Enriquillo returns to the tribe, leads an Indian revolt but submits peacefully when las Casas once again returns to the island. The novel is written with care for historical accuracy although this does not extend to the psychology of the period which the author fails to capture. Enriquillo's love of liberty is thoroughly Romantic. As he gazes at the mountains, he exclaims:

'Sí, amigos míos: allí está la libertad, allí la existencia del hombre, tan distinta de la del siervo. Allí el deber de defender esforzadamente esa existencia y esa libertad; dones que hemos de agradecer siempre al Señor Dios Omnipotente, como buenos cristianos.'
Esta corta alocución del cacique fue escuchado con religioso respeto por todos. El instinto natural y social obraba en los ánimos, haciéndoles comprender que su más perentoria necesidad era obedecer a un caudillo.†

The contradictions in this passage between 'nature' and Catholicism, between freedom and obedience within a natural hierarchy, are not only unacknowledged by the author but were probably not even conscious contradictions. *Enriquillo* remains an interesting attempt to understand the conflict between Indians and conquered rather than a great work of art.

* Heroes without salvation and without history, without tombs and laments. A stock that has been submerged gradually into the infinite hidden solitudes. Expiring light which dawn extinguished. Naked shadow dead among the thorns. Not even the stains of your blood does the land preserve.
† 'Yes, my friends, there lies freedom, there the existence of man—so different from that of the slave. There, there is the obligation to defend existence and liberty with courage,

Lucio Mansilla

Few nineteenth-century writers could do more than attempt a historical understanding of the Indian. Studies and works on the contemporary Indian were hardly attempted—with one notable exception. This was a report by an Argentinian army colonel, Lucio V. Mansilla (1831–1913), on an expedition to the Indians of Southern Argentina in order to sign a peace treaty. His report was published as *Una excursión a los indios ranqueles* [*An Excursion to the Ranquel Indians*] (1870) and constitutes one of the most interesting of nineteenth-century documents. Mansilla left on his mission with high ideals:

> Las fuerzas morales dominan constantemente las físicas y dan la explicación y la clave de los fenómenos sociales.*

His aim was to show the moral superiority of the Christians and so win over the Indians who believed the whites to be wholly treacherous. Mansilla succeeded in making contact with the Indians and carefully observed their customs, speech and attitudes, and attempted to explain to them the nature of government and constitution. Oddly enough, it is the Indians and not Mansilla who realise that the government are courting them for strictly practical reasons. As one of them points out:

> 'Que después que hagan el ferrocarril, dirán los cristianos que necesitan más campos al sur, y querrán echarnos de aquí, y tendremos que irnos al sur del Río Negro...'
> Doblando el diario y dándoselo, le contesté: 'Eso no ha de suceder, hermano, si ustedes observan honradamente la paz.'
> 'No, hermano, si los cristianos dicen que es mejor acabar con nosotros.'†

The words of the Indian were prophetic, for although Mansilla concluded a peace treaty this did not prevent the Argentinian Government from launching a war of extermination which virtually wiped out

---

for these are gifts for which we must, as good Christians, always be grateful to Almighty God.'
    This short speech of the chief was listened to with religious respect. The natural and social instinct worked on their spirits, making them understand that the most urgent need was to obey a chief.

* Moral forces always dominate physical ones and they provide an explanation and a key to social phenomena.

† 'When they have built the railway, the Christians will claim that they need more lands to the south and they will try and drive us out and we shall have to go south of the Rio Negro.'
    Folding the newspaper and giving it to him I replied:
    'That will not have to happen, brother, if you keep the peace honourably.'
    'No brother, the Christians say that it is better to finish with us.'

the Indians of Argentina. Even before this, Mansilla's own conscience had been awakened to the wrongs committed against the Indian and in the epilogue to his book, he wrote, 'No hay peor mal que la civilización sin clemencia' [There is no worse evil than a civilisation without clemency]. And he concludes:

Las grandes calamidades que afligen a la humanidad nacen de los odios de razas de las preocupaciones inveteradas, de la falta de benevolencia y de amor.

Por eso el medio más eficaz de extinguir la antipatía que suele observarse entre ciertas razas en los países donde los privilegios han creado dos clases sociales, una de opresores y otra de oprimidos, es la justicia.

Pero esta palabra seguirá siendo un nombre vano, mientras, al lado de la declaración de que todos los hombres son iguales, se produzca el hecho irritante de que los mismos servicios y las mismas virtudes no merezcan las mismas recompensas, que los mismos vicios y los mismos delitos no son igualmente castigados.*

Una excursión a los indios ranqueles cannot be classed as a work of literature, for it is more like a diary or a personal confession. Nevertheless, it gives a far more exact insight into the crisis of conscience which some intellectuals suffered over the Indian problem than any of the novels or poems on Indianist themes.

NATURE AND THE NOBLE SAVAGE

It was inevitable that the noble savage should have found a place in nineteenth-century Spanish–American literature. Indeed, *Martín Fierro* was something of a noble savage himself. However, the influence of Chateaubriand and Fenimore Cooper helped to attract attention to the living Indian of America. It was an Ecuadorian writer, Juan León de Mera (1832–94) who came closest to these European and North American models but in doing so, he also introduced many descriptions based on personal observation of tropical landscapes and peoples. In the preface to his novel, *Cumandá o un drama entre salvajes* [*Cumandá or a Drama among Savages*] (1879), he wrote:

Refresqué la memoria de los cuadros encantadores de las vírgenes selvas de oriente de esta República: reuní las reminiscencias de las costumbres de las tribus salvajes

---

* The great calamities which afflict humanity are born of hatred between the races, of inveterate drives, and of the lack of benevolence and love.

For this reason, the most effective method of stamping out the antipathy which is usually apparent between certain races where privileges have created two social classes, one of oppressors and the others of oppressed, is through justice.

But this sentiment will continue to be an empty one so long as men declare that all men are equal and at the same time there occurs the irritating fact that the same services and virtues do not reap the same rewards and that similar vices and crimes are not equally punished.

que por ellas vagan; acudí a las tradiciones de los tiempos en que estas tierras eran de España y escribí *Cumandá*.*

Mera made a praiseworthy attempt to achieve authenticity in this novel. He had lived on an estate where there were Indian labourers and he knew something of the Quechua language. However, he set his novel, not among the Indians of the sierra but among the more primitive jungle Indians, basing his plot on a legend of colonial times. The story is that of the monk, José Domingo Orozco, who had entered an order when all his family except a son, Carlos, had been killed by Indians. Orozco determined to convert the Indians and takes Carlos to the jungle where they meet the Indian girl, Cumandá, who is baptised and who on several occasions saves Carlos's life. The love between these two ends tragically with the girl's death, upon which it is learned that she is Orozco's daughter and Carlos's sister. We note at once the contradiction in this novel between the apparently Romantic plot and the unconscious taboos of the author, for, despite his sympathy for the Indians, he makes his heroine a Catholic with Spanish blood in her veins. As a supporter of the bigoted Catholic theocratic dictator of Ecuador, García Moreno, Mera could hardly accept the full implications of the noble savage theory which postulated the goodness of natural man. Instead the noble savage must be baptised before he or she could aspire to goodness. But such unconscious contradictions were a commonplace in Spanish America where writers had not lived the deeper ideological experiences of Romanticism. In any event, Mera's novel has been chiefly admired for the descriptions of the natural landscape and in particular of the *selva*:

Multitud de aves se acogen piando al abrigo de sus nidos o de sus pabellones de musgos y lianas, y una partida de micos mete una espantosa bulla al saltar de rama en rama en la precipitada fuga en que la pone la tempestad. Las nubes han bajado hasta tenderse sobre la superficie de la selva como un inmenso manto fúnebre; las sombras se aumentan, y comienza la lluvia. La primera descarga suena estrepitosa en los artesones de verdura, y solo desciende hasta el suelo tal cual gota acompañada de la hoja que se desprendió con ella. Pero en seguida el cielo del bosque arroja el agua que recibió de las nubes y la tempestad de abajo es más recia que la desencadenada encima. Hojas, ramas, festones enteros vienen a tierra; luego son árboles los que se desploman, y aún animales y aves que han perecido aplastados por ellos o despedazados por el rayo que no cesa de estallar por todas partes. Por todas partes, asimismo, corren torrentes que barren los despojos de las

* I refreshed my memory of the enchanting sight of virgin jungles in the east of the Republic; I gathered together my reminiscences of the customs of the savage tribes who wander there. I had recourse to the traditions of the years in which these lands belonged to Spain and I wrote *Cumandá*.

selvas, y los llevan arrollados y revueltos a botarlos a los ríos principales. Cumandá se ha guarecido bajo un tronco, único asilo para estos casos en aquellas desiertas regiones...

Una hora larga duró la tempestad. Cuando cesó del todo, la noche había comenzado, y era tan oscura que aún a la vista de un salvaje apenas podía distinguir los objetos en medio del bosque. A los relámpagos siguieron las exhalaciones que, rápidas y silenciosas, iluminaban los senos de aquellas encantadoras soledades. Al sublime estruendo de los rayos y torrentes sucedió el rumor de la selva, que sacudía su manto mojado y recibía las caricias del céfiro, que venía a consolarla después del espanto que acababa de estremecerla. Las plantas, como incitadas por una oculta mano, erguían sus penachos de tiernas hojas, y los insectos que habían podido salvarse de la catástrofe levantaban la voz saludando la calma que se restituía a la naturaleza...

¡Qué rumores, qué sonidos, qué voces! Quejas, frases misteriosas, plegarias elocuentes de la creación elevados a Dios que ha querido conmoverla con un tremendo fenómeno que ni la lengua ni el pincel podrán nunca bosquejar.*

The passage is a good illustration of Mera's virtues and defects. The description of the storm is powerful and effective but comes to grief with the childish humanisation of nature in such passages as 'sacudía su manto mojado' [shook its wet mantle], 'las caricias del céfiro' [the caresses of the zephyr] and worst of all, the naïve belief that the storm is the work of God 'que ha querido conmoverla con un

---

* A multitude of twittering birds shelter in their nests or in their pavilions of moss and liana, and a band of monkeys raise a fearful din as they jump from branch to branch in their precipitous flight occasioned by the storm. The clouds had come down so low that they stretch over the surface of the jungle like a great funeral shroud; the shadows lengthen and the rain begins. The first torrents resound noisily on the roof of vegetation and only fall to the ground as drops when the leaves come off with them. But afterwards the roof of the forest throws down the water which it has received from the clouds and the storm below is worse than that unleashed above. Leaves, boughs, entire festoons come to the ground, then there are the trees which fall and even animals and birds which have perished crushed beneath them or struck by the lightning which ceaselessly strikes all over. And everywhere there run torrents which sweep away the debris of the jungles and carry it turbulently and chaotically to throw it into the great rivers. Cumandá has sheltered under a tree trunk, the only cover in those deserted regions in such an event.

The storm lasted for a long hour. When it had stopped completely, night had fallen and it was so dark that even a savage's eyes could hardly distinguish objects in the middle of the forest. The lightning was followed by flashes which, swiftly and silently, lit up the depths of those enchanted solitudes. The sublime noise of thunderclaps and torrents gave way to the jungle noise as it shook its wet mantle and received the caresses of the zephyr which came to console it after the terror which had just shaken it. The plants, as if encouraged by a hidden hand, raised their crests of tender leaves and the insects which had been able to save themselves from the catastrophe raised their voices to greet the calm which had been restored to nature. What noises, what sounds, what voices! Complaints, mysterious phrases, eloquent prayers of creation raised to God who had wished to move it with that great phenomenon which neither tongue nor brush could ever describe.

D

tremendo fenómeno' [who wished to move it with a tremendous phenomenon].

IDYLLIC NATURE

As many more recent writers have pointed out, it was difficult to idealise Latin-American nature, which was infinitely more ferocious and savage than anything known in Europe. Yet the most successful Romantic novel was a love story set in the idyllic countryside of Colombia. The author, Jorge Isaacs (1837–95), came from a Jewish family which had been converted to Christianity and had settled first in Jamaica and then in Colombia. Jorge grew up on the family estate in the Cauca valley which is the setting for his novel, *María*, published in 1867 with the help of the literary circle, *El Mosaíco*, to which he belonged. The plot is inspired by the novels of Chateaubriand and by Bernardin de Saint-Pierre's *Paul et Virginie* but the setting of the Colombian farmstead gives the novel a fresh and original touch. The story is told by Efraín, son of a landowner who returns to the estate after an absence of six years spent as a student. He finds that a cousin, María, is living with the family and a pure idyllic love affair develops between them. But María is fatally ill and dies during Efraín's absence in London where he had gone to complete his studies. The charm of the story is partly attributable to the mood of gentle nostalgia with which Efraín relates the story, describing the scenes, the rivers and flowers that had been associated with María. All are part of an ideal landscape in which, except for the illness of María and the occasional storm, no evil wind blows:

Levantéme al día siguiente cuando amanecía. Los resplandores que delineaban hacia el Oriente las cúspides de la cordillera Central doraban en semicírculos sobre ella algunas nubes ligeras que se desataban las unas de las otras para alejarse y desaparecer. Las verdes pampas y bosques frondosos del valle se veían como a través de un vidrio azulado, y en medio de ellos algunas cabañas blancas, humaredas de los montes recién quemados elevándose en espiral, y alguna vez las revueltas del río. La cordillera de Occidente, con los pliegues y senos, asemejaba mantos de terciopelo azul oscuro suspendidos de sus centros por manos de genios velados por las nieblas. Al frente de mi ventana, los rosales y los follajes de los árboles del huerto parecían temer las primeras brisas que vendrían a derramar el rocío que brillaba en sus hojas y flores...Las garzas abandonaban sus dormideros, formulando en su vuelo líneas ondulantes, que plateaba el sol, como cintas abandonadas al capricho del viento. Bandadas numerosas de loros se levantaban de los guadales para dirigirse a los maizales vecinos.*

* I got up the following morning at dawn. The splendour which outlined the peaks of the Central Andes to the east glowed in a half-circle and gilded some light clouds which

Isaacs humanises nature just as Mera does and the passage is a mixture of conventional description and more felicitous and fresher observation like the picture of the herons, silvery and undulating in their flight. This idyllic setting shelters not only the lovers but also a contented human society in which each member knows his place. Thus, one of the humbler families in the district is presented as living in saintly simplicity:

La pequeña vivienda denunciaba laboriosidad, economía y limpieza; todo era rústico, pero cómodamente dispuesto cada cosa en su lugar. La sala de la casita perfectamente barrida; poyos de guadua alrededor, cubiertos de esteras de junco y pieles de oso; algunas láminas de papel iluminado representando santos, y, prendidas con espinas de naranjo a las paredes sin blanquear, tenía a derecha e izquierda la alcoba de la mujer de José y de las muchachas.*

The novel reflects the ideal of a patriarchal society, a vision of hierarchical order and harmony in which love only has a place as a stage in maturation. María's illness and her embarrassing Jewish ancestry are the shadows over the idyll. The tragic ending is inevitable.

Joaquín V. González

The note of nostalgia which predominates in *María* is found more intensely in an Argentinian work which was published in 1893. *Mis montañas* [*My Mountains*] was a series of sketches of life in La Rioja province by Joaquín V. González (1863–1923) who had already published *La tradición nacional* [*The National Tradition*] (1888) in which he had studied the origin of Argentinian myths and legends and had suggested that the 'tradición' could be instrumental in forming a national spirit.

broke off from one another to drift off and disappear. The green plants and leafy woods of the valley could be seen as if through a bluish glass and in the middle of them some white cabins and some smoke from recently burned hillsides which rose in spirals and here and there could be seen the bends of the river. The western Andes, with their folds and crevasses looked like a dark-blue velvet mantle suspended from the centre by the hands of a genii hidden in the clouds. In front of my window, the rose gardens and the foliage of the trees in the orchard seemed to fear the first breezes which would come to bring down the dew that shone on leaves and flowers. The herons abandoned their sleeping places and formed undulating lines that the sun silvered, resembling in their flight ribbons abandoned to the whim of the wind. Numerous bands of parrots flew up from the reed beds to make for the neighbouring corn fields.

* The little home bore witness to industriousness, thrift and cleanliness; everything was rustic but neatly in place. The living room of the little house was perfectly swept; bamboo seats stood covered with reed mats and bear skins; illuminated paper prints of saints were pinned to the unwhitewashed walls with sprays of orange tree; to the right and the left were the rooms of José's wife and the girls.

...es un elemento histórico y filosófico para explicar los grandes acontecimientos, es la historia misma de los pueblos que no tienen historia, es la costumbre de pueblos que no tienen leyes formales y por eso es culto, y por eso arraiga en el corazón y en la inteligencia y refleja el genio de la raza que le ha dado vida.*

The sketches of *Mis montañas* are based on González's childhood memories though his idyllic pictures of village customs, Andean landscapes and local characters are overshadowed by the threat of change. González's mystic attitude of communion with nature was associated with a feeling of apprehension at the forces that were threatening traditional values.

La tierra tiene un alma sensible y es dócil a las caricias de sus hijos y al riego regenerador de sus torrentes; ella se viste de gala y despide perfumes cuando los hombres se aman y santifican con su amor el hogar; ella se rejuvenece cuando siente el calor de las dulces afecciones domésticas, y el de ese otro grande y sublime sentimiento que nace de sus entrañas para encender el fuego creador de las naciones; ella guarda en sus recónditos abismos la patria del hombre, que comienza en el árbol solitario, sigue en la cabaña rústica donde arde ya la llama simbólica del hogar y se difunde en las agrupaciones...

Pero ¡cómo palidece y se decolora la tierra cuando sus habitantes, olvidando las leyes comunes del origen, dejan penetrar en el santuario de las familias las pasiones egoístas, las ambiciones sórdidas, la llama rojiza de las rivalidades y de los odios!†

Family and national harmony are, in González's view, the reflection of a national harmony. Many of his sketches deal with places which are associated with national legends or historical episodes for he sees a deep link between the land and its history. But the most interesting aspect of *Mis montañas* is in the nature descriptions, for here, almost for the first time in Spanish–American literature, are detailed and hitherto unobserved phenomena—the way the clouds pile up over the Andes at sunset, travelling in winter, the condor, hunting in the mountains,

* ...this is the historical and philosophical element which explains great events, the very history of peoples who have no history, the customs of the people who are without formal laws, and for this reason it is rooted in the heart and in the intelligence and reflects the genius of the race which has given it birth.

† The earth has a sensitive soul and is docile to the caresses of its sons and to the regenerative irrigation of its torrents; it is dressed in its best and emits perfumes when men love one another and sanctify the hearth with their love; it is rejuvenated when it feels the warmth of sweet domestic affections, and of the other lofty, sublime sentiment which is born in its entrails and fires the creative light of nations; she keeps in her hidden depths the fatherland which has its origins in the lonely tree and thence passes to the rustic cabin in which there burns the symbolic flame of the hearth and thence spreads into whole societies.

But how the earth pales and becomes discoloured when its inhabitants forget the common laws of their origin and allow selfish passions, sordid ambitions, the reddish flame of rivalry and hatred to invade the very sanctuary of the family!

the flowers of the region. Here, for instance, is his description of the 'flor del aire' [the air flower]:

'La flor del aire' no tiene hogar limitado: nace sobre la roca escueta como sobre el árbol centenario, sobre la corona rubia del cardón gigante, lo mismo que entre los espinosos follajes de los talas; su región es el espacio, su alimento un soplo de savia y de frescura comunicado por las otras plantas, o por la ráfaga mensajera; porque ella no tiene a descender a la tierra, sino a levantarse, a desvanecerse como su perfume mismo en el éter sutil; porque es, antes que una flor, un rayo de luz modelado en la forma, en la forma de los lirios místicos, con tres pétalos de suavísimo y casi volátil tejido, con la blancura y el aroma de la virginidad seráfica; porque es el alma de la tierra, y encarnada en tan delicioso cuerpo, vive encima de ella, impregnándola de su aliento, que es gracia y amor.*

SUMMARY

All the writing mentioned in this chapter was inspired to a greater or lesser extent by Romanticism, but it was a Romanticism appreciated more for its externals than intimately felt as a total change in sensibility. In *Martín Fierro*, the one work which fused native tradition with a theme that was both Romantic and universal, Spanish America produced a masterpiece, but ironically it was a masterpiece that went unrecognised by the élite. With the exception of *María*, novels were partial or wholly failures in their attempts to express American experience, since they failed to express this in a significant form and it is interesting that *Mis montañas*, cast in the form of loosely-knit sketches, succeeds where most novels failed in capturing the life of a region. Perhaps *Mis montañas* showed the lesson that was to be learned—that Spanish–American experience had to find its significant forms and that these might not be those of contemporary European writing.

* The 'air flower' has no precise home; it can grow on bare rock or on an age-old tree or on the red crown of the giant teasel, just as easily as among the thorny foliage of the hackberry; its region is space, its food the breath of sap and freshness transmitted by other plants or by the wafting breeze. For she has not to descend to earth but must rise and vanish like the very perfume into the subtle ether. For more than a flower, it is a ray of light modelled in the form, in the form of mystic lilies, with three petals of softest and almost volatile material, with the whiteness and perfume of seraphic virginity; for it is the soul of the earth and incarnated in such a delightful body, it lives above it, impregnating it with its breath, which is grace and love.

4 TO CHANGE SOCIETY

In 1880, the social structure of Latin America was still remarkably similar to that of the colonial period. Large estates, absentee landlords, exploited and illiterate peasantry formed the scaffolding of each country's economy, the shopkeeping and professional classes being for the most part isolated in urban enclaves. Instead of looking to the Spanish administration, the landowning classes now resorted to the *caudillo* or a military leader to maintain an often-precarious *status quo*, having little interest in improving the lot of the masses. The call for social change came largely from intellectuals, a few of whom (like the Peruvian, Manuel González Prada) were members of the landowning élite though the majority sprang from the professional and trading communities. And in Argentina and Mexico, at least, intellectuals such as Ignacio Ramírez, Guillermo Prieto, Sarmiento and Bartolomé Mitre played some part in bringing about social change.

The greatest changes that occurred in nineteenth-century Latin America, however, seem to have come about less through conscious reformist measures than through external factors. European and North American industrial expansion forced investors to look for new opportunities in the under-developed parts of the world and in the last decades of the century foreign capital began to flow into the mining industries, into railways and transport systems. Latin America became the supplier of raw materials and food products such as coffee, sugar and meat to the expanding populations of the old world. Inevitably there was an increase of prosperity among a few sectors, reflected in prestige building and the importation of luxury products. Probably the most spectacular changes were to be noted in Argentina with its booming meat-packing industry. As one commentator has it:

Carne y trigo a cambio de locomotoras, carrozas, elementos de mampostería, hilados, maderas y hasta aceites y otros productos alimenticios.*[1]

---

* Meat and wheat in exchange for engines, coaches, bits of masonry, cloth, timber and even oil and other food products.

Prosperity went hand in hand with economic dependence and, in addition, seemed most to favour the already privileged. The same critic pointed out:

El latifundista deja este aire semi-bárbaro, semi-feudal...y se convierte en en administrador científico, y con residencia alternada entre el casco de la estancia, la mansión de Buenos Aires y el hotel de París.*[1]

For their part, the majority of intellectuals accepted the assumption of continuous industrial and urban progress and sought ideologies which could account for the backwardness of Latin America and yet provide hope for the future, and these they found in Europe. First liberalism, later positivism and in the last decade of the nineteenth century, socialism and anarchism seemed to offer the hoped-for panacea.

LIBERALISM AND POSITIVISM

In Europe, liberalism was associated with free trade, *laissez-faire* and individualism. In Latin America, the conditions that had given rise to economic liberalism did not prevail, but a common cause was found in the attack against the Church which was both a major property-owner and the king-pin of the educational system. To the liberals the Church was a fortress of feudalism and obscurantism and if she could be weakened or deprived of her power, progress in other fields would then be achieved. Anti-clericalism was thus no side-issue but struck deep at the roots of reaction. Anti-clericalism was a characteristic of liberal movements all over the continent but in two countries—Ecuador and Mexico—it played a major political role. In Ecuador, liberalism was an important weapon in the attack against the fanatically Catholic dictator García Moreno, who had virtually made the country a fief of the Church. In Mexico, the Reform Movement, led by an Indian, Benito Juárez (1806–72), triumphed in 1855 and confiscated Church lands. But liberalism, even when successful, did not always bring social change. In Mexico, for instance, the confiscation of Church lands made the rich classes richer and did nothing to relieve the misery of the poor. And anti-clericalism could even become the weapon of a dictator. In Guatemala, Estrada Cabrera, one of Latin America's most formidable tyrants, called himself a liberal, built temples to the Goddess Minerva and defied religious orthodoxy.

Positivism, like liberalism, served both progress and reaction in

* The big landowner no longer has this semi-barbarous, semi-feudal air and becomes a scientific administrator alternating between his home on the estate, his Buenos Aires mansion and his Paris house.

Latin America. The philosophy originated in France, with the publication in 1830 of the *Cours de Philosophie Positive* by Auguste Comte and became important as a middle-class ideology both in France and in England, where Herbert Spencer fitted positivism into an evolutionist framework. Basic to both Comte's and Spencer's thought was the idea of progress in society. For Comte this progress was seen predominantly in intellectual terms, an awakening from primitive superstition to a positivist approach in which supernatural explanations of phenomena gave way to observation and laws deduced from observation. Spencer saw progress from simple to complex entities as being the basic law of the universe, a feature alike of biological evolution, of human consciousness, of societies and of institutions.

The ideas of Comte and Spencer quickly took root in Latin America where men like the Argentinian, Domingo Sarmiento, the Chilean, José Victorino Lastarria (1817–88) and the Mexican, Ignacio Ramírez (1818–79) had done much to prepare the ground. Like the positivists later, these men stressed the importance of practical knowledge and technical skills and hailed industrial progress. Soon there were many important groups of positivist thinkers such as the Comtians of Chile and the Spencerians of Uruguay. In these countries and in Cuba, they were progressive in their struggle for intellectual demystification but they could also become the ideologists of the *status quo*. Terms drawn from biological evolutionism like the 'survival of the fittest', the belief in the inevitability of progress, provided excellent justification for the élite in power. This was the case in Mexico, where the dictatorship of Porfirio Díaz had its foundations on the positivist slogan 'Order and Progress'. A group of *científicos* or positivist thinkers worked with his government and brought about educational reform. First Gabino Barreda, then Justo Sierra served as Ministers of Education and did some excellent work: Barreda founded the *Escuela Preparatoria* to provide the practical education for the technocracy he envisaged; and Sierra reopened the National University in 1910. But these reforms had to be made within a structure that was still predominantly feudal, in which the élite could maintain a good conscience by supporting a vague idea of inevitable progress whilst doing nothing to alter the structure. In Argentina, a new bourgeoisie found the justification of individualism in an evolutionist ideology of 'survival of the fittest.'[1] In short, positivism encouraged educational progress almost everywhere in the continent and helped to encourage secular schools and a more practical type of education. On the other hand, it failed to change the social structure except in so far as it encouraged rulers to look for quick and showy results by encouraging foreign capital and signing away concessions to foreign companies. Many Latin American countries awoke from an orgy of 'progress' to find themselves in a semi-colonial status with their natural resources in the hands of foreign companies who took most of the wealth out of the country. And financial speculation quickly brought about giant crises, notably in Chile and Argentina.

These social changes and the various ideologies of progress were reflected in the literature of the last two decades of the century. And though this literature does not constitute a 'movement', certain broad categories emerge:

1 A humanist literature which attacks dictatorship and fanaticism and sets up a more civilised code of behaviour. This is exemplified by the Ecuadorian, Juan Montalvo (1832–89).
2 A radical literature which saw salvation in a total change in the social structure and the incorporation of all races and sectors into national life. This is found in the writings of the Peruvian, Manuel González Prada (1040–1918) and the Cuban, José Martí (1853–95).
3 A literature which reflected rather than advocated social change. Examples of this are the Chilean and the Argentinian realist and naturalist novels.

Juan Montalvo

Montalvo is the supreme example of the nineteenth-century liberal polemicist. He was born in Ecuador, a small, sparsely-populated country with natural regions ranging from tropical jungle to high sierra, with a large Indian population and a tiny intelligentsia. From 1861 to 1875, this country was ruled by Gabriel García Moreno who had brought back the Jesuits of whom he was a devoted admirer, had dedicated the whole country to the Sacred Heart and did not hesitate to use extreme oppression in order to enforce piety and Christian living. Unlike Rosas in Argentina and General Páez of Venezuela, García Moreno was a learned man, a translator of the Latin poet Martial, and a witty writer; but believing that 'el hombre corrompido no puede ser libre' [the corrupt man cannot be free], he saw no contradiction between the Christian religion he upheld and the tyranny he exercised. García Moreno's chief opponent, Juan Montalvo, was an equally curious mixture. Born in the town of Ambato, his attacks on the dictator in the newspaper, *El Cosmopolita*, earned him exile and he lived abroad for the rest of his life. Even after García Moreno's assassination, he was against the rulers and (in Panama where he was then living) he published a series of polemical essays against them with the title *Catilinarias* (1889). From Panama he went to France, where he founded *El Espectador* (1886–8) and published his *Siete tratados* [*Seven Treatises*] (1882) which had been written some years earlier. A 'continuation' of Don Quixote, *Capítulos que se le olvidaron a Cervantes* [*Chapters which Cervantes Forgot*], was published posthumously.

Montalvo's work can be seen as an attempt to provide an inner-directed moral code in contrast to García Moreno's enforced morality. His *Siete tratados*, which were influenced by the writings of Bacon, dealt with such subjects as Nobility, Beauty, Genius, the Heroes of Emancipation. Their purpose was to provide standards, based on classical ideals, for the educated minority. These, by following the examples of the best, might themselves become models of dignity and civic virtue and thus raise the quality of Latin-American civilisation. Montalvo believed, therefore, in a moral aristocracy:

El mal no estaría en que hubiese entre nosotros clase aristócratica, sino en que ella no fundase su nobleza en la superioridad del carácter y la ilustración del espíritu, dirigidos sus esfuerzos al cultivo de las virtudes públicas y privadas.*

Unfortunately, as he pointed out, such men are not to be found in Latin America where

...nuestros principes repúblicanos son caballeros de capa y espada, que echan por el camino del menosprecio de las letras humanas†

And he concluded that 'no hay más nobleza que la de las virtudes' [there is no greater nobility than that of virtue]. For Montalvo, the 'best' were most likely to be learned men or saints:

Nosotros pensamos que no hay hombre dueño de su suerte si no son los sabios que están en contacto con la Divinidad por medio de la sabiduría, y los santos que tratan con ella mediante las virtudes practicadas con voluntad y conocimiento!‡

Inevitably Montalvo's consideration of which type of men constituted the best brought him up against the problem of race. He firmly

---

* The evil would not be in having an aristocracy among us, but in having one that is not based on nobility, superiority of character and enlightenment of spirit, whose efforts were directed to public and private virtues.

† ...our Republican princes are cloak and dagger gentlemen who follow the course of despising humane letters.

‡ We believe that there is no man who is master of his fate unless such be a wise man in contact with the Divinity through wisdom or the saint who is in touch with the Divinity through virtues which they practise by means of will and understanding.

rejected any racial prejudice, contrasting United States treatment of the Negro with Mexico's support of the Indian Benito Juárez who led the Reform Movement. At the same time, he admitted that the conquest made the Indian into a wretched outcast who now seemed too passive to better himself. He thus saw the complexity of the Indian problem and felt obliged to hold out to the Indian, in theory at least, the possibility of his joining the aristocracy of the best.

The quotations from Montalvo have so far come from his essay, 'De la Nobleza' and these are evidence enough of the way his ideology penetrates his literary style, leading him to adopt a slightly archaic Spanish (in the reference, for instance, to the 'caballeros de capa y espada' [gentlemen of cloak and dagger]). Just as his morality stems from a classical source and belongs to a long-standing humanist tradition, so his literary style echoes the Spanish of the Golden Age. This is particularly obvious in the *Capítulos que se le olvidaron a Cervantes* which is one of the most curious works of Latin-American literature. Montalvo wrote these further adventures of Don Quixote and Sancho Panza, imitating the style of Cervantes but incorporating his own opinions on a variety of questions. Characteristic, for instance, is the stoic attitude to good and evil fortune:

Bienes y males, venturas y desventuras, placeres y sinsabores, de todo se compone el mundo; y lo puesto en razón es no lamentarse uno demasiado de la adversa, ni engreírse con exceso de la buena fortuna.*

and his conviction that imprisonment or slavery is the worst of misfortunes:

La flor del viento, la luz matinal tomada en la campiña, son manjares que el alma saborea con ahinco; y hasta la verdura de los prados, la obscuridad de los montes lejanos contienen un delicioso alimento para el espíritu y el corazón del hombre que puede gozarlos segura y libremente.†

Montalvo's attack on the obscurantism of García Moreno thus led him to uphold rather than reject Spanish tradition because he saw in it not simply the Catholic apologists but also a humanist strain of which Cervantes had been the highest example.

---

* Good and evil, fortune and misfortune, pleasure and disappointment—all these make up the world; and the reasonable attitude is not to complain too much at adverse fortune nor to be too vain of good fortune.
† The wind flower, the morning light in the countryside, are the food which the soul savours eagerly; and even the green of the meadows, the darkness of the distant mountains are delicious food for the spirit and heart of the man who may enjoy them in security and freedom.

PROPAGANDA AND ATTACK IN PERU

Far more radical than Montalvo was the outstanding Peruvian intellectual of the period, Manuel González Prada (1848–1918), a man of wealthy and aristocratic family origins who became one of Peru's most revolutionary thinkers. Though his family were religious, he became extremely anti-clerical. As a young man, he left the seminary where he had been sent to be educated and he lived for some years on a family estate where he devoted himself to scientific studies. It was during the occupation of Peru by Chilean forces during the War of the Pacific (1879–83) that he began to take a more active part in political life. The war had revealed the appalling weakness of Peru and its precarious social structure in which an illiterate and largely Indian population were outside the mainstream of political life. Peru's urgent problem was the integration of these masses into national life and the development of national resources by governments which brought in a wider element than the creole aristocracy. It was González Prada who set out to achieve these aims by propagandist writings and by active political campaigning in a new party, La Unión Nacional. His programme was set out with forthright vigour in a speech he made in 1888 in which he declared his belief in scientific progress:

...que en sólo un siglo de aplicaciones industriales ha producido más bienes a la Humanidad que milenios enteros de Teología y Metafísica...*   .

and his conviction that the Indians must play a much greater role in national life:

No forman el verdadero Perú esas agrupaciones de criollos y extranjeros que habitan la faja de tierra situada entre el Pacífico y los Andes; la nación está formada por las muchedumbres de indios diseminadas en la banda oriental de la cordillera. Trescientos años ha que el indio rastrea en las capas inferiores de la civilización, siendo un híbrido con los vicios del bárbaro y sin las virtudes del europeo: enseñadle siquiera a leer y escribir; y veréis si en un cuarto de siglo se levanta o no a la dignidad de hombre.†1

* ...that a single century of industrial application has brought more good to Humanity than entire millennia of Theology and Metaphysics.
† The groups of creoles and foreigners who inhabit the fringe of land situated between the Pacific and the Andes do not form the real Peru; the whole Nation is formed by the two or three million Indians scattered along the eastern edge of the Andes. For three hundred years, the Indian has trailed on the lowest level of civilisation for he is a hybrid with the vices of the barbarian and without the virtues of the European; at least teach him to read and write and you will see in half a century whether or not he rises to the dignity of a man.

It was in this same speech that he uttered a slogan that was to become famous: 'Los viejos a la tumba: los niños y los jovenes a la obra!' [Old men to the tomb: children and young men to work!]

Although he retired from Peruvian life for a time and went to live in Europe, he returned even more radical in approach and became sympathetic to the anarchist movement. Militant to the last, he directly inspired two modern political thinkers, Haya de la Torre, founder of *A.P.R.A.* (*Alianza Popular Revolucionaria Americana*) and José Carlos Mariátegui, founder of the Peruvian Communist Party.

González Prada's influence was no less important in the literary field. In 1886, he founded the *Círculo Literario* in Lima with the declared aim of creating a committed nationalist literature of 'propaganda y ataque' [propaganda and attack], to which he himself contributed essays, many of which attacked the Church. The task of the writer, he declared was:

...mostrar al pueblo el horror de su envilecimiento y de su miseria: nunca se verificó excelente autopsia sin despedazar el cadáver, ni se conoció a fondo una sociedad sin descarnar su esqueleto.*[1]

He believed that a vigorous new writing on national problems must look to the future rather than the past and for this reason the Hispanic tradition must be rejected and a new language forged: 'Arcaísmo implica retroceso: a escritor arcaico, pensador retrógrado' [Archaism implies backwardness: the archaic writer is a retrograde thinker].[2] This language must reflect an industrial and scientific age:

Aquí en América y en nuestro siglo, necesitamos una lengua condensada, jugosa y alimenticia, como extracto de carne; una lengua fecunda, como riego en tierra de labor; una lengua que desenvuelva períodos con el estruendo y valentía de las olas en la playa; una lengua democrática que no se arredre con nombres propios ni con frases crudas como juramento de soldado: una lengua, en fin, donde se perciba el golpe del martillo en el yunque, el estridor de la locomotora en el riel, la fulguración de la luz en el foco eléctrico y hasta el olor del ácido fénico, el humo de la chimenea o el chirrido de la polea en el eje.†[3]

---

* ...to show the people the horror of their debasement and misery, a good autopsy was never made without dissecting the body, and no society can be thoroughly known without taking the flesh off the skeleton.

† Here in America in our century, we need a condensed language, juicy and nourishing like meat extract; a fertile language like irrigation upon tillage soil; a language whose periods unfold with the noise and valour of waves on a beach; a democratic language which is not afraid of proper names nor crude phrases like the oaths of a soldier, a tongue in short in which one may hear the blow of the hammer on the anvil, the noise of the locomotive on the rails, the glowing light of the electric lamp and even the smell of phenic acid, the smoke of the chimney and the creaking of the pulley on an axle.

Yet the poetry which González Prada published during his lifetime shows little evidence of militancy, perhaps because like the contemporary Modernists (see Chapter 5), he felt that poetry was a realm apart from everyday life: thus, in the introductory poem to his *Minúsculas* (1900), he wrote:

> ¡Paz y calma y sufrimiento!
> Que el bautismo del poeta
> Es la coz de algún jumento.
>
> Pues conviene resignarse.
> Resignémonos en prosa;
> Mas en verso, combatamos
> Por la azucena y la rosa.*

The poetry of *Minúsculas* and a later collection, *Exóticas*, meditates on death and time, or represents flights into the world of the imagination:

> Me alejo yo del hombre y de la Tierra,
> Por la región del águila y del cóndor.†1

In one sense, only, do they represent a break with the past—many of them are unrhymed and without assonance and are thus a novelty in Spanish literature. The poem 'La nevada' [The Snowfall], for instance, in which his own feelings are reflected in the cold, dead landscape, is written in unrhymed couplets:

> Con mis plantas en la nieve, con la nieve en cuerpo y alma
> Soy cadáver pisoteando la mortaja de un cadáver.
>
> En los seres y las cosas reina el frío de la muerte,
> Y es la Luna el epitafio de mi pecho y de la Tierra.‡

But González Prada wrote and sometimes published another kind of poetry, a poetry more closely related to his political ideas:

> O sociólogo profundo,
> Admiración del burgués,
> Tú que sabes lo insabible
> Tú me vas a responder:

---

* Peace, calm and suffering. For the poet's baptism is the kick of some ass.
  Since it is best to be resigned, let us be resigned in prose, for in verse, we fight for the lily and the rose.
† I leave man and the Earth for the region of the eagle and the condor.
‡ With my feet in the snow, with the snow in body and soul, I am a corpse treading the shroud of a corpse.
  In beings and things, there reigns the cold of death and the Moon is the epitaph of my heart and of the Land.

¿Por qué los unos ayunan
Y los otros comen bien?
¿Por qué a los unos el bodrio
Y a los otros el pastel?*[1]

Most interesting of all are his *Baladas Indias* [*Indian Ballads*] in which
the folk-ballad form was used very effectively to evoke the sufferings
of the Indians both of the past and in the present. 'El mitayo', for instance, is a dialogue between a son and his father who has been drafted
for forced labour, 'mitayo', in the mines:

'Hijo, parto: la mañana
Reverbera en el volcán;
Dadme el báculo de chonta,[2]
Las sandalias de jaguar.'

'Padre, tienes las sandalias,
Tienes el báculo ya;
Mas ¿por qué me ves y lloras?
A que regiones te vas?'

'La injusta ley de los Blancos
Me arrebata del hogar·
Voy al trabajo y al hambre,
Voy a la mina fatal.

Tú que partes hoy en día,
Dime ¿cuando volverás?
—Cuando el llama de las punas
Ame el desierto arenal.†[3]

González Prada, who turned his back so resolutely on Spanish literary
tradition, here captures perhaps more successfully than any other writer
the spirit of the Spanish folk-ballad and turns its into the instrument of
social justice.

Clorinda Matto de Turner (1854–1909)

In 1886, a young widow from Cuzco joined González Prada's *Círculo*

* O profound sociologist, admiration of the bourgeois. You who know the unknowable,
you are going to answer me. Why do some starve and others eat well? Why do some
get soup and the others cake?
† 'My son, I go. Morning reverberates on the volcano. Give me my stick of *chonta*, my
sandals of jaguar skin.'
    'Father, you have the sandals and your stick already. But why do you look on me and
weep? To what regions are you going?'
    'The unjust law of the white man snatches me from my home. I go to work and hunger.
I go to the fatal mine.'
    You who leave today, tell me when you will return? When the llama of the high
plateaux loves the desert sands.

Literario. She had married an Englishman and had lived in a small town in the sierra and in Arequipa. She had begun to write *tradiciones* in the manner of Ricardo Palma, and these were published as *Tradiciones y leyendas* [*Traditions and Legends*] (1884-6). She was to become unusually successful for a woman, for she was made editor of the influential *El Perú Ilustrado*. She came to share many of González Prada's ideas and stated, for instance, that:

El fomento del progreso material y la instrucción de un pueblo es el secreto para impulsar las bellas artes.*[1]

but her chief claim to fame is that she is the author of the first social protest novel on behalf of the Indian. This was her *Aves sin nido* [*Birds Without a Nest*] (1889). This is the story of a young married couple from Lima who go to live in a village of the sierra populated largely by Indians except for the 'holy trinity' of judge, priest, and governor. The husband, Fernando, has interests in the mines, the wife Lucía is often left to herself and begins to take an interest in the plight of Juan Yupanqui and his wife Marcela. From them she learns of the priest's ruthless exploitation of the Indians, but when she protests to him and to the governor, she finds herself up against a wall of ruthless self-interest. When Juan is killed and Marcela wounded in an attack on their house organised by the priest and his friends Lucía takes in Marcela, and on her death adopts the two daughters, one of whom, Margarita, is courted by the governor's son, Manuel, a young man who, unlike his father, has a good conscience. Disgusted with evil and exploitation, Lucía and Fernando leave for Lima and they are followed by Manuel who wishes to marry Margarita. At this point in the story, the melodramatic truth is revealed—both Margarita and Manuel are illegitimate children whose father is the evil priest. The novel is strongly anti-clerical and forthright in its denunciation of abuses; thus, one Indian woman says:

Nacimos indios, esclavos del cura, esclavos del gobernador, esclavos del cacique, esclavos de todos los que agarran la vara del mandón.†

On the other hand, the writer can offer little apart from personal solutions. The couple find the situation so overwhelmingly bad that they return to the civilisation of Lima, thus leaving the Indian popu-

---

* The encouragement of material progress and the instruction of a nation is the key to the encouragement of the fine arts.
† We were born Indians, slaves of the priest, slaves of the governor, slaves of the landowner, slaves of all those who hold the stick of the oppressor.

lation without even their slender protection. Fernando, indeed, sells his mine to 'a few Jews' and makes his escape with a clear conscience. The whole tone of the book is strongly paternalistic, a hardly surprising feature, perhaps, in view of the period in which it was written. Certainly what merits the book has lie in the fact that it was a pioneer work.

CUBA AND JOSÉ MARTÍ

As citizens of a Spanish colony, Cuban writers were almost of necessity thrown into the political combat, since no self-respecting man could accept this inferior status. But Cuba's greatest political and literary figure of the nineteenth century, José Martí (1853–95), not only fought actively for Independence, but looked beyond this to a free and integrated America in which each man's true worth and dignity could be recognised. There has been no finer Latin American than this Cuban, the son of a humble soldier of the Spanish garrison who retired to become a watchman. His son, José, was fortunate to attract the attention of an educational reformer, Rafael María Mendive (1821–86), founder of the *Revista de la Habana*, a magazine dedicated to poetic innovation. Mendive was a firm believer in educating the working masses of the country and it was his personal action, in persuading Martí's father to allow him to study at secondary school, that undoubtedly helped to start him on his career.

Early in his life, Martí found out what political oppression meant. Mendive was arrested after the uprising of Yara which took place shortly after the deposition of Isabel II of Spain in 1868. Revolution in Spain did nothing to ease Spanish oppression in Cuba and Martí at the age of sixteen was arrested when a letter from him was found amongst Mendive's belongings. During the trial, he accused the Spaniards instead of defending himself, and was condemned to six years' hard labour, being sent to work in a chain gang in a quarry. Among the prisoners were old men, boys of eleven and twelve, political prisoners as well as criminals. And many died when a cholera epidemic swept through their ranks. So at an age when most boys are still at school, Martí had experienced the worst of suffering. After a year, he was fortunate enough to be exiled in Spain where he could continue his studies and where he published a book, *El presidio político de Cuba* [*The Cuban Political Prison*].

The rest of Martí's life was spent fighting actively for Cuban Independence wherever he felt his presence was most effective. After being disillusioned by the Spanish Republicans who proved no less harsh in Cuba than the monarchists, he went to Mexico (1874–7), to Guatemala, New York, Venezuela (1877–80) and then once again to New York (1881–5) where he remained until the year of his death. Between 1874 and his death, he was three times in Cuba; the first time living under a false name; the second time in 1878 when there was a brief amnesty; and the third time when he landed there as a member of a Cuban expeditionary force of liberation. His dedication to the cause of Cuban freedom was total, as he wrote to his friend, Fermín Valdés Domínguez:

La verdad es, Fermín, que yo no vivo más que para mi tierra; pero refreno mil veces lo que el amor a ella me manda, para que no parezca que hago por interés mío o para ganar renombre.*[1]

This extreme integrity grew more and more intense as he prepared for the final expedition to Cuba. Writing to his mother the year before he set out, he said:

Mi porvenir es como la luz del carbón blanco, que se quema él para iluminar alrededor. Siento que jamás acabarán mis luchas. El hombre íntimo está muerto y fuera de toda resurrección, que sería el hogar franco y para mi imposible, adónde está la única dicha humana, o la raíz de todas las dichas. Pero el hombre vigilante y compasivo está aún vivo en mí, como un esqueleto que se hubiese salido de su sepultura; y sé que no le esperan más que combates y dolores en la contienda de los hombres, a que es preciso entrar para consolarlos y mejorarlos . . . La muerte o el aislamiento serán mi premio único.†[2]

Thus he accepts the sacrifice of a private life, notwithstanding his love for his family, and he accepts, too, the inevitability of a life of struggle and eventual death in the cause. But though dedicated, Martí was not a narrow fanatic. His immense correspondence, the vast number of articles (many written for *La Nación* of Buenos Aires between 1882 and 1891), reveal a great personality who was interested in every facet of life and particularly interested in the fate of the continent as a whole.

---

* The truth is, Fermín, that I no longer live except for my land; but a thousand times I hold back what love for her demands so that it does not seem that I do it out of self-interest or to win renown.

† My future is like the light of white coal which burns in order to illuminate its surroundings. I feel that my struggles will never end. The private individual is dead and beyond all possibility of resurrection; the open home where lies the only possible human happiness and which is the root of all happiness would be impossible for me. But the vigilant and compassionate man is still alive in me like a skeleton that might have come out of the tomb; and I know that only struggle and suffering await me in the human fight which I have to enter into in order to console and better mankind. Death or isolation will be my only prize.

He saw that Mexico had the seeds of an original culture in which indigenous and Hispanic elements would fuse, and he foresaw the threat that United States power offered for the future. His writings on race were profound and prophetic, for he realised that the white racialist bred the black racialist. He refused to identify men by their colour, believing that true man, white or black, will 'treat each other with faith and kindness because they love virtue'.[1]

The vigour of Martí's personality is just as evident in his literary criticism and in his own poetry. For him poetry was not an artefact, not something which could be considered separately from the society that produced it, for it was an expression of the collective spirit of humanity:

Poetry is durable when it is the work of all. Those who understand it are as much its authors as those who make it. To thrill all hearts by the vibrations of your own, you must have the germs and inspirations of humanity. To walk among the multitudes who suffer with love in your heart, and song on your lips, you must hear all the groans, witness all the agonies, feel all the joys and be inspired with the passions common to all. Above all, you must live among a suffering people...[2]

For this reason, he rejected the escapist tendency which he detected in Oscar Wilde whom he heard lecture in the United States:

Es cierto que yerran los estetas en buscar, con peculiar amor, en la adoración de lo pasado y de lo extraordinario de otros tiempos, el secreto del bienestar espiritual en lo porvenir. Es cierto que deben los reformadores vigorosos perseguir el daño en la causa que lo engendra, que es el excesivo amor al bienestar físico y no en el desamor del arte que es su resultado...*[3]

Every line of Martí's own poetry is indicative of this will to pursue a loftier goal than 'bienestar físico' [physical wellbeing]. In his poem, 'Odio del mar' [I Hate the Sea], he writes, 'Lo que me duele no es vivir; me duele vivir sin hacer bien' [what pains me is not living; it pains me to live without doing good]; existence is good even when it involves suffering:

> Buena es la tierra, la existencia es santa,
> Y en el mismo dolor, razones nuevas
> Se hallan para vivir.†[4]

* It is certain that the aesthetes are wrong in seeking with such strange persistence, the secret of future spiritual wellbeing in the adoration of the past and in the extraordinary features of other periods. It is certain that vigorous reforms should uproot the evil of excessive regard for physical wellbeing at its basic source and not attribute it to the lack of love for art which arises as a result of the former.

† Good is the earth, existence is holy and in suffering itself new reasons are found for living.

Martí's three major collections of poems are *Ismaelillo* (1882), dedicated to his infant son, *Versos sencillos* [*Simple Verses*] (1891), and *Versos libres* [*Free Verses*] written in the 1880s, but published posthumously.

The poems of *Ismaelillo* are in ballad form and recapture the simplicity and spontaneity found in the ballad poems of the Spanish Golden Age master, Lope de Vega. However, the dedication is wholly in the spirit of the nineteenth century:

Tengo fe en el mejoramiento humano, en la vida futura, en la utilidad de la virtud.*

The verses express the father's joy in his child in a direct and unsentimental manner, and the poet frequently breaks out of the ballad framework in search of a looser and freer form, as in the following 'Sueño despierto'.

> Yo sueño con los ojos
> Abiertos, y de día
> Y noche siempre sueño.
> Y sobre las espumas
> Del ancho mar revuelto,
> Y por entre las crespas
> Arenas del desierto,
> Y del león pujante,
> Monarca de mi pecho,
> Montado alegremente
> Sobre el sumiso cuello,
> Un niño que me llama
> Flotando siempre veo!†

The sea and the desert are formless, turbulent extensions, threatening storm and violence. The happy, playing child brings a new dimension into the poem, a sense of human joy which gives life purpose and meaning.

'El sueño despierto' [The Waking Dream] struck a completely fresh note in nineteenth-century Hispanic poetry not only because of the simplicity of form but also because of the allusiveness, the evocation of joy in images rather than by direct statement. Nevertheless, Martí was

---

* I have faith in human betterment, in life in the future and in the usefulness of virtue.
† I dream with my eyes open and both day and night I am always dreaming. And above the foam of the wide turbulent sea, over the curling sands of the desert and the mighty lion, the Monarch of my breast, mounted happily on my submissive neck, a child is there whom I always see calling me.

no poet of the élite, and in the preface to *Versos sencillos* he stressed the need for simplicity and directness in poetry:

...amo la sencillez, y creo en la necesidad de poner el sentimiento en formas llanas y sinceras.*

At the same time, he was more aware than many of his contemporaries (at least before Modernism) that form, language and content were an indivisible unity and that each subject had its unique poetic mould.

Mientras no pude encerrar íntegras mis visiones en una forma adecuada a ellas, dejé volar mis visiones. ¡ oh, cuánto aureo amigo que ya nunca ha vuelto. ! Pero la poesía tiene su honradez, y yo he querido siempre ser honrado... Así como cada hombre trae su fisonomía, cada inspiración trae su lenguaje. El verso ha de ser como una espada reluciente que deja a los espectadores la memoria de un guerrero que va camino al cielo, y al envainarla en el Sol, se rompe en alas...†¹

And he also declares that his verses were written 'en mi propia sangre' [in my own blood] not in 'tinta de academias' [academic ink].

Versos sencillos are poems which deal with all aspects of human experience—the countryside, freedom, poetry, the subconscious guilt and fears that haunt man. Indeed, Martí often plumbs deep under the surface of emotion as in the ballad, 'Yo tengo un amigo muerto'.

> Yo tengo un amigo muerto
> Que suele venirme a ver:
> Mi amigo se sienta, y canta
> Canta en voz que ha de doler.
>
> 'En una ave de dos alas
> Bogo por el cielo azul
> Una ala del ave es negra,
> Otra de oro Caribú.
>
> El corazón es un loco
> Que no sabe de un color:
> O es su amor de dos colores
> O dice que no es amor.

* ...I love simplicity and I believe in the necessity of putting feeling into plain and sincere forms.
† As long as I could not express my visions completely in the forms that are suited to them, I let my visions fly away. How many golden friends have never returned. But poetry has its honour and I have always wanted to be honourable...So just as each man has his features, each inspiration has its own language. Verse should be like a shining sword which leaves spectators with the memory of a warrior who goes to heaven and whose sword breaks into wings as he sheathes it in the sun.

Hay una loca más fiera
Que el corazón infeliz
La que le chupó la sangre
Y se echó luego a reir.

Corazón que lleva rota
El ancla fiel del hogar
Va como barca perdida,
Que no sabe a dónde va.'

En cuanto llega a esta angustia
Rompe el muerto a maldecir:
Le amanso el cráneo: lo acuesto:
Acuesto el muerto a dormir.*

The poem has the enigmatic quality of the best ballads. The bird which carries the poet's dead friend has two wings, one black and one gold, an allusion to the ambiguous nature of his love; which seems more of a destructive sexual passion than married love. But the most moving part of the poem is the last verse in which the agony of the dead man is overwhelming, and it is the poet who calms him and puts him to rest. Is the dead friend perhaps Martí himself, recalling for a moment the temptations and sorrows of erotic passion and then resolving to put such thoughts aside? Whether Martí himself or another person, what stands out is the tender sympathy of the poet for his dead friend. 'Putting the dead man to sleep' is a graphic image with disturbing associations for it suggests to us that the dead may still haunt us. At the same time it is an extremely vivid and concrete image for the expression of subconscious emotions which are difficult to verbalise. Elsewhere Martí uses with great effect the image of a stinking fish which mars the pleasure of the poet as he rows across a lake:

En el bote iba remando
Por el lago seductor
Con el sol que era oro puro
Y en el alma más de un sol.

---

* I have a dead friend who often comes to visit me. My friend sits down and sings. He sings in a voice that has to suffer.

'On a bird with two wings, I float in the blue sky. One wing of the bird is black, the other is of Caribu gold.

The heart is a madman which does not know only one colour; its love is of two colours or it says that it is not love.

There is a madwoman who is wilder than my unhappy heart. She it is who sucked my blood and then began to laugh.

The heart which has broken the faithful anchor of the home is like a lost boat which does not know where it goes.'

As he reaches this sorrow, the dead man begins to curse. I smooth his skull. I put him to bed. I put the dead man to sleep.

Y a mis pies vi de repente
Ofendido del hedor,
Un pez muerto, un pez hediondo
En el bote remador.*[1]

The fish, something that had once been alive in the lake and is now dead, disturbs the beauty of the present, just as dreams from the past or guilt may disturb the pleasure of the present. Or perhaps he is referring to the Cuban situation, marring the beauty of the present. Martí was successful in finding simple, everyday images and commonly experienced events through which he objectified conflicts. We shall see that the Modernists tried to express guilt and conflict through literary symbols and images and were frequently less effective than Martí who, by basing his imagery on everyday experiences, achieved universality. This is even true of his political poetry, a notoriously difficult genre. The cynical cruelty and oppression of the government, for instance, are attacked in lines that have the simplicity of a nursery rhyme:

La imagen del rey, por ley,
Lleva el papel del Estado:
El niño fue fusilado
por los fusiles del rey.

Festejar el santo es ley
Del rey: y en la fiesta santa
La hermana del niño canta
Ante la imagen del rey.†[2]

And in his most famous political poem, 'Sueño con claustros de mármol', he again takes us into a dream world in order to show how the example of the dead can spur on the present generation and keep the spirit of patriotism alive: the poet dreams of halls in which the statues of dead heroes stand. He speaks to them, telling them that there is no heroism left, whereupon the statues leap from their plinths to punish him. Once again Martí makes his subconscious fears and hopes come alive and he skilfully uses free verse lines with mid-line caesura and enjambment to express his agitated state of mind:

* In a boat I went rowing across the seductive lake with the sun which was pure gold and to the soul more than a sun.
    And at my feet I suddenly saw, outraged by the stink, a dead fish, a stinking fish in the rowing boat.
† Official paper by law bears the picture of the king. The boy was shot by the guns of the king.
    To celebrate the saint's day is a royal command. The boy's sister sings before the picture of the king.

Sueño con claustros de mármol
donde en silencio divino
los héroes, de pie, reposan;
¡de noche, a la luz del alma,
hablo con ellos: de noche!
Están en fila: paseo
entre las filas: las manos
de piedra les beso: abren
los ojos de piedra: mueven
los labios de piedra: tiemblan
las barbas de piedra: empuñan
la espada de piedra: lloran:
¡vibra la espada en la vaina!
Mudo, les beso la mano.

¡Hablo con ellos, de noche!
Están en fila: paseo
entre las filas: lloroso
me abrazo a un mármol: 'Oh mármol,
dicen que beben tus hijos
su propia sangre en las copas
venenosas de sus dueños!
¡Que hablan la lengua podrida
de sus rufianes! ¡Que comen
juntos el pan del oprobio,
en la mesa ensangrentada!
¡Que pierden en lengua inútil
el último fuego! Dicen,
oh mármol, mármol dormido,
que ya se ha muerto tu raza!'

Echame en tierra de un bote
el héroe que abrazo: me ase
del cuello: barre la tierra
con mi cabeza: levanta
el brazo: ¡el brazo le luce
lo mismo que un sol! resuena
la piedra: buscan el cinto
las manos blancas: ¡del soclo
saltan los hombres de mármol!★

★ I dream of marble cloisters, where in divine silence heroes stand at rest; by night, by the soul's light, I speak with them, by night. They are in rows. I pass between the rows, their stone hands I kiss, they open their eyes of stone, they move their lips of stone, their stone beards tremble, they grasp their swords of stone and weep. The sword trembles in the sheath. Silent, I kiss their hands.

I speak with them by night. They are in rows, I pass between the rows, weeping I embrace a statue, 'Oh marble, they say that your sons drink their own blood in the poisoned cups of their masters. That they speak the rotten tongue of their pimps, that

The violence of the last verse with the strenuous verbs—'asir', 'barrer', 'levantar', 'saltar' [seize, sweep, lift, leap]—is the violence of Martí as well as of the heroes and the expression of his conviction that heroism is not dead. So he shows that the past has an impact on the present and cannot simply be shut away and forgotten in the 'claustros de mármol' [marble cloisters]; at the same time, it is a poem that is humanist in the best sense for it shows how the virtues of the men of the past set standards in the present.

The posthumously published *Versos libres* testify that if Martí had not been a great political fighter, he might have been the first great twentieth-century poet, for he developed true originality—as in this charming love poem, 'Mantilla andaluza' [Andalusian mantilla]:

> ¿Por qué no acaba todo, ora que puedes
> Amortajar mi cuerpo venturoso
> con tu mantilla, pálida andaluza?
> ¡No me avergüenzo, no, de que me encuentren
> clavado el corazón con tu peineta!
>
> ¡Te vas! Como invisible escolta, surgen
> Sobre sus tallos frescos, a seguirte,
> Mis jazmines sin mancha y mis claveles.
> Te vas! Todos se van! Y tú me miras,
> Oh perla pura en flor, como quien echa
> En honda copa joya resonante,
> Y a tus manos tendidas me abalanzo
> Como a un cesto de frutas un sediento.
>
> De la tierra mi espíritu levantas
> Como el ave amorosa a su polluelo.*

The most striking image here is typical of Martí—the invisible escort of 'jazmines' [jasmines] and 'claveles' [carnations].

together they eat their bread of shame from the bloody table. That they waste their last fire in useless talk. They say, oh marble, oh sleeping marble, that your race is already dead!'
   With a blow, the hero I embrace throws me to the ground; he seizes my neck, sweeps the ground with my head, he raises his arm, his arm shines like a sun, the stone resounds, the white hands seek their waist; from their plinths leap the men of marble.
* O pale Andalusian woman, why does not everything end now that you may shroud my happy body with your veil. I am not ashamed, no, that they should find my heart pierced with your comb!
   You go away! Like an invisible escort, there arise to follow you, on their fresh stalks, my pure jasmine and carnations. You go away and everything goes with you. You look at me, oh pure flowering pearl like a sounding jewel dropped into a deep cup. And into your outstretched hand I throw myself like a thirsty man onto a basket of fruit; from the ground, my spirit rises like the loving bird to his young.

Many critics regard Martí's contribution to prose writing as of even greater significance than his contribution to poetry. Indeed nothing could be further from the archaic *casticismo* of Montalvo than Martí's sensitive prose in which language becomes the true instrument for the thought it must express. He wrote on every conceivable subject in articles, letters and travel diaries. Here is one example from the massive volume of his prose writing, a vigorous, vivid passage describing the adventures of the Venezuelan independence hero, General Páez:

Así iba ya, de jefe suelto, algo más libre que al principio de amigos traidores y jefes celosos, a la cabeza de su gente de lanza que le adora, que le para el caballo para pedirle lo que quiere, que le quita de las manos la lonja de carne que se lleva a la boca. Van por los ríos de noche, voceando para ahuyentar a los caimanes, por los esteros cenagosos, sacando a pujo de brazo su animal ahogado; por los llanos encendidos entre brotes de llamas, turbiones de humareda, bocanadas de polvo. No hay más comida que la res que matan; y los soldados, sin sombrero y vestidos de pieles, se apean, lanza en ristre, a disputarse el cuero fresco. La banda sigue al paso, cantando, afilando el chuzo de *albarico*,[1] asegurando la cuchilla floja. Páez va delante, 'descalzo y maltratado de vestido', con unas calzas de bayeta roídas hasta media pierna.

Cruzan los ríos con las armas y la montura a la cabeza: al que no sabe nadar le hacen bote de un cuero: si la carga es mucha, con tiras sin curtir recogen los bordes de una piel, echan lo pesado dentro, y al agua van, con su caballo de una mano y la cuerda en los dientes. Al salir a un yagual, descubren a un hombre encuclillado, con las manos en la maraña del cabello, con la mirada fija en tierra: tiene a sus pies mondados, los huesos de su propio hijo. De cuando en cuando se encuentran, colgada en una jaula o clavada en una escarpia, la cabeza de un patriota frita en aceite: un día, después de vencer, desclavan la cabeza de Alado, y sale volando un pájaro amarillo, como su bandera, que tenía allí su nido.*[2]

* So he went as a freelance chieftain, somewhat freer than at the beginning from trea-cherous friends and jealous rivals; he went at the head of his lancers who adore him, who stop his horse to ask him what he needs, who take the piece of meat from his hands to put it in his mouth. They go by river at night, shouting to frighten away the alliga-tors, across muddy estuaries in which they have to haul out their drowning horses; over burning plains through clouds of smoke and puffs of gunpowder. There is no food other than the cattle they kill and the bareheaded soldiers, dressed in skins, descend with their lances ready to fight over the fresh hide. The mob keeps up with him; they sing, sharpen their pikes of *albarico*, secure the loose knife. Páez goes before, barefoot, badly dressed with worn flannel breeches which reach half-way down his leg.

They cross rivers with weapons and saddles held high as their heads, for those who cannot swim, they make a leather boat; if they have a big load, they tie together the edges of a skin with strips of untanned leather and go into the water with their horse held by one hand and the cord between their teeth. As they emerge from a grove of palms, they find a man crouched with his hands in his knotted hair, with his eyes on the ground, at his bare feet, the bones of his own son. From time to time they find, hanging in a cage or nailed to a spike, the head of a patriot fried in oil; one day, after conquering, they take down the head of Alado and there flies out a yellow bird, which had nested there, like a flag.

What is new in this writing is the concrete detail; every word contributes to the final effect, as do the rhythm of the sentences which convey the restless life of Páez and his men. And the climax is the series of atrocities, enumerated in the last three lines, which bring the reader up sharply against the savagery of the opposition that Páez had to face. But notice that Martí unlike most of his contemporaries does not stop to exclaim over his subject matter, but allows the details to speak for him. If he had more imitators, the history of Latin-American literature in the nineteenth century would have been a good deal more exciting.

SOCIAL CHANGE AND THE NOVELS OF BLEST GANA

One of the first writers to attempt to describe social change in Latin American was the Chilean novelist, Alberto Blest Gana (1830–1920). The son of a doctor, he was sent to study military engineering in France and here fell under the influence of French realism and especially of Balzac. He returned to Chile in 1852 to teach mathematics in the Military Academy and in 1860 won a literary prize with *La aritmética en el amor* [*The Arithmetic of Love*]. One of the jurors was José Victorino Lastarria who praised the novel because:

Los personajes son chilenos, y se parecen mucho a las personas a quienes conocemos, a quienes estrechamos la mano, con quienes conversamos.*

In *La aritmética en el amor* and in two subsequent novels, *Martín Rivas* (1862) and *El ideal de un calavera* [*A Good-For-Nothing's Ideal*] (1863), Blest Gana depicted the Chilean upper and middle classes—merchants, landowners, army officers and a *demi-monde* of parasites and poor young men trying to improve their situation by marriage. In these early novels, class divisions are extremely important and marriage is the accepted way of bettering one's social status. In *La aritmética en el amor*, the hero, Fortunato, makes a cynical attempt to marry for money and neglects Amelia, his real love. Only at the end of the novel does he marry Amelia who, it transpires, has inherited a fortune. In *Martín Rivas*, fortune-hunting is made rather more respectable. The eponymous hero is a humble provincial who rises from obscurity through qualities of character which win him the respect of people and the love of a wealthy girl, Leonor, whom he eventually marries. Thus, implicitly, like González Prada, Blest Gana seeks a society in which worth rather than birth or money will prevail. At the same time,

* The characters are Chilean and are very like the people we know, the people we shake hands with and talk to.

the novel carefully documents the society of the period and brings in contemporary events such as the revolutionary uprising of the *Sociedad de la Igualdad* (1851)[1] and its suppression.

The third novel of this first series, *El ideal de un calavera*, is the story of the decline in fortune of a young man of respectable family, and thus represents the other side of the coin from Martín Rivas. The *calavera*, Abelardo Manrique, has no fortune and so cannot marry the woman he loves, Inés. Disillusioned, he joins the hussars and leads a gay life, playing practical jokes, visiting dances and the theatre until he seduces a girl who like himself is of a respectable but poor family. The butt of many of his jokes is Don Lino, a wealthy old man who is a complete cynic and libertine. Manrique's ideal—that of a perfect love— is unrealisable in a society in which only money counts, and the end of the novel is tragic, for the young man takes part in a revolutionary uprising and is shot by the execution squad when this fails.

The most unfortunate members of society in this as in Blest Gana's other novels are penniless girls. Blest Gana brings out clearly the heartlessness of the rigid social system in which women are the chief victims:

La clase social que en nuestro país designamos con el distintivo *de medio pelo*, entre la que naturalmente existe, como en todas, variedad de categorías, vive siempre cultivando la ilusión de que la amistad puede borrar el lindero que de la gente rica la separa. Ese lazo de unión entre ambas clases que forman los jovenes libertinos de la segunda y las jovenes, con pocos escrúpulos, sacrificadas, de la clase de medio pelo, será siempre para esta clase una ilusión que le dará la esperanza de la deseada igualdad, mientras que sólo introduce el desorden y la deshonra en sus hogares.*

Blest Gana's novels won him recognition and he was given posts in the civil service before joining the diplomatic corps. In 1866 he took up an appointment in New York and subsequently became ambassador in London and Paris and was never to return to Chile. For some time, his diplomatic work left him little time for writing and not until 1897 did he publish *Durante la reconquista* [*During the Reconquest*], a historical novel which he had begun in 1864. The published version was a total revision of the work which was set in 1814, during the struggles for Chilean Independence. In many ways, the novel closely

* The social class to which in our country we give the name *de medio pelo* [*demi-monde*] in which naturally there exists, as in all others, many categories, continually lives on the illusion that friendship can erase the barrier which separates them from the rich. The point of union between both classes that is formed by the young libertines of the one and the young women of doubtful morality, the victimised members of the *demi-monde*, will always be for the latter class the illusion that will give them hope of longed-for equality, although it only introduces disorder and dishonour into their homes.

resembles one of the *Episodios Nacionales* by the Spanish novelist, Pérez Galdós, for as in the Spanish novels, Blest Gana weaves actual historical figures into a story whose protagonists are fictional. Abel Malsira is a landowner's son in love with an ambitious Spanish woman, Violante. Abel's growing conviction that he must join the cause of Independence is accompanied by his growing disillusion with Violante and the awakening of his love for a cousin, Luisa Bustos, a fervent supporter of the Independence cause. The novel ends in tragedy for the lovers. A skilful piece of historical reconstruction, it is one of the best examples of the nineteenth-century historical novel.

Although Blest Gana wrote several other novels, one only is of outstanding interest—*Los transplantados* [*The Uprooted*] (1904) which deals with a theme familiar from the novels of Henry James—that of the cynical and impoverished European who courts the wealthy American woman for money. Mercedes Canalejas is a Spanish–American girl living in Paris with her wealthy and ambitious family who want to conquer the aristocratic world of Europe. Against her will, she is forced to marry an impoverished and cynical aristocrat and kills herself because her real love is for a young Latin-American student, Patricio. Mercedes thus fights against the false values of her family who love displaying wealth and think they can buy their way into nobility. But the odious family is characteristic of a type of Latin American whom Blest Gana criticises in all his novels—the materialists who believe that money is the key to all doors. Thus his novels, even though their characterisation is schematic and the writing clumsy on occasions, do represent a questioning of the values of the brash new societies that were emerging. And in *Los transplantados*, the fact that the Canalejas fortune is anything but secure adds to the absurdity of a family which has put its faith in material wellbeing. The attack on the materialism of the age is thus the common thread that runs through Blest Gana's novels.

ARGENTINA AND THE NATURALIST NOVEL

Nowhere in Latin America had society changed more drastically than in Argentina where the influx of immigrants, the rapid growth of Buenos Aires, and the success of the meat-exporting industry had created a type of urban prosperity unparalleled in the southern hemisphere. Compared with Buenos Aires, Lima and Bogotá were, at this period, still colonial cities. Yet the insecurity of this prosperity was soon sensed by writers who found literary models in the contemporary French naturalist novels, especially those of Zola which became extremely popular in Spanish America. One exemplary novel of this type was *La Bolsa* [*The Stock Exchange*] (1890) written by the journalist José María Miró (1867–96) who wrote under the pseudonym 'Julián Martel'. *La Bolsa* is the sad tale of the downfall of an opulent business man, Glow, who speculates too recklessly on the stock exchange. However, though the novel captures some aspects of the feverish life of Buenos Aires at the period, the technique is clumsy and Miró himself scarcely understood the forces involved, seeing the main enemies as the Jewish businessman and 'oro' [gold] against which there is a characteristic outburst:

...el oro es corruptor. Allí donde el dinero abunda, rara vez el patriotismo existe. Además de eso, el cosmopolitismo que tan grandes proporciones va tomando entre nosotros, hasta el punto de que ya no sabemos lo que somos, si franceses o españoles, o italianos o ingleses, nos trae, junto con el engradeci-miento material, el indiferentismo político, porque el extranjero que viene a nuestra tierra, naturalícese o no, maldito lo que se le importa que estemos bien o mal gobernados. Haya dinero, prospere su industria, esté bien remunerado su trabajo, él se ríe de los demás. Ahora bien lo peor del caso es que se nos ha contagiado este culpable egoismo importado; a nosotros, los argentinos.*

The polemic against 'foreigners' indicates that the influx of immigrants was already affecting the attitudes of the Argentinians. The materialism of the age is here blamed on the foreigners.

A contemporary of Miró, Eugenio Cambaceres (1843–88), the best of the Argentinian novelists, made a similar attack in his novel *Silbidos de un vago* [*Whistlings of a Vagabond*] (1881) which was less a novel than a series of ironic reflections on the society of Buenos Aires. Cambaceres also rails at the avariciousness of the trading classes, saying of one of their members:

Será incapaz de introducir materialmente la mano en el bolsillo del prójimo para sustraerle ni un peso ni diez millones, pero qué bonitamente le meterá cada clavo como un templo haciéndole creer que le cuesta mil y vende en cien, lo que no le cuesta diez ni vale uno.†

* ...gold is the corruptor. Where money is plentiful, patriotism rarely exists. Besides, cosmopolitanism which is making such great strides among us to the point where we no longer know who we are, whether French, Spanish, Italian or English, brings, along with material aggrandisement, political indifference, for the foreigner who comes to our land, whether naturalised or not, does not care a damn whether we are well or badly ruled. As long as there is money and industry prospers, as long as his work is remuner-ated, he can laugh at the rest. Now the worst of the case is that we have been injected by this blameworthy imported selfishness, we, the Argentinian people.
† He would be incapable of actually putting his hand in his neighbour's pocket and taking out one peso or ten millions, but he has no scruples in nailing him down another way

And he adds the moral reflection that the trader:

...ha cometido, es cierto, una iniquidad, pero eso se llama, en el medio donde vive, celebrar una transacción comercial, hacer un buen negocio.*

A second novel, *Música sentimental* (1884), the story of a prostitute regenerated through love, is set in France but two final novels, *Sin rumbo* [*Aimless*] (1885) and *En la sangre* [*In the Blood*] (1887) again have an Argentinian setting. In both the hero is a victim of forces over which he feels he has no control and they are perhaps most interesting as a reflection of the writer's own helplessness in a period of rapid change. *Sin rumbo* is, as the title suggests, the dilemma of the man who has lost traditional faith and who rides the tide of Schopenhauerian pessimism. Andrés, the protagonist, is a landowner who feels that life is a farce and love the pastime of fools:

Saber es sufrir: ignorar, comer, dormir y no pensar la solución exacta del problema, la única dicha de vivir.†

His knowledge leads him to the conclusion that we are the slaves of our instincts and he does little to control his own momentary passion for the daughter of one of the labourers on the estate, whom he seduces and then abandons. The next years are spent in Buenos Aires where he becomes the lover of an opera singer, but the refined luxury that surrounds this affair cannot ultimately mask the fact that low instincts are at work again. He returns, at last, to the farm to find his country sweetheart Donato has died and that their child survives. He finds momentary pleasure in his love for his daughter Andrea, but when she too dies, Andrés commits suicide in one of the most brutal suicide scenes in Latin-American fiction, for he cuts open his own stomach:

Un chorro de sangre y de excrementos saltó, le ensució la cara, la ropa, fue a salpicar la cama del cadáver de su hija, mientras él, boqueando, rodaba por el suelo...‡

The final scene sums up Cambaceres's belief that lack of moral or spiritual purpose in man's life reduces him to a biological machine

---

by making him believe that it is worth a thousand and he gets it for a hundred, when it costs ten and is not worth one.
* ...it is true that he has committed an evil but this is called in the circles in which he lives, making a commercial transaction or doing good business.
† Knowing is suffering: knowing nothing, eating, sleeping and not thinking of the exact solution of the problem is the only happiness in living.
‡ A stream of blood and excrement leapt out, dirtied his face and clothing and spattered the body of his daughter, while he, at his last gasp, rolled to the ground...

which propagates and evacuates without the intervention of human will. His only freedom is that of self-destruction.

En la sangre is even more mechanistic in its psychological approach. The opening chapter describes an Italian immigrant beating his wife and the closing chapter describes the immigrant's son, Gennaro, attacking his wife. In between, Gennaro, despite his good education, becomes a cheat and a rogue who deliberately seduces a girl of a wealthy family to force her to marry him. He soon spends her fortune and ends in the same brutish condition that his father had lived in. This mechanistic approach, so characteristic of the nineteenth century, is quite unacceptable today and the novel is of mainly sociological interest.

SUMMARY

Two of the writers mentioned in this chapter—Martí and Montalvo—were deeply influenced by Spanish literary traditions; two more, Cambaceres and Blest Gana, were influenced by contemporary French literature. In common with writers throughout the nineteenth century, they appropriated whatever foreign traditions they found suitable to their immediate purpose, whether that of the Spanish humanist tradition on which Montalvo drew or the naturalist novel which inspired Cambaceres. Only Martí, however, significantly enriched and transformed the sources on which he drew. He saw art neither as a propaganda tool nor as play but as the expression of a total experience which was communicable because universal. Yet this genuinely original poet and thinker had no followers and it was to be some time before his own optimistic statement that 'el libro importado ha sido vencido en América por el hombre natural' [the imported book has been vanquished in America by natural man] was truly applicable to the literature of the continent.[1]

5 MODERNISM

In the 1880s, a new phenomenon was to be observed in Latin America —the emergence of a number of poets who revolutionised the language and form of poetry. In Mexico, Salvador Díaz Mirón (1853–1928) and Manuel Gutiérrez Nájera (1859–95); in Cuba, Julián del Casal (1863–93); in Colombia, José Asunción Silva (1865–96) explored new areas of experience and sought a literary language that would embrace these. However, it was the publication of *Azul* (1888) by the Nicaraguan poet Rubén Darío which gave this movement of innovation the greatest impetus, and it was also Darío who defined the movement and gave it the name of Modernism. This was in 1890 when, in an article on Ricardo Palma, he wrote:

[Palma] comprende y admira el espíritu nuevo que hoy anima a un pequeño pero triunfante y soberbio grupo de escritores y poetas de la América española: el modernismo. Conviene saber: la elevación y la demostración en la crítica... la libertad y el vuelo, y el triunfo de lo bello sobre lo preceptivo, en la prosa, y la novedad en la poesía; dar color y vida y aire y flexibilidad al antiguo verso que sufría aniquilosis, apretado entre tomados moldes de hierro.*[1]

There have been few better definitions of Modernism. Here Darío puts into a sentence the three essential strands that bound together a disparate group of individual writers—1. the rejection of any overt message or teaching in art; 2. the stress on beauty as the highest goal; 3. the need to free verse from traditional forms. And Darío was the central personality of the whole movement, not only for his own experiments and innovations but also because his extensive travels through the American continent helped to link poets of different countries and give them a sense of solidarity. Not only this, he helped to found or contributed to many of the little magazines that sprang up all over

---

* [Palma] understands and admires the new spirit which today animates a small but triumphant and proud group of writers and poets of Spanish America: the spirit of Modernism. This implies: elevation and factual accuracy in criticism, in prose, freedom, imagination and the triumph of the beautiful over the didactic; originality in poetry and the infusion of colour, life, air and flexibility to old verse forms which suffered from repression for they were pressed between imitated iron moulds.

the continent as part of the campaign on behalf of the new poetry. He had helped to found the *Revista de América* in Buenos Aires, and contributed to the *Revista de Costa Rica*, *Azul* (Mexico) and *La Biblioteca* (Argentina).

The appearance of these and many other literary magazines—*Cosmópolis* (Venezuela), *Revista Moderna* (Mexico) and *Pluma y lápiz* (Chile)—was itself a totally new phenomenon, since never before had there been such an emphasis on art and literature. The slogan of 'Art for art's sake' is implicit in many of the editorials of these magazines; typical, in this respect, is the editorial to the first number of *Pluma y lápiz* which appeared in Santiago, Chile, in 1900.

Literatura y arte son nuestro campo:—todo lo que tienda a la agradable recreación intelectual y la sana alegría del espíritu. Con esto queda subentendido que prescindimos por completo de matices partidaristas y que queda proscrito cuanto no sea culto ni agradable, es decir, todo lo grosero y todo lo tonto.*[1]

Ephemeral though many of these magazines were, they helped to change the literary climate of the continent and did much to increase the importance of art and literature.

The high point of Modernism was marked by the publication of three important volumes of poetry: *Prosas profanas* (1896) by Darío; *Las montañas del oro* (1897) by Leopoldo Lugones (Argentina, 1874–1938); and *Castalia bárbara* (1899) by Ricardo Jaimes Freyre (Bolivia, 1868–1933). After 1900, Modernism tended to separate in a number of different strands, religious and meditative in the poetry of the Mexican, Amado Nervo (1870–1919), and the Uruguayan, Julio Herrera y Reissig (1875–1910), sensual in the poetry of Delmira Agustini (1886–1914), Americanist in the Peruvian, José Santos Chocano (1875–1934). But, broadly speaking, Modernism remained the dominant style of Spanish-American poetry down to the avant-garde movements of the '20s.

One significant aspect of Modernism was that it revolutionised the Spanish-American poets' attitude to art and society. Hitherto, most writers had regarded literature as a weapon in a social or political struggle. But the Modernist believed that contemporary society was in the wrong, since all over the continent governments deified material progress. No Modernist could bring himself to believe that material

---

* Literature and art are our field—all that tends towards agreeable intellectual recreation and the healthy joy of the spirit. This implies that we do away with partisan tendencies and that we forbid all that is not cultivated and agreeable; that is all that is coarse and stupid.

prosperity was a worth-while aim either for an individual or for a society, particularly as in Latin America this prosperity was unstable. The financial crises of the '90s proved the specious nature of the new wealth and some of the Modernist poets—Asunción Silva, Julián del Casal, Herrera y Reissig, and Leopoldo Lugones—suffered personally when their families lost money because of political or financial reverses. In contrast to societies which pursued the chimera of material progress, the Modernists sought values that were atemporal and eternal, and they found these values in art. The contrast between the 'cold' everyday world and the eternally beautiful realm of art was expressed by José Asunción Silva in a poem, 'Ars':

> El verso es vaso santo; poned en él tan sólo
>   Un pensamiento puro,
> En cuyo fondo bullan hirvientes las imágenes
> Como burbujas de oro de un viejo vino oscuro.

> Allí verted las flores que en la continua lucha
>   Ajó del mundo el frío
> Recuerdos deliciosos de tiempos que no vuelven,
> Y nardos empapados en gotas de rocío

> Para que la existencia mísera se embalsama
>   Cual de una esencia ignota
> Quemándose en el fuego del alma enternecida
> De aquel supremo bálsamo basta una sola gota!*

Art is thus the distilling flask in which is preserved only the purest and most beautiful of life's sensations.

SCHOPENHAUER AND HUGO

Directly or indirectly, much Modernist writing on art reflects the view of the German 'pessimist', Arthur Schopenhauer (1788–1860), whose thought had embodied both the determinism characteristic of much nineteenth-century thought and a high appreciation of art as a way of transcending this determinism. Schopenhauer believed that individuals were motivated not by rational thought but by unconscious drives (or Will) which worked for the betterment of the species. Men believed themselves to be individuals capable of making rational choices

---

* The poem is a holy vessel; put in it only pure thought. In its depths bubble and boil images like the golden bubbles of a dark old wine.

  There, pour flowers which the cold of the world has withered, delightful memories of times that do not return and spikenard soaked in dewdrops.

  So that miserable existence is thus perfumed as if with an unknown essence, burning in the fire of the heart that is moved; of that supreme balm, only a drop is needed.

when in fact these were determined by the Will. Realisation of their aims whether in love, ambition or on any other plane was bound to bring pain and suffering which could only be avoided when man abstracted himself from the flux of everyday life and contemplated eternal ideas. The artist was thus the most enviable member of society.

That this philosophy found acceptance among Spanish–American intellectuals in the '80s and '90s can be readily understood. We have already seen how the novel, *Sin rumba,* by Cambaceres embodied the deterministic aspects of this philosophy. In Modernism we see another aspect, the poet's attempt through art to liberate himself from the temporal flux in an act of communion with all that is eternal. But to the indirect influence of Schopenhauer on Modernism, there must be added the more immediate impact made by Victor Hugo with his view of the poet as a seer who could predict the future and who also mediated between the divine and the earthly. This Hugoan view of the poet is faithfully echoed in a poem by Salvador Díaz Mirón:

> El poeta es el antro en que la oscura
> síbila del progreso se revuelve,
> el vaso en que la vida se depura,
> y, libre de la escoria, se resuelve
> en verdad, en virtud y en hermosura.
> No hay gloria de más claros arreboles
> que la de ser, en la penumbra immensa,
> uno de esos crisoles
> en que la luz del alma se condensa
> como el fuego del éter en los soles.* [1]

So, whereas earlier generations of Latin Americans had put the political struggle first and believed that literature could only flourish in a changed society, the Modernists put literary creation first and placed the poet far above the statesman or the politician. However, the poet's rejection of society went much deeper than the political surface and became a rejection of all conventions whether of dress or behaviour. Indeed, defiance of superficial conventions—of dress, for instance— were merely symptoms of a deeper feeling of alienation from the moral standards of society. Certainly the poets made little effort to conform. Asunción Silva, the Colombian poet, was reputed to take drugs and to be in love with his sister. Julián del Casal used to burn

---

* The poet is the cavern in which the dark sybil of progress moves about, the cup in which life is purified, and, free of dross, is distilled in truth, virtue and beauty. There is no glory with a purer hue than that of being, in the immense darkness, one of these crucibles in which the soul's light is condensed like the fire of ether in suns.

incense before a statue of the Buddha. Scandals, suicides, even murders were features of the lives of the Modernists. Silva killed himself; Delmira Agustini, the Uruguayan poetess, was murdered. Darío, after two broken marriages, lived for years with a Spanish woman of humble stock.

These deviations from the accepted moral standards of the day are so persistent that we must obviously conclude that the Modernists' dissatisfaction went far deeper than mere literary matters. Indeed, two important critics, the Spanish poet, Juan Ramón Jiménez and Federico de Onís both see Modernism as one aspect of a deeper spiritual crisis. Juan Ramón, in particular, was emphatic in assigning to Modernism a role as important as that of Renaissance or Romantic thought. He declared that he differed from many critics who

... han sustentado el error de considerar el modernismo como una cuestión poética y no como lo que fue y sigue siendo: un movimiento general teológico, científico y literario.*[1]

For Federico de Onís, Modernism was part of a world-wide movement, one aspect of the crisis of Western civilisation. It was

... la forma hispánica de la crisis universal de las letras y del espíritu que inicia hacia 1885 la disolución del siglo XIX y que se había de manifestar en el arte, la ciencia, la religión, la política y gradualmente en los demás aspectos de la vida entera.†[2]

This crisis had arisen as a result of nineteenth-century intellectual progress. Scientific discovery had undermined the edifice of traditional belief yet it had failed to give any sense of purpose to the individual and to society; it had been unable to provide any other goal than material prosperity.

Far from offering a solution in this crisis, the reigning philosophy of positivism discouraged speculation and, in any case, had become vulgarised. 'The survival of the fittest' was scarcely a slogan that could appeal to the artist or thinker, and Darío was only voicing the opinion common among writers when he said: 'Hay que declarar la guerra al egoísmo. Hay que rehabilitar el ensueño y la fe' [War must be declared on egoism. Imagination and faith must be rehabilitated].[3] Hence one of the first tasks of the Modernist was to restore and rehabilitate imagination.

---

* ... have sustained the error of considering Modernism as a poetic matter and not as it really was and is—a general movement in theology, science and literature.

† ... the Hispanic form of a universal crisis of letters and the spirit which about 1885 initiated the dissolution of the nineteenth century and which was to manifest itself in art, in science, religion, politics and gradually in all the other aspects of life.

For the poet, the unknown—that fascinating area which the positivist refused to enter—was precisely the region that he found most fascinating. Many turned to spiritualism, to occult or esoteric philosophies, in order to open up new fields of exploration. Satanism, Rosicrucianism, Swedenborgian philosophy flourished in Paris and London. They offered attractive possibilities, often combining religion with a pseudo-scientific language (e.g. the ectoplasms of the spiritualists, the number symbolism of the gnostics). This pseudo-scientific language met the positivist's demand for proof and demonstration half-way. However, the supreme importance of such 'little religions' was that they defied traditional Christian attitudes. Sexual love, almost universally condemned as sinful by the orthodox, was not regarded as necessarily evil by some of the occult religions. Cruelty and egoism were far worse sins than the sexual union of male and female which in certain philosophies symbolised the wholeness and unity of the universe. The affirmation of joy in sexuality and in sensual experience was one way of meeting the threat of alienation in an industrial society.

In Latin America, the theme of sexual love and the sensuality of the new poetry represented something completely new in Hispanic literature. From Independence, heterodoxy had been the rule rather than the exception among intellectuals, but with the Modernists there is an attempt to explore hitherto taboo areas of experience. They anticipated the psychologists in their recognition of conflicts, aggression and violence, and so gave poetic recognition to forces which were still hidden from the rest of society. Whilst contemporaries tended to believe that material progress would improve human beings, the poets perceived conflicts that were independent of material well-being.

A NEW LANGUAGE

The most obvious aspect of Modernism—its renovation of literary language and poetic forms—is really a corollary of its moral and psychological explorations. The majority of Modernists were concerned with expressing eternal values (in contrast with the transitory aims of the everyday world) and at the same time they wanted a sensual poetry in which they could give voice to all those experiences which had never been put into poetry. That Spanish tradition could offer little guidance was abundantly clear. As Rubén Darío pointed out, no movement of innovation could come from Spain, where attitudes were still tied to tradition:

La evolución que llevara el castellano a ese renacimiento, habría de verificarse en América, puesto que España está amurallada de tradición, cercada y erizada de españolismo.*[1]

France, on the other hand, had undergone a literary revolution in the nineteenth century; the Romantic poets, Parnassians, Symbolists, great individuals such as Baudelaire, Rimbaud, Verlaine, offered a bewildering variety of techniques and poetic resources. The Modernists —and Darío in particular—learned from them all. From the Parnassians came the cult of perfection and the exotic symbols of princesses and swans, centaurs and Pierrot and Columbine; from Verlaine they learned the importance of musicality; from the Symbolists and from Mallarmé for whom 'tout, au monde, existe pour aboutir à un livre', they learned to sublimate the conflicts and variety of the real world into verbal syntheses or symbols. Yet we should beware of thinking in terms of plagiarism or mechanical imitation. When Darío wrote of the swan's melancholy,

> Melancolía de haber amado,
> junto a la fuente de la arboleda,
> el luminoso cuello estirado
> entre los blancos muslos de Leda...†

he moulds all these disparate influences into his own personal vision. The musicality is there. The swan and Leda are symbols which contain a whole complex of relationships between the animal and the human and the divine, yet this does not prevent the four lines being recognisably Darío.

Before turning to individual poets, there are two frequently-mentioned characteristics of Spanish–American Modernism that deserve comment—its cosmopolitan outlook and the cult of the exotic. Indeed Modernism, in its initial period at least, seems to turn its back on the nativist and regionalist trends which were such important features of Spanish–American literature. However, the Modernists' 'cosmopolitanism' was an inevitable consequence of their view of the poet as an outcast from bourgeois society and as a member of an international brotherhood of the arts. In a well-known passage, Julián del Casal identified himself not with bourgeois Paris but with the Paris that loved the artist—and the distinction is important. The Modernists

---

* The evolution which will bring Castilian to this rebirth must take place in America, since Spain is walled in tradition, besieged and beset by Hispanicism.
† The melancholy of having loved, by the fountain in the grove, his luminous neck outstretched between Leda's white thighs...

were not cosmopolitans because they preferred the foreign to the native, but simply because they regarded all art as cosmopolitan. Art might be the province of a special élite, but it was an élite which knew no frontiers. 'Exoticism' is simply another aspect of this. To take one's material from Greek myth, from the Orient, from Scandinavian legend or the France of the *fêtes galantes* was a way of abstracting the material from local or temporal associations. The Modernist attempted to give his poetry an atemporal and universal validity and hence he tended to avoid the particular, the contemporary and the local.

THE MODERNIST POETS

Generalisations about Modernism are particularly dangerous because the poets did not form a coherent movement with a definite poetic creed. The characteristics mentioned above are common to most of them, but further than that we cannot go. There is no way of studying Modernism except by reading the poems of each individual poet.

José Asunción Silva

Silva did not regard himself as a Modernist, and even poked fun at the *rubendarianos*, yet he shared enough common characteristics with them to have found a place in many anthologies of Modernism. He was born in Bogotá of a rich merchant family, his father, Ricardo, having been a member of the *Mosáico* literary group. José Asunción Silva spent two years in Paris and returned to find the family business on the verge of bankruptcy as a result of the 1885 civil war. For seven years after the death of his father he attempted to refloat the family business, but finally, after much fruitless effort, accepted a diplomatic post in Caracas where he stayed only for a few months. Misfortune dogged him, for on his return *l'Amérique*, the boat on which he was travelling, sank and with it went many unpublished poems and short stories. Shortly after his return, he shot himself.

Unamuno, the Spanish thinker, wrote of Asunción Silva that he felt something of the amazement of Adam on having been cast out of Paradise: 'He had tasted the suffering of Paradise'.[1] The observation is accurate, for Silva does seem to be reaching for some region outside time, a vision which he had glimpsed occasionally in childhood and in adult life. In his early poems, in which he is still under the influence of Romanticism, the nostalgia for the lost Golden Age is stated rather than evoked; thus 'Infancia' [Childhood] describes fairy-tales and the games of childhood on which the poet reflects:

Infancia, valle ameno;
De calma y de frescura bendecida
Donde es suave el rayo
Del sol que abrasa el resto de la vida.*

Childhood here is seen as a brief oasis before the desert of adult life. In his best poems 'Los maderos de San Juan' [The Bells of San Juan], 'Nocturno' [Nocturne], 'Día de Difuntos' [Day of the Dead], Silva uses subtle techniques to convey the effect of time and its passing and the constant presence of death. In 'Los maderos' and 'Día de difuntos', the sound of bells links the world of the living and the world of the dead. The first is a gloss on a nursery rhyme:

¡ Aserrín!
¡ Aserrán!
Los maderos de San Juan
Piden queso, piden pan,
Los de Roque
Alfandoque
Los de Rique
Alfeñique
¡ Los de triqui, triqui, tran!†

The rhyme recited by a grandmother as a memory of her own childhood is passed on to the grandchild who will in turn remember it. The grandmother is a living symbol of the lost past:

...son sus ojos turbios espejos que empañaron
Los años, y que, ha tiempos, las formas reflejaron
De cosas y de seres que nunca volverán.‡

In 'Día de difuntos', the temporal and the eternal are symbolised by two different bells; one set of bells tolls for the dead and reminds the poet of eternity; but over their sound tinkles that of the bell that chimes the hour, and this reminds the poet of all that is temporal and ephemeral. The poem skilfully mingles two emotions—the sadness and melancholy of death, which is intensified by the grey, rainy weather; and the joyful carelessness of the clock chimes which tell of pleasures, parties and balls. Here are the opening stanzas:

* Childhood, pleasant valley, blessed with calm and coolness, where the ray of the sun which burns the rest of our life is gentle.
† Ding, Dong, Ding, Dong, the Bells of San Juan ask for bread and cheese, those of Saint Roque candy and those of Saint Rique, barley sugar.
‡ ...her eyes are dark mirrors which the years clouded and which, for a long time now, have reflected things and beings who will never return.

La luz vaga...opaco el día,
La llovizna cae y moja
Con sus hilos penetrantes la ciudad desierta y fría,
Por el aire tenebroso ignorada mano arroja
Un oscuro velo opaco de letal melancolía,
Y no hay nadie que, en lo íntimo, no se aquiete y se recoja
Al mirar las nieblas grises de la atmósfera sombría,
Y al oír en las alturas,
Melancólicas y oscuras,
Los acentos dejativos
Y tristísimos e inciertos
Con que suenan las campanas
Las campanas plañideras que les hablan a los vivos
De los muertos!

Y hay algo angustioso e incierto
Que mezcla a ese sonido su sonido,
E inarmónico vibra en el concierto
Que alzan los bronces al tocar a muerto,
Por todos los que han sido!
Es la voz de una campana
Que va marcando la hora...*

Critics have not failed to point out that Asunción Silva's model was
Edgar Allan Poe's *The Bells*, but Silva's poem is far superior to that of
the North-American poet. The stanzas quoted above show how he
contrasts two totally antagonistic aspects of experience—an inner
brooding mysticism and melancholy and the 'algo angustioso o
incierto' which is associated with time.

...sigue marcando con el mismo modo
El mismo entusiasmo y el mismo desgaire
La huída del tiempo que lo borra todo!
Y eso es lo angustioso y lo incierto,
Que flota en el sonido,
Esa es la nota irónica que vibra en el concierto
Que alzan los bronces al tocar a muerto.†

* Vague light, an opaque day, drizzle falls and wets the deserted cold city with its penetrating threads; and in the shadowy air, an unknown hand throws down an obscure
veil of lethal melancholy. And there is nobody who, in his private self, does not grow
quiet and withdrawn as he sees the grey mists of the sombre atmosphere and hears in
the skies, melancholy and dark, the slow, immensely sad and hesitant sounds of the
ringing bells, the lamenting bells that speak to the living about the dead.
  And there is a certain anguish and doubt which mingles its sound with the other and
which dissonantly vibrates in the concerts which the bronze bells play as they toll death,
as they toll for those that have been. It is the voice of the bell which marks the time.
† ...it goes on indicating in the same way, the same enthusiasms and the same carelessness, the flight of time which erases all. And this is the anguish and doubt that floats

What distinguishes this poem from the many Romantic poems on time and death is that here the poet allows conflicting emotions and attitudes to speak entirely through the sound and the rhythm of the bells. We cannot separate the meaning of the poem from the language and rhythms in which it is expressed.

Asunción Silva's most famous poem, his 'Nocturno', was a startling innovation which abandoned all previously-known Spanish verse forms. Built up in groups of four syllables, the poem has lines that range from four to twenty syllables, its sinuous form being a perfect expression of the moonlight walk of the poet, first with his sister and later (after her death) alone. Baldomero Sanín Cano, a friend of the poet, wrote this of the origin of the poem:

El *Nocturno* nació de un incidente sencillo. Silva y su hermana paseaban a menudo a la luz de la luna, en su casa de campo, por una vereda alta de donde la sombra de los dos cuerpos se extendía, hasta desvanecerse en la planicie sembrada de trigos que quedaba muy abajo del camino. Alguna vez hizo Elvira la observación de cómo se extendían y se perdían sus sombras en el llano. A los tres años, este incidente se ligó en la memoria de Silva con el dolor de la pérdida, y produjo esta bella poesía.[*][1]

Some critics have made much of the supposed 'incestuous' love between Silva and his sister, but a reading of the poem makes it obvious that it does not depend on this biographical detail (whether true or false). For the poem is once again on Silva's favourite theme of the dead and the past, on the living and the present. The opening stanzas evoke the perfect communion of two people in time through images such as 'la sombra nupcial y húmeda' [the nuptial and humid shadow], and at the same time the unspoken anguish which accompanies any temporal union:

> Una noche
> Una noche toda llena de perfumes, de murmullos y de músicas de alas,
> Una noche
> En que ardían en la sombra nupcial y húmeda, las luciérnagas fantásticas,
> A mi lado, lentamente, contra mí ceñida, toda,
> Muda y pálida

in the sound, that is the ironic note which vibrates in the concert which the bronze bells play as they toll death.

[*] *Nocturne* arose out of a simple incident. Silva and his sister, when they were in their country home, often used to walk by moonlight along a high path on which the shadows of the two bodies stretched until they were lost in a wheat field which was lower than the road. Once Elvira noticed the way the shadows were lost on the plain. Three years later, this incident was linked in Silva's memory with his suffering at her loss and it produced this fine poem.

Como si un presentimiento de amarguras infinitas,
Hasta el fondo más secreto de tus fibras te agitara,
Por la senda que atraviesa la llanura florecida
   Caminabas.*

The uneven line-lengths are like the changing lengths of the shadows which follow the two and which finally merge into 'una sola sombra larga' [one single long shadow]. The shadow is the link which joins the temporal union of the poet and his sister with their union in memory after the death of the sister. In the second part of the poem, the poet walks alone after she has died: '...separado de ti misma, por la sombra, por el tiempo y la distancia' [separated from you by the shadow, by time and distance]. The warm images which had evoked harmony and beauty give way to images of cold; the sound of murmuring insects has become the croaking of frogs and the barking of dogs. But the poet's shadow which follows him on his solitary walk now symbolises a feeling of communion with his sister that transcends time and death:

¡Oh las sombras enlazadas!
¡Oh las sombras que se buscan y se juntan en las noches de negruras y de
                                                            lágrimas!†

The vocabulary, imagery and subject matter of the poem belong to Romantic tradition and offer little that is new, but both the form and the musicality of the verse were quite unprecedented. Silva's main contribution to a new poetry was his use of sonic effects and line-lengths in order to add a musical dimension which, in turn, greatly extended the scope and power of the words and images.

Silva's poems show, too, an awareness of the importance of childhood perceptions and of the mythic force of nursery rhymes and stories which he found 'mas durables que las convicciones de graves filósofos' [more durable than the convictions of grave philosophers].[1]

Less known than his poetry is José Asunción Silva's one work of fiction, *De sobremesa*, the diary of a poet whose attitudes are reminiscent of those of Silva himself. It is a tale of spiritual anguish, of a desperate search for faith—in art, in a new religion, in an ideal woman, a search

* One night, one night full of perfumes, murmurs and the music of wings, one night on which fantastic fireflies burned in the nuptial and humid shade, at my side, clasped close to me, all pale and silent as if the shadow of infinite bitterness shook your most secret fibres to the depths, you walked slowly along the path which crosses the flowering plain.

† O the embracing shadows, o the shadows which seek one another and are united on nights of darkness and tears.

that has no outcome. For the hero, Fernández, after the death of the ideal Helena, returns to business activities as the only way he has of keeping a grip on life. This curious ending of a man who had plunged into drug addiction, had seen the 'dark abyss of desperation' from which he had looked up to an 'inaccessible height of the ideal' can only be explained with reference to Silva's own existence. Business activities were only to prove a temporary narcotic, as his suicide in 1896 revealed.

Salvador Díaz Mirón (1853–1928)

Díaz Mirón, born in the state of Vera Cruz, Mexico, began his adult career as politician as well as poet, attracting attention by his brilliant speeches as deputy from 1884 to 1885. His poetry at this time reflected the influence of Victor Hugo, and he seems to have held Hugo's view of the poet as prophet and leader. His 'Sursum' written in 1884 prescribes a political and social task for the poet:

> Rompe en un himno que parezca un trueno
> El mal impera de la choza al solio;
> todo es dolor o iniquidad o cieno:
> pueblo, tropa, senado y capitolio.
> Canta la historia al porvenir que asoma,
> como Suetonio y Tácito la escriben...
>
> Para el poeta de divina lengua
> nada es estéril, ni la misma escoria.
> Si cuanto bulle en derredor es mengua,
> sobre la mengua esparcirás la gloria!*

This early and perhaps vainglorious phase ended abruptly in 1892 when Salvador Mirón killed a man in self-defence during the election campaign and was sent to prison, where he spent the next four years of his life. The poet of worldly glory became bitter and inward-looking. In 'Duelo' [Mourning], written on the death of his father, he voices words which seem like his own epitaph:

> Talento seductor; pero perdido
> en la sombra del mal y del olvido...
> Perla rica en las babas de un molusco

---

* Break into a hymn which is like thunder. Evil rules from the cabin to the throne, all is suffering, iniquity and mire; people, army, senate and capitol. History sings to the dawning future as Suetonius and Tacitus write it...
    For the poet of divine tongue, nothing is sterile, not even the dregs. If all that goes on around you is in decline, upon its decline you will spread glory.

encerrado en su concha y escondido
en el fondo de un mar lóbrego y brusco...*

The poems of this period and those in which he wrote on his release from prison were published as *Lascas* (1901) and have a much greater range and depth than his first poems. He experiments with form, as in the following mono-rhymed tercets of 'El fantasma':

Blancas y finas, y en el manto apenas
visibles, y con aire de azucenas,
las manos—que no rompen mis cadenas.

Azules y con oro enarenados,
como las noches limpias de nublados,
los ojos—que contemplan mis pecados.†

Although he moved away from social and political themes, some of the best poems of this collection are remarkable for their pitiless bitter realism, as in the following, 'El muerto' [The Dead Man]:

Como tronco en montaña venido al suelo,
Frente grandiosa y limpia, soberbia y pura.
Negras y unidas cejas, con la figura
del trazo curvo y fino que marca el vuelo

de un pájaro en un croquis que apunta un cielo.
Nariz igual a un pico de halcón. Albura
de canas. ¡El abeto, ya sin verdura,
dio en tierra y está en parte cinto de hielo!

El ojo mal cerrado tiene abertura
que muestra un hosco y vítreo claror de duelo,
un lustre de agua en pozo yerta en su hondura.

Moscas espanto y quito con el pañuelo;
y en la faz del cadáver sombra insegura
flota esbozando un cóndor al par que un vuelo.‡

---

* Seductive talent, but lost in the shade of evil and oblivion. Rich pearl in the mollusc's spittle, enclosed in its shell and hidden in the depths of the dark, rough sea.
† White and slender and hardly visible in your gown, like lilies, your hands—which do not break my chains.
     Blue, dusted with gold like nights that are clear of clouds, your eyes—which contemplate my sins.
‡ Like a tree-trunk brought down to earth on the mountain, the grandiose, clear, proud, pure forehead. Black and close-knit the eyebrows with a face that has the curved fine line that a bird's flight sketches in the sky. Nose like the falcon's beak. Whiteness of an old man's hair. The spruce tree that has lost its green has fallen to the earth, and is partly gripped in ice!

The poet begins conventionally enough with the comparison between the dead man and a fallen tree but this is followed by some realistic details unusual in Romantic poetry, the sharpening of the profile of the dead man, the semi-closed eyes with their glassy light, the flies which the poet flicks away with his handkerchief. And in the last line in which the face is already threatened with decomposition, the poet sees the 'sombra insegura' like a condor—a bizarre image that recalls the traditional picture of the soul flying from the body, but is far less comforting. Even more grotesque is his poem, 'Ejemplo' [Example], from the same collection in which he describes a man hanging from a gallows, converted into an object that hardly arouses even the curiosity of passers-by.

Though Salvador Díaz Mirón is less noteworthy than Asunción Silva as an innovator, his poems do carry certain Romantic preoccupations to a deeper level than any of his predecessors. After *Lascas* he wrote little, but he took up his political career again and became a deputy. He was also imprisoned again in 1910 for attempted murder, and was only released after the outbreak of the Revolution. He spent some years in exile during the Revolution but returned to Mexico in 1921.

Manuel Gutiérrez Nájera (1859–95)

Also born in Mexico, Gutiérrez Nájera attended a French school in that country and later wrote stories and verses impregnated with Gallic influence. He slaved as a journalist for most of his life, yet his prose writing does not seem to have suffered. Indeed, the stories of his *Cuentos frágiles* [*Fragile Stories*] (1883) and his *Cuentos color de humo* [*Smoke-coloured Tales*] which appeared in newspapers between 1890 and 1894 were written in a light and sparkling style that was quite new to Spanish. He wrote under two pseudonyms: the first 'Duque Job' epitomised two aspects of his life and art—his élitism and his suffering at the loss of religious faith; the second pseudonym was 'Puck' which was borrowed not directly from Shakespeare but from the contemporary French writer, Catulle Mendès. In 1894, he founded the *Revista Azul*, an important literary magazine in the history of the Modernist movement.

The part-closed eye has an opening that shows a gloomy vitreous clarity of mourning, the glint of water in a stagnant well in its depths.
I frighten away flies with my handkerchief and on the face of the corpse, there floats an uncertain shadow like the outline of a condor—but it is also a flight.

Gutiérrez Nájera is interesting for his extension of the literary language to embrace new areas of experience rather than for innovations in metrical form. He introduced a Gallic elegance and refinement into Spanish poetry, sometimes by the rather obvious device of using fashionable society slang as in 'Calicot':

> Mi duquesita, la que me adora,
> no tiene humos de gran señora
> es la griseta de Paul de Kock.
> No baila *Boston*, y desconoce
> de las carreras el alto goce
> y los placeres del *five o'clock*.*

Though proud of the freshness and naivety of his mistress, the poet also displays his familiarity with the latest fashion. We have here the poetic equivalent of the French-style opera-house and the villas that were springing up in Mexico City during the regime of Porfirio Díaz, placing a surface gloss of European elegance upon a city with the ruins of an Indian Empire at its foundations. Gutiérrez Nájera was also one of the first Latin-American poets to use colours as connotations of mood. An example is his 'El hada verde' [The Green Fairy] (1887), a poem in which he tries to capture the fatal seduction of bohemian life.

> En tus abismos, negros y rojos,
> fiebre implacable, mi alma se pierde;
> y en tus abismos miro los ojos,
> los ojos verdes del hada verde!
>
> Es nuestra musa glauca y sombría,
> la copa rompe, la lira quiebra,
> y a nuestro cuello se enrosca impía
> como culebra!†

The poem is a little too melodramatic for modern taste, but the use of 'verde' [green] in these lines, not merely to denote colour but also to suggest fatal attraction, represents an exploration in the direction of symbolism. Similarly, in the following poem, 'En un cromo' [Upon a Lithograph], 'blanca' [white] is used as a symbol of youthful

---

* My little duchess, the one who adores me, has no pretensions to be a great lady; she is the *grisette* of Paul de Kock. She does not dance the Boston and does not know the delights of the fashionable races and the pleasures of five o'clock tea.
† In your black and red abysses, implacable fever, my soul is lost; and in your abysses I see the eyes, the green eyes of the green fairy.
Our muse is glaucous and dark, it breaks the cup and smashes the lyre and wraps itself round the throat like a snake.

purity in a charming reworking of a traditional 'Gather ye Rosebuds'
theme which has the zest of popular poetry:

> Niña de blanca enagua
> que miras correr el agua
> y deshojas una flor,
> más rápido que esas ondas,
> niña de las trenzas blondas,
> pasa cantando el amor.

> Ya me dirás, si eres franca,
> niña de la enagua blanca
> que la dicha es el amor;
> mas yo haré que te convenzas,
> niña de las rubias trenzas
> de que olvidar es mejor.*

Gutiérrez Nájera's prose style also represented a break with the past,
although the themes of his stories are too sentimental for modern taste.
Dying children and consumptive maidens abound in them, and his
favourite theme was undoubtedly the contrast between the anguish of
death and the feverish gaiety of life that goes on. Here, for instance, is a
characteristic passage of a story, 'En la calle' [In the street], in which a
consumptive girl observes the passing throng:

Los carruajes pasaban con el ruido armonioso de los muelles nuevos: el landó,
abriendo su góndola, forrada de azul raso, descubría la seda resplandeciente de
los trajes y la blancura de las epidermis; el faetón iba saltando como un venado
fugitivo, y el *mail coach*, coronado de sombreros blancos y sombrillas rojas, con las
damas coquetamente escalonadas en el pescante y en el techo, corría pesadamente, como un viejo soltero enamorado, tras la griseta de ojos picarescos. Y
parecía que de las piedras salían voces, que un vago estrépito de fiesta se formaba
en los aires, confundiendo las carcajadas argentinas de los jóvenes, el rodar de los
coches en el empedrado, el chasquido del látigo que se retuerce como una víbora
en los aires, el son confuso de las palabras, y el trote de los caballos fatigados.
Esto es: vida que pasa, se arremolina, bulle, hierve; bocas que sonríen, ojos que
besan con la mirada, plumas, sedas, encajes blancos y pestañas negras...†¹

----

* Girl in a white petticoat, you watch the river running by and tear the petals off a flower,
oh girl of the blonde tresses, love sings and passes more swiftly than these waves.
  Now you will admit if you are frank, girl in the white petticoat, that love is happiness but I will convince you, maiden of the blonde tresses, that forgetting is better.
† The carriages passed with the harmonious noise of the newly-sprung landaus whose
open tops, lined in blue satin, discovered the splendid silks of the gowns and the whiteness of skin; the phaeton leapt like a fugitive doe and the mail coach, crowned with
white hats and red sunshades and with ladies coquettishly ranged on the outside and on
the roof, moved heavily like an old bachelor in love after mischievous girlish eyes. And
it seemed as if voices came out of the stones, as if a vague, festive noise formed on the
breeze, mingling the silvery laughter of the young, the rolling of coaches on the cobbles,

Here is a prose which appeals to the senses which, in every word and image, conveys colour and sound. Characteristic, too, is the way the author dwells on the civilised luxury of the scene, of the clothes and carriages and the way he introduces the foreign words 'griseta', 'góndola', to emphasise a cosmopolitan atmosphere. Gutiérrez Nájera, in short, exemplifies the sophisticated and the 'modern' aspects of the movement, which were themselves, perhaps, understandable attitudes for artists to take in countries still threatened by 'barbarism'.

Julián del Casal

A similar refinement and love of the artificial is present in the poetry of the Cuban, Julián del Casal. Casal came from a prosperous family who had lost their money when he was still a child. He was only able to spend one year at university, after which he earned his living as a clerk in a ministry. In common with many other Modernists, he detested his environment, the more so since Cuba was still under Spanish rule. Some of his first articles, which he signed 'El Conde de Camors', were so openly critical of the Spanish captain general of the island that he lost his job and copies of the paper were confiscated. After a brief visit to Madrid, he returned to La Habana where he published *Hojas al viento* [*Leaves in the Wind*] and he was preparing a second volume of poems, *Bustos y rimas* [*Busts and Rhymes*] (1893), when he died of tuberculosis. Casal was not only influenced by French poetry— the Parnassians, Gautier and Baudelaire in particular—but also by contemporary intellectual fashions such as the cult of the exotic. This interest in the exotic was in part the outcome of the cult of beauty in all its various manifestations, in part the outcome of the poet's admiration for civilisations in which art had reached such refinement and elegance. In few other Spanish–American poets do we find such a consistent preference for beauty in art over natural beauty. Indeed, he wrote a series of poems inspired by the work of the decadent French painter, Gustave Moreau, including one on a favourite *fin-de-siècle* topic, Salome. And in his 'La canción de la morfina' [The Song of Morphine], he praised the 'dicha artificial/que es la vida verdadera' [artificial happiness which is the true life] whilst in 'En el campo' [In the Countryside], he declared:

> the crack of the whip twisting like a viper in the wind, the confused sounds of words and the trotting of weary horses. That is: life passing, whirling, simmering, boiling; mouths that smile, eyes that kiss with a glance, feathers, silks, white lace and black eyelashes.

Tengo el impuro amor de las ciudades
y a este sol que ilumina las edades
prefiero yo del gas las claridades.*

This preference for city life, like his love for Chinese and Japanese art, was inspired by a conviction that the artificial was superior to the natural. The city, like art, testifies to man's ability to triumph over nature. And sensuality, which Casal incarnates in his 'Salome', is not animal bestiality when transmuted into a literary form. Many of the titles of Casal's poems—'Cromos' [Lithographs], 'Bustos' [Busts], 'Museo ideal' [The Ideal Museum]—are also indications of his desire to give words the more durable quality of painting and sculpture.

One of Casal's most interesting poems is, however, expressive of barely-controlled violence, and illustrates the narrowness of any view of Modernism which confines itself to stylistic innovation alone. The poem, 'Crepuscular' [Sunset], is an expressionistic description of nightfall on the coast:

> Como vientre rajado sangra el ocaso,
> manchando con sus chorros de sangre humeante
> de la celeste bóveda el azul raso
> de la mar estañada la onda espejeante.

> Alzan sus moles húmedas los arrecifes
> donde el chirrido agudo de las gaviotas,
> mezclado a los crujidos de los esquifes,
> agujerea el aire de extrañas notas.

> Va la sombra extendiendo sus pabellones,
> rodea el horizonte cinta de plata,
> y, dejando las brumas hechas jirones,
> parece cada faro flor escarlata.†

In each of the three verses, there are static, calm elements—the 'celeste bóveda' [celestial dome], the 'arrecifes' [cliffs], and the 'pabellones' [pavilions] of shadow, each of which is pierced and broken by a violent contrast of colour or sound—the red of the sun, the screeching of the seagulls, the colour of the lighthouse against the grey mist. Images

---

* I have the impure love of cities. I prefer the brightness of gas to that of the sun which has lit up the ages.
† Like a torn stomach, the twilight bleeds, staining the blue satin of the celestial dome and the reflecting wave of the blanched sea with its streams of steaming blood.
  The damp shapes of rocks rise where the shrill screech of seagulls mingled with the creaking of skiffs, pierces the air with strange notes.
  The darkness slowly extends its pavilions and a silver ribbon surrounds the horizon and, tearing the mist, each lighthouse seems to be a scarlet flower.

reinforce the ideal of violence. The sunset is like a torn stomach, the noise of the seagulls and the creaking of the boats 'make holes' in the air and the mists are torn to rags. The technique is thus expressionistic in that the landscape is described in terms of the poet's own fears and conflicts, with perhaps the suggestion that beauty and sensuality cannot harmonise with peace and stability.

Each of these poets—Silva, Díaz Mirón, Gutiérrez Nájera and Casal—attempted to explore new areas of experience; and occasionally their poetry represents a breakthrough either of form or language. But we now come to the virtuoso of Modernism—Rubén Darío—a man in whose poetry is to be found every facet of this highly complex movement.

Rubén Darío

Darío was born in 1867 in Metapa, Nicaragua, and grew up in the provincial town of León which had probably changed little since colonial times. He was educated in a Jesuit school and, since his parents were separated, he was brought up by an aunt. Even when still a child, his poems and improvisations attracted attention and he was invited to the Nicaraguan capital, Managua, given a post in the national library and at the age of fifteen invited to San Salvador. Through the Salvadorian scholar, Francisco Gavidia, he came into contact with contemporary European literature, especially with the poetry of Hugo, some of whose poems he translated. In 1885 he made a choice that was to be decisive. He went to Chile where he found himself in a far more sophisticated and cultivated society and where he greatly extended his reading of contemporary European writings. And it was here that he published a volume of stories and poems that established his literary reputation. This was *Azul* (1888), which earned him the praise of the influential Spanish critic Juan Valera, who also commented on the 'galicismo mental' of the author. Valera, who had little sympathy for the prevailing schools of naturalism and realism in the novel, was attracted to this poet who had rejected all didacticism in favour of pure art.

In 1890 Darío returned to Central America, and in 1892 visited Spain as correspondent for the Buenos Aires newspaper *La Nación*, and a short time later, on a second visit to Europe, he visited Paris where he met Verlaine. Until 1898 he was mostly in Buenos Aires working for *La Nación*, and it was here at his office desk that many poems were written. In 1896, he published his *Prosas profanas* [*Profane Prose*]; and

Los raros [*The Eccentrics*], a series of essays on the writers he admired, such as Verlaine, Huysmans and Leconte de Lisle. From 1898, he lived mostly in Spain where he published *Cantos de vida y esperanza* [*Songs of Life and Hope*] (1905). In 1907, there appeared *El canto errante* [*The Wandering Song*]. By now gravely ill, largely as a result of heavy drinking, his output grew smaller. The last volumes to appear in his lifetime were *Poema de otoño* [*Autumn Poem*] (1910) and *Canto a la Argentina y otros poemas* [*Chant to Argentina and Other Poems*] (1914).

Darío's technical brilliance was the quality which immediately attracted attention, and his innovations permanently enriched Spanish poetry. However, although some poems were written as virtuoso exercises, the majority of them wed technical innovations to his own spiritual crisis. In his life and in his art, Darío lived a crisis of faith; he prided himself on his 'sincerity', and for this reason every phase and mood has been recorded in poems or essays so that as a whole his work appears to be full of contradictions, waverings between pantheism and Catholic belief, between sensualism and guilt. But on carefully studying the chronological development of his poetry, we can follow certain broad preoccupations.

Darío's main problem throughout his life was moral and religious, and centred on the nature of evil. There is evidence that in his early years, even before his visit to Chile, and probably under the influence of Hugo, part of whose *Fin de Satan* he had translated, Darío began to question the Catholic dogma of original sin and the Catholic insistence on the evil which erotic love represented. A poem, 'El porvenir' [The Future] sees progress in Hugoan terms, with man conquering death by scaling the tree of knowledge. This optimistic evolutionism does not seem to have lasted long, although in *Azul* there is an attempt to celebrate the joy and innocence of sensual love while cruelty and the struggle for life are condemned as evil. Nowadays it requires something of an effort of the imagination to understand why *Azul* was regarded as so important and new. Much of the volume was devoted to stories and prose poems, and the 1888 edition included only a short cycle of poems on the four seasons and two other poems. Yet as we look at the first poem, 'Primaveral' there is indeed something remarkable in the first lines with their sinuous and sensual rhythm:

> Mes de rosas. Van mis rimas
> en ronda, a la vasta selva,
> a recoger miel y aromas
> en las flores entreabiertas.

> Amada, ven. El gran bosque
> es nuestro templo: allí ondea
> y flota un santo perfume
> de amor. El pájaro vuela
> de un árbol a otro y saluda
> tu frente rosada y bella
> como a un alma;*

By the use of enjambment and mid-line caesura, Darío had wrought
a remarkable change in the old-style ballad metre. Contrast the same
type of stanza in the hands of the Spanish Romantic poet, Zorrilla

> Muerte la lumbre solar,
> Iba la noche cerrando,
> Y dos jinetes cruzando
> A caballo un olivar.†

in which each line forms a natural phrase. Here there is a regular jog-
trot rhythm, while in Darío's poem the lines melt into one another,
expressing man's harmony with the whole of creation. The poem is a
hymn to love and creation with no stigma of sin attached to sensual
enjoyment.

> Allá hay una clara fuente
> que brota de una caverna,
> donde se bañan desnudas
> las blancas ninfas que juegan.
> Ríen al son de la espuma
> hienden la linfa serena;
> entre el polvo cristalino
> esponjan su caballera.‡

'Clara', 'blanca', 'cristalino' endow the verses with luminosity, so
that we cannot condemn this harmless joy in the senses. This is a poem
of fulfilled sexual love in which the poet rejects the frustrated loves of
Venus or the chastity of Diana which he finds represented on an
alabaster vase. Evil enters *Azul* not as sensuality but as cruelty. In
'Estival', the Prince of Wales shoots a female tiger in the middle of her

---

* Month of roses. My verses go round the vast wood to sip honey and perfumes from the
half-open flowers. Beloved, come. The great wood is our temple; there wafts and floats
a holy perfume of love. The bird flies from tree to tree and greets your rosy, beautiful
brow as if it were a soul.
† With the solar light dead, night began to fall, and two horsemen crossing an olive
grove.
‡ There is a clear spring which rises in a cavern, where white playing nymphs bathe
naked. They laugh at the sound of the foam and they cleave the serene water and in the
crystalline dust they sponge their hair.

jungle idyll with the male, and in the final poem, 'Ananke', the joyous dove is killed by a hawk after singing her hymn to creation. This notion of evil as part of the struggle for life, and expressed in cruelty, was quite possibly inspired by Hugo, who had propounded such views in *La Légende des Siècles* and *La Fin de Satan*, both of which Darío knew well.

Most of the stories included in *Azul* were in the nature of allegories either on the theme of love or on that of the artist as an outsider in the materialistic world of contemporary civilisation. One or two examples will suffice to illustrate the nature of these stories. 'El rubí' contrasts a false man-made ruby with the rubies made under the earth by the gnomes and which, as one of them relates, were stained red from the blood of an imprisoned princess who had been mortally wounded in an attempt to escape and meet her lover. The stones symbolise love and suffering, both of which spring from nature, and Darío ends the story with this apostrophe:

¡ Tú, oh madre Tierra !, eres grande, fecunda, de seno inextinguible y sacro, y de tu vientre moreno brota la savia de los troncos robustos, y el oro y el agua diamantina y la casta flor de lis ¡ Lo puro, lo fuerte, lo infalsicable ! ¡ Y tú, Mujer, eres espíritu y carne, toda amor !*

Two stories in the collection, 'El palacio del sol' [Sun Palace] and 'Palomas blancas y garzas morenas' [White Doves and Dark Herons] are in praise of sexual fulfilment.

The other important theme of the stories of *Azul*—that, for instance, expressed in 'El rey burgués' [The Bourgeois King] and 'El sátiro sordo' [The Deaf Satyr]—is that of the artist as outcast in a materialist society. Both bourgeois king and satyr represent philistine elements. 'La canción del oro' [The Song of Gold] is a prose poem which ironically praises gold and is sung by a beggar who is also a poet and who appeals to all the outcasts of the earth to join forces with 'the happy ones, with the powerful, the bankers, the demi-gods of the world'.

But possibly the pages of *Azul* which appeared most revolutionary to contemporaries were those which held no concealed message and simply bore titles like 'Acuarela' [Water Colour] or 'Paisaje' [Landscape] or 'Aguafuerte' [Etching]. This, for instance, is one of the landscapes:

---

* You, oh mother Earth, you are great, fertile; from your sacred and inextinguishable breast, from your dark womb springs the sap of robust trunks, gold and diamantine water and the chaste lily. The pure, the strong, that which it is impossible to counterfeit. And you, woman, are spirit and flesh, all love.

Sobre todo flotaba un vaho cálido, y el grato olor campestre de las hierbas chafadas. Veíase en lo profundo un trozo de azul. Un huaso robusto, uno de esos fuertes campesinos, toscos hércules que detienen un toro, apareció de pronto en lo más alto de los barrancos. Tenía tras sí el vasto cielo. Las piernas, todas músculo, las llevaba desnudas. En uno de sus brazos traía una cuerda gruesa y arrollada. Sobre su cabeza, como un gorro de nutria, sus cabellos enmarañados, tupidos y salvajes.*

Such a description appealed directly to the senses. Darío first of all conveys the scent of the countryside before springing upon the reader the dramatic vision of his sturdy peasant outlined against the sky. Visually the passage is extremely vivid while adjectives such as 'tosco', 'robusto', 'salvaje' add to the texture of the passage. Darío does not have to use an abstraction like 'noble savage' because he is able to convey this more immediately and concretely.

Between the publication of *Azul* and *Prosas profanas* (1896), Darío not only perfected his poetic technique but acquired a philosophy which satisfied his sensual need and yet gave him a religious faith. His reading of Hugo had already made him familiar with a philosophy which forecast the ending of evil. By 1890, he had also become interested in other heterodox philosophies, notably Orphaism and Pythagoreanism as described by Edouard Schuré in *Les Grands Initiés*. According to Schuré, the Pythagoreans had believed man to be part of a great chain of being which evolved from the humblest rocks to the divine. By means of Knowledge, Love and Death, man's spirit could draw nearer to God and the transmigration of the soul allowed man through successive rebirths to rejoin the divine. Meanwhile the earthly existence of ordinary men was fraught with contradictions, strife and suffering. The poet or seer who belonged to a higher order of humanity was alone in being able to transcend these contradictions and perceive the universal harmony.

One of the most important poems of *Prosas profanas*, 'El coloquio de los centauros', represents Darío's attempt to express this philosophy in poetic terms. It is a meditation on the conflicting aspects of existence, on the hidden harmony of the universe and on the evolutionary chain of being. The centaurs themselves—part animal, part human, part divine—symbolise the threefold nature of the human personality

---

* Over everything floated a hot vapour and the pleasant country smell of trampled grass. In the distance, there was a patch of blue. A robust peasant, one of those strong countrymen, a rough Hercules who can stop a bull, suddenly appeared right at the top of the ravine. Behind him was the whole of the vast sky. His legs, which were all muscle, were bare. On one of his arms, he held a thick coil of rope and on his head his thick, wild, tangled hair was like an otter hat.

which is composed of instinct, the spirit and the intellect. The finest lines of the poem aptly convey the sense of 'el misterio de las cosas' [the mystery of things], which is one of its themes. Here, for instance, is the passage which describes the striving of inanimate nature towards consciousness:

> He visto, entonces, raros ojos fijos en mí:
> los vivos ojos rojos del alma del rubí;
> los ojos luminosos del alma del topacio,
> y los de la esmeralda que del azul espacio
> la maravilla imitan; los ojos de las gemas
> de brillos peregrinos y mágicos emblemas.
> Amo el granito duro que el arquitecto labra
> y el mármol en que duerme la línea y la palabra.*

To understand 'El coloquio' is to understand that Darío seldom uses settings of pagan Greece or eighteenth-century France as mere trappings or as an escape from the present. In this poem are fused the philosophy which accepted spiritual conflicts as part of an existence whose true nature few people glimpsed and a poetic harmony which was the objective correlative of a spiritual harmony. And it was to pre-Christian Greece that Darío had to go because that society and those Gods had not found sexual love to be sinful.

Harmony, then, is one of the keynotes to *Prosas profanas*, a harmony of sound which expresses the harmony of soul which Darío achieved through his poetic creation if not in existence. Many poems—for example, the introductory 'Era un aire suave' [It was a soft tune...]—convey harmony by means of evocatively musical words and associations:

> Era un aire suave, de pausados giros:
> el hada Harmonía ritmaba sus vuelos,
> e iban frases vagas y tenues suspiros
> entre los sollozos de los violincelos.
>
> Sobre la terraza, junto a los ramajes,
> diríase un trémulo de liras eolias
> cuando acariciaban los sedosos trajes
> sobre el tallo erguidas, las blancas magnolias.†

---

* Then I saw strange eyes fixed on me; the live red eyes of the ruby's soul, the luminous eyes of the spirit of the topaz and those of the emerald which imitates the marvel of blue space; the eyes of the gems of weird lustre and magic emblems. I love the hard granite which the architect works and the marble in which sleeps the line and the word.

† It was a soft tune, of slow rhythm. The fairy, Harmony, moved her wings in time and there were vague phrases and tenuous sighs among the sobs of the cellos.

Upon the terrace, by the boughs, there seemed to be a tremulo of the Æolian harp when the white magnolias, erect on their stalks, caressed silken gowns.

Many of the words refer to musical instruments or sounds—cellos, sighs, tremulo, Æolian lyres. Against this background, Darío presents the 'marquesa Eulalia' who flirts with her admirers but reserves her true love for a poet. The poem is consciously elegant and refined, sensual on the one hand but on the other never falling into coarseness. In this way, Darío could treat an erotic theme whilst remaining on the side of 'civilisation' and against 'barbarism'.

In many poems of *Prosas profanas*, Darío uses a symbolism drawn from Greek mythology. The centaur, as we have seen, was one such symbol. These symbols were hallowed by tradition, and at the same time they had the necessary ambiguity to hide the dangerous implications of Darío's eroticism. Thus, another of his favourite symbols is the satyr, a mythical creature whom he associates with what was for him one of the most significant periods of human consciousness— the moment when the cry 'Great Pan is Dead' was heard throughout the pagan world. In Darío's version of the legend the satyr heard the cry and because of his musical gifts was accepted by the new religion of Christianity.[1] The legend reflects Darío's anxiety to reconcile Christian salvation and enjoyment. In human experience, conflict and guilt were unavoidable, but in the poem conflict and harmony could exist together like the different notes in a chord. Thus, in *Prosas profanas*, Darío moves towards the view of the poem as an artefact which presents conflicts and their resolution, but is not a direct expression of the poet's feeling. Many of these symbolic poems take the theme of the swan, which like the satyr and the centaur was a symbol that implied a whole history of classical reference and association. Jupiter had taken the form of a swan to rape Leda and from their union was born Helen of Troy. This act is frequently seen by Darío as having a significance equal to that of Christ's birth; the union of the divine and the earthly to bring forth beauty became, for him, the supreme symbol of poetry, and he was to dedicate poems not only in *Prosas profanas* but also in *Cantos de vida y esperanza* to this favourite theme. In the following 'Leda' poem, however, the emphasis is on sensuality, a sensuality which attains a shimmering beauty in the description of the swan at dawn:

> El cisne en la sombra parece de nieve;
> su pico es de ámbar, del alba al trasluz:
> el suave crepúsculo que pasa tan breve
> las cándidas alas sonrosa de luz.

Y luego en las ondas del lago azulado,
después que la aurora perdió su arrebol,
las alas tendidas y el cuello enarcado,
el cisne es de plata, bañado de sol.

Tal es, cuando esponja las plumas de seda,
olímpico pájaro herido de amor,
y viola en las linfas sonoras a Leda,
buscando su pico los labios en flor.

Suspira la bella desnuda y vencida
y en tanto que al aire sus quejas se van
del fondo verdoso de fronda tupida
chispean turbados los ojos de Pan.*

There is no moral comment here. The poet simply delights in translating sensuality into glowing, luminous language and if the word 'turbados' in the last line seems a comment on the anomaly of the event, this disturbing fact is never allowed to break the harmony of the whole, is always contained. Again, in one of a group of poems dedicated to swans, Darío makes the bird both a symbol of Olympian pride and also of melancholy, since Jupiter's rape of Leda had brought him down from his heights into the world of temporality. Yet this melancholy is again contained within the harmony of the whole and is never allowed to become tragic:

Las dignidades de vuestros actos
eternizados en lo infinito,
hacen que sean ritmos exactos,
voces de ensueño, luces de mito.

De orgullo olímpico sois el resumen,
oh blancas urnas de la armonía.
Ebúrneas joyas que anima un numen
con su celeste melancolía.

Melancolía de haber amado,
junto a la fuente de la arboleda,
el luminoso cuello estirado
entre los blancos muslos de Leda !†

* The swan in shadow seems of snow, his beak is of amber against the half-light of dawn; the soft twilight which passes so briefly casts a blush of light on his pure wings.
   And then in the waves of the bluish lake, when dawn has lost its first blush, his wings outstretched, his neck arched, the swan is of silver, bathed in sun.
   Thus he is, when he preens his silken plumes, an Olympian bird wounded by love and he violates Leda in the sounding water, seeking her flowering lips with his beak.
   The vanquished, naked beauty sighs and her complaints are wafted away on the breeze; from the green depths of thick fronds the eyes of Pan sparkle in fright.
† The dignity of your acts, eternalised in infinity, makes them exact rhythms, voices of dream, lights of myth.

It was, however, *Prosas profanas*, even more than the later *Cantos de vida y esperanza* which won the admiration of contemporaries for their stylistic virtuosity. The richness of the vocabulary, the introduction of exotic-sounding words such as 'parlar' [to speak], 'perlar' [lit. to pearl], 'liróforo' [lyre-player], 'ánfora' [amphora], etc., extended the range of the literary language enormously. There were also many innovations in verse forms like the adaptation of French verse forms in 'Responso a Verlaine' and the revitalisation of archaic Spanish forms as in the 'Dezires'.

This technical skill and virtuosity remain unquestioned, although other aspects of Darío's poetry (his persistent use of classical references, for instance) tend to make *Prosas profanas* less accessible to the modern reader. Often, indeed, it is his confession of doubt or failure rather than the creation of a perfect visionary world which nowadays has most appeal. The note he struck in 'Yo persigo una forma...' [I seek a form], the last poem of the collection, was to become more persistent towards the end of his life. Certainly the recognition rather than the denial of time lends the poem a more modern air. He begins with a glimpse of a vision of artistic beauty, symbolised in the Venus de Milo, but Darío works not in marble but in words and the nature of words makes them an impossible medium when the eternal is to be expressed in them:

> Y no hallo sino la palabra que huye,
> la iniciación melódica que de la flauta fluye
> y la barca del sueño que en el espacio boga;
>
> y bajo la ventana de mi Bella-Durmiente,
> el sollozo continuo del chorro de la fuente
> y el cuello del gran cisne blanco que me interroga.*

The fountain and the questioning curve of the swan's neck are there to remind Darío of time and the mystery of existence, the vast spaces into which his 'barca del sueño' [boat of dreams] has ventured.

In 1896, the year in which *Prosas profanas* had appeared, Darío had also published a series of articles on contemporary European writers which had previously appeared in *La Nación*. This was *Los*

You are the epitome of Olympian pride, oh white urns of harmony. Burnished jewels which a god animates with his celestial melancholy.

The melancholy of having loved, by the fountain in the grove, his luminous neck outstretched between Leda's white thighs.

* And I find only the fleeting word, the beginning of a melody which flows from the flute and the boat of dreams which drifts in space, and below the window of my sleeping-beauty, the continuous weeping of the fountain and the neck of the great white swan questioning me.

raros in which he discussed nineteenth-century writers such as Edgar Allan Poe, Leconte de Lisle, Verlaine, León Bloy, Paul Adam, Jean Moréas and many others. His greatest admiration was reserved for those like Verlaine who had been outcasts from society. 'Pauvre Lelian', he declared in his article on Verlaine, 'mitad cornudo flautista de la selva, violador de hamadríadas, mitad asceta del Señor' [part horned flautist of the jungle, violator of Hamadryads, part ascetic of the Lord]. In Verlaine's conflicts he saw his own reflected. But after 1896, there is evidence that Darío had come to realise that even art could not transcend conflict and suffering. Into a novel he began about this period, and which he never finished, he put some of his doubts. This was *El hombre de oro* [*The Man of Gold*], a work based on the adventures of Judas Iscariot after the death of Christ. The novel is set in Rome, and one of the characters, Lucio Vario, is undoubtedly the voice of Darío himself; hearing the sermon of St Paul condemning the temptations of the flesh, he protests sadly,

...mirad cómo la omnipotencia del Amor que procrea y fecunda se siente sobre todas las cosas, y todas las cosas están sujetas a ella. ¿Por qué vos, elocuente y sabio prodigais en contra de la naturaleza?...Yo soy un poeta, señor, y vuestro Dios, os lo confieso, si me quitan los labios de las mujeres y los cálices de las rosas, me da tristeza y me da miedo.*

This 'tristeza' and 'miedo' were, in fact, to be the predominant notes of his *Cantos de vida y esperanza* when they appeared in 1905. Though in this volume he included poems similar to those of *Prosas profanas*, and though he widened his scope to include political poems, yet there is a prevailing impression of sadness, as titles such as 'Nocturno', 'Melancolía', 'Lo Fatal', 'Thanatos' reveal. The opening poem of the collection was in the nature of a spiritual autobiography:

> Yo soy aquel que ayer no más decía
> el verso azul y la canción profana.†

He described how he had tried to reconcile his desire for immortality with his fleshly desires in the realm of poetry:

> Bosque ideal que lo real complica,
> allí el cuerpo arde y vive y Psiquis vuela:‡

---

* See how the omnipotence of Love which procreates and makes fertile is felt in all things and all things are subject to her. Why do you, eloquent and wise man, preach against nature?...I am a poet, sir, and your God, I confess, if they take away from me women's lips and the chalices of the roses, it makes me sad and frightens me.
† I am he who only yesterday recited the azure poem and the profane song.
‡ Ideal wood which the real complicates, there the body burns and lives and Psyche flies.

and how he had come to believe:

> el Arte puro como Cristo exclama:
> *Ego sum lux et veritas et vita!**

only to add the confession:

> Y la vida es misterio; la luz ciega
> y la verdad inaccesible asombra:
> la adusta perfección jamás se entrega,
> y el secreto ideal duerme en la sombra.†

In some poems there are glimpses of Christian hope, but in many, there is a note of sheer despair:

> Dichoso el árbol que es apenas sensitivo
> y más la piedra dura, porque ésta ya no siente,
> pues no hay dolor más grande que el dolor de ser vivo
> ni mayor pesadumbre que la vida consciente.‡

It is hardly surprising that he should have looked back nostalgically to the innocence of childhood in his 'La dulzura del ángelus', a childhood when there had been purity and an ingenuous faith. In adult life, there is an inevitable soiling of this innocence:

> El aureo ovillo vespertino
> que la tarde devana tras opacos cristales
> por tejer la inconsútil tela de nuestros males,
> todos hechos de carne y aromados de vino...§

This gloomy note might well have had its origin in Darío's sense of decline. Even his inventiveness had diminished, and his *Canto errante* (1907) included poems published many years previously. In these later poems, the mannerisms and the mythology of *Prosas profanas* have largely disappeared. And even an earlier poem now published for the first time in a complete version, 'Tutecotzimi', reveals an unexpected side of Darío's talent. This rich and sensuous interpretation of an Indian legend is an indication of what might have happened if, instead of absorbing Western tradition and Greek myth, the poet had found more

---

* Pure art like Christ exclaims: *Ego sum lux et veritas et vita!*
† And life is mystery, light blinds and inaccessible truth astonishes, harsh perfection never gives itself and the ideal secret sleeps in the shade.
‡ Happy the tree which is scarcely sensitive and more the hard stone because it no longer feels, for there is no greater pain than the pain of being alive, nor greater suffering than conscious life.
§ The golden ball of evening that the afternoon winds up behind panes of opaque glass, in order to weave the seamless cloth of our sins all made of flesh and flavoured with wine.

inspiration in his own continent. For, in these descriptions of tropical nature, Darío's sensuality can find expression in the lush environment. At the same time, there is some wonderfully vivid observation of insects and birds:

> Junto al verdoso charco, sobre las piedras toscas,
> rubí, cristal, zafiro, las susurrantes moscas
> del vaho de la tierra pasan cribando el tul;
> e intacta, con su veste de terciopelo rico,
> abanicando el lodo con su doble abanico,
> está como extasiada la mariposa azul.

> Las selvas foscas vibran con el calor del día;
> al viento el pavo negro su grito agudo fía,
> y el grillo aturde el verde, tupido carrizal;
> un pájaro del bosque remeda un son de cuerno;
> prolonga la cigarra su chincharchar eterno,
> y el grito de su pito repite el pito-real.*

But Darío was never convinced that this language could have universal and eternal significance. Hence his ambition to be the poet of 'ensueños y formas/que viene de lejos y va al porvenir' [a (singer of) dreams and forms who comes from afar and goes into the future]. But paradoxically those poems which were least consciously universal are those which now retain their appeal.

No other poet of the Modernist movement developed such a variety of techniques or drew on such a wealth of resources. His contemporary poets—Julio Herrera y Reissig (Uruguay, 1875–1910), Leopoldo Lugones, Ricardo Jaimes Freyre (Bolivia, 1868–1933), Delmira Agustini (1886–1914), Amado Nervo (1870–1919)—illustrate differing trends which had been prefigured in Darío.

Ricardo Jaimes Freyre

Jaimes Freyre is a poet of spiritual anguish. Though in public life he was one of the most fortunate of the Modernists, being the son of a Bolivian diplomat and himself destined to have a distinguished career as poet, scholar, diplomat and statesman, in his poetry he glimpses the

---

* By the greenish pool, upon the rough stones, ruby, crystal, sapphire, the whispering flies pass darting through the gauze of the earth's vapour; and intact, with its dress of rich velvet, wafting the mud with its double fan, the blue butterfly appears to be in ecstasy.

The angry jungles vibrate with the heat of the day, the black turkey sends his sharp cry into the wind and the cricket stuns the green, thick reed-grass; a woodbird imitates the sound of the horn, the cicada draws out its eternal chatter and the royal woodpecker repeats its call.

barren, bleak world of modern man. His career falls roughly into three parts. There was an early period when he lived in Buenos Aires and came under the influence of Darío, with whom he founded the *Revista de América* in 1894. This period culminated with the publication of *Castalia bárbara* in 1899. The second period of his life was spent as a professor of history and literature at the University of Tucumán where he worked on histories of Tucumán during the colonial period and on his *Leyes de la versificación castellana* [*Laws of Castilian Versification*] (1912). In 1921, he returned to Bolivia where he served as Minister of Education, then Minister of Foreign Affairs, and later as Ambassador, first in Chile and later in the United States. Undoubtedly, his most interesting creative work falls into the first period. In his *Castalia bárbara*, he borrowed from Norse mythology as Darío had from classical mythology in order to create a country of the mind. But unlike Darío he wrote in free verse, creating a rhythmic effect of repetition. Amongst the most striking of his poems is 'El canto del mal' [The Song of Evil] in which evil in the person of Lok is represented in an icy landscape with a dying victim who vainly stretches his hands towards the shadow of God:

Canta Lok en la obscura región desolada
y hay vapores de sangre en el canto de Lok,
El pastor apacienta su enorme rebaño de hielo
que obedece—gigantes que tiemblan—la voz del Pastor.
Canta Lok a los vientos helados que pasan
y hay vapores de sangre en el canto de Lok.

Densa bruma se cierne. Las olas se rompen
en las rocas abruptas, con sordo fragor.
En su dorso sombrío se mece la barca salvaje
del guerrero de rojos cabellos, huraño y feroz.
Canta Lok a las olas rugientes que pasan,
y hay vapores de sangre en el canto de Lok.

Cuando el himno del hierro se eleva al espacio
y a sus ecos responde siniestro clamor,
y en el foso sagrado y profundo, la víctima busca
con sus rígidos brazos tendidos, la sombra del Dios,
canta Lok a la pálida Muerte que pasa
y hay vapores de sangre en el canto de Lok.★

★ Lok sings in the dark and desolate region and there are vapours of blood in the song of Lok. The shepherd pastures his enormous, icy flock which—trembling giants—obey

The poem is much more than a description of a bleak northern scene. The shepherd, traditionally a symbol of Christ and salvation, is here associated with the God of evil, moving an icy flock and apparently indifferent to the appeal of the victim. Jaimes Freyre's poem presents us with a world without hope in which there is nothing warm, promising or alive and in which nature—sea, fog, rocks, ice—is seen in its most threatening and destructive aspects. In an equally striking poem, 'La noche' [Night], the human element disappears altogether and nature—the trees and clouds at night—is a nightmarish force:

> Agitadas por el viento se mecen las negras ramas
> el tronco, lleno de grietas, al rudo empuje, vacila,
> y entre el musgo donde vagan los rumores de la noche
> rompen la tierra y se asoman las raíces de la encina.
>
> Van las nubes por el cielo. Son Endriagos y Quimeras
> y enigmáticas Esfinges de la fiebre compañeras
> y Unicornios espantables y Dragones, que persigue
> la compacta muchedumbre de las venenosas Hidras;
> y sus miembros desgarrados en las luchas silenciosas
> ocultan con velo denso la faz de la luna lívida.
>
> Saltan sombras de las grietas del viejo tronco desnudo
> y hacia la selva en fantástica carrera se precipitan
> sobre el musgo donde vagan los rumores de la noche
> y amenazantes se yerguen las raíces de la encina.
>
> Extraños seres que visten singulares vestiduras
> y abandonan sus heladas, misteriosas sepulturas
> en el sueño pavoroso de una noche que no acaba.
> Mientras luchan en el cielo los Dragones y las Hidras
> y sus miembros desgarrados en los choques silenciosos,
> ocultan con velo denso la faz de la luna lívida.*

the voice of the shepherd. Lok sings to the icy winds that pass and there are vapours of blood in the song of Lok.

Dense fog comes up. The waves break on abrupt rocks, with dull crashes. On their dark backs rocks the wild boat of the red-haired warrior, wild and fierce. Lok sings to the roaring waves that pass and there are vapours of blood in the song of Lok.

When the hymn of iron rises to space and there replies a sinister clamour to its echoes and in the sacred deep pit the victim seeks with his rigid arms outstretched the shadow of God, Lok sings to pale Death who passes and there are vapours of blood in the song of Lok.

* Tossed by the wind, the black boughs rock, the cracked trunks waver at the hard assault and from the moss in which stirs the noise of the night, the oak trees' roots break the earth and emerge.

The clouds float in the sky. They are fabulous monsters and Chimeras and enigmatic Sphinxes, companions to fever, fearful Unicorns and Dragons who pursue the thick

F

Here the natural elements themselves—trees, clouds, nights—create a hallucinatory world of force and movement. The clouds whirl in the sky, roots break through the earth, the trees rear in the night, but significantly it is a world in which man is absent. Part of the success of the two poems quoted is due to the fact that they have a subliminal effect and this is what Jaimes Freyre sought:

La humanidad—he declared—vaga por un mundo poblado de fantasías. En todo espíritu hay un fondo fantástico y en las horas de la desolación, recorre las galerías siniestras de los fantasmas, va en busca del sueño que existe en la realidad, como los fenómenos físicos, esparcidos en el organismo del Universo. El Arte debe despertar, con estilo y emoción, ese sueño, donde él está, en el alma o del salvaje o el alma del culto.*

We can see here an anticipation of surrealist literary theory, and in fact of all the Modernist poets Jaimes Freyre is the one who, at his best, comes nearest to the modern world.

Julio Herrera y Reissig

In contrast to Jaimes Freyre, whose poetry often expresses flux and motion, Herrera y Reissig's most characteristic poems are expressive of timelessness. Born of an aristocratic family which fell into political disgrace, Herrera y Reissig deliberately isolated himself from his society, gathering in his apartment his 'Torre de las Panoramas', only those who, like himself, believed in the supremacy of art. His two main collections of poetry, *Los éxtasis de la montaña* [*The Ecstasy of the Mountain*] (1904–7) and *Los sonetos vascos* [*Basque Sonnets*] (1906), are volumes of pastoral poetry set in an idealised Basque country he himself had never visited. He chose this setting in order to describe a rural way of life in peasant communities in which for centuries the same

crowd of poisonous Hydras; and their limbs, torn in the silent struggles, hide the face of the livid moon with a dense veil.
    Shadows leap from the cracks of the old, naked trunk and rush in mad career towards the forest, over the moss where the noises of night and the threatening roots of the oak trees emerge.
    Strange beings which are clothed in strange garments, abandon their icy, mysterious tombs in the fearful dream of endless night. While the Dragons and Hydras fight in the heaven and, their limbs torn in silent combat, hide the face of the livid moon with a dense veil.
* Humanity wanders through a world peopled by fantasies. In every spirit there is an imaginative core and in the hours of desolation this passes along sinister, ghostly galleries, going in search of a dream which exists in reality like the physical phenomena scattered in the organism of the Universe. Art should awaken with style and emotion that dream, wherever it is, in the soul of the savage or that of the civilised.

customs and routine had prevailed. In 'La siesta', for instance, there is an atmosphere of sleepy but pleasant stagnation:

> No late más que un único reloj: el campanario
> que cuenta los dichosos hastíos de la aldea,
> el cual, al sol de enero, agriamente chispea,
> con su aspecto remoto de viejo refractario...
>
> A la puerta, sentado se duerme el boticario...
> En la plaza yacente la gallina cloquea
> y un tronco de ojaranzo arde en la chimenea,
> junto a la cual el cura medita su breviario.
>
> Todo es paz en la casa. Un cielo sin rigores,
> bendice las faenas, reparte los sudores...
> Madres, hermanas, tías, cantan lavando en rueda,
>
> las ropas que el domingo sufren los campesinos...
> y el asno vagabundo que ha entrado en la vereda
> huye, soltando coces, de los perros vecinos.*

Peace here is almost perfect, broken only by the one clock, the clucking hen, the song of the women and the runaway donkey. 'Hastío' [boredom] is 'dichoso' [happy] because it is an aspect of a world in which the structure is determined by nature and the seasons. Herrera y Reissig does not attack industrial progress directly. He simply shows us an idyllic world in which it has not even been thought of.

Delmira Agustini

The woman poet from Uruguay, Delmira Agustini, is the Modernist who carried furthest the sensuality and eroticism expressed in some of Darío's poetry. She was to die tragically, killed by the husband from whom she was separated and who afterwards killed himself, and the poems of most of her collections, *El libro blanco* [*The White Book*] (1907), *Cantos de la mañana* [Morning Songs] (1910), *Los cálices vacíos* [*Empty Chalices*], centre on the scarcely-disguised theme of sexuality.

---

* Only a single clock sounds; the bell which counts the happy boredom of the village, which in the January sun sparkles harshly with a remote look of an unruly old man.

At the door, the apothecary sits sleeping; in the sleepy village square the hen cackles and a trunk of hornbeam burns in the hearth by which the priest meditates over his breviary.

All is peace in the house. A temperate sky blesses the labours and distributes the tasks. In a circle, mothers, sisters, aunts sing as they wash the clothes which the peasants suffer on Sundays, and the vagrant ass which has entered the path flees kicking from the neighbouring dogs.

She accepts male evaluation of the woman as an object, saying that she is like 'un perro a tus plantas' [a dog at your feet]. Her rather melodramatic but forceful style is well illustrated in the following poem on the Romantic theme of Love and Death:

> Los lechos negros logran la más fuerte
> rosa de amor; arraigan en la muerte.
> Grandes lechos tendidos de tristeza
>   tallados a puñal y doselados
> de insomnio; las abiertas
> cortinas dicen caballeras muertas;
>   buenas como cabezas
> hermanas son las hondas almohadas:
> plintos del Sueño y del Misterio gradas.*

OTHER MODERNISTS

There were innumerable Modernist poets in Latin America and they cannot all be mentioned. Leopoldo Lugones and Santos Chocano, who are most noteworthy for their contribution to *Mundonovismo*, will be mentioned in a later chapter. In two Mexican poets, Amado Nervo (1870–1919) and Enrique González Martínez (1871–1952), we have examples of poets who became primarily meditative and introspective. The titles of their collections indicate their preoccupation with an inner quest. Amado Nervo published *Los jardines interiores* [*Inner Gardens*] (1908), *Serenidad* [*Serenity*] (1914), *Elevación* (1917); Enrique González Martínez, well-known for an attack on the Modernist aesthetic in a poem called 'Tuércele el cuello al cisne' [Twist the Swan's Neck], published volumes of meditative poems which he entitled *Silenter* and *Los senderos ocultos* [*The Hidden Paths*].

Modernism began as a revolt against the literary establishment, a revolt occasioned by the fact that the poets' experience had diverged widely from that of previous generations and called for a new language and form. The explorations of Darío and his contemporaries, the inspiration they drew from the French, enabled them to enter hitherto unexplored area of experience. Inevitably what began as an experimental movement became in its turn a literary establishment which was to be overthrown by the avant-garde of the '20s.

---

* Black beds bear the strongest rose of love; they are rooted in death. Great beds spread with sadness, carved with a dagger and canopied with insomnia; the open curtains speak of dead tresses; they are good, as twin heads, those deep pillows; plinths of sleep and steps of Mystery.

MODERNIST PROSE

No study of Modernism would be complete without considering the transformation in prose writing wrought by Darío, Gutiérrez Nájera and others. Some reference has already been made to this but perhaps the point can be further emphasised by comparing the *castizo* prose of Montalvo with a short extract from Darío's 'La canción del oro' [The Song of Gold]. Montalvo's style is highly abstract:

La nobleza se pierde moral y positivamente; así como los soberanos conceden títulos nobiliarios, y envisten de calidad señoril a una persona, así mismo dan carta desaforada. Una vez anulados los honores y prerogativas el noble queda plebeyo.*

Contrast Darío's baroque delight in rich detail:

Aquel día, un harapiento, por las trazas un mendigo, tal vez un peregrino, quizá un poeta, llegó, bajo la sombra de los altos álamos a la gran calle de los palacios, donde hay desafíos de soberbia entre el ónix y el pórfido, el ágata y el mármol, en donde las altas columnas, los hermosos frisos, las cúpulas doradas, reciben la caricia pálida del sol moribundo.†

Of course there is a vast difference in the effect the two writers are trying to achieve. Montalvo is arguing a case, Darío is trying to create the effect of opulence, the better to drive home his point that the worship of the Golden Calf has triumphed in the modern world. The appeal is to the senses and the emotions, not to reason.

But Modernism affected not only the style of prose writing but the whole approach. There was a new emphasis on perfection of style, and writers began to eschew didacticism. The artistic novel and short story were born. Gutiérrez Nájera's *Cuentos frágiles*, Darío's *Azul*, the *Cuentos de color* by the Venezuelan writer, Manuel Díaz Rodríguez, were often allegories, but the effect was achieved primarily by the use of evocative words, the creation of an impression rather than argument.

Enrique Larreta

One of the most interesting contributions to Modernist prose writing was a historical novel, *La gloria de don Ramiro* [*The Glory of Don*

* Nobility can be lost morally and practically. Just as sovereigns concede titles of nobility and bestow a gentleman's status on a person, in the same way can a letter of annulment be issued. Once the honours and prerogatives are annulled, the noble becomes a plebeian.
† That day, a man in rags, apparently a beggar, perhaps a pilgrim, perhaps a poet, passed under the shade of the high poplars to the great street of palaces where onyx and porphyry, agate and marble vie with one another, where the high columns, the beautiful friezes, the golden cupolas receive the pale caress of the dying sun.

Ramiro] (1908) by the Argentinian writer, Enrique Larreta (1875–1961). This is a reconstruction of Spanish life in the reign of Philip II which deals not only with Christian society but with the enclaves of Moors who carried on their religion under cover. The conflict of two cultures was precisely the subject that best suited a writer like Larreta who was interested not merely in historical events but in recreating the texture of life. His prose is characteristically Modernist in its accumulation of detail and in its appeal to the senses. Here, for instance, is a description of Don Alonso Blazquez, a nobleman who delights in his glass and ivory ware:

Algunos de aquellos objetos prolongaban el milagro de vivir centenariamente. Piezas del siglo anterior, arquetipos de la generación innumerable, habían sido exornados de mascarones y de imprevistas alimañas por la tenacilla de Vistori, de Ballorino, de Beroviero, en la gran época visionaria de la cristalería. Vidrios turbios, de un glauco tinte lodoso como el agua de los canales, de la cual aparentaban haber tomado toda su fantasía. Su manejo educaba la mano mejor que los marfiles. Don Alonso los tomaba con cuidado infinito, como si un movimiento poco armonioso pudiera quitarles la vida. Un amigo suyo, un pintor, formado en Venecia, a quien llamaban el Greco, habíale enseñado a mirarlos de noche en un rayo de luna. Sobre la vaga substancia la luz astral rielaba un reflejo fosforescente. Entonces, cual si hubiera caído en su pupila la gota de un filtro, don Alonso creía respirar el olor de la noche sobre las aguas, veía las escamosas estelas, las aturquesadas blancuras de los palacios, y la lobreguez de los pequeños canales internados en el misterio.*

We learn much about the character through his love of Venetian glass; we observe his aristocratic refinement, his appreciation of age and tradition and his love of beauty. Just as Modernist poetry had implied adherence to values which were alien to the bourgeois world, so did Larreta's prose writing dwell on aristocratic values which were outside the scope of the brash newly-rich.

But Modernist prose writing was also an instrument for conveying

---

* Some of those objects prolonged the miracle of living for centuries. Pieces of the previous century, archetypes of innumerable generations had been embellished with masks and with unexpected animals by the tongs of Vistori, of Ballorino, of Beroviero in the great visionary age of glass-making. Dark glasses, with a glaucous, muddy tint like the water of the canals from which they seemed to have taken all their fantasy. Handling them educated the hand better than the handling of ivory. Don Alonso took them with infinite care as if a slightly inharmonious movement could take their life from them. A friend of his, a painter, educated in Venice, who was called El Greco, had taught him to look at them by night in moonlight. Upon the vague substance, the astral light glistened in a phosphorescent reflection. Then as if a drop from a philtre had fallen in his eye, don Alonso thought he breathed the scent of night upon the waters, he saw the scaly wake, the turquoise and white of the palaces and the murkiness of the little canals plunged in mystery.

horror. Just as in poetry there was a sense of man's despair in a Godless universe, so prose writers, following the example of their master Poe, explored horror and fantasy. An outstanding Latin-American practitioner of the horror story was Horacio Quiroga whose work will be dealt with in a later chapter. Less known is Clemente Palma, son of the author of the *Tradiciones peruanas* whose 'El buzo' [The Diver] describes an hallucinatory journey through the sewers:

Su entrada produjo una verdadera revolución. Millones de cucarachas rojas se pusieron en movimiento...Había sitios en los que el muro se había derrumbado y formado pequeños montes de barro y piedras, y sobre los que tenía que pasar Feliciano; allí tenían los sapos su madriguera; allí también había culebras...y lombrices, que al ser pisadas por Feliciano se enroscaban a sus pies en los estertores de la agonía.

En otra calle...vió un animalejo del tamaño de un puño; dirigió la linterna hacia él; era una enorme araña en cuyo vientre podía caber un colibrí. La araña la miraba con sus ocho ojillos fulgurantes y emponzoñados, como las puntas de ocho flechas empapadas de curara. Estaban erizados sus pelos, y sobre el coselete se veía la palpitación ansiosa de un luchador que esperaba la agresión...*

Here nature is seen at its most savage. Snakes, spiders, frogs pullullate, procreate and devour one another. Man looks in vain for a design or a purpose. Though Clemente Palma is no doubt imitating contemporary European writing, it would not be long before Latin Americans realised that in their own continent, nature offered a spectacle of horror which outstripped man's imagination. The Modernists had revolutionised the language and techniques of Spanish–American literature. It now remained to apply these to the American scene.

* His entry produced a real revolution. Millions of red cockroaches began to move. There were places where the wall had tumbled down and had formed little heaps of clay and stones, over which Feliciano had to pass; there the toads had their lairs; there also were snakes and worms which, when Feliciano trod on them, wrapped themselves round his feet in their death agony.

In another street, he saw a beast the size of a fist; he shone his lantern on it; it was an enormous spider on whose stomach a humming bird could fit. The spider looked at him with its eight flashing and poisonous eyes, like the points of eight arrows soaked in curare. Its hair was on end and over the thorax could be seen the anxious palpitations of a fighter waiting for the attack.

6 THE REDISCOVERY OF THE NEW WORLD

In 1898, Spain lost Puerto Rico, Cuba and the Philippine islands, her last remaining colonies in the New World, a loss that was aggravated by her defeat at the hands of the United States. There was a dramatic change in the balance of power in the New World. The distant threat of Spain had been replaced by the more ominous threat of the vigorous young Anglo-Saxon power now incomparably wealthier and more industrially advanced than any other nation of the continent. The gloom of many intellectuals at the defeat of Spain was understandable. They had wanted Cuba liberated, but not by the United States, whose victory seemed to them to bear out contemporary racial theories which attributed superiority to the Anglo-Saxons and inferiority to racially-mixed societies. As Latin Americans looked towards their own societies, many of them torn by civil war, others suffering under dictatorships, all of them economically backward, they inevitably compared their position with that of the United States. They could take little pride in national tradition; Hispanic influence in the world had rapidly declined; and for a Bolivian, a Nicaraguan, a Uruguayan or any other Spanish–American nationality, there was little hope of rising to the forefront of world affairs.

THE ESSAY

However, in 1900, when the gloom was deepest, there appeared an essay whose forward-looking optimism was eagerly welcomed. This was *Ariel* by a young Uruguayan literature professor, José Enrique Rodó (1872–1917). In 1899, Rodó attracted attention with his perceptive criticism of Darío's *Prosas profanas*, in which he pointed out that while Darío was technically a virtuoso, he was not 'the poet of America'. Rodó was one of a new generation of Uruguayans, educated in a lay school, conversant with positivist theory and now alive to weaknesses as well as to the valuable aspects of positivism. Though partly self-educated (he was forced to leave school when his father died), he soon became one of Uruguay's leading intellectuals and helped to found *La revista nacional de literatura y ciencias sociales* in 1895. He became director of the National Library in 1900 and was twice a member of the Chamber of Deputies. He died in Europe, which it had been his life-time wish to visit. His essay *Ariel* was directed to the youth of the American continent whom he saw as the hope for the future. He based his work on a symbolism in which Ariel represented ideal values and Caliban the instinctual side of man, a symbolism which had probably been inspired by *Caliban*, one of the 'drames philosophiques' by the French thinker, Ernest Renan, who had, in turn, based his symbolism on the characters of Shakespeare's *Tempest*. For Rodó, man had his instinctual side, but the better individual transcended instinct and learned to act unselfishly and from the highest of motives. Indeed, Rodó believed that natural selection would encourage the development of this superior type of human being as he explains in his definition of Ariel.

Ariel es el imperio de la razón y el sentimiento sobre los bajos estímulos de la irracionalidad; es el entusiasmo generoso, el móvil alto y desinteresado en la acción, la espiritualidad de la cultura, la vivacidad y la gracia de la inteligencia— el término ideal a que asciende la selección humana, rectificando en el hombre superior los tenaces vestigios de Calibán, símbolo de sensualidad y de torpeza, con el cincel perseverante de la vida.*

Rodó does not seem to doubt that there is an evolutionist teleology nor that the disinterested ideal towards which man must strive is also the goal of societies. Indeed, he judges a society on the basis of its contribution to civilisation and hence considers Greece and Christian Europe to have offered most of value in the past. Both these had followed a disinterested idea, according to Rodó; the Greeks that of beauty and the Christians that of charity. Rodó seems to have inclined rather more to the Greeks, however, for he believed that beauty was not simply to be appreciated aesthetically but had a moral force. One could not love beauty (a form of harmony) and act evilly (since evil was a form of disharmony):

En el alma que haya sido objeto de una estimulación armónica y perfecta, la gracia íntima y la delicadeza del sentimiento de lo bello serán una misma cosa con la fuerza y la rectitud de la razón.†

* Ariel is the rule of reason and feeling over the low stimulus of irrationality; it is generous enthusiasm, the high and disinterested motive in action, spirituality in culture, vivacity and wit in intelligence—the ideal term to which human selection ascends, rectifying in higher man the tenacious vestiges of Caliban, symbol of sensuality and lewdness, with the persevering chisel of life.

† In the soul which has been the object of harmonious and perfect stimulation, the intimate

We now turn to the application of these ideas in an American context. Rodó wanted the continent to look beyond the mere selfish desire to become rich and prosperous towards a nobler goal. Though he had nothing against material wellbeing, he believed that it was useless to devote the whole of one's energies to this, and he pointed to the United States as an example of what happened when a nation adopts a purely utilitarian code. With all her technical efficiency, the United States had contributed no great art and no general scientific principle to the store of world culture:

Huérfano de tradiciones muy hondas que le orienten, ese pueblo no ha sabido sustituir la idealidad inspiradora del pasado con una alta y desinteresada concepción del porvenir. Vive para la realidad inmediata, del presente y por ellos subordina toda su actividad al egoismo del bienestar personal y colectivo.*

Latin America, Rodó felt, was destined for something better than this, for her roots were in the great Mediterranean cultures which had cultivated a love of beauty. If these Latin states were now constructed on democratic principles allowing for equality of opportunity in education, then the best man would inevitably rise to the top and guide the continent to a glorious future.

Using hindsight, it is easy to find much to criticise in Rodó's essay. It seems absurd, for instance, to offer cultural solutions to problems which are, in the main, economic and political. Moreover, there is no evidence to suppose that equality of opportunity would contribute to the formation of an exemplary élite. The meritocracy is not necessarily formed of men with 'disinterested ideals'. Nevertheless, the importance of *Ariel* cannot be over-emphasised. For generations, it was a seed-bed of ideas.

Looked at from another point of view, perhaps *Ariel* is simply a compendium of attitudes that were forced on intellectuals by the very fact that they were powerless to act or to affect the destiny of their continent except in the realm of ideas. The most influential notions propagated by the essay were:

   1 The identification of the United States with utilitarianism, and conversely the identification of Latin America with a nobler and more realistic continental ideal.

grace and delicacy of the sentiment of the beautiful will be the equivalent of force and rectitude of reason.
* Without deep traditions to direct her, this nation has not been able to substitute for the inspiring ideal of the past a high and disinterested concept of the future. It lives for the immediate reality of the present and subordinates all its activity to the selfishness of personal and collective wellbeing.

2 The notion that the nations of Latin America formed a cultural unity and that their roots were in Mediterranean civilisation.

3 That the task of the intellectual was to set a high example, both in the moral and the cultural sphere.

4 That the task of the intellectual was not only the creation of a Latin-American culture but also the preservation of the culture of the past.

5 That societies were shaped by guiding ideas.

6 The importance of education both as a training for the intellectual élite and also as a means of improving the masses.

The earnest moral tone of *Ariel* was to dominate the period until the outbreak of the Mexican Revolution and even beyond. Even Darío caught it. In 1905, he dedicated the first of his *Cantos de vida y esperanza* [*Songs of Life and Hope*] to Rodó, and doubtless stung by the latter's refusal to consider him 'the poet of America', he even turned his swan into the symbol of Latin America's enigmatic future, while in 'A Rooseveldt' he apostrophised the United States thus:

> Sois ricos
> Juntáis al culto de Hércules el culto de Mammón:
> y alumbrando el camino de la fácil conquista,
> la Libertad levanta su antorcha en Nueva York...
>
> Mas la América nuestra, que tenía poetas
> desde los viejos tiempos de Netzahualcoyotl
> que consultó los astros, que conoció la Atlántida
> cuyo nombre nos llega resonando en Platón,
> que desde los remotos momentos de su vida
> vive de luz, de fuego, de perfume, de amor...
> esa América...vive.*

Novelists too adopted a moralising tone, writing books which criticised shortcomings or which exposed injustice and evil. However, it was on essay writing that Rodó had most direct influence, as can be seen from the vast number of *Ariel*-type works which appeared. He himself contributed two more works before he died; the first, 'Motivos de Proteo' (1909), was a lengthy essay on psychological motivation and the idea of a vocation in the life of the individual; the second, *El*

---

* You are rich. You have joined the cult of Hercules to that of Mammon, and lighting up the road of easy conquest, Liberty raises its torch in New York...

But our America, which had poets from the ancient times of Netzahualcoyotl, who consulted the stars, who knew the Atlantides, whose name comes to us in echoes from Plato, which from the remotest period of its existence, lives on light, fire, perfume and love...this America...lives.

mirador de Próspero (1914) consisted of essays on great men which included several eminent Latin Americans such as Bolívar and Montalvo. The essays inspired by *Ariel* are legion, but they may be divided into the following types:

1 Those which described Latin America's cultural tradition and were designed to raise the stock of Latin-American civilisation in the eyes of the rest of the world. Examples are *Les démocraties latines de l'Amérique* (1912) by Francisco García Calderón (1883–1953) and *Les écrivains contemporains de l'Amérique Espagnole* (1920) by Francisco Contreras (Chile, 1877–1933).

2 Those which collected essays on 'great men' following the example of *El mirador de Próspero*. *Los optimistas* [*The Optimists*] by Jesús Castellanos (Cuba, 1879–1912) is of this type. Such essays followed a tradition of books of exemplary 'heroes' which the Modernists had initiated (especially Darío with *Los raros* and Enrique Gómez Carrillo (Guatemala, 1873–1927) in *Literatura extranjera* [*Foreign Literature*] (1895).

3 Those essays which analysed the historical and environmental factors affecting the continent and put forward a programme for the future. Such was 'La evolución política y social de Hispanoamérica' [The Political and Social Evolution of Spanish America] (1911) by the Venezuelan, Rufino Blanco Fombona (1874–1944) and 'El porvenir de América Latina' [The Future of Latin America] by the Argentinian, Manuel Ugarte (1878–1951). Analytical essays of this type were also written on the national situation, the most worthy of note being 'La restauración nacional' [National Restoration] (1910) by Ricardo Rojas (1882–1957) of Argentina and the para-sociological analysis of Bolivia, 'Pueblo enfermo' [Sick Nation] (1909) by Alcides Arguedas (1879–1946).

4 Educational essays: many of the analytical essays mentioned also offer educational solutions to Latin America's difficulties, since training (especially in civic affairs), a high level of literacy, and the right training of the élite were seen as the basis for a reform which would raise standards of civic morality. Carlos Vaz Ferreira's 'Moral para intelectuales' [Morality for Intellectuals] (1908), for instance, was directed towards the intelligentsia as an exemplary group.

The twin interest in analysis and reform was also reflected in imaginative literature. The Chilean critic, Francisco Contreras, was to coin the word *Mundonovismo* for the movement which he declared grew out of Modernism and strove for universality, but a universality rooted in

...grandes sugestiones de la raza, de la tierra o del ambiente que animan todas las literaturas superiores.*[1]

Poets began to express their emotions and conflicts not in terms of Greek myth or other archetypes but through elements drawn from their own environment. Novelists generally went further, and many of them attempted either to educate their public in national realities or to change society by showing its faults.

POETRY

Modernism had, in the '90s, attempted to break down the provincialism of Hispanic literature and graft it on to European tradition. But while a poet like Herrera y Reissig expressed his nostalgia for peace in an idealised pastoral world, others realised that this nostalgia, or the peace of provincial life, could equally well be conveyed in American terms. Two Modernist poets—Leopoldo Lugones (Argentina, 1874–1938) and José Santos Chocano (Peru, 1875–1934)—became thoroughly Americanist in their poetry.

Leopoldo Lugones

Lugones's long poem, *Las montañas del oro* [*The Mountains of Gold*] (1897), had been a Hugoesque hymn in praise of progress and poetry and undoubtedly a reflection of his view that the poet could be the leader of men in their struggle for a more just society. Soon after 1900, the extreme socialist convictions of his younger days began to waver, and he turned with increasing wonder and curiosity to his native land. At first this was expressed in his prose works—the *Guerra gaucha*, for instance—rather than in his poetry which still turned like a heliotrope to the sun of the European avant-garde. His *Crepúsculos del jardín* [*Twilight of the Garden*] (1905) recalled Samain and his *Lunario sentimental* (1909), Jules Laforgue; but in 1910, the centenary of Argentine Independence, he published a very different poetry. The *Odas seculares* were dedicated to his native land. Sections with titles such as 'A la patria' [To my Country], 'Las cosas útiles y magníficas' [Useful and Magnificent Things], 'A los ganados y las mieses' [To Cattle and the Corn], indicated his intention of celebrating the rural life of the

* ...these great suggestions of race, land or environment which inspire all the best literature.

Argentine. There was a picture, for instance, of 'el ruso Elías', the immigrant peasant:

> Pasa por el camino el ruso Elías
> Con su gabán eslavo y con sus botas,
> En la yegua cebruna que ha vendido
> Al cartero rural de la colonia. . .
>
> La fecundidad sana de su esfuerzo
> Se ennoblece en la tierra bondadosa,
> Que asegura a los pobres perseguidos
> La retribución justa de sus obras.*

Here the verse goes beyond description into a nationalist apotheosis as he sees the Argentine as a place of refuge for the persecuted of the world. From this point onwards, Lugones's poetry is increasingly nationalistic or descriptive of his native countryside. *El libro fiel* (1912) was followed in 1917 by *El libro de los paisajes* which presents an idyllic countryside. And with the publication of *Las horas doradas* [*The Gilded Hours*], the countryside had taken on a quasi-mystic beauty:

> Entre el cielo y la tierra azulada,
> Describían el vasto circuito
> La luz, el reposo y la nada.
>
> Apagóse, a lo lejos, un grito
> Que dejó la llanura más sola.
> En mi alma triunfó el infinito.
>
> Un silencio admirable llenóla
> Con su perfección. Ascendía
> Lento y hondo, a la vez, como una ola,
> Y era música y no todavía.†

In *Romancero* (1924), Lugones returned to the ballad-form, while *Poemas solariegos* (1927) sung 'of man and love and duty and the happiness of everyday life'. It included poetic portraits of characters such as the One-man Band whom Lugones remembered from his childhood or the harp-player, Ildefonso:

---

* The Russian, Elías, passes along the road with his Slav cape and his boots, riding on the dun mare that he has sold to the colony's postman. . .
  The healthy fruitfulness of his effort is ennobled in the fruitful earth which to the poor persecuted ones assures a just reward for their labours.
† Between the sky and the bluish earth, light, repose and nothingness made a vast circle.
  In the distance, a cry died away and left the plain more lonely. The infinite triumphed in my soul.
  A wonderful silence filled it with perfection and it ascended, at once slow and deep, like a wave—and its music was not music yet.

Que tocaba con empeño igual
Una chacarera o un responso.
Pues lo mismo oficiaba con el cura,
Que hacía buena figura
En la tertulia más arriesgada...*

His final compositions were published posthumously with the title *Romancero del Río Seco*. Lugones's poetry is poetry of a rural America already threatened by the immigrant horde and industrialisation. For him, the true Argentina was the countryside, its true tradition that of the *estancia* and these his poetry tried to preserve.

Very different is the Americanism of José Santos Chocano whose poetry is, however, a mere pallid reflection of a turbulent life. A political prisoner in his teens, his *Iras santas* [*Holy Wrath*] (1894) railed against his opponents. He loved the flamboyant and the colourful, and went to Mexico during the Revolution where he supported Pancho Villa, and later to Guatemala where his friend Estrada Cabrera was supreme dictator. Chocano's execution on the downfall of Estrada Cabrera was only averted by the protests and petitions that came from many parts of the world, but the experience seems to have left him unabashed. His private life caused continual scandal and when he resorted to a duel to defend his literary reputation, he killed his opponent and was forced to leave Peru and go to Santiago where he was to live for the rest of his life. His death was as violent as the rest of his life, for he was assassinated when riding in a tram-car.

Dramatic gestures had been a feature of the Modernist poets' attitude to existence and Santos Chocano was only following in a trend set by Darío when he saw himself as a superman. Much of his poetry, too, is a form of gesture. But he was one of the first poets to celebrate the history, landscape and the indigenous people of the continent. He published *Selva virgen* [*Virgin Jungle*] (1896), *Los cantos del Pacífico* [*Pacific Songs*] (1904), *Alma América* [*American Soul*] (1906) and *Primicias de oro de Indias* [*Offering of Gold from the Indies*] (1934) among other works which included a play and a body of polemical writing. Characteristic of his poetry is a nostalgia for the colonial past as well as appreciation of the glories of the Indian civilisation. In the following poem, 'Ciudad dormida', for instance, he presents us with a picture of the somnolent city of Cartagena, dreaming of the battle of long ago:

* With equal enthusiasm, he played a country dance or a response. For he would play in the same way for the priest as he would strum away at the most daring party...

> Cartagena de Indias: tú, que, a solas
> entre el rigor de las murallas fieras,
> crees que te acarician las banderas
> de pretéritas huestes españolas;
>
> Tú, que ciñes radiantes aureolas
> desenvuelves, soñando en las riberas,
> la perezosa voz de tus palmeras
> y el escándalo eterno de tus olas...
>
> ¿Para qué despertar, bella durmiente?
> Los piratas tus sueños mortifican,
> más tú siempre serena te destacas;
>
> Y los párpados cierras blandamente,
> mientras que tus palmeras te abanican
> y tus olas te mecen como hamacas...*

Like his compatriot Ricardo Palma, Chocano loved to recall the refinement and elegance of the Viceregal period, and there is no doubt that he regretted the lost heroism of the past. Yet he was also capable of writing evocative poetry describing the landscapes and the Indians of his native land. In the following poem, 'Las punas' [The Bleak Regions], he conjures up the immensity of the high plateau:

> Silencio y soledad...Nada se mueve...
> Apenas, a lo lejos, en hilera,
> las vicuñas con rápida carrera
> pasan, a modo de una sombra leve.
>
> ¿Quién a medir esa extensión se atreve?
> Solo la desplegada cordillera,
> que se encorva después a la manera
> de un colosal paréntesis de nieve.
>
> Vano será que busque la mirada
> alegría de vívidos colores,
> en la tristeza de la puna helada:

* Cartagena of the Indies: you who, alone in the grave circle of these savage walls, believe that the flags of former Spanish hosts caress you.
   You who are crowned with radiant aureoles discover, dreaming on the shores, the lazy voice of your palm trees and the eternal tumult of the waves.
   Why waken, sleeping beauty? Pirates disturb your dreams but you always rise serene and you close your eyes softly while your palm trees waft you and your waves rock like hammocks.

Sin mariposas, pájaros, ni flores,
es una inmensidad deshabitada,
como si fuese un alma sin amores...*[1]

Though describing the emptiness of the *puna*, Santos Chocano avoids obviously regionalist touches in his language. He uses a high-sounding literary Spanish which is effective as long as he is dealing with the grandiose. His declamatory style sets him somewhat apart from those of his generation who, in returning to the simple themes of provincial life, adopted a simple vocabulary and style. We shall now deal with the best of these *criollista*[2] writers—Baldomero Fernández Moreno, Carlos Pezoa Véliz and Ramón López Velarde.

Fernández Moreno (1886–1950)

Baldomero Fernández Moreno was born in Buenos Aires, but spent much of his childhood in Spain, and there is a Hispanic stamp on his poetry. Though he graduated as a doctor, he left the medical profession in order to teach literature and write poetry. His output has a remarkable unity, his main works being *Las iniciales del misal* (1915), *Aldea española* [*Spanish Village*] (1925), *Décimas* (1928), *Seguidillas* (1936), *Romances* (1936). Though much of this poetry is of comparatively recent date, in spirit it is very much of the 1900–18 period and illustrates the poet's search for stability in the simplicity of rustic life. Fernández Moreno abandons the decorative, rich verse favoured by some Modernists in favour of traditional Spanish metres and a plain unadorned language that reflects his love of the uncomplicated feelings and the simple life. Here, for example, is his 'Inicial de oro', a poem in which he recalls his grandmother—the very symbol of tradition, order and stability:

Nací, hermanos, en esta dulce tierra argentina
pero el primer recuerdo nítido de mi infancia
es este: una mañana de oro y de neblina,
un camino muy blanco y una calesa rancia.

Luego un portal oscuro de caduca arrogancia
y una abuelita toda temblona y pueblerina
que me deja en la cara una agreste fragancia
y me dice 'El mi nieto, qué caruca más fina!'

★ Silence and solitude...Nothing moves...Almost imperceptible in the distance, the vicuñas pass by with rapid step like light shadows.
  Who dares measure that spaciousness? Only the spreading range of mountains which is curved like a colossal bracket of snow; the eyes will seek the joy of lively colours in vain in the sadness of the icy plateau. Without butterflies or birds or flowers, it is an uninhabited waste like a soul without love.

Y me llenó las manos de castañas y nueces,
el alma de leyendas, el corazón de preces,
y los labios risueños de un divino parlar.

Un parlar montañés de viejecita bruja
que narra una conseja mientras mueve la aguja.
El mismo que ennoblece, hermanos, mi cantar!*

Carlos Pezoa Véliz

In Chile, even at the height of Modernism, poetry expressed humanitarian sentiments. The 'aristocratic' attitudes of a 'Duque Job' or a 'Conde de Camors' as Gutiérrez Nájera and Julián del Casal had called themselves, was far less evident in Chile, perhaps because many writers came from humbler sectors of the population and identified themselves with the poor and downtrodden. Chile's upper class was the most aristocratic in Latin America, but Chile was also the one country in which there was an emergent middle class who were shocked by the poverty of the mass of the population.

The two most interesting poets of the period were Magallanes Moure (1878–1924) and Carlos Pezoa Véliz (1879–1908). The latter achieved little distinction in his lifetime and his *Alma Chilena*, an interesting collection of poems, mostly on native themes, was published posthumously in 1912. The poems reveal a meditative man who expressed his sorrow at the poverty and misery he saw around him, not in a crude social-protest poetry, but by expressing the sadness in terms of landscape and scenery. He explained his poetic technique thus:

Si el poeta habla del agua con la voz misma del agua, hable también de los sedientes...Si quiere contar sus cuitas al paisaje, hable desde la tosca puerta del rancho carcomido, donde hay tapias, rosales, organismos y esperanza ruinosas... Cante el viento que arrastra el polen, principio de vida, y el ¡ay! de los desheredados, principio de muerte.†[1]

* I was born, brothers, in this sweet Argentine land, but the first clear memory of my childhood is this: a morning of gold mist, a white road and an ancient chaise.

Then a dark doorway of crumbling pride and a grandmother, trembling and rustic, who leaves a country fragrance on my face and says, 'My grandchild, what a delicate little face he has!'

And she filled my hands with chestnuts and nuts, my soul with legends and my heart with prayers and there was a divine speech on her smiling lips.

The mountain speech of a little old witch who tells a proverb while she plies her needle. The same speech that ennobles my song, brothers!

† If the poet speaks of water with the very voice of water, let him also speak of the thirsty ...If he wishes to sing the sorrows of the landscape, let him speak from the rough door of the decaying farm in which there are ruinous walls, rose gardens, ruined organisms and hope...Let him sing of the wind which carries away pollen, the germ of life and of the lament of the disinherited, the beginning of death.

From the Modernist movement, Pezoa Véliz had obviously drawn the lesson that poetry fails when it is overtly didactic and that the reader must be allowed to experience emotions of pity, indignation or melancholy through the associations suggested by the language and construction of the poem. 'El perro vagabundo' [The Stray Dog], 'La pena de azotes' [The Whipping Penalty] and 'Nada' [Nothing] (which tells of the funeral of a tramp) are undoubtedly intended as social protest, though this is conveyed indirectly. But his most successful poems are those that describe the desolate Chilean landscape, like the following, 'Entierro de campo' [Burial in the Countryside]:

> Con un cadáver a cuestas,
> camino del cementerio,
> meditabundos avanzan
> los pobres angarilleros.
>
> Cuatro faroles descienden
> por Marga-Marga hacia el pueblo,
> cuatro luces melancólicas
> que hacen llorar sus reflejos;
> cuatro maderos de encina,
> cuatro acompañantes viejos...
>
> Una voz cansada implora
> por la eterna paz del muerto;
> ruidos errantes, silhuetas
> de árboles foscos, siniestros.
> Allá lejos, en la sombra,
> el aullar de los perros
> y el efímero rezongo
> de los nostálgicos ecos.
>
> Sopla el puelche. Una voz dice:
> 'Viene, hermano, el aguacero'
> Otra voz murmura: 'Hermanos,
> roguemos por él, roguemos.'
>
> Calla en las faldas tortuosas
> el aullar de los perros;
> inmenso, extraño, desciende
> sobre la noche el silencio;
> apresuran sus responsos
> los pobres angarilleros
> y repite alguno: 'Hermano,
> ya no tarda el aguacero;
> son las cuatro, el alba viene,
> roguemos por él, roguemos.'

Y como empieza la lluvia,
doy mi adiós a aquel entierro,
pico espuela a mi caballo
y en la montaña me interno.

Y allá en la montaña obscura,
¿quién era? llorando pienso:
Algún pobre diablo anónimo
que vino un día de lejos,
alguno que amó los campos,
que amó el sol, que amó el sendero
por donde se va la vida,
por donde él, pobre labriego,
halló una tarde el olvido,
enfermo, cansado, viejo!*

The cold wind, the threatening storm, the melancholy landscape set the mood of the poem. The dead man is anonymous, destined to leave no trace of his passage on earth; and even in this last act of remembrance there is a suggestion of haste, since the mourners wish to get the funeral over before the storm begins. Human existence here is reduced to a brief passage with 'sol' [sun] and 'campos' [fields] before old age and death. And though there is no obvious social protest, Pezoa Véliz points a contrast between the lives and deaths of the rich and great and the unrecorded lives and deaths of the humble.

Ramón López Velarde (1888–1921)

The first collection of poems by Ramón López Velarde was published in 1916 during the Mexican Revolution. The author was a provincial

* With a body on their shoulders, on their way to the cemetery, meditatively advance the poor bearers.

Four lanterns descend down Marga-Marga towards the village, four melancholy lights whose reflections weep, four oak planks, four old attendants.

A tired voice implores for the eternal peace of death; wandering noises, silhouettes of sinister, frowning trees. Far away there, in the shadow, the howling of dogs and the ephemeral murmur of nostalgic echoes.

The *puelche* [wind from the Andes] blows. A voice says 'The storm approaches, brother.' Another voice murmurs, 'Brothers, let us pray for him, let us pray.'

The howling of the dogs ceases in the tortuous fells; immense, strange, a silence descends on the night; the poor bearers hurry their responses and someone repeats, 'Brother, the storm will not be long delayed; it is four, dawn is coming, let us pray for him, let us pray.'

And as the rain begins, I say goodbye to that funeral, I spur my horse and go up the mountain.

And there in the dark mountain, weeping I wonder, Who was he? Some poor anonymous devil who came one day from afar, one who loved the fields, who loved the sun, who loved the path along which life goes away, on which he, poor labourer, ill, tired and old found oblivion one evening.

lawyer and teacher who only settled in Mexico City in 1914. An admirer of Lugones, López Velarde felt a strong local patriotism, identifying, as Lugones had done, the good life with the simplicity and traditions of the provinces. Here, for instance, are his recollections of 'Mi prima Agueda' [My Cousin Agueda]:

> Mi madrina invitaba a mi prima Agueda
> a que pasara el día con nosotros,
> y mi prima llegaba
> con un contradictorio
> prestigio de almidón y de temible
> luto ceremonioso.
>
> Agueda aparecía, resonante
> de almidón, y sus ojos
> verdes y sus mejillas rubicundas
> me protegían contra el pavoroso
> luto...
>   Yo era rapaz
>
> y conocía la *o* por lo redondo,
> y Agueda que tejía
> mansa y perseverante en el sonoro
> corredor me causaba
> calosfríos ignotos...
> (Creo que hasta la debo la costumbre
> heroicamente insana de hablar solo)
>
> A la hora de comer, en la penumbra
> quieta del refectorio,
> me iba embelesando un quebradizo
> sonar intermitente de vajilla
> y el timbre caricioso
> de la voz de mi prima.
>   Agueda era
> (luto, pupilas verdes y mejillas
> rubicundas) un cesto policromo
> de manzanas y uvas
> en el ébano de un armario añoso.*

* My godmother invited my cousin Agueda to spend a day with us and my cousin came in a contradictory prestige of starch and of fearful ceremonial mourning.
Agueda appeared, resounding with starch and her green eyes and rubicund cheeks protected me against the fearful mourning.
I was a child and recognised the *o* because it was round and Agueda who knitted with patience and perseverance in the sonorous corridor caused unknown tremors in me (I think that I even inherited from her the heroically mad custom of talking to myself.)
At mealtimes, in the still half-light of the dining-room I was enchanted with the intermittent, fragile sound of dishes and the caressing sound of my cousin's voice.

Despite this picture of rustic simplicity, the technique is sophisticated, the poetic language complex. The picture of the cousin is contradictory. She is full of life and colour but is wearing mourning; she arouses sensuality but is one of the family. But the resolution of these contradictions is provided in the last lines, in which she is likened to a basket of fruit in an old cupboard. Within the formality of provincial life, the joy and fruitfulness of youth is contained without losing its quality and flavour.

This poem was included in the collection *La sangre devota* [*Reverent Blood*] (1916) which was followed in 1919 by *Zozobra* [*Anguish*]. A posthumous collection, *El son del corazón* [*The Sound of the Heart*] appeared in 1932. The best poems in all his works dramatise the conflict between sensuality and the ideal. One of the most forceful is 'Las hormigas' [The Ants] in which the ants are the symbol of his devouring sensuality. López Velarde indeed manages to convey complex reactions and conflicts through the provincial scenes of his childhood. One of the most striking of his poems is 'El retorno maléfico' [The Ill-Fated Return] in which the poet returns to the village of his childhood, the upturned 'Eden':

> Mejor será no regresar al pueblo,
> al edén subvertido que se calla,
> en la mutilación de la metralla.
>
> Hasta los fresnos mancos
> los dignatarios de cúpula oronda,
> han de rodar las quejas de la torre
> acribillada en los vientos de fronda.
>
> Y la fusilería grabó, en la cal
> de todas las paredes
> de la aldea espectral,
> negros y aciagos mapas,
> porque en ellos leyese el hijo pródigo
> al volver a su umbral
> en un anochecer de maleficio
> a la luz de petróleo de una mecha,
> su esperanza deshecha.
>
> Cuando la tosca llave enmohecida
> fuerza la chirriante cerradura,
> en la añeja clausura

Agueda was (mourning, green eyes and rubicund cheeks) a multicoloured basket of apples and grapes in the ebony of an ancient cupboard.

del zaguán, los dos púdicos
medallones de yeso,
entornando los párpados narcóticos
se mirarán y se dirán: '¿Qué es eso?'.*

The bullet-scarred houses, the rusty locks, are not simply evidence of the Mexican revolutionary fighting which had passed that way but also the revolution in time that had taken place. The poet's own hope is destroyed; in the countryside nature is ever-renewed:

el amor amoroso
de las parejas pares;
noviazgos de muchachas
frescas y humildes, como humildes coles
y que la mano dan por el postigo
a la luz de dramáticos faroles.†

From this, the poet is excluded by time and experience. The poems of López Velarde show that a local or regional setting did not necessarily mean simple or rustic sentiments.

THE NOVEL AND SHORT STORY

The novel and short story of this period were also primarily concerned with rural life and particularly the lives of the poor, although prose writing is characterised by a much greater tendency to didacticism. Many of the novelists of the period were men who came from wealthy or middle-class families, and though they had sometimes been brought up on country estates, nevertheless their interest in the lives of the peasants often sprang out of a feeling of disillusionment with city life. Like the poets, they looked to the countryside for an order and stability which seemed to be disappearing from modern societies. However, prose writing was also strongly influenced both by the Spanish school of *costumbrismo* (which emphasised descriptions of colourful types and

---

* It will be better not to go back to the village, to the upturned Eden which is silent in the mutilation of machine guns.
    Even the pruned ash trees, those dignitaries with a fine cupola, must surround a tower that complains and is wounded in the leafy winds.
    And the guns engraved black, fateful maps on the limestone of the walls in the spectral village so that on an ill-fated twilight the prodigal son might read his shattered hope, on his return home by the lamp light of the evening.
    When the rough and rusty key forces the creaking hinges of the ancient door lock, the two shamefaced plaster medallions with half-open drugged eyes will look at one another saying, 'What's this?'
† loving love of perfect couples, betrothed girls fresh and humble like humble cabbages who hold out their hands through the postern by the light of dramatic lanterns.

manners) and by contemporary French realism and naturalism. Hence, although the prose writer found a source of inspiration in the beauty of the landscape, his description of the peasants was not always idealised. Much more than the poet, the prose writer was also influenced by the moralising and didactic tone of the essayists. Novels and stories were frequently written with the purpose of exposing abuses and injustices. In fact, three broad streams of writing can be distinguished:

1 Novels and stories which record provincial life with warmth and humour, e.g. the novels of Tomás Carrasquilla of Colombia.

2 Novels and stories which expose either the sordidness of the life of the poor or arouse indignation at the exploitation of the poor, e.g. the stories of Javier de Viana of Uruguay and Baldomero Lillo of Chile.

3 The novel of intellectual frustration. *De sobremesa* [*At Dessert*] by José Asunción Silva was the prototype of the story in which a young writer or intellectual is broken on the rocks of society. Other novels of this type include *Los ídolos rotos* [*Broken Idols*] (1901) by Manuel Díaz Rodríguez (Venezuela, 1868–1927), *El terruño* [*The Homeland*] (1916) by Carlos Reyles (Uruguay, 1868–1938), and *El último Solar* (1920) by Rómulo Gallegos (Venezuela, 1884–1969) and the allegory, *Alsino* (1920) by the Chilean, Pedro Prado (1886–1952).

4 Some of the first novels of urban society were published during this period. Most of them dealt with the moral sickness of members of the middle classes. Examples are the novels of the Mexican, Federico Gamboa (1864–1939).

And since the novel of the period is related as never before to the national context, some of the main writers will now be considered with reference to the societies in which they were writing.

THE PLATE REGION

Argentina was the most urbanised of the Latin-American countries, and also the country which had admitted the greatest proportion of European immigrants. These two factors created problems of a wholly new type, chief among them being the problem of rootlessness and lack of tradition. The one characteristically Argentine stereotype— the gaucho—had become a farm labourer instead of a nomadic troubadour. On the other hand, the immigrants did not even have roots in Spanish tradition, and often their chief interest in coming to America was the amount of money they could make there. Amongst the Modernists, attacks on the materialism that prevailed, especially in Buenos Aires, had been common. Now it was echoed from all quarters. 'We have put our honour in trade' declared Leopoldo Lugones, and Roberto Payró planned a novel called 'Fuertes y ricos' [The Strong and the Rich] which was to deal with the 'power of money in our country'. And in both the novels of Payró and of Manuel Gálvez (1882–1962), this forms a major element of their social criticism.

Roberto Payró (1867–1928)

Payró was a journalist with experience of life in many different parts of the Argentine. He was a radical at first, later a socialist with anarchist sympathies, his political view being shaped by strong moral indignation against 'gamblers', 'thieves', 'violators' and 'assassins' who, he declared, went unpunished while those who protested against social injustice were persecuted. The writer's main task, he felt, was to fight this corruption and at the same time to record the American scene; and in particular

Esas costumbres que se pierden, esas razas que se extinguen, esas comedias y esos dramas políticos, guerreros y sociales que se han desarrollado en esta parte de América, son mina inagotable de lo pintoresco, que no se explota por momentánea ceguedad.*

His main works are three novels set in the provinces and based on his experiences of the town of Bahía Blanca; these are: *El casamiento de Laucha* [*Laucha's Marriage*] (1906), *Pago chico* (1908) and the *Divertidas aventuras del nieto de Juan Moreira* [*The Amusing Adventures of the Grandson of Juan Moreira*] (1910).

Payró's literary models were more Hispanic than French. *El casamiento de Laucha* derives from the picaresque and gives a masterly picture of the wily *criollo* who woos his employer, doña Carolina, the owner of a *pulpería* [provision store], goes through a fake marriage ceremony with her, helped by the rascally priest, padre Papagna, spends her money and then abandons her. Laucha tells his own story with the pride of a man who has always lived by his wits. Here is his description of being beaten in a horse-race when his rival is guilty of foul play. The description is colloquial and vivid:

* Those customs which are disappearing, those races which are in the process of being extinguished, these political, military and social dramas and comedies which took place in this part of America provide an inexhaustible source of the picturesque which is not exploited because of momentary blindness.

El tiro era de dos cuadras. Después de unas cuantas partidas, largamos y mi potrillo principió a sacar su ventajita, primero la cabeza, después un pescuezo, después medio cuerpo ¡sin castigar! ¡Contreras venía a dos rebenques, lonja y lonja!...Claro que el tordillo se le iba a aplastar, pero estaba ciego de rabia con la fumada...Asimismo saqué un cuerpo de ventaja, cuando ¡malhaya!, medio matando su tordillo, Contreras me alcanza, le mete pierna al zaino, que rueda largándome por las orejas y pasa como un refusilo sin parar hasta la raya. ¡Hijuna!...*

Payró's skill in this passage shows itself in his ability to give the impression of using popular speech without falling into incomprehensible dialect. Nor does he need to moralise explicitly. His short novel gives a succinct account of a society in which the rascals win and the virtuous lose.

Pago chico and the *Divertidas aventuras* are more openly moralising in tone. The first is the story of a small provincial town in which corruption and *caciquismo*[1] are rife. There is no plot in the traditional sense; instead there is a series of episodes which centre around an anecdote. One typical episode concerns an 'Eatanswill'-type election campaign in which the government party hires an assassin in order to intimidate the opposition. To everybody's dismay the 'gaucho matón' [gaucho killer] gets drunk and goes out into the street with a loaded shot-gun ready to fire at anybody. While Payró is here criticising a serious abuse, he does so with humour, stressing the comic and ridiculous aspects of the scene. At the same time, he does not allow the reader to forget that these hired killers can only flourish as long as they have official protection. Thus he declares:

Ha muerto a traición a tres o cuatro, en estos últimos años pero como nunca se ha atrevido con ningún oficialista, y siempre lo protegen los que lo utilizan como instrumento, el castigo mayor que se le ha dado hasta hoy, es el de hacerlo escaparse del partido en que 'se desgració', recomendándolo como 'hombre de acción' a las autoridades de cualquier otro.†

* The race was for two blocks. After a few bets, we set off and my little colt began to gain, first by a head then by a neck, then by half a length and without whipping. Contreras was two whip lengths behind...Of course he was going to knock out his grey but he was blind with rage at the defeat. I had a length advantage, when, curse it, half killing his grey, Contreras catches up on me, pushes my chestnut which rolls over and throws me over its ear and I fall over like a flash of lightning and don't stop until I get to the finishing post. Man!

† He treacherously shot three or four these last years but since he has never dared to do it against a government servant and they always protect him and use him as an instrument, the greatest punishment which has ever been meted out to him so far is to let him leave the region in which he has 'disgraced himself' recommending him as a 'man of action' to the authorities of some other place.

Payró pursued this same theme of corruption in an even more serious fashion in his *Divertidas aventuras del nieto de Juan Moreira*. In this novel, he tells the story of the rise of a modern politician who uses chicanery and intrigue to reach an influential position. He is totally without moral scruples, abandoning the girl he has seduced and who has borne his child in order to marry a wealthy heiress. The name of this upstart is Mauricio Gómez Herrera, but at the end of the book he is nicknamed 'the grandson of Juan Moreira' by a journalist who sees in him a modern version of the old gaucho bandit. Through the journalist's criticism of Mauricio, we come to understand the purpose of Payró's title, for he believes that the modern politicians are more sophisticated descendants of the wild, lawless gaucho chieftains. Mauricio is described in the following words:

> Tan ignorante y tan dominador como el abuelo, nació en un rincón de provincia, y creció en él sin aprender otra cosa que el amor de su persona y la adoración de sus propios vicios.
> Nunca entendió ni aceptó cosa alguna de la ley, sino cuando le convino para sus intereses y pasiones.
> Es la síntesis de la respetable generación que nos gobierna; y media sociedad si se viera en el espejo, se diría cuando pasa: 'Yo soy ése'.
> Tuvo de su abuelo el atavismo al revés, y así como aquél peleó contra la partida, muchas veces sin razón, éste pelea, siempre sin razón, con la partida, contra todo lo demás. Suprime sin ruido, hasta gobernadores, como el otro 'compadremente', facón en mano.*

The novel ends on a melodramatic note: the author of this article is Mauricio's illegitimate son. But the sentiments are undoubtedly those of Payró who in this same passage shows that his intention in writing a novel of social criticism is:

> ...acabar con el gauchismo y el compadraje, y no rendir culto a esos fantasmas del pasado.†

---

* As ignorant and as domineering as his grandfather, he was born in a corner of the provinces and grew up there without learning anything but self-love and the adoration of his own vices.
  He never understood or accepted any law except when it was convenient to his interest and passions.
  He is the epitome of the respectable generation which governs us; and half of society if it could see itself in the mirror, would say when he passes 'I am that man'.
  From his grandfather, he inherited an inverse atavism and so just as the former often fought against the men in power without any cause, he fights with a cause on behalf of the party in power against the rest. Noiselessly he suppresses even governors, as the other did, 'as a true gaucho', knife in hand.
† ...to finish with 'gauchism' with cliques and not to pay any tribute to these ghosts of the past.

Manuel Gálvez (1882–1962)

Like Payró, Gálvez knew the Argentine provinces well, having been born in Paraná. His first important novel was *La maestra normal* [*The High School Teacher*] (1914) which described the hypocrisy and pettiness of small-town life. The novel was set in La Rioja, the protagonist being a young man who after living for many years in Buenos Aires had been obliged to take a job in the provinces because of his bad health. His first sight of La Rioja is depressing:

> Los alrededores de la ciudad eran un espectáculo de pobreza y desolación. Los ranchos miserables; las criaturas, cuyas desnudeces quemaba un sol atroz; la indolencia y la suciedad de aquella gente de rostros tostados y ojos negros; la tierra cenicienta; las palmeras solitarias; las desigualdades del suelo, en cuya mayor hondura yacía la ciudad; todo sugería al viajero visiones del Oriente.*

Solís falls in love with one of the school teachers from the *Escuela Normal*. Raselda is a dreamy, idealistic and ingenuous provincial who falls into the trap, allows herself to be seduced and is then abandoned when Solís is transferred. She herself suffers the inevitable ostracism of an abandoned woman in a small town and when the novel ends is living in a remote Andean village where her 'past' continues to haunt her. Gálvez's novel is one of the best evocations of provincial life with its boredom, its small-town characters and its narrow moral code. It is written without the didacticism that characterised Payró's novels, although the entire plot implies a criticism of the way in which the Argentinian provinces had been neglected and forgotten by Buenos Aires. Gálvez was to have a long literary career. His *El mal metafísico* [*Metaphysical Sickness*] (1916) and *Nacha Regules* (1918) were set in Buenos Aires, the first being the story of a frustrated intellectual, the second that of a prostitute. In the '20s he published a trilogy of historical novels on the nineteenth-century wars against Paraguay with the title *Escenas de la Guerra del Paraguay* (1928–9) while his *Miércoles Santo* [*Ash Wednesday*] (1930) was about a day in the life of a parish priest.

Alberto Gerchunoff (1884–1950)

The flight from Buenos Aires was even made by the immigrant. One of the most unusual Argentinian novels of this period was *Los gauchos*

---

* The surroundings of the city offered a spectacle of poverty and desolation. The miserable huts, the children whose naked bodies were burned in the terrible sun; the idleness and filthiness of that people with sunburned faces and dark eyes; the ashy earth, the solitary palm trees, the uneven ground in whose deepest hollow lay the city; everything suggested visions of the East to the visitor.

judíos [*The Jewish Gauchos*] by Alberto Gerchunoff which was published in 1910, the centenary year of Argentinian Independence. The novel consists of a series of sketches which hinge upon life in a colony of Russian Jews who had escaped from the Tsarist Russian pogroms in order to start anew in Argentina. Gerchunoff shows the colonists slowly adapting themselves to life on the land, abandoning the merchant activities which they had devoted themselves to in Russia and learning to look after cattle and till the soil. For Gerchunoff, the peasant life is the good life. Though a relative newcomer to Argentina (he arrived there when he was a few years old), he shared the common attitude that the life lived near to nature was superior to the life of the city.

URUGUAY

Uruguayan writers, too, had turned to provincial themes at this period. Two writers, Carlos Reyles (1868–1938) and Javier de Viana (1868–1926) illustrate two different tendencies. The first, a wealthy *estanciero*, came to idealise the peaceful and wholesome life of the countryside; the second, son of an *estanciero*, described with brutal realism its poverty and sordidness. To modern tastes, Reyles's work is uneven and too closely influenced by contemporary European naturalism. His main novels are *Beba* (1894), *La raza de Caín* [*The Race of Cain*] (1900), a melodramatic exposition of the 'mal de siglo', and *El terruño* [*The Homeland*]. This latter novel, written after Reyles had experienced disillusionment in political life, describes the failures of an intellectual, Tocles, whose efforts to impose his ideas on his fellow-countrymen through his teaching and writing have met with no success. Tocles appears to be a minor Rodó, and his failures in this novel contrast with the success of his mother-in-law, Mamagela, a woman of sound practical ability whose success in running her farm not only brings personal benefits but is seen as a far more effective contribution to national wellbeing than Tocles's intellectual efforts. Reyles afterwards published *El embrujo de Sevilla* [*The Enchantment of Seville*] (again characteristic of this generation in its return to Hispanic tradition) and *El gaucho Florido* (1932), the portrait of an ordinary gaucho which is probably his best novel.

Javier de Viana was a short-story writer rather than a novelist, and one whose early work is superior to his later stories which became mechanical in technique and repetitive in theme. Viana attempted to deal honestly with life in the Uruguayan countryside and what he reveals, above all, is the laziness and neglect of the *criollos*. Here, for instance, is Bentos Sagrera speaking of one of his women:

Cuasi no podía ir al rancho: se volvía puro llorar y puro echarme en cara lo que había hecho y lo que no había hecho, y patatrís y patatrás, como si no estuviera mejor conmigo que lo que hubiera estao con el polecía que se iba a acollarar con ella, y como si no estuviera bien paga con haberle dao población y con mandarle la carne de las casas todos los días, y con las lecheras que le había emprestao y los caballos que le había regalao!...¡No, señor, nada! Que 'cualquier día me voy a alsar con el primero que llegue!'...Que 'el día menos pensao me encontrás augada en la laguna...'*

Viana gives us a picture in which life is lived at a primitive level, in which women are objects to be taken on or packed off without fuss. When there is no woman in the house, the neglect is even worse. Here, from *En familia* [*In the Family*], is the picture of such a farmhouse:

El pobre rancho de techumbre pajiza ennegrecida por el tiempo, y de paredes de terrón carcomidas por las lluvias, iba adquiriendo aspecto de tapera con la proliferación de yuyos que lo circundaban; vigorosa vegetación de gramíneas que, extendiéndose con cautela al ras de la tierra, dominaba casi el que antes fue patio, rodeaba los muros a manera de golilla esmeraldina, y en partes atrevida, osada, aprovechando una grieta, trepaba por la pared y miraba con envidia la solera donde las golondrinas hacen sus nidos y dejan sus piojos. Cuando soplaba viento no podía soportarse en el rancho el olor que traía del basurero inmediato, donde se pudrían las sobras de carne, los residuos de la comida y los pedazos de guasca y cuero inservibles.†

Viana here concentrates on age, decay, neglect. Even the birds leave fleas behind them and the scent of the countryside is that of rotting flesh. This sordidness is, in part, the result of the character of the inhabitants, the lazy and ignorant half-caste creoles, but there is also

---

* I could hardly go back to the farm; it was always the same—fits of weeping and throwing in my face what I had done and what I hadn't done and so on and so forth, as if she weren't better off with me than she would have been with the policeman who was going to yoke her and as if she weren't well enough rewarded with the children I gave her and with the meat from the houses I sent her every day and with the dairymaids that I lent her and the horses I gave her!...No sir, nothing! What with 'I'm going off with the first man who comes!'...And, 'One of these days you're going to find me drowned in the lake'....

† The poor hut, with the straw roofs blackened with time and the earth walls weathered by the rains, acquired the look of a ruin with the proliferation of weeds which surrounded it—a powerful vegetation of grasses which, carefully spreading over the surface of the ground, almost covered what had once been the yard, surrounded the walls like a green ruff and in some places, venturesome and daring, taking advantage of a crack, it climbed over the wall and looked with envy towards the beam where the swallows make their nests and leave their fleas. When the wind blew it was impossible in the hut to bear the smell from the nearby rubbish heap, where leftovers of meat rotted with the remains of meals and useless pieces of rawhide and leather.

the implication that the élite have allowed the rural areas to fall into this state. Without being presented as overt criticism, Viana's stories nevertheless imply discontent with the *status quo*.

CHILE

Baldomero Lillo

In Chile, too, the intellectuals flew to the countryside. Indeed, one group of writers attempted to found a Tolstoyan colony and return to the simple life of the peasant.[1] As in Argentina and Uruguay, there was a distinct moralising tendency in the writing of the period, the most interesting example being that of Baldomero Lillo (1867–1923), a man of humble family who was born in the provincial town of Lota and who worked in a *pulpería* [provision store] in a mining district.

Writers of comparatively humble origin were still a rarity in Spanish–American literature. In Chile, the majority had been from wealthy and even aristocratic family backgrounds. Lillo, on the other hand, was very close to the people of whom he was writing, and perhaps for this reason his stories have a strength and an authenticity unusual at this period. He published two volumes of stories—*Sub terra* (1904) and *Sub sole* (1907), the first being almost totally devoted to life in mining communities.

Lillo's stories are the first in Spanish–American literature to picture man as a victim of industrialisation. Two stories are particularly interesting in this respect. In 'La compuerta número 12' [Gate Number 12], a father is forced to take his young son to work in the mine. The boy does not understand why he is being taken below the surface and is at first half-afraid, half-fascinated by what he sees, but on realising that he must work there, he is overcome by terror and has to be tied to the rock. The father's anguish at having to act in this way is expressed not in words but in the way he hacks at the coal face, wounding himself masochistically in the process but ultimately powerless to change the situation:

No se detuvo sino cuando se halló delante de la veta, a la vista de la cual su dolor se convirtió de pronto en furiosa ira, y, empuñando el mango del pico, la atacó rabiosamente. En el duro bloque caían los golpes como espesa granizada sobre sonoros cristales, y el diente de acero se hundía en aquella masa negra y brillante, arrancando trozos enormes que se amontonaban entre las piernas del obrero, mientras un polvo espeso cubría como un velo la vacilante luz de la lámpara.

Las cortantes aristas del carbón volaban con fuerza, hiriéndole el rostro, el cuello y el pecho desnudo. Hilos de sangre mezclábanse al copioso sudore que inundaba su cuerpo, que penetraba como una cuña en la brecha abierta...*

In this passage, it is interesting to note the way the man's body has become an implement, a wedge driven into the rock. The picture is one of complete alienation.

'El chiflón del diablo' [The Devil's Cave] relates the story of a dangerous mine in which many workers have been wounded, the tragic story of a miner who is forced to work because it is the only job available, and his death in an accident. One of the most striking passages in this story describes a day of sunlight on which the men who had been wounded in the mine come out to sun themselves:

Sentados en un banco de madera que recibía de lleno los rayos de sol, sus pupilas fatigadas, hundidas en las órbitas, tenían una extraña fijeza. Ni una palabra se cruzaba entre ellos, y de cuando en cuando, tras una tos breve y cavernosa, sus labios cerrados se entreabrían para dar paso a un escupitajo negro como la tinta.

Se acercaba la hora del mediodía, y en los cuartos las mujeres atareadas preparaban las cestas de la merienda para los trabajadores, cuando el breve repique de la campana de alarma las hizo abandonar la faena y precipitarse despavoridas fuera de las habitaciones...

Las habitaciones quedaron desiertas. Sus puertas y ventanas se abrían y se cerraban con estrépito impulsadas por el viento. Un perro atado en uno de los corredores, sentado en sus cuartos traseros, con la cabeza vuelta hacia arriba, dejaba oír un aullido lúgubre como respuesta al plañidero clamor que llegaba hasta él, apagado por la distancia.

Sólo los viejos no habían abandonado su banco calentado por el sol, y mudos e inmóviles, seguían siempre en la misma actitud, con los turbios ojos fijos en un más allá invisible, y ajenos a cuanto no fuera aquella férvida irradiación que infiltraba en sus yertos organismos un poco de aquella energía y de aquel tibio calor que hacía renacer la vida sobre los campos desiertos.†

* He did not stop until he was in front of the seam at the sight of which his sorrow became furious anger and seizing the handle of his pick, he attacked it in a rage. The blows fell on the hard block like a thick hail upon sounding crystals and the steel tooth sank into that black, brilliant mass, tearing out great pieces which piled up between the worker's feet whilst a thick dust covered the hesitant light of the lamp like a veil.

The cutting chips of coal flew forcefully, wounding him in the face, the neck and the naked breast. Threads of blood mingled with the copious sweat that bathed his body, which penetrated the open breach like a wedge.

† Seated on a wooden bench which received the full rays of the sun, their eyes weary and sunken in their orbits had a strange fixity. Not a word passed between them and from time to time after a brief cavernous cough, their closed lips half-opened to emit a gob of spittle that was black as ink.

Midday approached and in the rooms, busy women were preparing the lunch baskets of the workers when the brief ring of the alarm bell made them abandon their work and rush in alarm out of their houses...

The rooms were left empty. Their doors and windows opened and shut noisily, pushed by the wind. A dog tied up in one of the corridors sitting on its hind legs, its

The tragedy that is taking place in the distance is made even more sombre because contrasted with these human wrecks who have been reduced to a kind of vegetable life.

Mariano Latorre (1886–1955)

A younger contemporary of Lillo, Mariano Latorre felt compelled to write of the lives of the peasant and fisherman and to describe the scenery of Chile when he discovered the gulf between the life around him and the European-orientated education he had received. In his autobiography, he described his discovery of the Chilean people and landscape in these words:

> ...al observar esta disparidad entre una enseñanza sin savia y un pueblo que era superior a ella, se despertó en mí un afán casi místico de viajar por todos los rincones de mi tierra, conocer paisajes y hombres por mis propios ojos y no a través de libros o referencias y, por último, verterlo en novelas, cuentos o ensayos y darlo a conocer a los propios chilenos y a los estudiantes que, por vivir en él, no se había enterrado de que existía.*

The main theme of Latorre's stories is man's fight against nature, hence his preference for sea stories or for stories set in the Andes. Latorre is by no means a great writer. His descriptions of landscape seldom break out of traditional literary imagery; 'una laguna de esmeralda' [an emerald lake], 'un intenso verdor de terciopelo' [an intense velvety green], etc. His virtue is that of a pioneer opening up new territories for literature. In his best stories there is the excitement of completely new themes as in 'La epopeya de Moñi' [The Epic of Moñi], which relates a young shepherd's fight to the death with a condor which is trying to steal his sheep. The *criollista* literature which he helped to initiate was to be the main school of Chilean literature down to 1950.

---

head upturned, howled mournfully as a reply to the lamenting clamour which came to it, muffled by the distance.

    Only the old men had not abandoned their sun-warmed benches and silent and motionless, stayed in the same attitude, their troubled eyes fixed on the invisible distance and alien to everything that was not that ardent radiation that filtered into their rigid organisms a little of that energy and mild warmth that made life bloom again in the deserted fields.

* On observing the disparity between the flavourless education and a nation that was superior to this, there was awakened in me an almost mystic urgency to travel to all the corners of my land, to get to know the landscapes and men with my own eyes and not through books or references, and, finally, to put this in novels, stories and essays and to make it known to the Chileans themselves and to students who, while living in the country, had not found out that it existed.

G

THE ANDEAN REPUBLICS AND MEXICO

Though no outstanding novel appeared in either the Andean Republics or Mexico during the period before 1920, an awakening interest in the lives of those who lived outside the capital cities led to some of the first novels and stories on Indian life, and some of the first descriptions of the scenery of these areas.

As in most contemporary novels, there is a strong moralising tendency, and there are a number of exemplary novels which show the corruption of certain sectors of the community and the healthy moral attitude of those who devote themselves to honest toil in the land. An example of this type of novel is *A la costa* (1904) by Luis Martínez, an Ecuadorian writer who recorded the frustrations of a poor law student in Quito and had his hero leave the city to work as a foreman on a banana plantation in the tropics. As in Reyles's novel, *El terruño*, work on the land is seen as a contribution to national wellbeing as well as to the hero's personal happiness. In Mexico, Federico Gamboa (1864–1939), Emilio Rabasa (1856–1930) and López Portillo y Rojas (1850–1923) attacked the moral corruption which they believed was the source of the nation's backwardness. In *La parcela* [*The Piece of Land*] (1898), López Portillo y Rojas made a contrasting study of two landowners, one virtuous and kind to his labourers, the other corrupt and lawless. He thus suggested that moral weakness on the part of the ruling landowning élite was responsible for the prevailing evils in Mexico and that a change of attitude on their part would lead to reform on a national scale. The Mexican Revolution was to shatter this illusion.

Perhaps more interesting, in the light of subsequent developments, were the first tentative explorations of Indian life. Although the Indian of the past and the glories of the pre-Columbian eras had already figured prominently in nineteenth-century writing, the contemporary Indian had had little place in literature except as the ferocious opponent in poems such as *La cautiva* and *Martín Fierro*. However, the conscience of the middle classes was slowly awakening. In Peru, González Prada had recognised that the Indian must be integrated into national life if Peru were to advance as a nation. In Mexico, while the official policy of the Porfirio Díaz government tended to favour the European sectors of the population, men such as Justo Sierra affirmed that the Indian must be drawn into national life. One of the most interesting testimonies of the repiod, was a novel written by a young ex-lieutenant in Porfirio Díaz's army. Heriberto Frías (1870–1928) had been sent as lieutenant in a company to quell an Indian uprising and found himself more in sympathy with the underdogs than with his fellow soldiers. He was amazed at the courage of the Indians, at their sincere though unorthodox religious convictions, and at their bitter opposition to the troops of the central government which attempted to force their allegiance. He recorded his reactions in a novel, *Tomóchic* (1892), which is more interesting as a social document than as a work of literature, but reveals with startling directness what could happen when a sincere man came into close contact with the Indian. However, it was only after the Revolution that there was any appreciable attempt to understand the Indian on the part of the majority of Mexican intellectuals.

In the Andean countries, most writers showed a paternalistic attitude to the Indian. This is the case in the stories of Ventura García Calderón, collected and published as *La venganza del cóndor* [*The Condor's Revenge*] (1924). There lingered, too, the inheritance of Modernism in *Los hijos del sol* [*Children of the Sun*], a collection of stories by Abraham Valdelomar (1888–1918) many of which are poetic allegories which use words from Quechua but relate to Modernist themes. In 'El alfarero' [The Potter], for instance, he tells the story of an artist who bleeds himself to death trying to reproduce the colours of nature. Here, the theme recalls the stories of Darío's *Azul*, and the Indian setting and the Quechua vocabulary are incidental.

The most conscientious attempt to record Indian life accurately at this period was made by the Bolivian historian and sociologist Alcides Arguedas (1879–1946) whose *Wata-Wara* was begun as early as 1904 but later revised and published as *Raza de bronce* [*Race of Bronze*] in 1919. The story centres around the love story of Wata-Wara and Agiali, two Indians of the Lake Titicaca region. Their love affair and marriage is overshadowed by their relations with their white and *ladino*[1] overlords. They are the feudal chattels of an estate owner, Patoja, and of the bailiff of the estate. Arguedas links the exploitation of the Indians with political oppression and makes the Patoja family associates of the dictatorship of Melgarejo through whom they had risen to power. The landowner has all the evil qualities of the ruling élite which Arguedas had exposed in his 'Pueblo enfermo':

El indio carecía para él de toda noción de sentimiento y su única superioridad sobre los brutos era que podía traducir por palabras las necesidades de su organismo. No sabía ni quería establecer distinción alguna entre los servicios de la bestia y del hombre. Sólo sabía que de ambos podía servirse por igual para el uso de sus comodidades. . . Indolente para realizar ninguna tentativa que rompiese con la secular rutina, y menos para innovar, se contentaba con recoger cada año el producto de las cosechas y cumplir con desgano los menesteres que su empleado la decía indispensables. . .*

The central incidents of the novel relate Wata-Wara's violation by the bailiff while her *novio*, Agiali, is on a journey to the lowlands; her marriage to Agiali despite the fact that she is expecting the bailiff's child; and her death after attempted mass rape by the young Patoja and a group of his friends. In the course of the story, Arguedas amply describes the life and customs of the people and a series of cruel acts perpetrated against them by the whites and the *ladinos* which at the end of the book provokes an uprising during which the landowner's house is burnt to the ground. Arguedas's attack is directed mainly against the cruelty and indifference of whites and *ladinos*, and it is cruelty rather than economic exploitation alone which leads the Indians to rebel. At the same time, the author is at pains to show how different is his approach from that of the Modernists. He even introduces a poet, Suárez, who visits the landowner's estate in order to write about the Indians; one of Suárez's works is included in the novel and is clearly a parody of Modernist writing. Influenced by Marmontel's book, *Los Incas*, Suárez idealises Indian civilisation and is without the training necessary to observe the Indians around him. The idealised Indian legend that he writes is reproduced in the chapter preceding the attempted rape of Wata-Wara as a deliberate contrast. Yet is Arguedas's picture of the Indian any more true? Though he makes a valiant attempt at interpreting Indian thoughts and speech, the study of anthropology was still in its infancy, and sentences such as the following merely transpose the author's own thoughts into the mind of the Indian.

También he pensado que sería bueno aprender a leer, porque leyendo acaso llegaríamos a descubrir el secreto de su fuerza; pero algún veneno horrible han de tener las letras, porque cuantos las conocen de nuestra casta se tornan otros, reniegan hasta de su origen y llegan a servirse de su saber para explotarnos también

---

* For him, the Indian lacked any notion of feeling and his only superiority to animals was that he could translate the necessities of his body into words. He did not know how or want to establish any distinction between the services of beasts and that of man. He only knew that both served him equally for the use of his comforts. . . Lazy when it came to making any effort that would break with the century-old routine, and even less able to change, he was content to take in each year the proceeds of the harvests and to perform with reluctance the services that his bailiff thought indispensable.

...Entretanto...nada debemos esperar de las gentes que hoy nos dominan, y es bueno que a raíz de cualquiera de sus crímenes nos levantemos para castigarlos...*

However the novel marks an important stage in the growing awareness of the Indian problem and foreshadows the Indianist novels of the '30s and '40s.

VENEZUELA AND COLOMBIA

In Venezuela and Colombia, the period after 1900 was dominated by *criollismo* in literature. Indeed it was the Venezuelan writer, Rufino Blanco Fombona (1874–1944), who defined *criollismo* with some justice as

la pintura, *à outrance*, de las costumbres populares, con los tipos y en el lenguaje del bajo pueblo†

and he added that the *criollistas* 'fomentan nuestra literatura del porvenir' [stimulate the literature of the future].[1] As was so often to be the case in Latin-American literary movements, a literary review helped to encourage the movement. *El cojo ilustrado* [*The Illustrated Lame Man*] though founded in 1892 quickly developed into Venezuela's leading periodical and particularly encouraged stories of Venezuelan life. The two best *criollista* writers were Luis Manuel Urbaneja Achelpohl (1872–) and José Rafael Pocaterra (1892–). Rufino Blanco Fombona also wrote a few short stories depicting life in rural areas although he was best known for his historical essays and for the novels *El hombre de hierro* (1907) and *El hombre de oro* (1915) in which he exposed the *arriviste* society of his country.

In Colombia, the province of Antioquia and the city of Medellín became the centre for a lively group of writers, one of whom, Tomás Carrasquilla (1858–1940), managed to transcend the moralising and didacticism which elsewhere was one of the most tiresome features of *criollista* writing.

Tomás Carrasquilla

Carrasquilla grew up and lived his life in a tightly-knit provincial society in which the way of life was very similar to that of a Spanish

---

* I too, have thought that it would be good to learn to read because perhaps by reading, I would manage to find the secret of their power; for some horrible poison must there be in letters since all those of our caste who know them turn into others and deny their origin and use their knowledge to exploit us in their turn. Meanwhile, we must hope nothing of the people who rule us and it is good that on the excuse of any one of their crimes we should arise and punish them.

† the painting, carried to extremes, of popular customs with the types and language of the lower class.

provincial town. A voracious reader, it did not occur to him to write until comparatively late in life, when a heated literary discussion on whether or not provincial life offered suitable material for the novelist stimulated him to try his hand:

...escribí un mamotreto, allá en las reconditeces de mi cuartucho. No pensé tampoco en publicarlo: quería probar solamente que puede hacerse novela sobre el tema más vulgar y cotidiano.*[1]

But Carrasquilla's strength as a writer was the fact that he was able to draw on a Spanish literary tradition—that of the picaresque novel—and the *costumbrista* story as well as on a storehouse of folk-legend which was also Spanish in origin. His interest in the eccentric characters of his native province did not demand a totally new and original form, since the material lent itself to traditional genres. His first novel, *Frutos de mi tierra* [*Fruits of my Land*] (1896), was an amusing and racy account of the triumph of a girl of humble family who falls in love with a student and eventually marries him despite the intrigues and jealousy of a neighbourhood family. The plot is basically a Cinderella story and is merely a framework for Carrasquilla's main interest—the portrayal of small-town bigots, eccentrics and hypocrites. Indeed, his talents were perhaps best displayed in short stories where he fused acute psychological perception with the storyteller's skills. His tales often have the charm and flavour of folk-tales and the basic anecdotes sometimes have a folk origin though they are never merely folksy. One of the best examples of his stories is 'En la diestra de Dios Padre' [On the Right Hand of God the Father], a tale that is surely mediaeval in origin although in Carrasquilla's version it becomes an amusing study of the wily Antioquian peasant. The hero of the story, Peralta, has received a visit from St Peter and Christ who are disguised as travellers. They leave money which the honest peasant returns to them, and in recompense they offer him three wishes. St Peter expects Peralta to ask for salvation, but the peasant has other ideas.

Peralta...se puso a pensar a ver qué pedía. Todos tres se quedaron callaos como en misa, y a un rato...dice San Pedro: 'Hombre, Peralta, fijáte bien lo que vas a pedir, no vas a salir con una buena bobada', 'En eso estoy pensando, Su Mercé', contestó Peralta, sin nadita de susto. 'Es que si pedís cosa mala, va y el Maestro te la concede; y, una vez concedida, te amolaste, porque la palabra del Maestro no puede faltar...'
A un ratísimo, voltea a ver al Señor y le dice, 'Bueno Su Divina Majestá; lo

* I wrote a little rubbish, there in the depths of my little room. I did not think of publishing it either. I wanted only to prove that a novel could be written upon the most ordinary and everyday theme.

primerito que le pido es que yo gane al juego siempre que me dé la gana'. 'Concedido' dijo el Señor. 'Lo segundo' siguió Peralta 'es que cuando me vaya a morir me mande la Muerte por delante y no a la traición'. 'Concedido' dijo el Señor. Peralta seguía haciendo la cuenta en los dedos y a San Pedro se lo llevaba Judas con las bobadas de ese hombre: él se rascaba la calva, él tosía, él le mataba el ojo, él alzaba el brazo y, con el dedito parao, le señalaba el cielo: Peralta no se daba por notificao. Después de mucho pensar, dice Peralta: 'Pues bueno, su Divina Majestá, lo tercero que me ha de conceder es, que yo pueda detener al que quiera en el puesto que yo le señale y por el tiempo que a yo me parezca'.*

Needless to say, Peralta's three wishes enable him to outwit both Death and the Devil. As in *Martín Fierro*, the use of a living folk tradition enables Carrasquilla to present peasant psychology with far more verisimilitude than the contemporary naturalistic and realistic writers. At the same time, implicit in this story, there is the recognition of peasant virtues over the apparently more sophisticated attitudes of St Peter.

Carrasquilla was not content simply to extol country or provincial life, however. He was equally aware of the bigotry, the hypocrisy and cruelty that life in the provinces encouraged, and his story 'El padre Casafús' [*Father Casafús*], though not without humour, shows how merciless small-town life can be. The priest, who is basically a good man, is tactless and bad-tempered and having offended the most powerful lady of the parish, he is hounded out of his parish and dies of starvation.

Carrasquilla's most ambitious work is the novel *La marquesa de Yolombó* which he completed in 1926. Set in the colonial period, Carrasquilla condemns the waste and frustration of the colonial era when 'sólo tenían por riqueza oro, plata y pedrería' [only gold, silver and precious stones were considered to be riches]. His remarkable heroine, a woman of great talent and beauty, marries a good-for-

---

* Peralta began to think what he should ask. They all three remained silent as at a mass and after a while Saint Peter says: 'Come, Peralta, think carefully of what you are going to ask and don't come out with anything stupid'. 'I am thinking, sir', replied Peralta, not a bit afraid. 'It's just that if you ask for something bad and the Master agrees, once it's agreed, you'll be finished, because the word of the Master can never be broken'...
After a while, he turns to see the Lord and says, 'Well, your Divine Majesty, the first thing I ask for is to win at cards whenever I want'. 'Agreed' said the Lord. 'The second' went on Peralta, 'is that when I am going to die, that Death will be sent to me face to face and not behind my back.' 'Agreed' said the Lord. Peralta went on adding up on his fingers and Saint Peter nearly flew off the handle at the stupidity of the man; he scratched his bald head, he coughed, he rubbed his eye, he raised his arm and with his finger stretched up, he pointed to heaven. Peralta did not appear to notice. After much thought, Peralta says: 'Well, your Divine Majestry, the third thing that you must concede me is that I can detain anybody in whatever place I indicate for as long as I like.'

nothing and symbolises the country's reckless waste of its potential.

Carrasquilla came nearer to being Latin America's great novelist than any of his contemporaries, perhaps because his material fitted into traditional moulds. By drawing on the language of folk-tale and proverb and the wealth of story and legend handed down through oral tradition he was able to penetrate below the surface of peasant life. The difficulty came when writers tried to extend their scope to areas of experience hitherto unrecorded in literature.

THEATRE

A review of *criollista* literature would be incomplete without mention of the theatre which put down its first native roots at this period. Theatre had been popular throughout the nineteenth century in the big towns—in Buenos Aires and Mexico City, for instance—and visiting European companies, especially opera companies, were eagerly welcomed. Plays on native themes by native dramatists—apart from the fact that they were very bad—were not considered worthy of attention by the élite. However, both in Mexico and Buenos Aires, people began to want their own dramas and problems to be reflected on the stage; the Buenos Aires theatre produced one dramatist of note, Florencio Sánchez (1875–1910), a Uruguayan writer whose plays were written in Argentina and performed with great success in Buenos Aires. Sánchez was acquainted with contemporary European drama—that of Ibsen, for instance—but he owed his success to the fact that he brought typical Argentinian and Uruguayan problems to the stage: particularly the clash between the immigrant and the old-style gaucho, an issue that was obviously of major interest to his audiences. Sánchez was an anarchist by conviction, so that his plays reflect not only the social situation but also the moral crisis of the intellectual élite. This is particularly evident in his first play, *M'hijo el dotor* [*My Son, the Doctor*] (1903) which, as the socialist, José Ingenieros declared:

...lleva a la escena una página de audaz filosofía, bajo el manto ordinario de escenas propias de nuestra vida criolla.*

Undoubtedly it was the use of Argentine dialect and the typical *criollo* characters which account for the success of the play, for the plot is based on a 'new morality' which could scarcely have pleased the majority of the audience. The story is that of Julio, son of an old

* ...brings a page of daring philosophy to the stage beneath the ordinary cloak of scenes from our creole life.

farmer, Olegario. Julio, having absorbed advanced idea in the course
of his city education, returns to the farm, seduces a girl and refuses to
marry her because he doesn't love her. The clash between this new
morality and the old leads to tragedy, since Julio stubbornly refuses to
marry the girl until his father is on his death-bed. To the modern mind,
Julio's reasoning on behalf of the 'new morality' has an old ring.
Like Cambaccres's hero in *Sin rumbo*, he regards his seduction of the
girl as something that is outside his control since he was driven by
instinct. Hence he refuses to accept responsibility for his action. The
'new morality' as interpreted by Julio is little more than shoddy self-
interest and compares badly with Olegario's traditional morality
which has the virtue of protecting the victim.

In each of Sánchez's main plays the progressive and the new appears
inhuman, ruthless, as against the old and out-dated. Yet this need not
imply that the author's anarchism was insincere. In common with many
of his generation, Sánchez deplored the materialistic nature of contemporary life, while finding himself equally opposed to the idealisation of the past and the literary exaltation of the gaucho. In his plays,
he attempts to show the passing of one age and the beginning of
another rather than to offer solutions to the ills of society. In *La gringa*
(1904),[1] the ruthless materialistically-minded immigrant family clash
with the easy-going creole Cantalicio, who, however, has been unable
to run his farm successfully. The immigrants bring new methods and
triumph through sheer hard work, but they are cold and inhuman
people. The Romeo and Juliet love-affair between Cantalicio's son
Próspero and Victoria, the daughter of the immigrants, is little more
than a convenient dramatic device that carries far less conviction
than the basic situation—that of the gulf between two conflicting
cultures. However, it enables Sánchez to end on an optimistic note
with the union of the two:

Hija de gringos puros...hijo de criollos puros...De ahí va a salir la raza fuerte
del porvenir...*

Sánchez's most successful play is *Barranca abajo* [*Downhill*] (1905), the
aptly-named drama of the decline and death of don Zoilo, a creole
farmer of the old school. Zoilo's downfall and suicide are precipitated
not only by the forces of a new age which he does not understand but
also by his family. His one sympathetic daughter, Robustiana, is con-

* Daughter of pure immigrants, son of pure creoles. Thence will come the strong race
of the future.

sumptive and dies during the course of the drama. His wife Dolores, his sister Rudecinda, and his daughter Prudencia are all against him. But the real tragedy is the loss of his land in a lawsuit and the resultant loss of hope and self-respect. So when arrested, he tells his family:

¡Si al menos ustedes me respetaran! Pero ni eso, canejo. ¡ Ni los míos me guardan consideración! Soy más viejo Zoilo pa ustedes, que pal más ingrato de los ajenos. ¡Vida miserable'. . . ¡Y yo tengo la culpa! ¡Yo!¡ Yo! Por ser demasiado pacífico.*

The hostility of his family is only a microcosmic version of the hostility of a new society in which the old creole virtues have disappeared. Zoilo hangs himself because the world he has grown up in and the one he understands, is on the way out:

Agarran a un hombre, sano, güeno. . . honrao, trabajador, servicial. . . lo despojan de todo lo que tiene, de sus bienes amontonaos a juerza de sudor, del cariño de su familia, que es su mejor consuelo, de su honra. . . canejo!, que es su reliquia, lo agarran, le retiran la consideración, le pierden el respeto, lo manosean, lo pisotean, lo soban, le quitan hasta el apellido. . . †

Thus Zoilo sings the swan-song of rural Argentina.

Sánchez also wrote a number of plays which dealt with the urban poor and the middle classes, the most interesting being *En familia* [*In the Family Circle*] (1905) and *Nuestros hijos* [*Our Sons*] (1907)—in both of which there is a vigorous criticism of middle-class life.

SUMMARY

Criollismo in poetry, prose and drama indicates a totally new phase in Latin-American literature. Modernism had helped to raise the prestige of literature; the founding of little magazines all over the continent had helped to stimulate poetry and the short story as never before. *Criollismo* marks the canalisation of this literary activity into American themes; and with this went an increasing consciousness of the poverty and injustices under which the majority of the population suffered. Writers had begun to explore the hinterland of their countries and though their implements were often crude, they helped to shape the tradition which was to culminate in the great regionalist novels of the '20s.

* If only you would respect me! But not even that, you wretch. Not even my family respect me. I am 'old Zoilo' more to you than to any other ungrateful person outside the family. Miserable life! And it is my fault! For being too peaceful.
† They take a healthy, good, honoured, hard-working, serviceable man, they take all he has from him, all his goods acquired by the sweat of his brow, the affection of his family which is his best consolation, his honour. . . which is his talisman, they seize him, take away respect and consideration, they mishandle him, trample on him, they pummel him and even take away his name.

7 REGIONALISM IN THE NOVEL AND SHORT STORY

THE BACKGROUND

In the 1920s, a number of regionalist novels written in Latin America attracted international attention. *Doña Bárbara* (1929) by Rómulo Gallegos, *Don Segundo Sombra* (1926) by Ricardo Güiraldes and *La vorágine* (1924) by Eustasio Rivera were amongst the first Latin–American novels to be translated into the European languages and to be read by a public which had no first-hand knowledge of the areas which the authors described. The translation and publication of these novels in Europe and North America not only marks the coming-of-age of the Spanish American novel but marked the beginning of a change of attitude on the part of Europeans towards non-European cultures.

Vast and momentous changes took place in the decade between 1910 and 1920 in both hemispheres. The Mexican Revolution (1910–17), the Russian Revolution of 1917, the First World War (1914–18), marked the end of a European hegemony, the upsurge of quite new forces both of class and race. To many, the First World War signalled the decline of Europe which would now be obliged to make way for new civilisations, perhaps in the Americas. And in Mexico and Russia, the underdogs had demonstrated that they were capable of over-throwing governments and taking power. The intellectual read the writing on the wall. If Europe was to fail, he must put his faith in America, and not in the America of landowners and financiers but in that of the peasant and the worker. The Spanish–American novel of the '20s was to be characterised by an Americanism that went much further than the creolism of an earlier generation, and by a total change of heart towards the humbler members of society. The following new attitudes emerged among the novelists:

1 The belief that literature was an agent of national integration and that through it, divergent areas and peoples could be brought into the stream of national culture.

2 The recognition that American racial mixtures and landscape were totally different from those of Europe and that a new approach was needed if literature was to be an expression of this experience.

3 The belief that, out of American experience, totally new values for a new type of civilisation could arise.

4 The conviction that a potential national public existed for which it was appropriate to create a literature using regional linguistic variants, and referring to a precise regional setting.

5 The belief that literature need not be overtly didactic to arouse opinion against injustice and that the exposure of injustice was inseparable from regional literature.

The era of imitating Europe was over. Culturally, Spanish Americans now stood on their own feet.

THE MEXICAN REVOLUTION AND LITERATURE

For many reasons, Mexican literature is of special interest during this period, for Mexico was the one country in which the social revolution had taken place and where the conditions for a new type of culture existed. The Revolution was itself an event that was without parallel in Europe. It had begun as a liberal revolt against the dictatorship of Porfirio Díaz. The liberal leader Francisco Madero fought for free elections and believed that the people wanted liberty rather than bread, but his revolution was quickly swept aside by a greater one. Pancho Villa in the north and Zapata in the south represented the hungry masses, and when Madero was assassinated in 1913 they and not the liberal middle classes were the driving force of the revolution. Madero's assassin, the right-wing Victoriano Huerta, who aspired to take the place of Porfirio Díaz, failed to stem the united revolt of Pancho Villa, Venustiano Carranza and Alvaro Obregón in the north and Zapata in the south and was defeated in 1915. From 1915 to 1917 in-fighting broke out between Villa and Carranza and was to end only with the victory of the latter.

The most important achievement of the Revolution was the Constitution of 1917, which laid a basis for the expropriation of land and its distribution to the peasants, for free education, for the future nationalisation of foreign-owned mines and petroleum.

Mexico had taken a step into the twentieth century. Though the poor were still poor, the social structure had undergone such radical changes that there could be no return to the large estates and the serfdom of the Díaz era. The big estates were to be broken up, the landowning families had fled, churches were destroyed and new laws prevented the clergy from resuming their old privileges. And a new class came to the fore, a class that was not always scrupulous and idealistic but was pledged to the ideal of 'La Revolución'. Amongst these were artists and writers who, now that there was no aristocratic élite, must address themselves to a new public, one that was thirsty for education but whose ideas were still primitive and uncomplicated. For these, a school of mural painters decorated public buildings with scenes from national history. Writers were slower to adapt to the new era but even they gradually began to digest and to work on the new material that the Revolution offered.

José Vasconcelos

The optimistic nationalism of the early post-Revolutionary period was epitomised in the work and writing of José Vasconcelos (1882–1959), a lawyer who had supported Madero and who became Minister of Education in the post-Revolutionary government of Obregón (1920–4). His was the unique case of an idealist and theorist who, briefly, was allowed to put his ideals into practice. In two of his essays, 'Pitágoras' (1916) and 'La raza cósmica' (1925), he had put forward his belief that creativity was the highest point of human endeavour and that humanity was destined to progress to an 'aesthetic' stage of civilisation that would far surpass the present era. In his view, Latin America was destined to reach this stage first of all. Hence, as Minister of Education in a post-Revolutionary government pledged to large-scale social reform, he had an unsurpassed opportunity to initiate Mexicans not only into the basic skills of reading and writing but also in the appreciation of literature, art and music. His Ministry was too shotr-lived for him to achieve all he wanted to do, but he did succeed in opening new schools, in giving music, drawing and dance an important place in the curriculum, in publishing big editions of the classics and in commissioning the first murals by Mexican artists. Vasconcelos was later to come under criticism; yet, he is in many ways a prototype of a generation of intellectuals with no standing among the traditional élite and with a sense of duty towards the poor and the illiterate. The fervent nationalism of his autobiography, *Ulises criollo* (1936) springs from his own identification with a new Mexico.

But it was the Mexican painters rather than the writers who dominated the '20s, becoming the iconographers of a new ideal, the creators of the mythology of the Revolution in which Moctezuma and Cuauhtemoc were the suffering heroes and the Spaniards were the villains. The painters, unhindered by the illiteracy of the public, gave direct expression to totally new values which exalted the poor and the humble, attributed beauty to the Indian rather than the European and covered walls with the flora and fauna of Mexico.

For writers, the Revolution offered different opportunities. The raw material was there in their own personal experience, but they had to learn how to exploit this material and to do so without guidance from Europe. Since their work was not directly commissioned by the government—unlike that of the painters—they were less directly identified with its aims and were freer to express their doubts or the ambiguities of the situation. Yet, when novels of the Revolution gradually began to appear, they too offered the face of a new Mexico. They dealt with the lower sectors of society, the mass emerged as the chief protagonist and, in order to give the feeling of violent upheaval, traditional chapter structures and character description disappeared to give way to brief, dissociated scenes.

Mariano Azuela

The pioneer of this new type of novel was Mariano Azuela (1873–1952), a doctor who had begun to write novels before the Revolution. On the outbreak of the Revolution he was a supporter of Madero, and after the latter's assassination, he served in the campaign against Huerta, an experience which served as the basis for his most famous novel, *Los de abajo* [*The Underdogs*]. The novel, published in a Texas newspaper, *El Paso de Norte*, in 1916, went unnoticed until it was republished in Mexico in 1925. Meanwhile, Azuela had brought out two other important novels, *Los caciques* [*The Bosses*] (1917) and *Las moscas* [*The Flies*] (1918), both on themes connected with the Revolution. Throughout his long life, he continued to write, was to experiment continually as in *La malhora* [*The Evil Hour*] (1923), *El desquite* [*The Revenge*] (1925), *La luciérnaga* [*The Firefly*] (1932) and to attempt novels of the urban working-class as in *Pedro Moreno el insurgente* (1933). But none of the later works has the power of his earlier revolutionary novels.

The most carefully structured and successful of Azuela's novels is *Los de abajo* in which the central event of the Revolution—the battle of Zacatecas where Huerta was defeated by Carranza, Pancho Villa and Obregón—is also the central event in the life of the protagonist, Demetrio Macías. *Los de abajo* is about the rise and fall of Macías and his guerrilla band. Macías, an illiterate peasant, has desperate courage and ferocity which attract a group of fellow-rebels to his side. Knowing every inch of the terrain on which they fight, they have no difficulty in defeating superior numbers of government troops, in taking and sacking towns and in acquitting themselves well at the battle of Zacatecas. Macías becomes a self-styled general, but from this point on his downfall begins. For courage, recklessness and ignorance cannot serve him in the complex struggle of interests between Carranza, Villa and Obregón that now follows. He joins Villa and is defeated and killed on the very spot where he had won his first battle. The pattern of the novel is thus circular. The battle of Zacatecas is the point at which the blind forces which had set the Revolution in motion might have been harnessed to an ideal; but in this battle the one idealist in the novel, an intellectual, Alberto Solís, is killed. The death symbolises Azuela's belief that what happened after the battle spelt the ruin of any revolutionary ideal. Self-interest was to win the day, a self-interest that took advantage of the ignorance of the peasants and used their courage to further selfish ends. This self-interested element is epitomised by Luis Cervantes, a medical student who joins the revolutionaries when they seem likely to win, carefully keeps clear of any battle and with looted diamonds that he picks up after a town has been plundered lays the foundation of his own future education and career. Cervantes does not share the tragic fate of Macías because he is clever and cynical enough to get away in time.

Each member of Macías's band represents some aspect of Mexican society. Pancracio belongs to the prosperous peasant class; Venancio is an ex-barber. Then there are the women: Camilia, the ignorant but loyal and long-suffering Mexican peasant girl; and La Pintada the prostitute. It is significant that the corrupt characters—Cervantes, La Pintada, and Margarito, an ex-waiter who has joined the Revolution so that he can rape and torture freely—are all townspeople and not peasants. Demetrio is no noble savage but he is not corrupt either. Azuela seems to suggest that those who might have guided the peasant out of his ignorance were simply missing from the scene or had no sense of responsibility.

Characters and history then are inseparable in *Los de abajo*. And both the style and technique of the novel reflect the swiftness of events and the revolutionary momentum in which individuals had significance only as part of a great movement. Constructed like a film out of a series of brief episodes, each short section is a compressed episode. There is no self-indulgent description, only functional references. Even time appears contracted, for there is no leisure for events to evolve or characters to meditate on the past. Instead, all takes place in the present so that the reader has a sense that something is happening as he reads—the actuality of a film. Abrupt transitions from one episode to another increase the impression of speed. Here is an example, taken from the opening of the novel in which Demetrio fights his first action against a contingent of government troops:

Entre las malezas de la sierra durmieron los veinticinco hombres de Demetrio Macías, hasta que la señal del cuerno los hizo despertar. Pancracio la daba de lo alto de un risco de la montaña.

'Ora si, muchachos; pónganse changos', dijo Anastasio Montañés, reconociendo los muelles de su rifle.

Pero transcurrió una hora sin que se oyera más que el canto de las cigarras en el herbazal y el croar de las ranas en los baches.

Cuando los albores de la luna se esfumaron en la faja débilmente rosada de la aurora, se destacó la primera silueta de un soldado en el filo más alto de la vereda. Y tras él aparecieron otros, y otros diez, y otros cien; pero todos en breve se perdían en las sombras. Asomaron los fulgores del sol, y hasta entonces pudo verse el despeñadero cubierto de gente: hombres diminutos en caballos de miniatura.

'¡Mirenlos qué bonitos!' exclamó Pancracio. '¡Anden muchachos: vamos a jugar con ellos!'

Aquellas figuritas movedizas ora se perdían en la espesura del chaparral ora negreaban más abajo sobre el ocre de las peñas.

Distintamente se oían las voces de jefes y soldados.

Demetrio hizo una señal; crujieron los muelles y los resortes de los fusiles.

'Ora!' ordenó con voz apagada.

Veintiún hombres dispararon a un tiempo y otros tantos federales cayeron de sus caballos. Los demás, sorprendidos, permanecían inmóviles, como bajorrelieves de las peñas.*

* In the undergrowth of the mountain Demetrio Macías's twenty-five men slept till a signal of a horn made them wake up. Pancracio sounded it from the top of a mountain peak.

'Now, boys, on guard', said Anastasio Montañéz, checking the springs of his rifle.

But an hour passed without their hearing anything other than the sound of the cicadas in the grass and the croaking of frogs in the hollows.

When the white of the moon disappeared in the light pink fringe of the dawn, the first silhouette of a soldier stood out on the highest section of the path. And behind it appeared others, and another ten and another hundred; but all were quickly lost in shadows. The ray of the sun came out and only then could the slope be seen, covered with men, diminutive men on miniature horses.

'Look how nice!' Pancracio exclaimed. 'Come on, boys, we're going to play with them.'

Those little moving figures were sometimes lost in the thickness of the *chaparro* trees, sometimes looked blacker, lower down against the ochre of the peaks.

The voices of officers and soldiers could be heard distinctly.

Here the short sentences, the brief descriptions of nature, the rapid exclamations all contribute to give an effect of rapid motion. The action cuts back and forth, as in a film, between Demetrio and the Federal army. Few words are said, but those few serve to give a vivid close-up of the character. Demetrio speaks only to give orders. For Pancracio the fight with the miniature soldiers is just like a game.

Los de abajo is, perhaps, the first example of a Spanish-American novel in which the subject matter imposed a new style and in which the author successfully fused structure and subject matter. The innovation extended to language, which was completely fresh. Concise and economic in narrative and descriptions, the language also captured the different types of speech used by ordinary Mexicans. There were even subtle variations in the language used by different characters. Camila has the thickest accent, Luis Cervantes speaks the most rhetorically. And certain words and expressions like 'currito' have class and political associations. The word means 'dandy' and is used by Demetrio's men to stereotype their opponents.

If for no other reason, *Los de abajo* earns a place in the literature of Mexico as a pioneer work.

In *Las moscas*, Azuela focused attention on the opportunities of the Revolution. Again the novel is skilfully structured, unity of theme being provided by the train on which most of the action takes place. This choice of background was brilliantly perceptive. Trains played a major part in revolutionary strategy and had transformed troop mobility. But in *Las moscas*, the train underpins the irony of the story, for it is loaded with retreating 'flies', the parasites who have lived off the dead corpse of their country and are now fleeing before the advance of Obregón and his troops into Mexico City. The period of the action is some time after 1915, when the revolutionaries had already begun to fight amongst themselves; and on the train, reactionaries who had supported Porfirio Díaz rub shoulders with Villa's generals. Azuela's spotlight, however, falls particularly on the family of a widow with her three children, and highlights their grotesque efforts to ingratiate themselves with anyone who momentarily can help them. They first try to win over a doctor so that they can be allowed to travel in the hospital compartment, then a general who is well provided with

---

Demetrio gave a signal; the springs and locks of the rifles creaked.

'Now!' he said in a low voice.

Twenty-one men fired at the same time and as many Federals fell from their horses. The rest, in surprise, remained motionless, like bas-reliefs on the rocks.

food and drink. However, when they reach Irapuato, they gradually realise that their general, a supporter of Villa, might be on the losing side and as the train moves off, the mother pushes her adolescent son back on the line so that he can go back to Irapuato and ingratiate himself with an Obregón supporter he had met there. Like Luis Cervantes in *Los de abajo*, this 'familia decente' and their friends are far more ruthless and opportunist than the generals and prostitutes they so heartily despise. Here, for instance, is the scathing description of a fleeing bureaucrat who mistakes the shadowy telegraph poles for the revolutionary army and trembles in terror. He symbolises a whole class of people who have not the courage to fight and whose only instinct is for self-preservation.

El señor Ríos, que no puede pegar las pestañas porque la idea de un asalto intempestivo se le ha metido entre ceja y ceja, tiene sus miradas fijas en la oscuridad del valle. De pronto un estremecimiento le sorprende y agarrota: ha creído ver siluetas sospechosas, tendidas a distancia, a lo largo de la vía. ¡Gran Dios! Los carrancistas! Quiere dar voces, pero es inútil su esfuerzo; sus labios ya no son suyos. Por otra parte, ¿a qué llamar la atención de nadie? Los militares vienen perfectamente ebrios. El señor Ríos saca fuerza de su misma angustia para preguntarse si no será víctima de alguna alucinación. ¡Veintiocho horas sin comer! ¡Su temperamento tan nervioso! Y se restrega los ojos y vuelve a explorar el campo atentamente. Y he ahí una vaga sombra que de pronto se alza del suelo, crece, se agiganta en un instante y con igual rapidez se aleja, empequeñece y se pierde, Y luego otra, y otra, y otra...*

The passage successfully conveys the impression of a train passing quickly through the night, laden with drunken soldiers. Beneath the objective description, however, Azuela probes deeper into the nightmare thoughts which reveal the psychological impact of the Revolution on members of the middle class who are unused to fighting, or going without food. And as in *Los de abajo*, short, clipped sentences and exclamations contribute to creating a feeling of excitement.

In *Los caciques*, Azuela takes us back to the period of Madero and to a

---

* Señor Rios, who could not close his eyes because the idea of a sudden assault was on his brain, had his eyes fixed on the darkness of the valley. Suddenly, he is overcome by trembling and a feeling he is choking. He thought he saw suspicious silhouettes stretched out along the track. Carranza's forces! He wants to shout but his effort is useless. His lips are not his own. Anyway, what's the use of attracting anybody's attention? The soldiers are all completely drunk. Sr. Rios finds strength in his anguish to wonder if he is not the victim of an hallucination. Twenty-eight hours without food. He has such a nervous temperament! And he rubs his eyes and carefully explores the countryside again. And there is a vague shadow which suddenly rises from the ground, grows, towers suddenly and with equal rapidity recedes, grows small and is lost. Then another and another and another...

small provincial town dominated by a pair of ruthless capitalists, the Del Llano brothers. The Madero Revolution hardly affects their power, and during the period of repression that follows the assassination they are able to get rid of the one person in the town, Juan Rodríguez, who offers a threat to their power. They then proceed to bankrupt and break a rival shopkeeper whose two children at the end of the novel set the Del Llano store on fire as the approach of revolutionary troops promises deliverance from 'Los caciques'.

These are Azuela's major novels of the Revolution. Implicit in them is the author's moral condemnation of an upper and middle class who have failed to show interest in national progress. Their failure is stressed in *Los caciques* and *Las moscas* and through the character of Luis Cervantes in *Los de abajo*. On the other hand, Azuela's portrayal of the revolutionaries is utterly unsentimental. They are too ignorant and backward to lead the nation and so are at the mercy of the opportunists who will inevitably rise to the surface. But whether we agree with this pessimistic outlook or not, Azuela's novels capture, as no other novelist had done, the movement and exitement and the abrupt changes of fortune of the revolutionary period.

Martín Luis Guzmán

The Revolution also gave rise to a hybrid genre of literature which was novelised autobiography or autobiographical novel. In *El águila y la serpiente* [*The Eagle and the Serpent*] (1928) Martín Luis Guzmán (1887–) describes his own experiences, when during Huerta's oppression in Mexico City, he escaped to Cuba, thence to the United States and entered Northern Mexico to join the revolutionary forces. Unlike Azuela, Guzmán gives us little insight into the fighting, being more interested in the personalities of the generals and revolutionaries among whom he sought the great leader who would shape the future of the country. The story is one of failure, as in a series of telling scenes and anecdotes Guzmán reveals the shortcomings of these men. Carranza is too vainglorious. Villa is pictured as cool and courageous but more like a panther or tiger than a man. On one occasion he hangs a poor man who has no money because he argues that this will frighten the rich men of the locality into giving up their wealth. One of his generals performs a mass execution single-handed though it takes him the whole day to do it, just out of sheer pleasure in the killing. Zapata and his men are simply peasants completely out of place in the National Palace. The book is really a collection of brilliant anecdotes, but they are anecdotes which fix forever the personality of the principals and also shed a curious sidelight on what it was like to live in the provincial towns and cities during the Revolution. But fundamentally what Guzmán reveals is the discomfort of the middle-class intellectual at finding his values overturned and disregarded, and his alarm at the new forces that have come to the fore in national life. One of the most vivid scenes in the book is one in which the narrator goes out after dark in a town occupied by revolutionary troops. It is pitch black but in the darkness, a peasant soldier takes hold of him and he is pushed into a silent, seething mass of revolutionaries. The middle-class individualist is horrified at the sensation of being absorbed into the mass:

...tropecé con algo—al parecer con las piernas de un cuerpo recostado contra la pared—y me fui de bruces hacia el lodo. Pero al extender los brazos en el curso de la caída, mis manos, abiertas en anticipación del suelo, dieron milagrosamente en la ropa de otro cuerpo, al que me agarré. Este segundo cuerpo estaba a pie firme, según noté en seguida, y fue a sus piernas a lo que me mantuve asido mientras mis rodillas se posaban en el lodo con fresca blandura. Mi salvador invisible pareció entender lo que me pasaba, pues sentí una mano fuerte que me cogía por una axila, que me ayudaba a enderezarme y que, por último, me soltaba un instante para convertirse en brazo echado sobre mis hombros, brazo cariñoso, brazo que me apretaba el cuello con inesperado afecto, sensación que se desvaneció en mí en el acto para resolverse en la de un olor humano desagradabilísimo y a vueltas con el tufo de mezcal.*[1]

Notice how the feeling of gratitude at having been saved from a fall changes into one of surprise at the affection his companion shows and then into disgust when he smells the liquor. A light reveals his companion to be a ragged soldier who proceeds to drag him into a street in which many others like himself had crowded:

La oscuridad me cegaba ahora más que antes. La multitud en cambio, gracias a la acción de un nuevo sentido, se volvió para mí más perceptible. Dentro de su perímetro, que yo no veía, pero que sentía, se formó un alma de unidad colectiva: la muchedumbre se incorporó y comenzó a agitarse como un cuerpo solo, empezó

---

* ...I tripped over something—apparently over the legs of a body leaning against the wall—and I fell headlong in the mud. But as I stretched out my arms in the course of my fall, my hands, opened in anticipation of the ground, miraculously came up against the clothes of another body which I caught hold of. This second body was standing, as I immediately realised and I went down to his legs which I seized whilst my knees rested in the cool softness of the mud. My invisible saviour seemed to understand what was happening for I felt a strong hand that took me under the arms, which helped me to stand up and finally let me go for a moment only to be replaced by an arm thrown around my shoulders, an affectionate arm, an arm which squeezed my neck with unexpected affection, a sensation which in me at once disappeared as it became a very disagreeable human odour which mingled with the stink of *mezcal*.

a ondular, a mecerse a bambolearse, todo en el corazón de un ruido espeso y opaco.*

Caught inextricably in the mass, forced to drink by his companion, Guzmán feels himself slowly advancing as part of this great human wall.

¡ Extraña embriaguez en masa, triste y silenciosa como las tinieblas que la escondían! Embriaguez gregaria y lucífuga, como de termites felices en su hedor y en su contacto! Era, en pleno, la brutalidad del mezcal puesto al servicio de las más rudimentarias necesidades de liberarse, de inhibirse. Chapoteando en el lodo, perdidos en la sombra de la noche y de la conciencia, todos aquellos hombres parecían haber renunciado a su humanidad al juntarse. Formaban algo así como el alma de un reptil monstruoso, con cientos de cabezas, con millares de pies, que se arrastrara, alcohólico y torpe, entre las paredes de una calle lóbrega en una ciudad sin habitantes...†

Here is the climax of the scene. Guzmán is not moved by a sensation of human solidarity, for he hates the feeling of being dragged along in the mass, the feeling of having lost his individuality, of only forming part of a collective consciousness. Yet, despite his hostility, there is something impressive in this scene which conveys vividly what it was like to be one of the mass and the unexpected warmth and fraternity that Guzmán found there, despite himself.

Of the many other writers of novels of the Revolution, Gregorio López y Fuentes (1897–1967) is worth mentioning for *Tierra* [*Land*] (1932), one of the few novels to attempt the depiction of the agrarian revolution and Zapata. Unfortunately, he had no direct experience of this and his writing is lifeless and clumsy. A previous novel, *Campamento* [*Bivouac*] (1931), which was based on personal experience is far better. Here he attempted only to evoke a single night in the life of a revolutionary army, who are to go into action on the morrow. The characters are anonymous voices heard in the night around the camp-

* The darkness blinded me now more than before. On the other hand, the crowd, thanks to the action of a new sense, became perceptible to me. Inside its perimeter that I could not see but which I felt, the soul of a collective unity was formed; the crowd stood up and began to move like a single body, it began to undulate, to sway and rock, all in the heart of a thick and opaque noise.

† Strange mass intoxication, sad and silent as the shadows which hid it! Gregarious drunkenness which fled the light like ants happy in the smell and contact. This was entirely the brutality of *mezcal* put to the service of the most rudimentary necessity for liberating themselves and inhibiting themselves. Splashing in the mud, lost in the shade of night and consciousness, all those men seemed to have given up humanity in order to unite together. They formed something like the soul of a monstrous reptile with hundreds of heads, with thousands of feet which dragged itself, drunken and clumsily, between the walls of the murky street in a city without inhabitants.

fires, but certain moments of drama arise during their wait. An unruly *caudillo* and his men try to cause trouble but their power is broken and next day a united army moves off to join the battle.

As the Revolution faded into Mexico's past, new themes began to occupy the attention of the novelist—the integration of the Indian into the nation, the 'Cristero' war of the 1920s in which a group of Catholic fanatics held out against government attacks on the religion; and—most important of all among these novelistic themes—that of the frustration of revolutionary hopes and the rise of a new class of leaders who appeared ready to restore old dictatorial methods. The danger that this new type of leader presented was dealt with in *La sombra del caudillo* [*The Shadow of the Leader*] (1929) by Martín Luis Guzmán, *Mi general* (1934) by López y Fuentes, and *El resplandor* [*Sunburst*] (1937) by Mauricio Magdaleno (1906–   ) who describes the rise of a local boss who had himself been one of the underdogs. The novels of Guzmán and López y Fuentes refer particularly to the period around 1928 when President Calles, having finished his term of office, called on Obregón to serve a second term. When Obregón was assassinated, Calles ruled through a succession of puppet presidents, a move which writers were quick to criticise, seeing in it a return to authoritarian rule.

José Rubén Romero (1890–1952)

Perhaps the best Mexican writer to emerge during this post-revolutionary period was José Rubén Romero whose novels often touch on the Revolution although he rarely makes it his main theme. Born in a small town in the state of Michoacán, his father was a merchant of modest means who also held administrative posts. Romero joined the Madero Revolution and became secretary to Miguel Silva, Governor of Michoacán. After the Revolution, he served as representative to the assembly which drew up the Constitution, and he later became editor of *El Universal*. In 1930, he was appointed Consul in Barcelona and he rose in 1939 to the rank of Ambassador to Cuba. This brief biography reveals Romero to have been one of the 'new men' of the Revolution, yet, paradoxically, his novels betray attitudes that were far from revolutionary.

Significantly, his major works were written while he was abroad. Most of them are based on his childhood and adolescent experiences in Michoacán, the first three—*Apuntes de un lugareño* [*Notes of a Provincial*] (1932), *El pueblo inocente* [*The Innocent Village*] (1934) and *Deshandada* [*Flight*] (1934)—being a series of anecdotes and sketches describing the life and characters of a small town. In two of these, *Apuntes de un lugareño* and *Desbandada*, the Revolution erupts with devastating brutality. In the first, the narrator is almost shot; in the second the village is sacked by a revolutionary force, his property is destroyed, and neighbours and members of his family killed. The swiftness and senselessness of the disaster speak for themselves. The one Romero novel that is most closely connected with a revolutionary theme is *Mi caballo, mi perro y mi rifle* [*My Horse, my Dog and my Rifle*] (1936), the story of a widow's son who grows up with a chip on his shoulder and hates the rich. His childhood experiences teach him that there is one law for the rich and another for the poor; but one day, news of the Revolution comes to him in a most unexpected fashion:

Apareció doña Concha la Reyes y soltó la noticia con esa tranquilidad con que los viejos dicen las cosas más graves:
'Por *aí* viene la revolución. Acaba de oírlo a unos señores que platicaban en la botica.'
La frase dicha así tan sencillamente paralizó nuestros movimientos, y quedamos como una fotografía familiar iluminada a colores: Andrea con la cuchara en la boca del niño, y yo mordiendo un plátano de Costa Rica tierno y sonrosado como carne de mujer.*

But the narrator feels

un impulso de potro salvaje que rompe el freno y echa a correr sin rumbo y salta sin cordura.†

For him the Revolution is a force which

pueda arrasar todas las cosas que yo odio. Deseo que haya revolución y que venga hasta nuestro pequeño mundo a remover viejas miserias.‡

The Revolution means for him the ending of petty injustice, the ending of the power of landowner and priest. He likens it to an enormous hand taking the pieces of a chess set and mixing them up until knight, bishop and castle are all the same. From the Revolution the young man

---

* Doña Concha la Reyes appeared and gave the news with that calm with which old people speak of the most serious things.
'The revolution is coming this way. I have just heard some men talking in the drug store.'
The sentence, spoken with such simplicity, paralysed our movements and we remained like a domestic colour photograph; Andrea with the spoon in the baby's mouth and I biting a Costa Rican banana, tender and rosy as a woman's flesh.
† the instinct of a wild stallion which breaks the bridle and begins to run without aim and to jump senselessly.
‡ may destroy all the things that I hate. I want there to be a revolution and that it should come into our small world in order to stir up old sources of trouble.

gains his horse, his rifle and his dog, the possessions which, for a moment, make the struggle worth while; but at the end of the novel, he returns to his native village to find the old forces are still in power while he himself has lost the horse, the dog and the rifle he had once possessed.

Romero was undoubtedly a bitter man who felt that social organisation inevitably encouraged the hypocrite and the opportunist. This led him to sympathise with the outsider and to make a village drunkard, Pito Pérez (based on a real-life character), into a spokesman for his attack on certain social conventions. *La vida inútil de Pito Pérez* [*The Useless Life of Pito Pérez*] (1938) has its origin in the picaresque and is an amusing yet bitter account of the drunkard's defiance of all the norms of small-town life. The very title *La vida inútil* [*The Useless Life*] flouts middle-class assumptions as to the desirability of leading a 'useful life'. Instead Pito Pérez lives the life of a 'beat' or a drop-out who practises what he preaches, whilst the rest of society preaches respectability and adherence to Christian norms—but when they have the opportunity behave quite differently.

Pito Pérez's self-portrait is characteristic of his wry self-deprecation:

Perdí la flauta en algúna cárcel, o en algún sitio de tantos que me han servido para dormir las monas. Porque debo advertirle, con la honradez que ha caracterizado mi desvergüenza, que ya no soy un borracho respetable, ni siquiera ingenioso. Me escarnecen los chicos, me roban los tenderos, me humillan los gendarmes, y cuando quedo tendido en las banquetas con *la botica abierta* y el *boticario dormido* no hay alma caritativa que extienda sobre mis desnudeces el abrigo de un periódico. Las personas decentes huyen de mí con asco; asco de mi aspecto repugnante, de mi hedor a vino agrio, de mis manos negras, que ni los amigos quieren estrechar, simulando que llevan las suyas ocupadas con el pañuelo.*

Pérez is at the lowest stratum of society, a dirty drunkard. Because he is this, he can see through the externals and comes to understand the real degradation of society. In one sombre incident, he is made to play Christ in a Crucifixion play which ends as a drunken orgy. But when Pito Pérez asks to be let down from his cross, he is laughed at:

---

* I lost my flute in some prison or in some of the many places where I have slept off my drunkenness. Because I should warn you with the honesty that has characterised my shame that I am not a respectable drunkard nor even a clever one. The kids make fun of me, the shopkeepers rob me, the police humiliate me and when I lie stretched out on the benches with the 'shop open' and the 'shopkeeper asleep' there is not a charitable soul who covers my nakedness with a newspaper. Decent people run away from me in disgust; disgust at my repulsive appearance, my smell of sour wine, my black hands which not even my friends want to shake, pretending that theirs are occupied with a handkerchief.

...reían de mi angustia y me daban la espalda con la misma indiferencia con que la humanidad ve morir a Jesús, pendiente del madero...*

He loves only his faithful 'La Caneca', a skeleton which he has stolen from a hospital. When he dies, his body is found, fittingly, on a rubbish dump and his last will and testament is discovered to be one more blistering attack on the establishment and on the poor:

...Para los pobres, por cobardes, mi desprecio, porque no se alzan y lo toman todo en un arranque de suprema justicia. ¡Miserables esclavos de una iglesia que les predica resignación y de un gobierno que les pide sumisión sin darles nada en cambio! ¡Libertad, Igualdad, Fraternidad!

Que farsa más ridícula! A la Libertad la asesinan todos los que ejercen algún mando; la Igualdad la destruyen con el dinero, y la Fraternidad muere a mano de nuestro despiadado egoismo.†

No one class can ever save Mexico since from top to bottom humanity is corrupt and worth only the contempt that Pito Pérez had always shown it:

Humanidad, yo te robé unas monedas; hice burla de tí, y mis vicios te escarnecieron. No me arrepiento, y al morir, quisiera tener fuerzas para escupirte en la faz todo mi desprecio.‡

Romero has no faith in institutions either of the past or of the present, either in the Catholic Church or in the new revolutionary governments. Human beings are always weak, ambitious, egoistical, incapable of putting into action the deeds and principles they preach. That is why Pito Pérez stands as a living judgment on them. And even in structure, Romero drives home his point by constructing a sort of anti-novel which sometimes takes the form of Pito's reminiscences, sometimes the form of a questionnaire on love or prison life. The sombre tones, the 'desengaño' are strongly reminiscent of the Spanish picaresque, but a picaresque that is firmly transplanted into Mexico.

Many critics believe *Rosenda* (1946) to be Rubén Romero's best novel. It is an uncomplicated story of a country girl who sacrifices herself

---

* ...they laughed at my anguish and turned their backs on me with the same indifference that humanity watched Christ hanging from his Cross.

† ...To the poor for their cowardice, I leave my contempt, for they do not rise up and take everything in one blow of supreme justice. Miserable slaves of a church which preaches resignation and of a government which asks for their submission without giving anything in exchange. Liberty, Equality, Fraternity. What a ridiculous farce! Liberty is killed by all those who exercise some office, equality is destroyed by money and fraternity dies at the hand of our pitiless egoism.

‡ Humanity, I stole some money from you, I made fun of you and I warned you of your vices. I do not repent and as I die I should like to have the strength to spit in your face with all my contempt.

to a lover without losing her dignity and strength of character. Well-written the novel certainly is, though Rosenda herself is the kind of female stereotype often produced in a male-dominated society.

Rubén Romero was the best and most original novelist to emerge from Mexico before 1940. His technique was drawn from Hispanic sources both *costumbrista* and picaresque, but he was able to mould these to the requirements of the post-revolutionary Mexican scene.

VENEZUELA AND COLOMBIA

Outside Mexico there was no social revolution, but the novel still played an important part as a comment on society. In both Venezuela and Colombia—vast countries with hinterlands of mountain, plain and jungle—writers made a serious attempt to break out of the bounds of city society and understand life in backward areas. They saw the novel as having a positive and integrating role, bringing forgotten regions before the attention of the reading public.

The prototype of the new regionalist novel of the '20s was *La vorágine* [*The Vortex*] (1924). Written by a young lawyer, Eustasio Rivera (1889–1928), who had first-hand experience of both plains and jungle, the novel first attracted attention for its descriptions of the *selva*. The story tells of the flight of a young poet, Arturo Cova and his mistress, Alicia, from Bogotá, and from the restrictions of middle-class life which are a bar to their marriage. But once outside Bogotá, social and religious conventions are replaced by the law of survival of the fittest. Cova and Alicia first find shelter with the cattle-rancher Franco and his wife, Griselda, and here come face to face with a rough cowboy existence. At this time, Cova spends hours daydreaming, and in his dreams he sees himself acclaimed by the public, showing off his manliness or overcoming potential rivals. Childish such dreams may seem, but we should remember that Romanticism and Modernism have propagated a mythology of the poetic bohemian life which Cova inherits only to find the myth shatters at the first touch of brutal reality. Indeed, one of the major themes of the novel is the destruction of the Romantic personality; the process begins on the cattle ranch where Cova finds himself among men who are only impressed by action. He comes up against Barrera, his rival for Alicia and the man who recruits labour for the jungle rubber exploiters. Cova is no match for Barrera for he merely strikes attitudes while Barrera quietly goes to work recruiting his workers. Even the nature which Cova as a poet admires, turns against him. This is no nature to be contemplated in the Romantic manner, but a nature that is usually cruel and death-dealing. The poet realises that his broodings on the 'spirit' are quite irrelevant when he witnesses the abrupt death of a man in round-up in which the head is torn off the body:

...esa risa sin rostro y sin alma, sin labios que la corrigieran, sin ojos que la humanizaran, me pareció vengativa, torturadora, y aun al través de los días que corren, me repite su mueca desde ultratumba y me estremece de pavor.*

But this horror is nothing compared to what Cova and Franco experience when they set off in the jungle in pursuit of Alicia and Barrera. All trace of civilisation and humanity now disappear. They find themselves in primeval chaos, in a nature without consciousness, endlessly reproducing and devouring itself. As they drift down the river into the green hell, Cova feels that he is being sucked into 'the vortex of nothingness'. The European concept of nature civilised by art and literature, the nature of Cova's literary musings, has nothing in common with the purposeless chaos which makes nonsense of notions of destiny, or providence:

Entretanto, la tierra cumple las renovaciones sucesivas. Al pie del coloso que se derrumba, el germen que brota; en medio de los miasmas, el polen que vuela; y por todas partes el hálito del fermento, los vapores calientes de la penumbra, el sopor de la muerte, el marasmo de la procreación.

¿Cuál es aquí la poesía de los retiros, dónde están las mariposas que parecen flores traslúcidas, los pájaros mágicos, el arroyo cantor? Pobre fantasía de los poetas que sólo conocen las soledades domesticadas.

¡Nada de ruiseñores enamorados, nada de jardín versallesco, nada de panoramas sentimentales. Aquí, los responsos de sapos hidrópicos, las malezas de cerros misántropos, los rebalses de caños podridos. Aquí la parásita afrodisíaca que llena el suelo de abejas muertas; la diversidad de flores inmundas que se contraen con sexuales palpitaciones y su olor pegajoso emborracha como una droga... liana maligna cuya peluza enceguece los animales, la *pringamosa* que inflama la piel, la pepa del *curujú* que parece irisado globo y sólo contiene ceniza cáustica; la uva purgante, el coroso amargo.†

* ...that smile without a face or soul, without lips to moderate it, without eyes to make it human seemed to me vengeful, torturing and even after days had passed, its otherwordly grimace comes back to me and fills me with horror.
† Meanwhile the earth accomplishes its successive regenerations, at the foot of the falling colossus is the growing seed; in the midst of the miasmas, the pollen which flies; and everywhere the breath of ferment, hot vapours of the twilight, the lethargy of death, the stupor of procreation.
　Where is the poetry of the wilds, where are the butterflies like translucent flowers, the magic birds, the singing stream? Poor fantasy of poets who only know domesticated solitudes.
　There is nothing of love-sick nightingales or gardens like those at Versailles, no sentimental views. Here, the chant of hydropic toads, the undergrowth of misan-

As in Schopenhauer's philosophy, sex merely serves the species. Whatever human society exists in this environment is totally degenerate. Bands of escaped convicts fight amongst themselves for control of the rubber. Charity, social control, human feeling have disappeared. Slave workers extract the rubber until they die. But evil as humans are, nature exceeds them in its ferocity:

La cadena que os muerde los tobillos es más piadosa que las sanguijuelas de estos pantanos; el carcelero que os atormenta no es tan adusto como estos árboles que nos vigilan sin hablar !*

Cova cannot escape from the jungle as he had from Bogotá. What he thought of as his 'personality' and his sense of identity are threatened. He no longer acts in the way he believed men should behave. He shows complete indifference when his Indian guides are drowned before his eyes. When delirious, he rushes into the jungle, even forgetting the basic instinct for self-preservation. By the time he finds Alicia, he is like an animal and in the fight in which he kills Barrera and watches the body being devoured by piranha fish, he is no different from the animals and vegetation around him. It is fitting that he and Alicia and their newly-born child should die in the jungle whence they have hidden so as to avoid sharing their food with a boat full of plague-stricken men.

Rivera's knowledge of life in the plains and the jungle had come about almost by chance. He had trained as a lawyer and visited the *Llanos* as a legal representative. He was later sent on a boundary commission into the jungle. The emotion of his novel is utterly genuine and it is an emotion of horror at what nature is and what man can be reduced to without the super-ego. If *La vorágine* has a message, it is that nature is more powerful than civilisation in Latin America.

Rómulo Gallegos

In contrast, Rómulo Gallegos (1884–1969) is more optimistic, although during his formative years there was little cause for hope in Venezuela.

---

thropic hills, stagnant waters with rotting reeds. Here the aphrodisiac parasite which fills the ground with dead bees; the variety of filthy flowers which contract with sexual palpitations and their sticky odour intoxicates like a drug... malignant liana whose hair blinds animals, the *pringamosa* which inflames the skin, the seed of the *curujú* which looks like a rainbow-coloured globe and only contains caustic ash, the purgative grape and the bitter nut.

* The chain which bites your ankles is more merciful than the leeches of these marshes; the warder who torments you is not as severe as these trees which watch us without speaking.

Until 1936, Venezuela was in the grip of dictatorships, first of Cipriano Castro then of Vicente Gómez. Gallegos, of a modest family, never completed his university education, but while a student he had joined a literary circle which founded a magazine, *La Alborada*, and which was dedicated to social and educational reform. His early thinking was shaped by Rodó's generation and he did in fact become a teacher, believing that the nation would progress only when there was a higher level of culture and literacy. In 1920, he published his first novel, *Reinaldo Solar* (the original title was *El último Solar*), whose theme is similar to that of many novels of the Arielist generation. Reinaldo is a man with great ambitions for himself and his country, but both the environment and his own character work against him. He jumps from one scheme to another, trying farming, literature and finally political militancy. He joins a revolutionary force and dies after being attacked by his own men who have refused to follow him in a suicidal advance. The novel is thus expressive of frustration and the general tone is pessimistic. Gallegos's personal frustration was increased in the 1920s, when despite the discovery of oil and the consequent increase of national wealth, the country remained the personal domain of Vicente Gómez, the dictator who wasted rather than contributed to the national potential. Yet Gallegos believed that the novel must reflect faith in the country's future and not simply present a despairing picture. This was why in *La trepadora* [*The Climber*] (1925), and in subsequent novels, he always ended on a note of hope, however slender. In *La trepadora*, the mulatto, Hilario Guanipa is a sturdy, intelligent man who through hard work becomes manager and then owner of a large estate. In his rise to power, he married Adelaida, a white creole of good family whose aristocratic ways conflict with Hilario's semi-barbaric energy. He himself will never be completely accepted into Venezuelan society, despite his power and wealth. It is his daughter, Victoria, who is to effect the fusion of the races and their integration into Venezuelan society through her marriage into the nation's Europeanised élite.

In 1929, Gallegos published *Doña Bárbara*, a novel based on a real-life character and set in the plains of Venezuela, where there was a cowboy society somewhat similar to that of the Argentine pampa. A group of symbolic characters incarnate the struggle between civilisation and barbarism. Santos Luzardo, a city-educated lawyer, returns to his country estate because of the encroachments of the lawless Doña Bárbara who has a band of ruthless men ready to obey her orders. Her lack of sentimentality, her skill as a horsewoman are the qualities which allow her supremacy in a male-dominated society, and she is more than a match for the lawyer, who after trying to obtain justice against her has to resort to strong-arm methods in order to defeat her. The message of the novel is that taming the frontier cannot be achieved without some violence, but violence can also be overcome by education. Santos Luzardo educates Doña Bárbara's illiterate daughter, Marisela, and eventually marries her.

The international success of *Doña Bárbara*, however, was attributable more to the exotic nature of the material than to the theme. The descriptions of cowboy activities and customs, of floods and storms, of Venezuelan flora and fauna opened up a new world. Here, for example, is a description of dawn, in which Gallegos uses many local words:

> Avanza el rápido amanecer llanero. Comienza a moverse sobre la sabana la fresca brisa matinal, que huele a mastranto y a ganados. Empiezan a bajar las gallinas de las ramas del totumo y del merecure;[1] el talisayo[2] insaciable les arrastra el manto de oro de ala ahuecada y una a una les hace esponjarse de amor. Silban las perdices entre los pastos. En el paloapique de la majada una paraulata[3] rompe su trino de plata. Pasan los voraces pericos, en bulliciosas bandadas; más arriba, la algarabía de los bandos de guiriríes,[4] los rojos rosarios de corocoras;[5] más arriba todavía, las garzas blancas, serenas y silenciosas.*

The intention of such passages is plainly that of naming birds, flowers and trees which had never previously been named in literature.

After the publication of *Doña Bárbara*, Gallegos found it prudent to go into voluntary exile in order to escape an official post which the dictator, Vicente Gómez, wanted him to accept. He left for Spain where he published *Cantaclaro* (1934) which was set in the *Llanos*, and then *Canaima*, 1935, a novel of the jungle. Both describe little-known areas of Venezuela and at the same time expose obstacles to national regeneration.

In *Cantaclaro*, the two central characters are the minstrel Florentino and the *caudillo*, Juan Crisóstomo Payara. The first incarnates all the lyricism in the life of the cowboys. He is a wanderer whose work as a herder takes him to the estate of the mysterious Payara, a man who had once seemed likely to attain political power. But he had retired dis-

---

* The rapid dawn of the plains advances. The fresh morning breeze begins to move over the savannah and brings the scent of mint and cattle. The hens begin to come down from the branches of the callabash tree and from the *merecure*; the insatiable *talisayo* drags from them the golden mantle of its hollowed wing and one by one sponges them with love. The partridges go into the meadows. On the fence of the cattle field, a *paraulata* breaks into a silvery trill. The voracious parrots fly in noisy groups; further up, the gabble of flocks of *guiriríes*, the red rosaries of *corocoras*; and even further white herons, serene and silent.

illusioned from public life 'al desierto y a su aislamiento con todas las esperanzas frustradas' [to the desert and to his isolation with all his frustrated hopes.] Florentino rescues Payara's daughter from this doom-haunted atmosphere and takes her to live with his own family, but a happy ending is hardly possible. A revolutionary war once more tears the *Llanos* apart, the family house is burned down, men and women massacred. Florentino, alone once more, disappears into the *Llanos*.

From this brief summary, it will be obvious that this is not a novel with a plot in any ordinary sense. The gaucho minstrel, Florentino, is its only unity. Characters have little control over their own fate but are abruptly overwhelmed by natural, political or social catastrophes over which there is no control.

Canaima is Gallegos's most ambitious novel and its hero, Marcos Vargas, embodies all the potentiality and all the frustrations of the Orinoco region in which he was born. However, this novel departs from Gallegos's earlier novels in that the theme of self-development and discovery is linked in a total fashion with the theme of national (or rather regional) regeneration.

Vargas comes from a penniless family who have never prospered in the Guayana region. The father sends Marcos to study in the British island of Trinidad, an education that proves of little value and does little to fit him for the life he is to live. From the moment of his return from Trinidad, Vargas's biography is a micro-structure of Guayana history since the conquest. He makes the same errors, follows the same illusions as Guayana itself has done in the course of its history.

Vargas begins his career as a trader with a mule train, but soon finds that he has to compete against the Ardavines, the political bosses who control the area, and their brutal henchman, Cholo Parima, who has already killed his brother, and who now kills his best friend, Manuel Ladera. Vargas proves his *machismo*[1] by killing Parima and standing up to the Ardavines but *machismo* is no answer to his own or his country's problems. He goes to work as foreman in a rubber plantation owned by the Italian Vellorini brothers, but though he runs the rubber business successfully and treats the workers humanely this, too, is no solution. His labours only help to enrich the foreign capitalist, and though Vargas is attracted to Araceli Vellorini, the father will not allow her to marry a native Venezuelan, thus indicating that the foreign immigrant exploits national resources but puts down no permanent roots. Vargas takes one more false path—he goes off to prospect for gold—but by this time he has learned that extracting material wealth from the land is not the way to enrich either the individual or the country, and when he strikes gold he gives it away.

In contrast to the *machos* and those interested only in material exploitation, there are many characters in the book who show how life should be lived in the region. There is Gabriel Ureña, a man who refuses to accept violence and killing and quietly cultivates his own estate. Such men are the pioneers of the future. There is Juan Solito, a huntsman whose knowledge of the jungle and its animal life is such that he is wholly identified with nature and no longer speaks of himself in the first person. There is the mysterious Count Giaffero who shows how man can release the evil passions within himself without harming other people. Marcos Vargas learns something from all of these, but he finally goes to live with an Indian tribe from whom he learns the ancient lore of the land and a form of communal living which provided, perhaps, a constructive alternative to the egoistic *machismo* which had hitherto been the prevailing regional way of life. Vargas marries an Indian woman, and it is their son who returns to civilisation to be educated and thus fuses the best of both Indian and European cultures. This hopeful conclusion is, however, overshadowed by the theme of frustration—that of Guayana and that of Vargas whose talents are spent in vain. And both the beginning and the end of the novel describe the mighty Orinoco flowing unproductively into the sea, a symbol of the wasted potential of the region:

Guayana frustrada... la que todavía no ha sido y la que ya no es. La de los caudalosos ríos desiertos, por cuyas aguas sólo navegan las sombras de las nubes, la de las inmensas energías baldías de los fragorosos saltos desaprovechados y la de los pueblos tristes sin tránsito por el día ni luz por la noche, donde el guayanés suspira y dice al forastero: 'Esto fue.'

Por los caminos del Yuruari, sembrados de baches, ya las colleras de las mulas no entonan el canto de la abundancia y en los paraderos donde ahora nadie se detiene están abandonados a la intemperie los carros de los antiguos convoyes. Los sustituyó el progreso aparente del camión, pero sólo muy de trecho en trecho y de tiempo en tiempo jalona el silencio el alarido del bocinazo, y en Upata de los carreros la gente suspira y murmura:

'Esto fue!'

La del caucho sin precio para ganancias, que ya no se explota, la del oro que poco aparece y sólo para enriquecer avariciosas manos extrañas, la de la sarrapia,[1] apenas, que continúa manteniendo la ilusión de riqueza conquistable sólo con unos meses de montaña.

'Esto fue!'

¿Qué se habrá hecho? ¡Aquella esperanza fallida! Aquella fuerza gozosa que se convirtió en atormentada!*

In this concluding chapter is summarised the theme of the book— that of the 'fuerza gozosa' that became 'atormentada'.

Curiously enough, Gallegos was to experience at first hand the difficulties of establishing the rule of law in Venezuela, for in 1936 he served a short term as Minister of Education before being forced to resign. And in 1947, after he had been elected President of the Republic, a military coup overthrew his government after a very brief period in office.

Though involved in political activity, he continued to write novels and published *Pobre negro* [*Poor Negro*] (1937), the story of the plantation Negro, Pedro Miguel Candelas, and his defiance of the landowning society which refuses to recognise his humanity. Gallegos's other novels include *El forastero* [*The Stranger*] (1942), *Sobre la misma tierra* [*Over the Same Earth*] (1943) which was a novel of Indian life, and *La brizna de paja en el viento* [*Straw in the Wind*] (1952) based on his first-hand experience of Cuba during the dictatorship of Machado.

Gallegos is undoubtedly one of the most distinguished regionalist novelists of Latin America, a man who put Venezuela on the literary map by exploring life in different regions, and whose novels, often diffuse and broad in scope, always give a vast cross-section of life. In order to judge his contribution to Venezuelan letters and the originality of his novels, it is perhaps worth comparing his work with that of a contemporary woman novelist, Teresa de la Parra (1891–1936), a fine writer whose two novels, *Ifigenia. Diario de una señorita que escribió*

---

* Frustrated Guayana...that which has not yet been and what no longer exists. Guayana of the great deserted rivers on whose waters there only floats the shadows of the clouds; that of the immense wasted energies of the unused, roaring waterfalls and that of the sad villages with no traffic by day and no lights by night, in which the Guayanian sighs and says to the foreigner: 'Those were the days.'

Along the roads of the Yuruari, strewn with potholes, the strings of mules no longer intone the chant of abundance and in the inns where now nobody stops, the carts of the old mule trains are abandoned to the elements. The apparent progress of the truck has taken their place but it is only here and there and from time to time that the howl of a motorhorn tears the silence, and in Upata, once the centre of the mule trains, the people sigh and murmur: 'Those were the days.'

The region of priceless profits in the rubber that is no longer exploited, that of the gold which seldom is struck and then only to enrich the avaricious hands of foreigners, that of the *sarapia* which scarcely helps to preserve the myth of unconquerable riches after only a few months in the mountains.

'Those were the days.'

What has happened? That lost hope! That joyful strength which became a tortured strength!

H

porque se fastidiaba [*Ifigenia. The Diary of a Young Lady Who Wrote Because She was Bored*] (1924) and *Las memorias de Mamá Blanca*, were both set in Venezuela but written from a 'European' point of view. The first describes the difficulty experienced by a young lady who finds herself unable to settle down in provincial, backward Caracas after a period in Europe. The second is based on her childhood memories of life on a paternalistically-run sugar-cane plantation. She shows herself unashamedly nostalgic for the old plantation life which she describes as a kind of paradise ruled by the good-natured 'Mama Blanca'.

Nuestra situación social en aquellos tiempos primitivos era, pues, muy semejante a la de Adán y Eva, cuando, señores absolutos del mundo, salieron inocentes y desnudos de entre las manos de Dios. Sólo que nosotros seis teníamos varias ventajas sobre ellos dos. Una de esas ventajas consistía en tener a Mamá, quien, dicho sea imparcialmente, con sus veinticuatro años, sus seis niñitas y sus batas llenas de volantes era un encanto. Otra ventaja no menos agradable era la de desobedecer impunemente comiéndonos a escondidas, mientras Avelyn almorzaba, el mayor número posible de guayabas sin que Dios nos arrojara del Paraíso, cubríendonos de castigos y de maldiciones.*

Apart from the mention of the *guayabas*, there is little indication here that we are in Venezuela; the reference to the Garden of Eden and the Fall places the extract firmly in a Western tradition.

THE PLATE REGION

In the Plate region, the regionalist novel could draw on a long-standing tradition of gaucho literature as well as on the more recent post-Modernist writing in which poets and prose writers had turned to rural life. Though nature was not so threatening as in Venezuela or Colombia, nevertheless there were still regions where she was untamed and where only the hardy pioneer could survive. One such was Misiones, a northern tropical region along the Paraná bordered by Brazil and Paraguay. It is the area which provides the setting for some of the best regional short stories of Latin America—those of Horacio Quiroga.

---

* Our social situation in those primitive times was very similar to that of Adam and Eve when, absolute lords of the earth, they went out innocent and naked from the hands of God. Only we six had many advantages over those two. One of these advantages was Mama, who, speaking objectively, was delightful, with her six children, her frilly dresses and her twenty-four years. Another no less delightful advantage was that of being able to disobey without punishment and secretly: while Avelyn was lunching to eat the greatest possible number of *guayabas* without God ever casting us out of Paradise and covering us with punishments and curses.

Horacio Quiroga (1878–1937)

Quiroga was born in Salto in Uruguay and first wrote under the influence of the Modernists (especially Lugones) and also under that of Edgar Allan Poe. However, from the first, he showed an interest in the human personality in extreme or abnormal situations. This interest might have led him to Paris and the Decadents and, indeed, he did spend a few months in the French capital, only to find that the 'bohemian' life was not for him. On his return to Montevideo he published a volume of Modernist poetry, *Los arrecifes de coral* [*The Coral Reefs*] (1902), and he had begun to write stories in the manner of Poe, when a bizarre accident occurred which determined the course of his future writing. He accidentally killed one of his best friends when examining a gun, and had to go to live in Buenos Aires. Here he became a frequent visitor to Lugones's house and Lugones encouraged him to join an expedition to the northern territory of Misiones. Thus Quiroga came upon a part of the world where the individual, in his lonely struggle against nature, lived a life of dramatic intensity. He returned to the tropics to settle there and lived first in the Chaco and then in Misiones.

An essential factor in good regionalist literature is that the natural environment should be more than a setting for a human drama. The great regional novels, *La vorágine*, *Canaima*, *Don Segundo Sombra*, are those in which the human drama and the environment are inseparable. This is also true of Quiroga's best stories. From his early model, Poe, he had learned to concentrate on human personalities at breaking-point. After settling in the tropics, he began to write stories in which individuals found themselves in extreme danger or hardship, for people tended to show their real worth when natural hazards enabled them to display qualities that would otherwise have lain dormant. In *Cuentos de amor, de locura y de muerte* [*Stories of Love, Madness and Death*] (1917), *Anaconda* (1921), *El salvaje* [*The Savage*] (1920), *Los desterrados* [*The Exiles*] (1926), the situations are often as bizarre as those of Poe, but they arise out of the combination of human weakness and carelessness, accident and a pitiless natural environment.

In both the Chaco and Misiones, man cannot control nature. He can only study the environment and hope to survive by pitting his courage, tenacity and resourcefulness against the overwhelming natural hazards. An accident or a moment of carelessness can change a normal working day into a fierce struggle for life. It was this that fascinated Quiroga. Nowhere else could he have found situations in which chance or accident, human will and natural force were all to play their part. Even the best human beings have defects which an accident can convert into tragic flaws.

A great majority of Quiroga's stories, then, follow a similar pattern. The protagonist is never an intellectual. He is usually a pioneer, a farmer or labourer in the Misiones or Chaco going about his daily work. The accident happens: a snake bites him, the river waters rise, a long period of drought alters the conditions of life. Suddenly he becomes a lonely man fighting for life.

Two of Quiroga's best stories follow this pattern: 'A la deriva' [Drifting] and 'Un hombre muerto' [A Dead Man]. In both these stories, a fatal accident occurs in the first few lines and the protagonist dies at the end. The death struggle forms the only theme or plot. But in neither story is the death quite 'accidental'. In 'A la deriva' a man bitten by a deadly snake paddles frantically down-river to get help, but he had quarrelled with his nearest neighbour. His cries for help are not answered, and he floats helplessly away between the dark cliffs along the Paraná. The snake-bite was an accident, but the man had in a sense contributed to his own death when, years before, he had quarrelled with his nearest neighbour. In 'El hombre muerto', a man who is tired after a day's work in the banana plantations slips and falls on a machete knife. The entire drama consists of the attempts of the man's 'I' to retain its hold on reality until the final disintegration of the personality when the plantation, 'his' knife and 'his' horse cease to be 'his'. But again the accident arises out of the man's character. Obsessed with clearing his banana plantation, he had neglected to see to the handle of his knife which needed replacing and was overtired when the accident took place; and there is a certain dramatic irony in the fact that the plantation of which he is so proud indirectly brings about his death. Here, for instance, is a fine passage in which the dying man watches the almost motionless leaves on 'his' plantation:

El hombre resiste, ¡ es tan imprevisto ese horror! Y piensa: ¡ Es una pesadilla, esto es! ¿Qué ha cambiado? Nada. Y mira: ¿No es acaso ese bananal su bananal? ¿No viene todas las mañanas a limpiarlo? ¿Quién lo conoce como él? Ve perfectamente el bananal, muy raleado, y las anchas hojas desnudas por el viento. Pero ahora no se mueven... Es la calma de mediodía; pronto deben de ser las doce.

Por entre los bananos, allá arriba, el hombre ve desde el duro suelo el techo rojo de su casa. A la izquierda entreví el monte y la capuera de canelas. No alcanza a ver más, pero sabe muy bien que a sus espaldas está el camino al puerto nuevo, y que en la dirección de su cabeza, allá abajo, yace en el fondo del valle el Paraná dormido como un lago. Todo, todo, exactamente como siempre: el sol

de fuego, el aire vibrante y solitario, los bananos inmóviles, el alambrado de postes muy gruesos y altos que pronto tendrá que cambiar...
¡ Muerto ! Pero ¿es posible?*

And we see how, though dying, the man still assumes that he is owner of the property, how his mind still cannot adjust to the idea of death but goes on making plans for the future, for repairing the wire fence. At the same time, notice that the author never presents any thought too complex for the mind of a simple farmer.

Though Quiroga is not directly concerned with society in his stories, criticism of social organisation is often implicit. For Quiroga, all man-made institutions are fallible, fragile and ultimately unimportant, when set beside the mightiness of nature but he expresses this view indirectly, often by showing the failure of human organisation when confronted with natural hazards. In 'Los fabricantes de carbón' [The Charcoal Burners], two men plan to set up a charcoal-burning furnace in Misiones and the story ironically comments on their careful calculations—the structure of the furnace, temperatures, etc.—and the natural and human elements which defy calculation. There is thus a conflict between human reason and will which seeks to plan, structure and control the environment, and nature which defies such control. This also helps to explain why Quiroga should so often choose animals as the protagonists of his stories, since their instinctual knowledge and acts are totally opposed to the willed and motivated actions of human beings. This conflict is the subject of 'Anaconda', a story in which the snakes rise up to fight a war to the death with a group of men in charge of a laboratory which manufactures snake serum. The snakes instinctively defend the natural order. Men seek to destroy this in order to bring nature under their control. In this story, the humans win a victory, but usually defiance of nature brings punishment,

---

* The man resists; this horror is so unexpected. And he thinks: It is a nightmare, that is what it is. What had changed? Nothing. And he looked. Isn't this banana plantation his plantation? Doesn't he come here every day to clear the ground? Who knows it as he does? He can see his plantation perfectly; very sparse—and the broad leaves naked from the wind. But now they are not moving. It is he midday calm; soon it will probably be twelve o'clock.
Between the banana plants, up there, the man sees the red roof of his house from the hard ground. To the left, he glimpses the bush and the cinnamon fence. He cannot see more, but he knows quite well that behind him lies the road to the new port and that in the direction of his head, down below, the Paraná, calm as a lake, lies in the depths of the valley. Everything, everything is exactly as always; the burning sun, the vibrating, solitary air, the motionless banana plants, the wire fence with its very thick high posts that he will soon have to change.
Dead ! Is it possible?

as in 'La insolación' [Sun-stroke] where Mr Jones drives himself pitilessly to clear his cotton plantation during a hot spell. His dogs instinctively realise that they must conserve their energy and rest in the shade whereas their master kills himself from sunstroke in his anxiety to get a job done. In stories such as this, nature is no passive element but an actively destructive force, a threat to human identity. Here, for instance, is Mr Jones attempting to walk through the cane-brake in the burning sun:

> ...Llegó al riacho y se internó en el pajonal, el diluviano pajonal del Saladito, que ha crecido, secado y retoñado desde que hay paja en el mundo, sin conocer fuego. Las matas arqueadas en bóveda a la altura del pecho, se entregaban en bloques macizos. La tarea de cruzarlo, seria ya en día fresco, era muy dura a esa hora. Mister Jones lo atravesó, sin embargo, braceando entre la paja restallante y polvorienta por el barro que dejaban las crecientes, ahogado de fatiga y acres vahos de nitratos.*

The human figure struggling across the cane-brake seems almost derisory in comparison with the nature he is struggling against—in this case a mass of plants that have grown untouched for centuries. In this passage one cannot talk of a natural 'background'; here as in other stories natural hazards take on the role of the Fates in the Greek drama, visiting on the human protagonist the punishment his own nature has destined him for.

Though social protest has no place in Quiroga's stories, he does not avoid stories about economic exploitation. His attitude towards social organisation inevitably led him to see the dehumanising effect of the semi-slave conditions in which many labourers worked, and several of his most striking stories illustrate this. 'Los mensús' is about two *mensuales*—labourers hired on a monthly basis—who contract debts in a company store, are forced to work off the debts on a plantation where they are ruthlessly driven to work even when ill, and who escape. One of them dies during the escape bid, the other finds his way to the river port, only to contract debts and start the same fatal trajectory once again. In 'Una bofetada' [A Blow], Quiroga tells a monstrous story of hatred between a foreman and an Indian labourer.

---

* He reached the stream and went into the cane-brake, the antediluvian cane-brake of Saladito which has grown, dried out and resprouted for as long as there ever has been cane in the world and without ever being burned. The clumps, arched in a dome chest-high, were tangled in solid blocks. The task of crossing, difficult even on a cool day, was very hard at this hour. Mr Jones crossed it, nevertheless, swimming between the crackling dusty cane over the clay left by the floods, gasping with fatigue and the bitter vapour of nitrates.

The foreman slaps the labourer, who harbours his hatred for years until circumstances put the foreman in his power. The Indian manages to disarm him of his gun and whip, and proceeds to beat the man to death along the lonely tracks between the plantations. Often in Quiroga's stories the landscape has symbolic features, as in the following passage:

Korner no se movía más. El mensú cortó entonces las amarras de la jangada y subiendo en la canoa, ató un cabo a la popa de la almadía y paleó vigorosamente.

Por leve que fuera la tracción sobre la inmensa mole de vigas, el esfuerzo inicial bastó. La jangada viró insensiblemente, entró en la corriente y el hombre cortó entonces el cabo.

El sol había entrado hacía rato. El ambiente calcinado dos horas antes, tenía ahora una frescura y quietud fúnebres. Bajo el cielo aún verde, la jangada derivaba girando, entraba en la sombra transparente de la costa paraguaya, para resurgir de nuevo a la distancia, sólo una línea negra ya.*

The dead foreman has reached the end of life's journey. The *peon* he had once beaten is now triumphant but no emotion is shown other than the quiet preparations to float the body downstream. All the emotional content of the passage lies in the description of the twilight and the boat floating away down the river. The heat has died down, the hours of torment are over, the peace and coolness of death have come. It is precisely this objectification of the emotions that gives the story a power that many orthodox social-protest stories do not have. For here we are shown how men behave under humiliation and oppression and we are shown this without rhetoric.

Quiroga's most bizarre and probably his best collection is *Los desterrados* [*The Exiles*], particularly the section he called 'Los tipos' which gives sketches of characters whom he had known in Misiones. Here we meet the dregs of humanity, drunkards and dipsomaniacs who have come to end their lives away from social censure. These 'real-life' stories have more horror in them than the fantasy stories Quiroga wrote under the influence of Poe. One of the characters, for instance, dies of exposure after drinking wood alcohol out of a lamp; another dies in a dipsomaniac delirium; a labourer disappears and all that is ever found of him are his boots hanging from a tree. These

* Korner no longer moved. The *mensú* then cut the ropes of the raft and getting into the canoe, he tied an end to the stern of the raft and paddled vigorously.

Despite the slightness of the drag on the immense mass of logs, the initial impulse was enough. The raft turned slightly, entered the current and then the man cut the end.

The sun had gone in some time before. The burning atmosphere of two hours before had now a funereal freshness and quiet. Beneath the sky which was still green, the raft drifted and turned round; it entered into the transparent shadow of the Paraguayan coast to reappear again in the distance as a mere black line.

lonely desperate men were probably not unlike Quiroga himself after the loss of his first wife, who committed suicide in 1915, or the Quiroga of later years, ignored by the younger generation of writers, poor and almost friendless, who returned from Misiones to Buenos Aires ill with cancer. Characteristically, he killed himself before the disease reached its last stages.

Quiroga's importance is not only his contribution to regional writing but also his contribution to the art of the short story. His *Decálogo del perfecto cuentista*[1] stresses the need for economy and intensity and shows that he was conscious of the scope and limitations of the genre. He can certainly be counted one of the Latin-Amer can masters of the genre.

Ricardo Güiraldes

The greatest regional novel of this century is *Don Segundo Sombra* by Ricardo Güiraldes (1886–1927) and it is regional in the sense that Quiroga's stories were regional, in that the pampa is an essential element in the human drama.

Güiraldes came from a family of wealthy landowners, and spent part of his childhood in Europe, part on the family *estancia* where he lived with gauchos and met the man who was to become the model for Don Segundo. The scenes of his childhood—Europe and the pampa— were to play significant if conflicting roles in his development. His first writings, published in 1915, were the poems and prose poems of *El cencerro de cristal* [*The Glass Bell*], and stories, the *Cuentos de muerte y de sangre* [*Stories of Death and Blood*]; some of these were anecdotes which illustrated the character of historical figures such as Rosas or Urquiza. These first publications had no success with the Argentine public although they contained the seeds of his later and more successful works. They reveal not a simple 'back to nature' attitude but a religious need for spiritual equilibrium and peace evocatively stated in the brief poem, 'Quietud' [Quietude].

> Tarde, tarde,
> Cae la tarde,
> larga, larga
> se aletarga
> En derrumbe silencioso
> como mirada en un pozo.*

---

* Evening, evening. Evening falls, long, long, it grows drowsy. In silent decline like a glance in a well.

The tension in Güiraldes's mind between the Europeanised way of life his education had accustomed him to and the stoic, manly qualities developed in the pampa was first expressed in a novel, *Raucho* (1917), which was based closely on his personal experience. The story is of a young man's disillusionment with Europe and his return to Argentina where, back on the *estancia*, he experiences a sense of inner peace such as he had never known when away from home. This is the significant passage:

Raucho piensa cómo quiso ser todo menos lo que era. Su chiripá,[1] sólo desprendido de la faja, se habrá envilecido en el polvo de caminos extranjeros.

Raucho se sienta bajo un sauce, cerca de una tosca,[2] donde el agua habla de misterios serenos.

Un pato silbón pasa perforando noche con gritos agudos.

Raucho inefablemente quieto, se duerme de espaldas, los brazos abiertos, crucificado de calma sobre su tierra de siempre.*

Though he describes Raucho as 'serenely crucified' this is not a picture of agony but of bliss.

It is obvious that Güiraldes had serious doubts as to the quality of the progress achieved by Western civilisation. In his *Rosaura* (1918), a simple, idyllic love story, the novel ends with the heroine's death under a train which symbolises a type of progress that destroys simpler more traditional forms of life. And it is clear too that Güiraldes felt that attainment of inner peace and maturity was the individual's main task in life. This conviction led him to take an interest in Eastern religions which emphasised meditation, and he had paid a visit to the East in 1910. The recording of inner experience is also uppermost in *Xamaica*, a love story published in 1923 and set on board a ship sailing to Jamaica. The union of the lovers brings them an experience of having transcended the individuation principle similar to that of the mystics:

Tengo de pronto la certeza de que el infinito está presente. Lo veo y abrazo en mí, con una facultad momentánea más fuerte que toda razón. Se definitivamente lo que es. A pesar del desenlace forzoso de mi vida, comprendo que he vencido la muerte y el tiempo en ese instante en que, fuera de mi limitación individual,

---

* Raucho thinks how he had wanted to be less than he was. His *chiripá*, undone at the waist, must have been soiled in the dust of foreign roads.

   Raucho sits down under a willow tree near a *tosca* in which the water speaks of calm mysteries.

   A whistling duck passes by, perforating the night with shrill cries.

   Raucho, ineffably quiet, sleeps on his back, his arms wide open, serenely crucified upon the eternal earth.

unido con Clara, he sido el amor mismo en todo su poder abstracto, que rige el universo nacido de su serenidad.*

Is it an exaggeration to see *Don Segundo Sombra* as a spiritual preparation for the good life? Certainly the strong, mystical strain is also evident in the poetry of Güiraldes's last years, published posthumously in 1927 as *Senderos* [*Pathways*].

Why was it that this sophisticated man who once declared himself to have been influenced by Spanish and French Romantics, by Schopenhauer, Samain, Anatole France, Nietzsche, Gorki, Dostoievsky, Maupassant, Dickens, Spencer, Zola and others,[1] who was well aware of all the latest cultural trends, why is it that such a man should have turned to the gaucho? The answer lies partly in the fact that he felt Europe had taken the wrong direction; partly in his conviction that American experience could give a man a valid set of standards to guide his life. Above all, he felt that American experience had never been recorded. Writing to his friend, the French writer, Valéry Larbaud, in 1921, he declared:

Me parece que hay tanto por decir en este país, que me desespera no ser un hombre orquesta, capaz de desentrañar el aspecto poético, filosófico, musical y pictórico de una raza inexpresada.

En Europa, el problema está en ver las cosas bajo el prisma de un temperamento interesante. Muchos se torturan en buscar una forma de arte novedosa. Aquí todo el secreto estaría en apartarse de normas ajenas y dejar que los sujetos mismos fueran creando en uno la forma adecuada de expresarlos. Y pensar que en cada una de las formas del arte hay un alma que está esperando su palabra.

En el lenguaje pulcro y malicioso del gaucho el embrión de una literatura viva y compleja. Todo estaría en ser capaz de llevar estas enseñanzas a una forma natural y noble.†[2]

---

* I suddenly have the certainty that the infinite is here. I see it and embrace it in me with a momentary faculty that is stronger than any reason. I know definitely what it is. Despite the ineluctable outcome of my life, I understand that I have conquered death and time in that instant, in which transcending my individual limits, united with Clara, I have been love itself in all its abstract power which rules the universe born of its serenity.

† It seems to me that there is so much to say in this country that I am desperate, because I am not a one-man band able to bring out the poetical, philosophical, musical and pictorial aspects of an unexpressed race.

In Europe, the problem is in seeing things through the prism of an interesting personality. Many torment themselves trying to find a form of original art. Here the whole secret will lie in getting away from foreign models and allowing the themes themselves to create in one the proper form for expressing them. And to think that in each one of the forms of art, there is a soul that is awaiting its word.

In the neat malicious language of the gaucho, there is the germ of a living complex literature. Everything would depend on being able to express these teachings in a natural and noble form.

Notice the difference that Güiraldes sees between European art—which cannot draw on new material, only on new perspectives—and American art in which experience is still waiting to be expressed in the right forms. This is what he tried to do in *Don Segundo Sombra*.

Don Segundo Sombra is a *Bildungsroman* (literally, a 'formation novel'; that is, one in which the central character undergoes a series of key experiences and thus achieves maturity). Güiraldes describes a process that is universal, but relates this to a regional experience. The hero of the novel is a boy, Guacho, so nicknamed because he is illegitimate and does not know who his father is. He lives with two 'aunts' in a small town and is well on his way to becoming a juvenile delinquent at the time when the novel begins. He is saved from this by his hero-worship for Don Segundo Sombra, a gaucho he sees riding into town one day and who proceeds with stoic calm and dignity to disarm a drunkard who tries to pick a fight. Guacho runs away from home to follow Don Segundo Sombra, who becomes his 'tutor' and takes him on a long cattle drive across country. The boy's boastfulness, his vanity and impudence are soon tempered when the long rides and the round-ups teach him that these have no place in gaucho society, where real skills are all that count. But Don Segundo Sombra teaches him more than this. He shows him the threat that women offer since they help to provoke quarrels between men or try to enslave them to passion. He teaches him, too, that acceptance of death is the only way to transcend fear. When, after five years, Guacho returns to the small town where he had once lived he is a man in the fullest sense of the word. Here he discovers the identity of his father, a landowner who had died and left him his estate. But he is now able to meet this responsibility, while Don Segundo Sombra, his work done, rides away.

The journeys which are the basic pattern of *Don Segundo Sombra* are, of course, analogues of human life. They have the advantage of giving the novel a familiar structure, one which has the force of myth. Yet the pattern which *Don Segundo Sombra* recalls is that of *Huckleberry Finn* rather than any European archetype. Here, as in *Huckleberry Finn*, we are confronted with a male world, one in which women, towns, officials of any kind, represent a threat. Indeed *Don Segundo Sombra* tells a story in which human misery is described as being essential, since, when misery disappeared from earth, 'abogaos, procuradores, jueces de paz, curanderos, médicos y todos los que son autoridá' [lawyers, solicitors, justices of the peace, quacks, doctors and all those who are authority] began to die of hunger. Notice that nearly all these parasites are associated with social organisation.

Yet Güiraldes does not present a simple 'back to nature' philosophy as the alternative. Nature is not benevolent in the novel. Indeed it is a blind force, obeying the law of survival of the fittest. There is no religious awe of nature in this striking passage, which describes the colony of spider-like crabs which appear to pray to the sun:

El sol se ponía. De cada cueva salía una de esas repugnantes arañas duras, pero más grandes, más redondas que las del cañadón. El suelo se fué cubriendo de ellas. Y caminaban despacio, sin fijarse unas en otras, dadas vuelta todas hacia la bola de fuego que se iba escondiendo. Y se quedaron inmóviles, con las manitos plegadas sobre el pecho, rojas como si estuvieran teñidas en sangre.

¡ Aquello me hacía una profunda impresión! ¿Era cierto que rezaban? ¿Tendrían siempre, como una condena, las manitos ensangrentadas? ¿Que pedían? Seguramente que algún vacuno o yeguarizo, con jinete, si mal no venía, cayera en aquel barro fofo minado por ellos.*

Nature without man is chaotic, even vile. When the narrator comes across a herd of wild cattle, he notices how many of them are scarred and maimed and comments, 'Esos animales nunca fueron curados por mano de hombre' [Those animals had never been tended by the hand of man]. Nor can man exist in complete solitude. Don Sixto, a man they come across living on his own, is half-mad.

Thus Güiraldes does not see either lone nature or lone man as capable of achieving perfection. Man reaches maturity by learning to control nature, which includes controlling his own nature, and this he does through his contact with the external world and his fellow men. However, it is also clear that Güiraldes believed that certain environments provided more favourable opportunities than others in this process of maturation.

Many critics have commented that in *Don Segundo Sombra*, Güiraldes idealised a style of life that was dying. In fact, this matters little. Like all major novelists, Güiraldes had the power to transform elements he had drawn from reality; what he says in *Don Segundo Sombra* is valid

---

* The sun was setting. Out of each hole came one of those repugnant hard spiders, but bigger, rounder than those of the ravine. The ground was gradually covered with them. And they walked slowly without noticing one another, all turned towards the fiery ball which was going down. And they stayed motionless with their small hands crossed over their breasts looking red as if they were stained with blood.

That made a deep impression on me. Was it true that they prayed? Would they always have, like a curse, those bloodstained hands? What did they ask for? Surely that some mare or head of cattle might fall in that soft clay that they had mined.

and understandable, whether the society he drew his inspiration from still existed or not.

To most contemporaries, *Don Segundo Sombra* was an excellent example of a work that was written in a style recognisably American and yet not narrowly regional in scope. The following passage describes the dawn preparations for departure on the cattle-drive and is a good example of Güiraldes's style:

Respiré hondamente el aliento de los campos dormidos. Era una oscuridad serena alegrada de luminares lucientes como chispas de un fuego ruidoso. Al dejar que entrara en mí aquel silencio me sentí más fuerte y más grande.

A lo lejos oí tintinear un cencerro. Alguno andaría agarrando caballo o juntando la tropilla. Los novillos no daban aún señales de su vida tosca, pero yo sentía por el olor la presencia de sus quinientos cuerpos gruesos.

De pronto oí correr unos caballos; un cencerro agitó sus notas con precipitación de gotera. Aquellos sonidos se expandían en el sereno matinal, como ondas en la piel soñolenta del agua al galope de algún cascote. Perdido en la noche, cantó un gallo, despertando la simpatía de unos *teros*.[1] Solitarias expresiones de vida diurna, que amplificaban la inmensidad del mundo.

En el corral, agarré mi petiso, algo inquieto por el inusitado correr de sus compañeros libres. Al ponerle el bozal sentí su frente mojada de rocío. Sobre el suelo húmedo oí rascar las espuelas de Goyo que andaba buscando alguna prenda.

'Güen día, hermano,' dije despacio.

'Güen día.'

'¿Se te ha perdido algo?'

'Ahá, el arriador.'*

There is a synthesis here of heightened poetic language which evokes the silence of the early morning and the regional language used in the

---

* I breathed deeply of the breath of the sleeping fields. It was a calm darkness gladdened with shining patches of light like sparks of a noisy fire. When I let the silence enter into me I felt stronger and taller.

In the distance, I heard a bell tinkling. Somebody must be going along holding a horse or getting together the drove. The steers as yet gave no signs of their rough life, but I scented the presence of their five hundred fat bodies.

Suddenly I heard some horses running; a bell sounded its notes like drops of water dripping fast. Those sounds expanded in the morning calm, like waves off the sleeping skin of water at the gallop of some hoof. Lost in the night, there sang a cock, awakening the sympathy of some *teros*. Solitary expressions of daily life that widened the immensity of the world.

In the corral, I took my colt that was rather restless because of the unaccustomed galloping of her free companions. When I put on the muzzle, I felt the forehead wet with dew. Upon the damp ground I heard Goyo dragging his spurs as he went in search of some equipment.

'Good day, brother,' I said slowly.

'Good day.'

'Have you lost something?'

'The whip.'

conversation of the gauchos. Neither is out of place, each sets the other off.

While no other writer attained the artistic mastery of Güiraldes, many excellent novels of rural life were written during the '20s and '30s. Benito Lynch (1885–1951) was an accurate recorder of the language and customs of the gaucho. Unlike Güiraldes, who showed the gaucho attaining mastery and control over his own nature, Lynch's characters are often victims of fatal passions. His best-known novel, *El inglés de los güesos* [*The Englishman of the Bones*] (1924) is the tragedy of a simple country girl who falls in love with a 'gringo', an Englishman who is investigating prehistoric remains. *El romance de un gaucho* [*The Romance of a Gaucho*] (1930), considered by many to be his best novel, is another story of love between two people of totally different cultures—in this case the gaucho and a sophisticated woman of the city. The tension between urban Westernised forms of life and rural attitudes, implicit in many of Güiraldes's stories and his novel, is explicit in the works of Lynch.

SOCIAL CHANGES AND THE NOVELS OF AMORIM

Reflection of the social changes through which the Plate region was passing is not to be found in either Güiraldes or Lynch, but in the novels of the Uruguayan writer, Enrique Amorim (1900–60). A prolific writer who was born in Salto, Uruguay, he spent many years in Buenos Aires and there began his literary career. From the first, conflict and social change were his main preoccupations and he is the kind of novelist whose works need to be judged as a whole. When judged singly, the novels have good moments but appear defective in structure. Taken as a whole, they give an epic picture of the Uruguayan countryside, transformed by the immigrant and industrialisation, torn by political strife, the home of both millionaires and poor labourers as well as of men descended from old pioneer stock and newcomers who scarcely speak Spanish. But though social change is an important subject, nature is still strong enough to influence men and their history. In *El paisano Aguilar* [*The Compatriot, Aguilar*] (1934), the eponymous protagonist returns to the farm from the city and is slowly absorbed by the life of the countryside in a trajectory that is not unlike that of many of D. H. Lawrence's characters. In *El caballo y su sombra* [*The Horse and his Shadow*] (1941) an Italian immigrant whose son has been killed by a *criollo*, stabs the latter to death and thus shows how deeply he has been altered by his new country. But in a late, ambitious novel,

La desembocadura (1958), man appears, at last, to dominate. Though short, this novel has a broad sweep. It opens with a description of a mound of earth, the burial place of the narrator's grandfather who had pioneered in that part of the country. This is how the narrator expresses his sense of communion with his great-grandfather and through him with his native land:

...los campos de 'El Moreno' no eran como los demás. Las tormentas marcaban los límites, y las aguas iban a juntarse en las gargantas de los arroyuelos, luego en la boca mansa del arroyo, entre peñascos, para marchar serenas, entre altas riberas de colores, hacia la desembocadura.

Mi bisabuelo siguió ese curso natural de la tierra, y dejaron sus restos en una loma que mira insistente el curso de las aguas, misterioso por sereno, triste siempre, siempre melancólico, a veces enlutado de sombras.

Yo trepé a la loma hasta el montículo que está dejando ver los huesos, más bien dicho el polvo de los huesos de mi bisabuelo. Detenido sobre su prodigiosa tumba recorrí las manchas blancas que dibujan su cuerpo. Una mano, quizás la derecha a flor de tierra, perfila el esfuerzo de aquel hombre al arrojar la botella al Uruguay. Sigo el curso de ese objeto en el aire. Lo veo caer en las aguas y oigo el disparo que me impide escuchar el choque de cristal en las aguas serenas.*

The bottle to which the passage refers contained documents which the great-grandfather had been about to throw in the river as he was shot. The voice of the grandfather now takes up the tale following the fortunes of himself and his dependants down to the present as bulldozers move in to destroy his grave and bring irrigation and a new life to the land. But it is he who has the last word as he declares

Yo el único de todos los de mi sangre que ha tenido la fortuna de abonar la tierra.†

The novels of Amorim reveal to us how closely Argentinians and Uruguayans continued to identify themselves with country life even when Buenos Aires and Montevideo had absorbed the greater part of the population.

---

* ...the fields of 'El Moreno' were not like the rest. Storms marked the boundaries and the waters came together in the throats of the streams, then in the calm mouth of the stream, between peaks, to run serenely between high-coloured banks to the confluence.

My great-grandfather followed the natural course of the earth and left his remains on a hill that watches the flow of the waters insistently, mysterious because serene, always sad, always melancholy, sometimes darkened by shadows.

I climbed the slope to the little hill which reveals the bones, or rather the dust of my grandfather's bones. Motionless on his great tomb, I went over to the white stains that marked his body. A hand, perhaps the right hand, on the surface of the ground outlines the strength of that man as he threw the bottle into the Uruguay River. I follow the course of that object in the air. I see it fall in the waters and I hear the shot that prevents me from hearing the sound of glass on the serene waters.

† I the only one of those of my blood who have the good fortune to fertilise the earth.

CHILE

In Chile no major regionalist novelist emerged during this period, though there abounded stories and novels in the *criollista* tradition which painted rural manners and types. A vast number of writers recorded lives in remote parts of the republic from the extreme south described in some of the novels of Juan Marín (1900–63), to the varied aspects of the lives of the peasant and the poor described in the novels and stories of Rafael Maluenda (1885–1963), Luis Durand (1895–1954) and Marta Brunet (1901–). Curiously, however, the two best regionalist novels were written by writers who had made their reputation in quite a different field. Eduardo Barrios (1888–1963), best known as a psychological novelist, published his *Gran Señor y Rajadiablos* [*Gentleman and Hell-Raiser*] (1948) towards the end of his long writing career and Pedro Prado (1886–1952), Modernist poet and author of several symbolic and poetic novels wrote and published *El juez rural* [*The Rural Judge*] in 1924.

The last is perhaps more interesting as document than as an artistic work, being the day-to-day life of a country magistrate. The former is set in the nineteenth century when rural overlords such as the 'Gran Señor' of the title were at the height of their power and influence. The novelist shows a certain nostalgia for the good old days of lusty and vigorous men who were able to manipulate others as they willed.

SUMMARY

In this chapter we have been concerned with the major regional novels published in the '20s and the '30s. The best of these, as we have seen, dealt with men and situations which were of universal interest although they were at the same time totally integrated into a particular region. Don Segundo Sombra could not be anything but a gaucho, but we do not have to be particularly interested in gaucho lore and customs to find his story understandable. However, because the lives of the country-dwellers were often lived in great misery, the regional novel flows into the social protest novel and the two are not always separable.

8 REALISM AND THE NOVEL: ITS APPLICATION TO SOCIAL PROTEST AND INDIANIST WRITING

In the nineteenth century, realism had been the technique of the bourgeois novelist who wished to show with as much verisimilitude and objectivity as possible the relationship between the individual and his society. In the '30s realism took on a new meaning. Its purpose was to show not only the workings of society but in particular economic exploitation, the class-struggle and the new forces among working class and peasantry who were to change the situation. This type of realism was known as socialist realism. However, even among writers who were not Communists, the prevailing mood of economic depression encouraged a concentration on those sectors of society which seemed actually or potentially the most militant.[1] In Europe these were the years of the 'proletarian' novel whose heroes were miners and factory workers. In Latin America, where the proletariat was almost non-existent, some writers found their Latin-American equivalent in the small industrial enclaves such as oil and mine fields, amongst the dockers or the city *Lumpenproletariat*: more often, the writer found his material among the peasants and agricultural workers or the Indians.

Novels about Indians, agricultural workers or even poor city-dwellers were not exactly new in Spanish–American literature. Clorinda Matto de Turner, Heriberto Frías and Alcides Arguedas had already registered their protest at the treatment of the Indians; the *criollista* writers had covered almost every area of peasant life. But for the *criollistas* and the early *Indianista* writers, the fault lay in character weaknesses either of the upper or the lower classes. The socialist realists still depicted wicked or heartless landowners, but the momentum of the plot depended on the inexorable development of an economic situation. Expulsion from the land or mechanisation of agricultural methods and its repercussions tended to replace the seduction or rape as a plot device. Very often, too, the purpose of such novels was much more than to expose injustice; they also aimed at showing the emergence of new class situations and even at arousing people to action. Here, however, they found themselves in a paradoxical position, since the high number of illiterates in Latin America reduced the public they most wanted to reach. The Ecuadorian realist writer José de la Cuadra criticised the more extreme manifestations of socialist realism precisely on the grounds that they were ineffective:

De la presentación veraz, en ocasiones hasta fotográfica, de la realidad montuvia, deviene una literatura de protesta y de denuncia francamente tendenciosa, que adjetivamente se enruta al plantamiento de las reivindicaciones campesinas, y aún lucha por ellas en el grado en que vale hacerlo en un país donde quienes leen son, en su mayor parte, aquellos que no necesitan saber literalmente, esto es, por vía literaria, lo que saben ya por vías más obvias. Y por demás, es decir que el propio interesado, el montuvio, tampoco lee.*[1]

Nevertheless, socialist realism was practised by writers all over Latin America. (For characteristic works, see reading list to this chapter.) In order to examine this type of novel more closely, I have chosen to concentrate on Ecuadorian realism, since for various historical and social reasons, realism became the reigning school of writing.

ECUADORIAN REALISM

In 1931, a group of writers, Demetrio Aguilera Malta (1905–), Enrique Gil Gilbert (1912–) and Joaquín Gallegos Lara (1911–) published a joint collection of short stories with the title *Los que se van. Cuentos de cholos y del montuvio* [*Those Who Go Away. Stories of Cholos and Montuvios*]. Literary critics found the realism of their stories too crude and violent, yet they heralded a new phenomenon in Ecuadorian writing. To begin with they were all from Guayaquil, a port town which served a tropical agricultural region and was inhabited by a trader class which resented the political dominance of Quito and landowners of the sierra. Further, the lower classes in the Guayaquil region were totally different from the silent, oppressed sierra Indians. Here were the *montuvios* with Negro and Indian blood in their veins, and the *cholos* or Indian half-breeds. It was in this region, too, that the first strikes took place and there were also violent political battles. Obviously, for the novelist interested in social change there was much to exercise his attention, particularly after 1928 when the old liberal

* From the truthful and sometimes even photographic representation of *montuvio* reality there arises a literature of protest and denunciation which is frankly tendentious and which through adjectives orientates [the reader] towards the demands of the peasants. The novel even fights for them as far as it can do in a country in which those who read are usually those who literally do not need to know, that is, through literature, what they already know by more obvious means. And besides, there is the fact that the most interested person, the *montuvio*, cannot read.

oligarchy was overthrown and a new Constitution proclaimed which promised to help the hitherto submerged sections of the community. Angel Rojas, the Ecuadorian critic, has summed up the multiple social and political themes of the novel of this period as:

... el feudalismo, el gamonalismo,[1] el problema del indio en la sierra y el montuvio en la costa; la lucha entre la ciudad y el campo; la tragedia del cholo; el mundo explotado en el suelo y el subsuelo, el imperialismo, el mitín político y la huelga; el cuartelazo y la especulación, la miseria del suburbio y los intereses en juego en la apuesta política de las oligarquías; el panorama de un país semicolonial productor de materias primas y dependiente en forma casi exclusiva de sistema solar norteamericano.*

These themes of feudalism, of economic struggle and foreign domination were the core of the realist novel, and—not surprisingly—two novelists, Gil Gilbert and Gallegos Lara, were members of the Communist Party.

The Ecuadorian writers who emerged during the '30s included Demetrio Aguilera Malta, José de la Cuadra and Alfredo Pareja Diezcanseco as well as the three authors of *Los que se van*. All wrote of the coastal region. At the same time a group of sierra writers arose, the best known of whom was Jorge Icaza (1906–   ) who wrote of the sierra Indians and *cholos*. But though their works gave a certain common stamp attributable to the subject matter, each author made an individual contribution to realist writing in Spanish America.

José de la Cuadra (1904–41)

José de la Cuadra was a short-story writer who had in 1931 already published two collections of stories, *El amor que dormía* [*The Love that Slept*] (1930) and *Repisas* [*Shelves*] (1931). In 1932 he published *Horno* [*Oven*] and in 1933 his most powerful work, a short novel, *Los Sangurimas*. His final collection of stories, *Guasintón*, appeared in 1938. Of all the Ecuadorian writers of the period, he was perhaps the one who was most concerned with the art of the story and the novel and the one least concerned with the ideological method. He chose as his subject matter the *montuvio*, the racially-mixed inhabitants of the coastal regions on whom he published a sociological study, *El montuvio*

* Feudalism, *gamonalism*, the problem of the Indian in the mountain and the *montuvio* on the coast; the struggle between city and the countryside, the tragedy of the *cholo*; the exploited world, exploited both in its soil and its subsoil, imperialism, the political meeting and the strike, the military *coup d'état* and speculation, the poverty of the outskirts of the cities and the play of interest in the political gamble of the oligarchies; the panorama of a semi-colonial country, producer of raw materials and almost exclusively dependent on the North-American solar system.

ecuatoriano. He was not tied to conventional realism; one of his most successful stories, 'Guasintón', is about a giant lizard, 'señor feudal de las aguas montuvias' [the feudal lord of the *montuvio* waters] and his death with the coming of progress. But even in a more obviously political story, it is not an ideological point but the illumination of the character of the *montuvio* which provides the main centre of interest. In 'El santo nuevo' [The New Saint], for instance, a peasant who witnesses a Communist's successful defiance of the boss's son lights a candle before the portrait of Lenin and attributes the miracle to this new saint.

Los Sangurimas is one of the best examples of Ecuadorian realist writing. The novel relates the history of a violent family, the sons and grandchildren of Nicasio Sangurima, who had been born and brought up in a violent vendetta atmosphere. He was the son of a white foreigner and an Indian mother; his father had been killed by one of his mother's brothers, she, in her turn had killed the murderer and fled to the wild, uncultivated lands where Nicasio grew up and which he came to dominate as a feudal baron. His sons and their children form a veritable tribe at war with one another and with the surrounding countryside, until one night a granddaughter is carried off by three of her cousins, raped and killed. The resulting scandal brings the police to the region, the men are rounded up and Nicasio's power broken. The novel was undoubtedly based on an actual backlands incident which de la Cuadra elaborates into a powerful, ruthless drama that pivots on the character of the old patriarch Nicasio, a man who is identified with the beauty and destructive force of nature and who favours among his children and grandchildren those who are as violent and cruel as the land he loves. Here, for example, is a description of the river which runs through Nicasio's estate and which like Nicasio himself is both destructive and beautiful:

El río de los Mameyes debe más vidas de hombre y animales que otro río cualquiera del litoral ecuatoriano.

Durante las altas crecientes, se ven pasar velozmente, aguas abajo, cadáveres humanos, inflados, moraduzcos, y restos de perros, de terneros, de vacas y caballos ahogados. En cierta época del año, para los llenos del Carnaval y la Semana Santa, sobre todo, se ven también cadáveres de monos, de jaguares, de osos frente-blanca y más alimañas de la selva subtropical. Sin duda, para entonces, el río de los Mameyes hincha sus cabeceras y se desparrama sobre la selva lejana, haciendo destrozos.

El río de los Mameyes sabe una canción muy bonita y la va cantando constantemente.

Al principio, encanta al eschucharla. Luego, fastidia. A la larga termina uno
por acostumbrarse a ella, hasta casi no darse cuenta de que se la está oyendo.
Esta canción la hacen sus aguas al rozar los pedruscos profundos.
Parece que esa canción tuviera dulces palabras, que el río fuera musitando.*

This passage shows that Ecuadorian realism was not without lyrical
quality, nor in the case of José de la Cuadra was it without objectivity.
The novelist nowhere invites the reader to side with the police against
the Sangurimas nor with one faction of the Sangurima family against
another. They seem no more responsible for their violence than nature
itself.

Demetrio Aguilera Malta and Enrique Gil Gilbert

The novels of Aguilera Malta and Gil Gilbert have a more obvious
ideological bias than the works of José de la Cuadra. Two of Aguilera
Malta's novels, *Don Goyo* (1933) and *La isla virgen* (1942), are set in the
tropical islands off the coast of Ecuador. As in *Los Sangurimas*, the central character reflects the power, violence and fecundity of nature.
Don Goyo is the self-appointed leader of a group of islanders who fish
and cut mangrove, and at his death he becomes a legendary figure,
whose shadow is still seen walking the land. By making Don Goyo a
mythical figure, Aguilera Malta avoids one of the difficulties faced by
the socialist realist writer who wishes to end his novel on a positive
note although there was in reality little hope of changing the economic
situation. Nevertheless, the novel leaves us in little doubt that Don Goyo
and his men represent an enclave of relative economic freedom which
does not apply to the rest of the country. Aguilera Malta shows this
through the adventures of Cusumbo, an escaped serf whose early life
is described in the first part of the novel. It is a life of sheer slavery:

...él siguió pagando. Todos los días, todas las semanas, todos los meses, todos
los años.

---

* The Mameyes River is responsible for more lives of animals and men than any other
river of the Ecuadorian coast.
  In the high floods, one can see passing swiftly downstream human bodies, bloated
and darkish and the remains of drowned dogs, of calves, of cows and horses. During
certain times of the year, during the Lent and Easter floods especially, there are also the
bodies of monkeys, jaguars, white-headed bears and other beasts of the subtropical
jungle. Doubtless at this time, the headwaters of the Mameyes River are swollen and
spread out over the distant jungle, doing damage.
  The Mameyes River knows a pleasant song which it sings continuously.
  At first it is beautiful to listen to, then boring, and finally one gets used to it until
one almost forgets that one hears it.
  This song comes from the waters rubbing against the deep pebbles.
  It is as if the song had sweet words that the river mumbled.

Fue a manera de un rosario de labores. Siempre sobre él la voz autoritaria del amo:
'Cusumbo. Anda a desyerbar. El arrozal está lleno de monte.'
'Ta bien, patrón.'
Desde la mañana hasta la noche. En cuclillas. Separando bien las calles de las plantas lanceoladas. Bajo el sol o bajo la lluvia. Sudoroso, jadeante. Rumiando en silencio su dolor y su desgracia. Mirando distraídamente el vuelo de los tíos-tíos. Hasta que la campana sonara, anunciando el final de la jornada. Y al regresar. La misma voz-látigo del amo.
'Cusumbo. Anda a vaquear. Anda solo. Vos no necesitás que te ayuda nadie.'*

This emphasis on the physical suffering of the workers is a characteristic of the majority of these realistic novels, as is the detailed description of the serf's agricultural tasks. Gil Gilbert's *Nuestro pan* [*Our Bread*] (1941), a novel set in the rice-fields, is an excellent example of this combination of documentary techniques with an ideological framework which shows the rise of a family of rice 'barons'. Here, for instance, is the description of the rice harvest, with its emphasis on the courage and the suffering of the labourers:

Apenas emergían desde sus pechos. Las mujeres tenían sus senos junto a las espigas. Los sombreros de los chicos salían un poco más alto que los pechos de los hombres.
El sol venía aún rojo. Casi desde la altura del suelo enviaba sus rayos. Era increíble que la sombra se proyectaba hacia abajo en vez de ser hacia arriba.
Iban cortando la espiga. Dorada, llena de vainillas pequeñas en cada una guardaba un grano de arroz blanco. Cortaban el tallo, y lo metían en un cajón que estaba en su delante, junto al pecho y la barriga...
El negro Pío no lleva cajón. Un saco de cabuya le cuelga sobre una pierna y allí deposita el grano que arranca. Con la boca llena de humo de cigarro lo echa con una canción bronca. Nunca nadie había oído cantar al negro. Por eso ahora lo escuchaban. Su canción recuerda el galope lejano de un bombo. No dice palabras. Se espanta los mosquitos. A él acuden porque es negro. Está tiznado de blanco donde tiene lodo. Su piel está escamosa, como de culebra. A veces sale de allí una gotita roja de sangre igual a la cabeza de esos alfileres que la tienen de vidrio rojo.†

---

* ...He went on paying. Every day, every week, every month, every year.
It was like a rosary of labour. The authoritarian voice of the boss always over him:
'Cusumbo. Go and weed. The rice field is full of weeds.'
'Alright, boss.'
From morning to night. Crouched down. He separates the rows of lance-shaped plants carefully. In sun or rain. Sweating, panting. Mulling silently over his pain and hard luck. Absent-mindedly watching the flights of the *tío-tíos*. Until the bell rang that announced the end of the day. And on his return the same whip-like voice of the boss.
'Cusumbo! Go and bring the cows in. Go alone. You don't need anyone to help you.'
† They just emerged chest-high. The women's breasts were on a level with the shoots. The children's hats emerged higher than the breasts of the men.

Like José de la Cuadra, Gil Gilbert does not divide his exploiters and exploited into black and white figures. The rice baron and former bandit Hermógenes Sandoval is a vigorous, larger-than-life character whose energy and fecundity is that of tropical nature. Sensuality, so predominant in these tropical novels, is an integral factor of life, as in this scene where Captain Sandoval courts his future wife:

Desde el río llegaba una brisa rumorante. Mariposas de terciopelo azul y rojo volaban alocadas en busca de polen. Ramas de ciruelo deshojadas y llenas de fruta pulposa, manchaban ya el día de rojo y amarillo. Caminaron juntos. A veces el pelo de Magdalena rozaba la piel de Sandoval. Latigazo en caballo chúcaro. Arponazo en tiburón. Relámpago en noche negra.*

The rise of a workers' movement at the end seems almost incidental in a novel whose main emphasis is on the inexhaustible fertility of tropical nature.

Alfredo Pareja Diezcanseco

Pareja Diezcanseco is the widest ranging of the Guayaquil writers. His main works include *Río arriba* [*Downriver*] (1931); *El muelle* [*The Dock*] (1933); *La Beldaca* (1935)—the story of a small freighter; *Baldomera* (1938); *Hechos y hazañas de don Balón de Baba y de su amigo Inocente Cruz* [*Facts and Deeds about Don Balón de Baba and his Friend, Inocente Cruz*] (1939); *Hombres sin tiempo* [*Men Without Time*] (1941)— an ambitious political novel in three volumes—and *Las tres ratas* [*The Three Rats*]. While for most of the Ecuadorian realists woman only exists as an object of male lust, Pareja Diezcanseco drew a number of outstanding female characters of the lower classes. The eponymous

---

The sun was still red. Its rays were shining almost level with the ground. It was incredible that the shadow fell downwards instead of upwards.

They were cutting the shoots. Golden, full of small husks, in each one there was a grain of white rice. They cut the stalk and put it in a box which was in front near their chests and stomachs.

The negro Pío had no box. A hemp sack hangs on one of his legs and there he deposits the grain he cuts off. With his mouth full of cigarette smoke, he throws it in with a joking song. Nobody had ever heard the negro sing. But now they listened to him. His song is like the distant gallop of a drum. He does not sing in words. He brushes off mosquitoes. They come to him because he is black. He is daubed with white where he is muddy. His skin is scaly like a snake's. Sometimes a little red drop of blood comes out like the head of a pin with a red glass head.

* From the river came a murmuring breeze. Blue and red velvet butterflies flew madly in search of pollen. Branches of leafless plum, full of pulpy fruit, already stained the daylight with red and yellow. They walked together. Sometimes the skin of Magdalena brushed the skin of Sandoval. Whiplash on a wild horse, harpoon in a shark, lightning on a black night.

heroine of *Baldomera* is a mulatta who makes a heroic self-sacrifice on behalf of her lover during the 1922 workers' massacre in Guayaquil. *Las tres ratas* is the tragic story of three sisters who come to live alone in Guayaquil. The heroine of *El muelle* is a simple cook and washer-woman, María del Socorro, whose beauty attracts the attention of a landlord and capitalist, Angel Mariño. Her refusal to put up with Mariño's attentions brings ruin on herself and her husband. The lust of Angel Mariño contrasts with the more innocent and joyous sensuality of María del Socorro's employer, doña Florencia, as she sits watching labourers carry sacks of cocoa beans with their delicious smell:

...se moría de gusto cuando el cacahuero se echaba sobre los hombres desnudos los dos quintales y salía trotando y trotando hasta la calle por llevarlos al muelle, donde un lanchón esperaba la carga que conducía al buque anclado en medio río.
Y qué fragancia! Era lo que más le gustaba. Toda la casa de Doña Florencia se envolvía en el olor de cacao, agridulce acariciante. Hinchaba sus delgadas narices y lanzaba suspiros con los ojos entrecerrados.*

With Jorge Icaza, Pareja Diezcanseco is one of the few writers to set the plot of his novel within the wider framework of international politics. *El muelle* includes scenes set in New York during the depression and the fate of María Socorro and her husband are linked with a world economic crisis. And the trilogy, *Hombres sin tiempo* [*Men Without Time*], set in Quito, deals with the revolutionary years of the late '20s and early '30s and with the social changes of this period.

Jorge Icaza (1906–)

Probably the most internationally famous of the Ecuadorian realists is Jorge Icaza, author of the Indianist novel *Huasipungo* (1934) which will be considered in the next section. His main theme was the exploitation of the sierra Indian and the situation of the *cholo*. *En las calles* [*On the Streets*] (1935) was based on an actual historical incident of the 'four-day battle' between two opposing political factions. It concerns an Indian who joins the army to find himself shooting against his own people. He dies urging the soldiers on his side not to shoot at their

---

* She was overcome with joy when the cocoa workers lifted the two-hundredweight sacks on his bare shoulders and went trotting, trotting to the street to carry them to the dock where a lighter awaited the load to take it to the boat anchored in midstream.
And what fragrance! That was what she liked most. The whole of doña Florencia's house was enveloped in the scent of cocoa, bittersweet and caressing. She dilated her thin nostrils and sighed, her eyes half-closed.

fellows. *Cholos* [*Half-breeds*] (1938) has a similar theme. In this case, the *cholo* protagonist identifies himself with Montoya, the contrabandist and exploiter, against the Indians, until Montoya's ruthlessness forces him to see the evil of the situation and identify himself with the oppressed.

In style, Icaza is the most uncompromising of the Ecuadorian realists. There is little lyricism in his works. The style is terse and the concentration wholly on the sordidness of life. He uses dialect and transcription of Indian pronunciation far more than his compatriots. The following short passage is a good example of what Spanish critics term 'infrarealism', that is, a realism that concentrates on the basest aspects of life.

Sonó la mañana en la torre. Las misas empezaron a sucederse. Toda la gente estaba en pie. La limosna cayó sobre los charoles de la iglesia. Una decena de clérigos rezaban responsos por veinte centavos y un sucre.[1] Casi todos los romeriantes tenían sus muertos queridos, y el negocio fue redondo para la clerigalla.

   'Por el alma del Jacinto, taita curita.'
   '¿De a cómo?'
   'Di'a sucre ha de ser taita curita para que salga pronto.'
   'Por el alma de Ricardo.'
   'De mi mama, tan.'
   'De mi hijita, tan. . .'*

We notice how much more loaded this type of description is with criticism of the exploiting class than were the passages quoted from other Ecuadorian writers. The use of words like 'clerigalla' and the priest's preoccupation with money sway the readers' sympathies irresistibly. This type of realism is very far from José de la Cuadra's attempt at objectivity.

SUMMARY

This brief survey of Ecuadorian realism is intended to show that terms such as 'realism' or 'social protest' have little validity in themselves and can only be considered in relation to specific novels. Icaza's

---

* The morning bell sounded in the tower. Masses began to be celebrated one after another. The people stood. Money fell onto the enamelled dishes. About ten priests prayed for twenty centavos and a *sucre*. Almost all the pilgrims had beloved dead ones and business boomed for the priesthood.
   'For the soul of Jacinto, father priest.'
   'How much?'
   'For one *sucre*, father, so that he'll come out soon.'
   'For the soul of Ricardo.'
   'For my mother.'
   'For my little daughter.'

realism is based on a careful and narrow selection of sordid details and cruel incidents. José de la Cuadra sees man and the environment as one, and therefore avoids explicit or implicit judgments on his characters. In Aguilera Malta's and Gil Gilbert's novels, lyrical and sensual aspects of nature temper the theme of exploitation. In Aguilera Malta's *Don Goyo* there is even an anticipation of the 'realismo mágico' which will be discussed in the next chapters. Pareja Diezcanseco's realism extends beyond the local and regional to include the impact of other societies and their economies on Ecuador.

This variety even within the confines of Ecuadorian realism applies to all social-protest and realistic writing, which should be seen within the context of the national literature if it is properly to be understood. However, the following is a brief guide to some social-protest novels in other countries.

COSTA RICA: Carlos Luis Fallas (1911–) in *Mamita Yunaí* (1941) tells the story of the exploited peasant masses, especially in the banana plantations.

PUERTO RICO: Enrique A. Laguerre (1906–) described the Puerto Rican peasant in *Solar Montoya* (1947).

MEXICO: José Mancisidor (1895–1956) wrote a Communist interpretation of the Revolution, *La asonada* [*The Demonstration*] (1931).

MANUEL ROJAS AND CHILEAN REALISM

Realism was not invariably linked with social protest and didacticism. The work of Manuel Rojas has some of the qualities of Gorky; like the Russian author, Rojas's own life is an inexhaustible source of material. Born in Buenos Aires in 1896, he crossed the Andes on foot in 1912 in order to find work in Santiago. Here he lived with a number of anarchists, learned to paint doors and windows and also became an electrician, and he later worked on boats in Valparaiso, before joining a theatre company as prompter. From this raw material, he constructed his best books, *Lanchas en la bahía* [*Boats in the Bay*] (1931) and *Hijo de ladrón* [*Thief's Son*] (1951). The first is about a boy who works as a watchman on the barges and later as a docker and stevedore. He takes a prostitute as a mistress, fights over her, is put in prison and then released. The story is told in the first person in a laconic style devoid of sentimentality and emotionalism, with few adjectives and more action than description. This is a realism that concentrates on the events of a man's life, on work relationships and techniques, and on the pressures that the objective world places upon him. *Hijo de ladrón* which is also a first-person story, is the story of the wanderings of a young man who at the beginning of the novel leaves prison in Valparaiso. Interspersed with his first meetings and jobs after leaving prison is an account of his childhood in Buenos Aires, where his father was a burglar. In Chile, he works at a variety of jobs, finds himself in prison after a riot and finally with two friends, the 'philosopher' and a painter Cristían, he leaves to work on the coast.

The novel has the unity of life; the events are imposed by work and by the necessity of earning money, or they happen by chance. The burglar father is caught; the youth finds himself in the streets during rioting and plundering and attacks the police because he has seen them beating a man. Rojas's realism is thus quite different from the 'directed' realism of Icaza, since unlike the latter, he does not seem to want to show us anything except the movement of life as it is lived by the poorest city-dwellers. Here, for instance, is a passage in which quite suddenly, without knowing how, the youth finds himself in the middle of a rioting city:

Las calles perpendiculares al mar se veían desiertas, como si fueran de otra ciudad y no de aquélla, y esto sin duda porque en ellas no había negocios o los había en muy pequeña cantidad; a pesar de ello, pocos faroles conservaban aún sus vidrios. Las paralelas a la playa, en cambio, estaban llenas de gente, sobre todo la avenida a que llegué, en donde ardía, en pleno fuego, la violenta llama: ya no eran cincuenta sino quinientos o mil quinientos los hombres que llenaban la cuadra en que me sorprendiera la carga de la caballería policial: habían bajado quien sabe desde qué cerro y por qué callejones o quebradas, Lecheros o Calaguala, Las Violetas o La Cárcel, El Barón o la Cabritería o quizá surgido de los talleres, del dique, de los barcos, de las chatas; algunos llevaban aún su saquillo con carbón o leña y se veía a varios con los pantalones a media pierna, mostrando blancos calzoncillos; otros iban descalzos y un centenar de ellos bullía alrededor de dos tranvías que eran destruidas centímetro por centímetro; primero los vidrios que la gente pisaba y convertía al fin en una especia de brillante harina.*

* The streets that went straight down to the sea were deserted as if it were some other city not that one, and this doubtless because in these streets were no shops or if there were, only in small numbers. Despite this, few lamp-posts still had glass in them. On the other hand the streets parallel to the shore were full of people, especially the avenue in which I had arrived and in which blazed the violent flame. There were no longer fifty but five hundred or fifteen hundred which filled the block where the police cavalry charge had surprised me. They had come down who knows from what hill, by which alleys and ravines, Lecheros or Calaguala, Las Violetas or La Cárcel, El Barón or La Cabritería, or perhaps they had come up from the workshops, from the quay, from the boats, from the barges. Some still carried sacks of coal and wood and there were many wearing their trousers rolled half-way up their legs showing white underpants. Others were barefoot, and about a hundred rushed around two trams which they had destroyed centimetre by centimetre; first the windows which the people trampled to pieces, and made finally into a sort of brilliant flour.

The scene begins in deserted silent streets and ends with the sudden violence of the mob pulverising the trams, but the violence appears to come from nowhere as if conjured by the city itself.

Rojas is the major realist writer of Latin America, the technique he chooses being perfectly moulded to the exigencies of material that is very near to working life.

THE INDIANIST NOVEL

One special branch of regional and social-protest novels is that which deals with the Indians. Indianist literature has been written entirely by non-Indians and has inevitably suffered because of this. But since the publication of *Aves sin nido* by Clorindo Matto de Turner and *Raza de bronce* by Alcides Arguedas there has been increasing accuracy and depth in such writing. Realism was an instrument in achieving accuracy although it finally proved inadequate.

Since the 1920s, Indianism in literature has gone through a number of stages:

1 Simple documentary exposure of conditions, and particularly of inhumanity in the treatment of the Indian. Examples of this literature are the stories of López Albújar in Peru and *El indio* by the Mexican novelist, Gregorio López y Fuentes.

2 The Indians seen as the equivalent of the proletariat and the source of future revolutionary militancy. Examples of this are *El mundo es ancho y ajeno* [*The World is Broad and Alien*] by Ciro Alegría (Peru, 1909–67) and *Huasipungo* by Jorge Icaza (Ecuador).

3 The sociological study of the Indian in *Juan Pérez Jolote* (1952) by Ricardo Pozas.

4 The attempt to comprehend the Indian mind through his mythology, poetry and legend. This has given rise to the best Indianist writing to date, as exemplified in novels by Rosario Castellanos (Mexico), Miguel Angel Asturias (Guatemala) and José María Arguedas (Peru), whose novels break with realism.

The Mexican Revolution transformed the national stereotype from a predominantly white Europeanised Mexican to a dark, predominantly Indian type. The roots of Mexican national culture were sought not in European but in pre-Columbian tradition, and a school of mural painters which emerged after the Revolution covered walls of public buildings with paintings many of which depicted the Indians of the past or present in their characteristic dress, or glorified Indian chiefs like Cuauhtémoc. Contemporary European interest in non-European cultures further stimulated interest in pre-Columbian civilisations and modern Indian customs. In other countries with large Indian populations—Peru, Ecuador, Bolivia, Guatemala—left-wing nationalist movements emerged which stressed the importance of the cultural contribution of the Indian to national life. In Peru, for instance, the Communist politician and essayist, José Carlos Mariátegui, wrote a number of important essays in his review, *Amauta*, on the Indian and on the place of Indianists in Peruvian literature.

The first stage in coming to some understanding of the Indian was undoubtedly through knowledge and understanding of his way of life. This could only be done by attempting to see the Indian within his own culture and not with the eyes of an outsider. *El indio* [*The Indian*], by the Mexican Gregorio López y Fuentes, is a *costumbrista* description of the daily life of an Indian village which the Revolution leaves almost unchanged. In Peru, *Cuentos andinos* [*Andean tales*] (1920) and *Nuevos cuentos andinos* [*New Andean Stories*] (1937) by Enrique López Albújar (1872–) consisted of carefully-observed anecdotes of Indian life by a man who had served as judge in the hill town of Huanuco. He differs from 'ideological' Indianist writers in that he is less concerned than they are with economic exploitation and prefers anecdotes which reveal Indian character. Usually the anecdote is based on a crime or court-case where the author's first-hand experience had given him valuable source material on the Indian character. He thus tends to show us events through the point of view of the Indian himself. In 'Ushanan-Jampi', for instance, he describes the Indian communities' expulsion of a thief and the vengeance they wreak on him. The author makes no judgment but limits himself to observation of the way the Indians behave. 'El licenciado Aponte' [The Lawyer Aponte], for instance, concerns an Indian's return to his native community after serving in the army and his failure to adapt himself to the life of the village which forces him to become an outlaw. Even here, where the central character is an outlaw, he is an outlaw who has belonged to an Indian community and who allows us insight into it. The Indians of the *Cuentos andinos* are totally different from the whites in attitude but they nevertheless had dignity and an authentic way of life that does not need to draw on European or Western religious and moral codes. Here, for instance, is the elder of a tribe drinking poisoned *chicha*[1] rather than give his consent to the election of Ponciano Culqui as headman.

El indio, olímpicamente desdeñoso apuró, a grandes tragos la bebida fatal, mientras los demás *yayas*,[1] pálidos, sudorosos, trémulos, vacilantes, con las pupilas casi apagadas por el soplo de la muerte, aprobaban, con marcados movimientos de cabeza, este apóstrofe del feroz Huaylas:

'Ponciano Culqui, alcalde hechizo y mostrenco, aprende a morir como nosotros para cuando te llegue la hora, que deseamos pronto...'*

Icaza and Alegría

Both Jorge Icaza's *Huasipungo* and Ciro Alegrías *El mundo es ancho y ajeno* [*Broad and Alien is the World*] use the expulsion of Indians from traditionally-owned lands as the pivot on which the action of their novels turns. In *Huasipungo*, the Indians are without humanity. Treated like beasts, they behave like beasts. The novel takes place on the estate of Alfonso Pereira who, having found himself in financial difficulties, decides to accept help from an American petroleum company. But this is only given on condition that he build a road through his property and clears away the Indian *huasipungos* or holdings in order to make way for buildings. The novel describes this operation in which many Indian lives are lost on the road-building and in which famine hits the village when there is no longer food produced on the land. The Indians finally rise in protest, only to be defeated by troops sent against them. Icaza is not concerned with showing human Indians since the situation he describes is essentially inhuman. Both oppressor and victim had become degenerate, and the Indians are invariably used as if they are animals or objects. For instance, the wife of an Indian is taken as wet nurse by the white woman and her own child starves. In places too difficult for horses to pass, the Indians carry their masters on their shoulders. The degradation reaches its lowest when the Indians steal rotten meat to satisfy their hunger and one of them dies. The first glimpse of the Indian village almost at the beginning of the novel sets the note of sadness and sordidness which pervades the whole book:

Atardecía cuando la cabalgata entró en el pueblo de Tomachi. El invierno, los vientos de páramo de las laderas cercanas, la miseria y la indolencia de las gentes, la sombra de las altas cumbres que acorrallan, han hecho de aquel lugar un nido de lodo, de basura, de tristeza, de actitud acurrucada y defensiva. Se acurrucan las chozas a lo largo de la única vía fangosa; se acurrucan los pequeños a la puerta de

* The Indian with Olympian disdain drank with great draughts the fatal drink, while the other *yayas*, pale, sweating, tremulous, hesitant, with their pupils almost extinguished by the breath of death, approved with firm movements of the head this apostrophe of the ferocious Huaylas:

'Ponciano Culqui, evil-doing and monstrous mayor, learn to die like us when the hour arrives that we hope will be soon.'

las viviendas a jugar con el barro podrido o a masticar el calofrío de un viejo paludismo; se acurrucan las mujeres junto al fogón, tarde y mañana a hervir la mazmorra de *mashca* o el locro de *cuchipapa*;[1] se acurrucan los hombres de seis a seis, sobre el trabajo de la chacra, de la montaña, del páramo o se pierden por los caminos tras de las mulas que llevan cargas a los pueblos vecinos; se acurruca el murmullo del agua de la acequia tatuada a lo largo de la calle, de la acequia de agua turbia donde sacian la sed los animales de los huasipungos vecinos, donde los cerdos hacen camas de lodo para refrescar sus ardores, donde los niños se ponen en cuatro para beber, donde se orinan los borrachos.*

The whole village and everything in it is pictured as crouching down in humiliation; animals and men live on the same level, and the high Andes, magnificent as the mountains are, only serve as a wall which encircles the prison of the village.

Although fundamentally the novel follows the same plan at *Huasipungo, El mundo es ancho y ajeno* by Ciro Alegría is far from the infrarealism of Icaza. Alegría had spent his childhood on his grandfather's estate, where he gained first-hand knowledge of the Indians. Later in life, he worked at a variety of jobs, including journalism and he was also an active member of the A.P.R.A. party, as a result of which he was first imprisoned and later went to Chile into exile. His first publication was the novel *La serpiente de oro* [*The Golden Serpent*] (1935) set among the river villagers of the Marañón, the tropical region where he had been born. This was followed in 1938 by *Los perros hambrientos* [*Hungry Dogs*], set among the sierra Indians. In 1941 he won a North-American literary prize with his *El mundo es ancho y ajeno* [*Broad and Alien is the World*].

This novel closely reflects the political programme of A.P.R.A.— at least in its earlier days. A.P.R.A. was a left-wing nationalist party whose leader, Haya de la Torre, adhered to certain Marxist principles although he did not wish to found a Communist Party. What he wanted was an alliance between left-wing intellectuals and workers,

* It was growing dark when the cavalcade entered the village of Tomachi. Winter, the winds of the wastelands from the nearby slopes, the poverty and indolence of the people, the shadow of the high peaks which hemmed it in, have made that place a nest of mud, rubbish, sadness, of crouching and defensive attitudes. The huts crouch by the side of the one muddy road; the little ones crouch at the door of the houses to play with rotting earth or to get over the shivering left from a past attack of malaria. The women crouch at the fire, night and morning to boil the porridge of *mashca* or the stew of *cuchipapa*. The men crouch from six in the morning till six at night in the work of the farm or the mountain or the plain or they are lost along the roads behind mules which carry loads to neighbouring towns; the murmur of water from the drains tattooed the length of the street also crouched—the drains of muddy water in which animals from the neighbouring *huasipungos* drank, in which pigs made mudbeds to refresh their hot skins, in which children went on all fours to drink, in which the drunks made water.

and for this reason he named his party *Alianza popular revolucionaria americana* (hence, A.P.R.A.). In *El mundo es ancho y ajeno* there are reflected two important characteristics of Peruvian life as propounded by contemporary political thinkers. Firstly, the importance of the Indian communal spirit which, they believed, made the Peruvian Indians singularly fitted to accept some form of socialism. Secondly, the importance of education and experience of the world outside the Indian community if the Indians were to become integrated into a modern Peru.

El mundo es ancho y ajeno is thus divided into two parts. In the first part, the Indian commune exists as it had always done under the leadership of Rosendo Maqui who has inherited the accumulated wisdom of his race. But Rosendo's traditional knowledge is powerless when a covetous landowner uses all the resources of modern law and state organisation to gain control of the communal lands. The Indians appeal to the white man's law but find it does not work in their favour. Rosendo is put into prison when he tries to resist, and he dies there after being beaten by the guards after another prisoner had escaped. The second stage of resistance is carried on by Benito Castro, Rosario's adopted son and the offspring of a white father. Benito is able to carry on the struggle at a more sophisticated level because he has lived outside the village, knows how to read and write and has worked in trade union and other organisations. Thus he has the ideological training necessary to organise the village commune, settle it on new lands and teach the Indians about the modern state. But his efforts also fail. This time troops are sent against the commune, and when the Indians resist they die to the last man.

Compared with Icaza, Alegría's picture of Indian village life before its destruction by the white man is an idyllic one. The source of evil is 'bad governments': the solution is to reform in order to bring real democracy into effect:

Estas autoridades de este distrito son explotadores e incondicionales instrumentos también de explotación de los gamonales. Los distritos son las pequeñas células de nuestra nacionalidad donde en primer lugar se incuban los gérmenes del mal; estoy seguro de que si en cada uno de estos diminutos pueblos llegáramos a extirpar radicalmente el mal en toda su amplitud, llegaríamos a constituir una verdadera democracia llena de justicia y libertá.*

* These authorities of this district are exploiters and are also unconditional instruments of the exploitation by the bosses. The rural districts are the small cells of our nation where the germs of evil are first incubated; I am sure that if in each of these diminutive communities we could manage to radically uproot the evil in all its extension, we should manage to constitute a true democracy full of justice and liberty.

Unlike Icaza, Alegría shows us an Indian communal life that is more rather than less human than that of more sophisticated people. The very simplicity seems a virtue. Contrast, for instance, this view of a village with the passage previously quoted from *Huasipungo*:

Va cayendo la tarde y el sol toma un tinte dorado. Abajo, en el caserío, el vaquero Inocencio está encerrando los terneros y las madres lamentan con inquietos bramidos la separación. Una india de pollera colorada va por el senderillo que cruza la plaza. Curvado bajo el peso de un gran haz, avanza un leñador por media calle y ante la puerta de la casa de Amaro Santos se ha detenido un jinete. El alcalde colige que debe ser el mismo Amaro Santos quien le pidió un caballo para ir a verificar algunas diligencias en el pueblo cercano. Ya desmonta y entra a la casa con andar pausado. El es.*

This is not so much a description of village life as it actually is but of an ideal community in which one man feels responsible for his neighbour. Yet, as Alegría recognised, the ideal was impossible in modern Peru, and he illustrates this graphically by the ending of the novel in which the dying Benito is interrogated by his wife.

'¿Adónde iremos? ¿Adónde?' implora Marguicha, mirando con los ojos locos al marido, al hijo, al mundo, a su soledad.
Ella no lo sabe y Benito ha muerto ya. Más cerca, cada vez más cerca, el estampido de los máuseres continúa sonando.†

The novel gives an idealised rather than a fully realistic picture of the Indian, yet it is undoubtedly a landmark in the Indianist novel for it avoids the sordidness of Icaza's approach and the reader's consequent alienation from the Indian victims while at the same time avoiding the other extreme of *costumbrista* picturesqueness.

THE SOCIOLOGICAL VIEW: 'JUAN PÉREZ JOLOTE'

The logical outcome of the novelists' attempts to portray the Indian with verisimilitude was the sociological approach. In novels such as

---

* Night is falling and the sun has a golden tint. Below in the village, the cowman Inocencio is shutting the calves in, and their mothers lament the separation with restless lowing. An Indian woman with a coloured skirt is going along the little path that crosses the square. Bent below the weight of a great bundle, the woodcutter advances up the middle of the street and before the door of Amaro Santos's house a horseman has stopped. The mayor guesses that it is that same Amaro Santos who asked him for a horse to go and do some business in the nearby town. He dismounts and enters the house with slow steps. It is he.

† 'Where shall we go? Where?' implores Marguicha, looking at her husband, at her son, at the world, at her solitude with distraught eyes.
She does not know, and Benito has already died. Nearer, ever nearer, the explosion of the Mausers continues to resound.

Aves sin nido [*Birds Without a Nest*], the author had had to depend on his own observation and had no scientific guide to Indian life and customs. It was not until the 1950s, when sociological surveys of Indian villages had been made, that the novel incorporated his new knowledge. The anthropologist Francisco Rojas González (1905–51) published a series of short stories *El diosero* [*The Godmaker*] in 1952 and in these gave an accurate picture of Indian attitudes. In the same year there appeared *Juan Pérez Jolote*, a novel which described the life of a Chamula Indian, whose author Ricardo Pozas (1910–), was a trained social anthropologist who had made detailed academic studies of the Indian and had done field work in the area he described. Yet *Juan Pérez Jolote* has novelistic elements. It is written as a first-person narrative and the narrator undergoes certain personal as opposed to merely typical experiences. For instance, he takes part in the Mexican revolutionary fighting and hence comes to learn about life outside the village and to speak Spanish. However, as the author insists, the character is typical in all other respects:

No es una biografía excepcional; por el contrario, es perfectamente normal dentro de su medio, salvo las causas que obligaron a nuestro biografiado a salir de su pueblo.*

From a literary point of view the most interesting aspect of the work is the attempt to reproduce Indian psychological attitudes in the Spanish language. Here for instance is a characteristic passage:

Todos los días, desde que llegué, iba con mi mamá a traer leña al monte. Una vez fuimos los tres, mi papá, mi mamá y yo, a traer leña; llevábamos una bestia que era muy cimarrona; no se dejaba cargar; yo detenía el lazo de la bestia; pero mi mamá no aguantaba la carga de leña que iba a ponerle encima; entonces mi papá cogió una raja de leña y nos dio con ella. A mi mamá le pegó en la cabeza y el sacó sangre. Volvieron a cargar la bestia, y después de pegarle también a ella, recibió la carga.†

We notice here a great contrast with Ciro Alegría's attempts to record the thoughts passing through an Indian mind. This Chamula makes

---

* It is not an unusual life-story. On the contrary, it is a perfectly normal case within the environment, except for the reasons which obliged our protagonist to leave the village.
† Every day after I arrived I went with my mother to bring wood from the woods. Once we all three went—my father, my mother and myself—to bring wood. We took an animal that was very wild. It would not let us load it. I held the animal's halter but my mother could not carry the load of wood that she was going to put on top. Then my father took a piece of wood and hit us with it. He hit my mother on the head and drew blood. They went on loading the animal and after hitting it as well, it took the load.

no generalisations, nor does he enter into his father's emotions. It is the behaviour and its consequences that he records, using only simple sentences and repeating the key words many times. Pozas manages to maintain this simplicity even when dealing with more complex subject matter. Here, for instance, is Jolote's account of his difficulty in adapting himself to village life after serving in the army during the Revolution.

Yo les hablaba palabras en castilla y palabras en la lengua, porque no podía decirlo todo en la lengua. Ellos se reían de mí porque no decía bien las cosas en la lengua.*

Juan Pérez Jolote returns to the village, takes a wife, and accepts official positions in the village community. Because of his knowledge of Spanish, acquired in years of living outside his village, he even becomes school teacher. Yet he is still to some extent a victim of his environment. Village ceremonial requires much drinking of *aguardiente* [cane spirit] and he realises, without being able to avoid this, that he is doomed to die, as his father had done, from drink. His biography thus ends on a sad note:

A mi casa vienen a beber todos los días compañeros que llegan a comprar; me dan de lo que toman, y con todos tomo yo. 'Ya no tomes más', me dicen mi Lorenzo y mi Domingo, pero yo no puedo dejar de tomar. Hace días que ya no como... Así murió mi papá. Pero yo no quiero morirme. Yo quiero vivir.†

In these simple lines are summarised the complexity of the Indian problem in Mexico. The Indian has his identity, his language, his customs which have been handed down over centuries. But as never before, the Indian is assaulted by claims from a world outside his community, a world of laws and government which erodes his own culture. Inevitably his attitudes will change. Juan Pérez Jolote is the Indian of a transitional period, still an upholder of tradition, yet, whether he is conscious of it or not, awakening to the new. So, while he accepts the ritual drink of *aguardiente* as part of Chamula custom, his defiant 'Yo quiero vivir' [I want to live] already implies a criticism of the attitude of resignation with which his father had accepted such

---

* I spoke to them in Spanish and in words in my own tongue, but I could not say everything in my tongue. They laughed at me because I did not say things well in my own tongue.
† Friends who come to buy come to drink every day at my house. They give me what they drink and I drink with all of them. 'Don't drink any more', Lorenzo and Domingo say to me but I cannot stop drinking. I have not eaten for days. My father died like that. But I do not want to die. I want to live.

matters. The desire to live and the acceptance of a ritual that will prove harmful to him are the contradictions which will give rise to the new.

MYTH AND PSYCHOLOGICAL TRUTH

As long as the non-Indian interpreted the Indian mind through the language and literary forms of an alien culture, he was bound to present only a poor approximation. *Juan Pérez Jolote* attempted to create a language based on behaviour and its consequences rather than on abstractions and general concepts which the Indians may not have had. It was thus a step in the direction of accuracy. But a group of writers chose a quite different path, and one that was to be extremely fruitful. Miguel Angel Asturias (Guatemala, 1899–), Rosario Castellanos (Mexico, 1925–) and José María Arguedas (Peru, 1911–) are three authors who break with realism precisely because of the limitations of the genre when it came to representing the Indian. All three had lived in Indian areas, where they came into contact with Indian language, myth and song. Asturias went to Paris to study Maya language and anthropology at the *Musée de L'Homme*. Arguedas spoke Quechua before he spoke Spanish. All three found that by abandoning realism they gained in verisimilitude.

Miguel Angel Asturias

Asturias is a novelist whose scope extends far beyond Indianist writing and the body of his work will be dealt with in Chapter 9. His first published work, *Leyendas de Guatemala* [*Legends of Guatemala*] (1930), gave lyrical recreations of Guatemalan folk-lore many of which drew their inspiration from pre-Columbian and colonial sources.

Asturias's first Indianist novel was *Hombres de maíz* [*Men of Maize*] (1949) in which he resorted to legend but this time of his own creation. Using his knowledge of pre-Columbian literature, he reconstructed the story of the oppression of the Indians, the expropriation of their lands by men intent on the commercial exploitation of maize, and their gradual degeneration. This theme, apparently similar to the realist novel, was however expressed in terms of Indian myth; each stage in the degeneration of the Indian being presented in the form of a different myth-figure. And the time scheme of the novel is a mythic time in which many thousands of years may be compressed and seen as a single moment. The language, too, was a Spanish so structured as to be analogous to Indian languages.

Gaspar Ilóm, the first of the myth-figures presented by Asturias, is an Indian chief of the old type, completely identified with his land, able to communicate with plants, animals and the earth which are as sentient as himself. In the following passage, Asturias represents Ilóm with 'his head separated from his body', his thoughts being not simply identified with the earth but being the earth itself.

Así lo hablaba con la cabeza separada del cuerpo, picuda, caliente, envuelta en estropajo canoso de luna. Envejeció el Gaspar Ilóm mientras hablaba. Su cabeza había caído al suelo como un tiesto sembrado de piecitos de pensamientos. Lo que hablaba el Gaspar ya viejo era monte. Lo que pensaba era monte recordado, no era pelo nuevo. De las orejas le salía el pensamiento a oír el ganado que le pasaba encima.*

The technique here is more akin to poetry than to traditional prose writing, but we feel that this is a more authentic way of representing the Indian mind than, for example, the prose of Alegría.

Gaspar Ilóm leads a rebellion against the maize planters, is poisoned by his enemies but lives as a folk-hero. His enemy, Colonel Godoy, dies in the blazing forest, but his death appears as a magical act, the vengeance of nature.

Sólo el Coronel, clavado poro por poro en una tabla por los ojos de los buhos que seguirán viéndolo fijamente, quedará intacto con sus orejas, sus párpados, sus labios. Ni la ceniza del puro se le caerá. Manos de tiniebla esgrimiendo dagas lo obligarán a suicidarse.†

But the resistance of the Indians comes to an end. The next episodes of the novel deal with their alienation and this is presented through the character of the blind Indian Goyo Yic whose wife María Tecún has left him. A witch doctor cures his blindness so that he can look for his wife, and he has a vision of her, but whenever he approaches her she turns to a pillar of salt. In allegorical form the story is that of the Indians' alienation from the land which they have now lost. In the last part of the book, the central character, Nicho, is a postman who is also in search of his lost wife. Nicho's guardian spirit is a coyote

* Thus he spoke with his head separated from his body, pointed, warm, wrapped in the grey mop of the moon. Gaspar Ilóm grew old as he was speaking. His head had fallen to the ground like a flower pot sown with little feet of thoughts [*pensamientos* also means pansies]. Gaspar, now old, spoke and it was forest. What he thought was forest, it was not new hair. From his ears came his thought (pansy) on hearing the cattle passing over him.

† Only the colonel nailed pore by pore on a plank by the eyes of the owls that will go on staring at him, will remain intact with his ears, his eyelids, his lips. Not even the ash from his cigar will fall. Hands of the darkness, fencing with daggers, will make him commit suicide.

and he leaves his postman's bag and turns into a coyote in order to pursue his search. Nicho represents a third stage in the degeneration of Indian cultures, since as a postman he is a member of the white society, although he feels a strong, atavistic need to return to nature. At the end of the novel, the magic world of Indian legend has been lost. The characters, many of whom find themselves far from their country of origin in a penal colony near the coast, have lost not only liberty but also nearly all traces of their true culture. Though they foresee a distant time when Ilóm's son 'erguida estará en el tiempo que está por venir' [will stand erect in a time that is to come], the novel ends on a sombre note.

Volvieron pues, a Pisigüilito. Horconear de nuevo para construir un rancho más grande, porque sus hijos casados tenían muchos hijos y todos se fueron a vivir con ellos. Lujo de hombres y lujo de mujeres, tener muchos hijos. Viejos, niños, hombres y mujeres, se volvían hormigas después de la cosecha, para acarrear el maíz, hormigas, hormigas, hormigas, hormigas...*

The final tragedy of the Indian is that he had lost his legends and culture and without them is a mere labouring insect like an ant.

Rosario Castellanos

Less original in form that the novels of Miguel Angel Asturias, those of Rosario Castellanos nevertheless draw on the Indian legends and religious practices from the Chiapas region of southern Mexico. She is less concerned, however, with the interpretation of Indian attitudes than with the interpenetration of Indian and non-Indian cultures. Childhood experiences and the stories told her by her Indian nurses are the doors through which she enters the Indian world, but she generally shows this in conflict with the white or mestizo world. *Balún Canán* (1957) is told partly through the experiences of a seven-year-old girl whose family are landowners, threatened with expropriation when one of the post-revolutionary governments plans to distribute lands to the peasants. The child has an intuitive understanding of the Indian, since the deepest experiences of her childhood are connected with an Indian nurse. The novel is less successful when the author abandons the child narrator and adopts a third-person narration in order to show the growing self-confidence and defiance of the Indians when they realise that they have government backing. They set fire to the sugar press

---

* So they went back to Pisigüilito. Putting up poles again to construct a bigger hut because the married sons had many sons and all went to live with them. The men, the women, to have many children. Old men, children, men and women became ants after the harvest to transport the corn, ants, ants, ants, ants.

and their masters are driven from the estate to spend their time petitioning uselessly for the return of their lands. Now it is the non-Indian who is dispossessed, influenced more deeply than he knows by the indigenous culture which his conscious mind refuses to accept. The conflict of cultures is again the subject of a second novel, *Oficio de tinieblas* [*Office of Shadows*] (1962) in which the Indians resort to secret religious practices as a defence against the non-Indian's abuses. They are finally goaded to open rebellion and the rebellion is crushed; another sad defeat for the race.

José María Arguedas

With Asturias, Arguedas is the greatest living Indianist writer. As a child, he was brought up largely by Indians with whom his father, a lawyer who defended Indian rights, left him for long periods. He learned Quechua before he learned Castilian, became an expert on Indian music, song and customs, and early in his career published an anthology of Quechua lyrics with an introduction in which he defended the 'true' culture of Peru (i.e. Quechua culture) as against the imported culture. He claimed that the folk-music and poetry of the Indians was not only the predominant culture in the Indian villages of the sierra but that even non-Indians had been deeply affected by this. The true Peruvian culture, he felt, must be based on Quechua tradition since this was the only indigenous tradition in Peru. From the beginning, Arguedas found himself in difficulty, not knowing whether his stories should be written in Spanish or Quechua. If written in Spanish, they would lose authenticity. In a preface to a later edition of his first stories, he explained his difficulties:

¿En qué idioma se debía hacer hablar a los indios en la novela? Para el bilingüe, para quien aprendió a hablar en quechua, resulta imposible, de pronto, hacerlos hablar en castellano; en cambio, quien no los conoce a través de la niñez, de la experiencia profunda, puede quizá concebirlos expresándose en castellano. Yo resolví el problema creándoles un lenguaje castellano especial, que después ha sido empleado con horrible exageración en trabajos ajenos. ¡Pero los indios no hablan en ese castellano, ni con los de lengua española ni mucho menos entre ellos! Es una ficción. Los indios hablan en quechua. Toda la sierra del sur y del centro, excepción de algunas ciudades, es de habla quechua total. Es pues falso y horrendo presentar a los indios hablando en el castellano de los sirvientes quechuas aclimatados en la Capital. Yo, ahora, tras veinte años de esfuerzo, estoy intentando una traducción castellana de los diálogos de los personajes andinos de habla quechua.*

* In what language should one make the Indians speak in the novel? It is altogether impossible to make them speak Spanish if one is either bilingual or a native Quechua speaker. On the other hand, those who do not know them from childhood, through

Like Asturias, Arguedas was thus faced with the problem of finding a literary language analogous to Quechua, though he solved this in a manner totally different from the Guatemalan writer. His first story 'Agua', published in 1935, was amply sprinkled with Quechua phrases, and the Indians spoke in a kind of broken Spanish. The protagonist was a young boy stung to defiance by a landowner who refuses to distribute water to the Indians so that they can water their lands. This story, and his first novel, *Yawar Fiesta* (1940), which related the expulsion of a group of Indians from their communal lands, were similar in theme if not in language to many novels of protest. Arguedas's major works are two novels, *Los ríos profundos* [*Deep Rivers*] (1958) and *Todas las sangres* [*All the Bloods*] (1954). The first of these was closely based on biographical material. The young protagonist's father is a lawyer who is called to a distant village and leaves his son at a boarding school in a small town whose population are mostly Indian or *cholos*. The school is run by a religious order; its dour, anti-natural discipline, its isolation from the rest of the life of the town, have an evil effect on the boys. Their sexual repressions are released thanks to a poor imbecile who works in the kitchens; bullying and obscenity are commonplace. But outside there is another world, a world of great natural beauty, that of 'los ríos profundos' [the deep rivers], the world of the Indian with this poetry and his music. It is this world which has caught the imagination of the boy protagonist and to which he constantly escapes.

Arguedas's novels cannot only be discussed, however, in relation to Indian culture. Both his theme and technique go far beyond the limits of social protest and are better seen in relation to contemporary experiments in the novel.

SUMMARY

Realism rarely produces the greatest novels in Latin America. The treatment of the exploitation of the Indian, for example, was limited

---

deep experience, can perhaps conceive of them expressing themselves in Spanish. I solved the problem by creating a special Spanish for them, which has since been horribly exaggerated in other people's writing. But the Indians do not speak in that Spanish to other Spanish-speaking people, much less among themselves. It is a fiction. The Indians speak Quechua. All the southern highlands and the central highlands, except for some of the cities, are totally Quechua-speaking. Therefore it is horrible to represent the Indians speaking in the Castilian of Quechua servants who are acclimatised to the capital. After twenty years of effort, I am now trying a Spanish translation of the conversations of Andean people who speak Quechua.

rather than illuminated when the writer confined himself to an external verisimilitude. Significantly, most of the finest Spanish–American novels were to be published after the 1940s when writers finally began to explore new techniques with great freedom and to allow their 'balloons of fantasy' to slip further away from the ground.

THE AVANT-GARDE IN POETRY

THE BACKGROUND

In 1909, the Modernist poet Leopoldo Lugones published a volume of poems called *Lunario sentimental* [*Sentimental Lunarium*] in which he used free verse (still rare in Spanish), parody, comic metaphor and contemporary references to trams and policemen. The now tired Modernist idiom was abandoned, to be replaced by startling images and grotesque descriptions like the following lines on a chorus of cats:

> Mayando una melopea insana
> Con ayes de parto y de gresca,
> Gatos a la valeriana
> Deslizan por mi barbacana
> El suspicaz silencio de sus patas de yesca.*

'Yesca' is tinder which strikes a spark and starts a fire in the same way that the cat's claws can suddenly spark and become deadly weapons. The image is unusual, accurate and slightly comic. In the preface to this collection, Lugones had stressed the importance of investing these new images:

> ...hallar imágenes nuevas y hermosas, expresándolas con claridad y concisión es enriqucer el idioma, renovándolo a la vez...El idioma es un bien social, y hasta el elemento más sólido de las nacionalidades.†

While Lugones anticipates in these lines many of the theories of the avante-garde of the '20s, he was by no means an isolated experimenter. Even before 1920, poets were relatively unaffected by the didacticism and the realism of the novel. Under the influence of the French symbolists, they began to reject the view that poetry was a direct expression of feeling and to write poems that were like artefacts. Some of the

---

* Miaowing an insane chant with birth-pang groans and quarrels, valerian cats slide through my fortress on the suspicious silence of their tinder feet.
† ...to find new and beautiful images and express them with clarity and concision enriches the language and revives it. The language is a social good, and even the most solid basic element of nationality.

brief poems included in *Flores de cardo* [*Thistle Flowers*] by Pedro Prado, for instance, were of this type, like the following, 'Honey':

> La miel: aroma de flor
> con rayos de sol,
> de un rubio cristal
> de grato sabor.*

This sort of poetry grew naturally out of Modernism. Poets such as Pedro Prado (1886–1952), Guillermo Valencia (Colombia, 1873–1943), Porfirio Barba Jacob (Colombia, 1883–1942) and Lugones had had their roots in Modernism but greatly extended the range of symbols and metaphors. In Mexico, José Juan Tablada (1871–1945) experimented with the *haiku* of Japanese origin, taking yet another step towards 'pure poetry'. However, he did not go beyond a surface picturesqueness, as in his 'Sandía' [Watermelon].

> Del verano, roja y fría
> carcajada
> rebanada
> de sandía.†

Poetic experiment was further encouraged, perhaps, by the isolated position of the Spanish–American poet who was untrammelled by the criticism of a reading public. Indeed, there were cases of poets who developed along very personal lines, working for their own satisfaction and without thought of fame or public recognition. In Argentina, Enrique Banchs (1888–   ) and in Peru, José María Eguren (1874–1942) were almost poetic recluses in their disregard of fashion or rewards. Both poets spent a lifetime working at their poetry. Eguren's first collection, *Simbólicas* (1911) still bore the traces of Modernist symbols in his 'blonde princesses', 'red kings' and 'dead towers' but this was only a basis on which he constructed the edifice of his own imagining as in 'Favila':

> En la arena
> se ha bañado la sombra.
> Una, dos
> libélulas fantasmas
>
> Aves de humo
> van a la penumbra
> del bosque.‡

* Honey; scent of flower and sun-rays, of blond glass, of delightful taste.
† The red, cold grin of summer—slice of watermelon.
‡ In the sand the shadow has been bathing. One, two, phantom dragonflies. Birds of smoke pass into the shade of the wood.

The isolation of Eguren and Banchs from the rest of the literary world was, however, exceptional. After 1900, poets had an abundance of little magazines through which they kept in touch with what was going on in Europe. But the 1914–18 war was to change perspectives radically. In Europe the end of the war saw an explosion of creative energy, and Dadaism and Futurism were quickly followed by Surrealism. In all the arts, the emphasis was on innovation and experiment. This new avant-garde had an impact on Spanish America, as will be shown. But perhaps the most immediate effect of the 1914–18 war was in its encouragement of a new sense of nationalism and of national confidence among Latin-American intellectuals who in the declining star of European civilisation foresaw their own future fortunes. In the novel, cultural nationalism gave an impulse towards works set in the American countryside, and in poetry, too, there was some emphasis on 'Americanism'. However, the most famous poet of the '20s, Gabriela Mistral, succeeded in fusing a discreet use of regional vocabulary with universal themes.

Gabriela Mistral (1889–1957)

Born Lucila Godoy Alcayaga, Gabriela Mistral started her adult life as a provincial school teacher. She came from the valley of Elqui in northern Chile and drew public attention in 1914 when her *Sonetos de la muerte* [*Sonnets of Death*] won a prize. In 1922, she published *Desolación* [*Desolation*] to which she was later to make additions whenever it was published. Her two other collections of poetry were *Tala* [*Destruction*] (1938) and *Lagar* [*Wine-press*] (1954). She won the Nobel prize and was the first Spanish–American writer so to do. During her lifetime she had a continental reputation as a poet and as a humanitarian with a strong sense of the cultural union of Spanish America.

Gabriela Mistral's poetry, which initially sprang out of an unhappy personal experience, deals with the archetypal themes of love, death, maternal love, sterility, nature. Her poems have a rude, plain strength, an ascetic quality far removed from the baroque magnificence of her fellow Chilean, Pablo Neruda. Her main links with the avant-garde movements of the time are in her naturalism and in her reverence for childhood. She enters with wonderful directness into a child's fantasy as the following poem, 'La Manca' [The Girl Without a Finger] shows:

> Que mi dedito lo cogió una almeja
> y que la almeja se cayó en la arena
> y que la arena se tragó el mar.

Y que del mar la pescó un ballenero
y el ballenero llegó a Gibraltar:
y que en Gibraltar cantan pescadores
'Novedad de tierra sacamos del mar,
novedad de un dedito de niña.
La que esté manca lo venga a buscar'

Que me den un barco para ir a traerlo,
Y para el barco me den capitán
para el capitán que me den soldada,
y que por soldada pide la ciudad:
Marsella con torres y plazas y barcos
de todo el mundo la mejor ciudad,
que no será hermosa con una niñita
a la que robó su dedito el mar,
y los balleneros en pregones cantan
y están esperando sobre Gibraltar.*

The appeal of a poem like this is in its nearness to nursery rhyme, and indeed in her best poems there is always a reminiscence of folk-poetry in the simplicity of her vocabulary and the allusiveness of this apparent simplicity. Her major theme was that of frustrated motherhood, but she was also sensitive to the earth, to all plants, trees and animals which she observed with loving care as in the little poem, 'The Strawberry':

La fresa desperdigada
en el tendal de las hojas,
huele antes de cogida;
antes de vista se sonroja...
La fresa, sin ave picada,
que el rocío del cielo moja.

No magulles a la tierra
no aprietes a la olorosa,
Por el amor de ella abájate,
huélela y dale la boca.†

* A mussel took my finger and the mussel dropped in the sand and the sand was swallowed by the sea and from the sea it was fished by a whaler and the whaler arrived in Gibraltar and in Gibraltar the fishermen sing. 'We brought a marvel of the earth from the sea, a marvel of a girl's little finger. She who has one missing, come and get it.'
  Let them give me a boat to get it and a captain for the boat and wages for the captain and for wages he asks a city. Marseilles with towers, squares and boats, the best city in all the world, will it not be beautiful with a little girl whose finger was robbed by the sea and for whom the whalers sing and cry and who is awaited at Gibraltar?
† The strawberry scattered in the awning of the leaves, smells before it is picked and blushes at the gaze. The strawberry pecked by no bird, and which the dew of heaven wets. Do not trample the earth, do not crush the sweet-smelling [fruit]. For love of it, bend down, smell it and give it your mouth.

This is a poetry concerned with conveying emotion rather than with play or formal experiment.

DADA, SURREALISM, AND THEIR IMPACT

Gabriela Mistral's poetry had grown from the basic preoccupations of human life as it had always been lived. But she was not a city-dweller. Her experiences were not those of the urban individual, and in a sense her poetry looked backwards. But in Paris, London, and later in Spanish America, human life had come to seem so fragmented, machines and cities had brought about such changes, communications had become so rapid, that totally new types of art were needed to meet the experiences of a new age. With 'Futurism', an art movement that came out of Italy, locomotives, telephones and aeroplanes made their assault on painting and poetry. The Dada movement, centred first in Switzerland then in Paris, brought in a kind of art that was as expendable as a paper handkerchief. The Dadaists crashed right through the theory that painting and literature were some holy kind of activity and declared that any object could be looked on as a work of art. They hung spades up in art galleries, made poems out of pure sounds and played practical jokes against their enemies—the bourgeoisie. But in Latin America, where there was no bourgeois or artistic establishment to attack, Dada had no immediate impact. On the other hand, Cubism and Surrealism did.

The Cubists introduced four new concepts into painting that were later taken up by poets:

1 Instead of painting the objects as they saw them, they painted them as they thought them—just as certain African primitives had done.

2 Since we perceive many things simultaneously, they tried to introduce this simultaneity into art.

3 They introduced the ideal of *collage* in the use of ready-made elements such as the postage stamp or the newspaper.

4 They aimed to create new visions rather than to imitate what they saw around them.

The French poet Guillaume Apollinaire was interested in Cubism and wrote an early study of the movement, and he introduced some of its theories into his poetry. He made startling new juxtapositions of images, employed typographical devices which could convey simultaneity of perceptions, and he also used 'ready made' elements to create a *collage* effect. In 1917, Apollinaire had founded the magazine

Nord-Sud which had among its contributors a young Chilean poet, Vicente Huidobro (1893–1948). Critics have begrudged Huidobro his role as a pioneer of the avant-garde in Spanish America; it is true that he wrote many poems in French and his base was Paris, but he was a tireless propagandist on behalf of the avant-garde; a lecture he gave in Spain helped to sow the seeds of experiment in that country and ultimately in the Hispanic world.[1] Declaring that the poet no longer imitated nature but created new associations, he founded a movement known as *Creacionismo* and in his poetry invented startling new metaphors and associations, as in

> El mar electrizado
> > Y las piletas de ballenas clavadas.*

He practised simultaneity:

SALE LA LUNA
> > Un astro maltratado
> > Se desliza†

and his poems are constructed as a series of associations:

> Ahogado encantador qué hora es?
> Dínos la consistencia de los sueños
> Intercambiables en caos civil
>
> La quietud está llena de lanas de oveja
> Y yo no sé nada
>
> Junto a las angustias en marcha de la vida
> Las ropas blancas se secan día y noche
> Sobre la cuerda del horizonte
> (Por ahí se va muy lejos)
>
> Ahogado encantador
> La bella música de los equinoccios arrastra a los amantes
> Sólo la ley de la gravitación
> Descuelga los muros del salón.‡

---

* The electrified sea and the batteries of nailed whales.
† THE MOON COMES OUT
> > An ill-treated star slides down.
‡ Drowned enchanter, what time is it? Tell us the consistency of dreams that are interchangeable in civil chaos. The calm is full of the fleece of sheep and I do not know anything. Along with the advancing sorrow of life, the white clothes dry night and day upon the rope of the horizon. You can go far away from here. Drowned enchanter. The beautiful music of the equinoxes draws away the lovers. Only the law of gravity brings down the walls of the drawing-room.

We can understand why this poem was disconcerting to those not familiar with avant-garde techniques. There is no apparent link between the series of statements and the reader has to eschew logical deductions. But the poem is in fact a series of contrasts between 'sueño' [dream], 'quietud' [quietude], 'horizonte', 'La bella música de los equinoccios' [The beautiful music of the equinoxes] on the one hand, and on the other, an everyday, agitated world.

Huidobro's poems still express a romantic view of life despite the odd and disconcerting new techniques. It was only with the advent of César Vallejo that there was to be a 'new sensibility' which demanded revolutionary new techniques.

Avant-garde techniques were Hispanised by a group of writers known as the Ultraists who contributed to a number of Spanish magazines.[1] Among them was an Argentine poet, Jorge Luis Borges, who was to return to Buenos Aires in 1921 to become one of the leading figures in Argentine literary circles. The avant-garde theories already familiar in Europe soon began to appear in the magazines of Buenos Aires. Nosotros, for instance, published an Ultraist manifesto which explained that in the new poetry the poem was to be reduced to its first element—the metaphor; that there was to be an abolition of intermediary phrases, ornamentation and didacticism.

The avant-garde movement which had the most profound and lasting influence on Spanish–American poetry was Surrealism. André Breton's first Surrealist manifesto was published in 1924 and involved not only questions of technique but much more basic questions. He believed that the subject was in danger of becoming a slave to practical necessity and that dream and imagination were instruments of human emancipation. Since logic and reason had failed man, chance and spontaneity were the openings through which he entered new areas of the subconscious. 'Automatic writing' in which the conscious, organising mind of the poet was to be suspended so that the subconscious could take over was one method by which hitherto unknown forces could be appropriated by the poet. Surrealism thus implied extreme freedom, almost to the point of the abolition of grammar and syntax.

In Spanish America, Surrealism had an important liberating effect on language, and perhaps because of the special position of the artist in relation to society came to be regarded as a movement of inner freedom which the objective world sought to deny.

Despite the important influence of Dada, Cubism and Surrealism, however, it is misleading to talk of Cubist or Surrealist movements in Spanish America. As with Modernism, the '20s and '30s were a period during which poets appropriated techniques and theories from abroad, but invariably modifying them or developing them in personal ways. We shall therefore first look at three focal points of the avante-garde— Mexico, Buenos Aires and Cuba and then at the work of three poets— Vallejo, Neruda and Octavio Paz—who have absorbed avant-garde techniques and converted them into a wholly personal style.

MEXICO AND 'CONTEMPORÁNEOS'

In Mexico, both painting and the novel in the '20s and '30s centred on the recent experience of the Revolution. Poetry stood aloof. The poets alone had no new public. Nevertheless, avant-garde experiment quickly made its appearance. The 'estridentistas' of the early '20s filled their poems with contemporary vocabulary and revolutionary slogans, but they were soon eclipsed by an altogether more serious movement— that which centred round the magazine, *Contemporáneos*. The editor of this magazine was Bernardo Ortiz de Montellano (1899–1949) and the main contributors were Xavier Villaurrutia (1903–50), Jaime Torres Bodet (1902–), José Gorostiza (1901–) and Salvador Novo 1904–).

With the exception of some of the early playful poems of Salvador Novo, the predominant tone of the poetry of this group was one of deep gravity. Though not against revolutionary governments— Torres Bodet had been a government employee—they were not much concerned with social themes, but retreated into areas which society and social problems hardly touched. These areas were common to all poetry and hence they assumed a cosmopolitanism that brought them under fire from many of their contemporaries.

The poetry and even the imagery of the group has a remarkable consistency. A long rhythmic free-verse line forms the scaffolding on which they constructed meditations or reproduced the quality of dream or nightmare. They used Surrealist techniques to penetrate these regions. Characteristic in this respect is the 'Segundo sueño' [Second Dream] by Ortiz de Montellano which was written after he had undergone an operation and had been under an anaesthetic. The poem re-creates his loss of a sense of identity and finally breaks into a series of adjectives:

> alúcida   veloz   clara   ceñuda
> desnuda   sofocada   misteriosa

menuda pura impura deseada
libre precisa frágil despojada
sola solemne solitaria alma

alúcida veloz cálida oscura
orgullosa dolida apasionada
ávida tímida arrojada sobria
sensible fina libre leve dueña
multiforme constante sangre sangre.*

The question of personal identity was indeed one of the central themes of the *Contemporáneos* group as they sought vainly for an irreducible essence. Thus, Torres Bodet's desperate poem, 'Dédalo' begins:

Enterrado vivo
en un infinito
dédalo de espejos
me oigo, me sigo
me busco en el liso
muro de silencio.†

The infinite search in an infinite series of mirrors creates a sense of nightmare which again recurs in more than one poet. In Xavier Villaurrutia's 'Nocturno de la Estatua' [Nocturne of the Statue], the nightmare feeling is yet more intense:

Soñar, soñar la noche, la calle, la escalera
y el grito de la estatua desdoblando la esquina.
Correr hacia la estatua y encontrar sólo el grito,
querer tocar el grito y sólo hallar el eco,
querer asir el eco y encontrar sólo el muro
y correr hacia el muro y tocar un espejo.
Hallar en el espejo la estatua asesinada,
sacarla de la sangre de su sombra,
vestirla en un cerrar de ojos,
acariciarla como a una hermana imprevista
y jugar con las fichas de sus dedos
y contar a su oreja cien veces cien cien veces
hasta oirla decir: 'estoy muerta de miedo'.‡

---

* polished speedy clear gilded naked suffocated mysterious small pure impure desired free necessary fragile stripped alone solemn solitary soul polished speedy warm dark proud pained passionate avid timid hasty sober sensible fine free light owner multiform constant blood blood.

† Buried alive in an infinite labyrinth of mirrors, I hear myself, I follow myself, I seek myself on the smooth wall of silence.

‡ To dream, to dream the night, the street, the staircase and the cry of a statue turning the corner. To run towards the statue and find only the cry, to want to touch the cry and to find only the echo, to want to seize the echo and to find only the wall, to run towards the wall and touch the mirror. To find in the mirror the assassinated statue, to take it out

The poem is one of utter frustration, the kind of frustration one encounters in dream. The statue externalises the poet's fear and anguish. But the external world can never be reached by the poet. When he reaches the 'assassinated' statue, he dresses and embraces it as if it were 'an unexpected sister' but he can only communicate his own fears to this lifeless object. The poem is thus utterly solipsistic.

In 'Poesía', poetry itself is the echo of the poet's own voice bouncing back to him:

> Tu voz, hoz de eco
> es el rebote de mi voz en el muro.*

Communication with any world outside the self becomes even less possible because of the nature of words. Words become distorted. In 'Nocturno en que nada se oye' [Nocturne in which nothing is heard], the poet's voice comes back to him like a distorted echo.

> Y en el juego angustioso de un espejo frente a otro
> cae mi voz
> y mi voz que madura
> y mi voz quemadura
> y mi bosque madura
> y mi voz quema dura.†

The most ambitious poem written by a member of the *Contemporáneos* group, 'Muerte sin fin' [Endless Death] by José Gorostiza (1901–), brings together all their preoccupations in a long meditation on a glass of water. Water within glass is Gorostiza's image for pure form, a form which only exists so long as the glass is there. But form implies a chaos that has been contained and shaped and to which water and glass must return. Indestructible form, which the mind tries to conceive, is mere lifelessness:

> oh inteligencia, páramo de espejos,
> helada emanación de rosas pétreas
> en la cumbre de un tiempo paralítico
> pulso sellado.‡

of the blood of its shadow, to dress it in the twinkling of an eye, to embrace her as if she were an unexpected sister and to play with the counters of her fingers and to tell her ear a hundred times, a hundred, hundred times until she is heard to say, 'I am dead with fear'.

* Your voice, a sickle of echo is my voice bouncing back on the wall.
† And in the anguished play of one mirror in front of another, my voice falls and my voice which ripens and my voice which burns and my mature wood and my voice burns hard.
‡ o intelligence, desert of mirrors, icy emanation of stone roses at the summit of paralysed time, the sealed pulse.

In the first part of the poem, death without end is identified with God who is pure intelligence and who is symbolised in the empty glass. But glass is nothing by itself. Neither is water. Water seeks form and is contained in the glass but the moment the glass is taken away it returns to its origins in a 'frenesí de muerte' [mad desire for death]. The poem thus moves continually between the opposing poles of form and chaos, glass and water, word and silence, reason and imagination in a process that is a 'death without end'. Written in an abstract and pure style, the poem has been aptly described by Octavio Paz as the 'monument that Form has erected to its own death'.[1]

The importance of the *Contemporáneos* group lay in their insistence on high aesthetic standards at a time when, in other arts, formal considerations had been subordinated to the didactic.

ULTRAISM

In Buenos Aires, the Ultraist movement has a similar role to that of the *Contemporáneos* group in Mexico. Borges and his associates helped to found and encourage a number of little magazines such as *Proa* and *Prisma*, and later in the '20s founded the influential *Martín Fierro* which claimed to be interested in 'everything new under the sun' and further that everything new was interesting if looked at with modern eyes and expressed in a 'contemporary accent'.

Martín Fierro was succeeded by *Sur* (founded 1931) which down to the present has fulfilled an important role in bringing the best of contemporary world literature to the attention of the Argentine public. The playful poems of Oliverio Girondo are characteristic of the early period of the Buenos Aires avant-garde, but Jorge Luis Borges, its most talented spirit, was to turn from poetry to the short story form. His work will be discussed elsewhere.

CUBA

In Cuba, the *Revista Avance* also promised literary revolution, but here avant-garde theories happened to coincide with social preoccupations. The Paris fashion for Negro art was taken up by white Cuban intellectuals and there was born the Afro-Cuban poetry movement. The Afro-Cuban style was also to be taken up by Luis Palés Matos (1898–1959) of Puerto Rico and also had influences as far as Ecuador. In Cuba itself, after the initial experiments with poems that imitated rhumba rhythms, the movement gained depth and seriousness in the poetry of the mulatto poet, Nicolás Guillén (1902–) whose early compositions were influenced by the Spanish poet García Lorca. Guillén drew on African lore, on Cuban folk-poetry and on the speech rhythms of ordinary people. Thus his 'Sensemayá' was based on a Yoruba rite which had become part of Cuban Negro folk-lore, a rite in which a procession dances around the effigy of a boa. Guillén's poem combines African words and beats with a Spanish gloss:

> ¡Mayombe-bombe-mayombé!
> ¡Mayombe-bombe-mayombé!
> La culebra tiene los ojos de vidrio;
> la culebra viene y se enreda en un palo.*

Elsewhere, he transcribes Cuban Negro and mulatto pronunciation as in 'Búcate plata':

> Búcate plata
> búcate plata.
> porque no doy un paso má:
> estoy a arró con gayeta
> na má†

He was later to move away from this humorous light verse to poems in which he identified himself with the poor of Cuba and expressed his feelings about his mixed race. But indirectly he reflected the re-valuation of the Negro culture which had initially come from Europe.

THREE MAJOR FIGURES

César Vallejo (1892–1938)

César Vallejo is the Spanish American poet who made the most revolutionary break with tradition and created the most original style. A Peruvian who came from a modest *cholo* (part Indian-, part Spanish-descended) family from the small town of Santiago de Chuco near Trujillo, his first poems were written when he was still a student. In 1918 the early poems were collected and published as *Los heraldos negros* [*The Black Heralds*]. But these poems only gave a hint of his later work. A decisive turning point in his life was his imprisonment in 1920 on charges of 'incendiarism, assault, attempted homicide, robbery and riot'. These were unproved charges, but he nevertheless spent 112 days in prison before being released. The experience marked him,

---

* Mayombe-bombe-mayombé. Mayombe-bombe-mayombé. The snake has eyes of glass. The snake comes and winds round a stick.
† Go and find money, go and find money, because I am not going a step further. I am down to rice and bread, that's all.

but some of the most complex and finest poems of *Trilce* (1922) were written in prison. In 1923 he left for Europe, where he spent the rest of his life, a life dogged by poverty. He twice visited the Soviet Union and at one point was prevented from re-entering France from Spain because of his left-wing activities. He joined the Communist Party in 1931.

For some years in the late '20s and early '30s his political militancy led him to try genres—the novel and the theatre—which were didactic and could express a political message. But the works were not successful. In 1936, the Spanish Civil War broke out, and Vallejo went to Spain where he took part in a Writers' Congress before returning to Paris to work on behalf of the Republicans. But he was already a sick man. His later poems are often death-haunted. They were not to appear in his lifetime but were published as *Poemas Humanos* [*Human Poems*] after his death which took place in 1938. The poems he wrote on the Spanish War were also published posthumously as *España, aparta de mí este cáliz* [*Spain, Take Thou this Chalice from me*].

From *Los heraldos negros* onwards, Vallejo struggled to write poems about modern man. At first he worked within Modernist forms and vocabulary. Sections of his first collection, particularly a group of poems on the Indian which he called 'Nostalgias imperiales' [Imperial Nostalgias] recall the sonnets of Herrera y Reissig. Like the Modernists, he used vocabulary drawn from Christianity—the Mass, the Crucifixion, Christ—to express personal passion and anguish. Yet even in *Los heraldos negros* there are poems which are totally original. The style of these poems can best be described as 'dramatic' for in them emotions or feelings are presented through an objective conflict. In 'La araña' [The Spider], the wounded spider lies on the edge of a stone, unable to move. Eyes and legs are equally useless.

> Es una araña enorme, a quien impide
> el abdomen seguir a la cabeza
> Y he pensado en sus ojos
> Y en sus pies numerosos...
> Y me ha dado qué pena esa viajera!*

But the spider's struggle is reminiscent of the human predicament, when in certain situations brain and intelligence are divided and powerless.

* It is an enormous spider whose abdomen is prevented from following its head and I have thought of his eyes and his numerous feet and this traveller has given me so much pain.

In 'Agape', another poem of this collection, feelings of guilt and separation are dramatised in the poet's anxious questions to those who pass outside his door:

> Hoy no ha venido nadie a preguntar;
> ni me han pedido en esta tarde nada.
>
> No he visto ni una flor de cementerio
> en tan alegre procesión de luces.
> Perdóname, Señor: qué poco he muerto!
>
> En esta tarde todos, todos pasan
> sin preguntarme ni pedirme nada.
>
> Y no sé qué se olvida y se queda
> mal en mis manos, como cosa ajena.
>
> He salido a la puerta,
> y me da ganas de gritar a todos:
> Si echan de menos algo, aquí se queda!
>
> Porque en todas las tardes de esta vida
> yo no sé con qué puertas dan a un rostro,
> y algo ajeno se toma el alma mía.
>
> Hoy no ha venido nadie;
> y hoy he muerto qué poco en esta tarde!*

There is an anguished feeling of insufficiency as the poet watches people pass without being asked to give or communicate with them. A number of key words act as the scaffolding to the emotion—'nadie' [nobody], 'nada' [nothing], 'ajeno' [alien], 'muerto' [dead], 'tarde' [with its dual meaning of late and afternoon]. These words are words of negation, the positive being left unexpressed. Fullness, plenitude, communion are inferred because they are lacking. The open-

---

* Nobody came to ask today, this afternoon no-one has asked anything of me.
  I have not seen even a flower from the cemetery in this happy procession of lights. Forgive me, Lord, how little I have died!
  This afternoon, they all pass, without asking me anything or asking anything of me.
  And I know not what is forgotten and what is left uneasy in my hands like an alien thing.
  I have gone to the door and I want to shout to everybody. If anything is missing, here it is.
  Because on all the afternoons of this life, I know not what doors are closed in the face and something alien takes over my soul.
  Today nobody has come to ask anything and today how little I have died this afternoon.

ing and closing door also symbolises the offering and rejection which characterises the relationship of the individual and the objective world. The individual's non-participation gives rise to a feeling of insufficiency. He must 'die' in order to live fully. The poem is thus truly dialectical.

Christian imagery of communion is used in some of the poems of *Los heraldos negros*—for instance, 'El pan nuestro' [Our Daily Bread] and 'La cena miserable' [The Poor Supper]—generally as symbols of human brotherhood; but it was in the family and in family life that he was to find the analogue for the state of wholeness and perfection that he found lacking in adult existence. The 'Canciones de hogar' [Songs of Home], a group of poems that come at the end of *Los heraldos negros*, are about members of his own family and his own childhood. The father and the mother 'dos viejos caminos blancos' [two white roads] represent the Providence which brought him into the world, into the happiness, warmth, promise and fullness of childhood which tragically do not persist into adult life. His brother Miguel was the first member of the family to die, and one of the most moving poems of the section is a lament on his death, presented dramatically through the evocation of a game of hide-and-seek in which the brother hides and is never found again. The closing lines have a tragic irony, since the reader knows that the brother will never emerge from his hiding-place:

> Oye, hermano, no tardes
> en salir. Bueno? Puede inquietarse mamá.*

Los heraldos negros was an uneven collection, vacillating between the old and the new. *Trilce* was frankly disconcerting.[1] Isolated from contact with other poets, even from a reading public during his weeks in prison, Vallejo experimented in total freedom, and in doing so went far beyond the limits set by other Hispanic poets. New words were invented, traditional syntax and typography disappeared, the back of Spanish rhetoric was broken. But the dialectical or dramatic presentation that had made its appearance in *Los heraldos negros* was now extended, so that the poem became a sort of action or event. Yet Vallejo was not interested, as many of the avant-garde were interested, in experiment for its own sake. For him, experiment only had meaning if it sprang from the 'latido vital y sincero' [vital and sincere beat] of the poet. He wrote scathingly of those members of the Spanish-

---

* Listen brother, don't be late coming out. Right? Mummy might get anxious.

American avant-garde whose new techniques hid the hollowness of their attitudes:

> La actual generación de América es tan retórica y falta de honestidad espiritual como las anteriores generaciones de las que ella reniega'.*¹

The poetry of *Trilce*, therefore, springs out of burning emotion, out of sheer anguish, and it is this that provokes the unusual vocabulary and technique.

Trilce is a vast extension of the mood of 'Canciones del hogar'. The sexual act brings the human individual into the world. In the family he lives in a state of communion with his parents and brothers but time threatens this Eden. Inevitably he or they must leave. The individual enters upon his 'mayoría inválida' [useless majority]; alone and isolated, he comes to consciousness in a world that is without sense.

> Regocíjate, huérfano, bebe tu copa de agua
> desde la pulpería de una esquina cualquiera.†

Love—not sexual love but brotherly love or the love of mother for her child is the only binding force. This is what enriches childhood. A symbol of this love is the inexhaustible supply of biscuits which the mother takes from the oven:

> Tahona estuosa de aquellos mis bizcochos
> pura yema infantil innumerable, madre.‡

But in adult life, we pay for this; we pay for

> el alquiler de este mundo donde nos deja
> y el valor de aquel pan inacabable.§

But why? This is the mystery of life for Vallejo, that having been given existence, man must pay for this through suffering.

> Y nos lo cobran, cuando, siendo nosotros
> pequeños entonces, como tú verías
> no se lo podíamos haber arrebatado
> a nadie; cuando tú nos lo diste,
> ¿dí, mamá?¶

---

* The present generation of America is as rhetorical and lacking in spiritual honesty as the previous generations which it denies.
† Enjoy yourself, orphan, drink your cup of water from the bar on any old corner.
‡ Glowing oven of those my biscuits, pure infantile yoke, innumerable, mother.
§ The rent of this world in which we are abandoned and the value of that unfinished bread.
¶ And they make us pay when we, who were young, then, as you see, we could not have taken it away from anyone, when you gave it to us, isn't that so, Mummy?

Man feels guilty because something he has possessed has been taken from him. He has come into his 'mayoría inválida' and feels forever as if punished for something he had once done wrong, perhaps simply for having once been a child and known love and communion with others. Thus in one poem, Vallejo speaks of this state as if it were that of a child separated from his school friends:

> que dentro de dos gráfilas oscuras y aparte,
> por haber sido niños y también
> por habernos juntado mucho en la vida,
> reclusos para siempre nos irán a encerrar.
>
> Para que te compongas.*

The prison in which he wrote many of his poems with its 'cuatro paredes' [four walls] which always added up to the same number, thus became a symbol for this adult life in which love was lacking. 'Amor; este es el cuadro que faltó' [Love; this is the frame which was lacking]. Without it life is a grey plain, history and events have no sense, time is meaningless succession.

> Oh valle sin altura madre, donde todo duerme
> horrible mediatinta, sin ríos frescos, sin entradas de amor.
> Oh voces y ciudades que pasan cabalgando en un dedo
> tendido que señala a calva Unidad. Mientras pasan de
> mucho en muchos, gañanes de gran costado
> sabio, detrás
> de las tres tardas dimensiones.
>   Hoy Mañana Ayer
> (No, hombre).†

The last line is the poet's desperate protest against the three iron dimensions of past, present and future.

To Vallejo time is infinitely complex, perpetually pushing us to death or giving a deceitful impression of recapturing the past in memory. His ironic use of dates in the poems—'Dobla el dos de noviembre [The second of November tolls], 'Estamos a catorce de Julio' [It is the 14th of July], 'Junio eres nuestro' [June you are ours], 'altos de a 1921' [in 1921]—often underline the fact that existence cannot be

---

* between two dark edges and apart, for having been children and also for having been very close together in life, they will shut us away in solitary for life. To make you behave.

† O valley without commanding heights where everything sleeps, dreadful half tones which have no cool rivers or openings of love. O voices and cities which pass galloping on an outstretched finger which points to bald Unity. While there pass all the time the workmen of a great, wise, rib, behind the three slow dimensions. Today, Tomorrow, Yesterday (No, man).

dated. And in one remarkable poem, he objectifies the dialectic of the human personality.

Me da miedo ese chorro
buen recuerdo, señor fuerte, implacable
cruel dulzor. Me da miedo
Esta casa me da entero bien, entero
lugar para este no saber dónde estar.

No entremos. Me da miedo este favor
de tornar por minutos, por puentes volados.
Yo no avanzo, señor dulce,
recuerdo valeroso, triste
esqueleto cantor.

Qué contenido, el de esta casa encantada
me da muertes de azogue, y obtura
con plomo mis tomas a la seca actualidad.

El chorro que no sabe a cómo vamos
dame miedo, pavor.
Recuerdo valeroso, yo no avanzo
Rubio y triste esqueleto, silba, silba.*

Here memory fills the poet with fear. He refuses to step into the stream which will take him back 'por puentes volados' [over blown-up bridges] protesting that his present is perfectly satisfactory. The past is like a skeleton that sings or whistles, beckoning him back, but only to bring the realisation that all that has gone is indeed dead. But the present, symbolised in the house, is also 'enchanted'; here, too, he suffers deaths with the passing of each moment. What is remarkable in this and in other poems by Vallejo is the way in which what in other poets might be an abstract lament on memory and the passing of time becomes a situation fraught with drama, a situation in which the poet and the reader are immediately involved; the poet as actor, the reader as helpless spectator.

Abstraction, generalisation are indeed alien to Vallejo's whole attitude to life. For him human reason is insufficient, for though it

---

* This stream frightens me, good memory, strong lord, implacable, cruel sweetness. It frightens me. This house I feel good in, it is a good place for this not knowing where to be.

Let us not go in. I am afraid of this gift of going back in minutes over blown-up bridges. I am not going on, sweet lord, courageous memory, sad singing skeleton.

What strange contents those of this enchanted house. They give me deaths of mercury and I solder with lead my seizure of dry actuality.

The stream which does not know at what speed we go makes me afraid, frightened. Courageous memory, I am not going on. White and sad skeleton, whistle, whistle.

teaches us to count and measure and attach names to phenomena, the real nature of phenomena escapes it. Like his references to dates, the use of scientifically-exact words has an ironic connotation. 'Dicotyledon', 'Osmosis', 'lactic glands' may be scientifically useful terms but they shed no light on human existence. Reason can only tell us of externals. Thus when, on the 'Monday of reason', he examines his own self, he finds nothing but empty suits of clothes hanging in a wardrobe:

> En los bastidores donde nos vestimos
> no hay, no Hay nadie: hojas tan sólo
> de par en par.
> Y siempre los trajes descolgándose
> por sí propios, de perchas
> como ductores índices grotescos,
> y partiendo sin cuerpos, vacantes,
> hasta el matiz prudente
> de un gran caldo de alas sin causas
> y lindes fritas.
> Y hasta el hueso!*

The poem seems to put in doubt the existence of the self as an absolute entity. In the wardrobe, the poet finds only suits of clothes hanging until they decay into chaos.

Vallejo once stated that a new poetry could only arise out of a new sensibility. The 'dramatic' presentation of situations, the use of a scientific vocabulary or of colloquialisms are all strictly linked with the vital attitudes of the poet. There is no self-indulgence. And this is the case even with the typographical experiments which might at first sight seem part of an avant-garde game. Thus in the second poem of *Trilce*, 'Tiempo, tiempo' [Time, time], he shows how time makes nonsense of the substantive for nouns exist as if time did not. He asks a question for which there is no possible answer.'¿Qué se llama cuanto heriza nos?' [What is it called how much that bristles us?] and this contradictory and impossible question he answers by applying a name 'Se llama Lomismo que padece nombre nombre nombrE' [it is called The same that suffers name name namE]. The capital letter which usually distinguishes a proper noun is put at the beginning of the meaningless Lomismo and at the end of 'nombre', thus ironically underlining

---

* In the wings where we dress, there is not, there is nobody. Only wide-open doors and the clothes always descending by themselves from hangers, like grotesque guiding fingers, bodiless, vacant, leaving for the prudent shade of a great soup of causeless wings and fried limits and to the bone!

the fact that names are not identical with the experience they purport to categorise. Similarly his spacing out of words like 'sombra   a   sombra' [shadow   to   shadow]¹ is only used when the visual effect is an integral part of the poem. In this case, he is talking of a door opening and closing, and indirectly of the sexual act.

Typographical devices are, nevertheless, much rarer in *Poemas humanos*. And though the technique of dramatising conflicts is still used, the poems have taken on an apocalyptic and prophetic tone. In many of them, the presence of death already seems to have touched the poet physically:

> Ay, cómo la sensación arruga tanto
> ay, como una idea fija me ha entrado en una uña.*

But there is another new element. Vallejo is no longer talking of a general 'mayoría inválida' but of a particular situation. The shadow of the depression hung over Europe, unemployed lined the streets, the industrial society was at a standstill, leaving millions to suffer:

> Execrable sistema, clima en nombre del cielo del bronquio y la quebrada,
> la cantidad enorme de dinero que cuesta el ser pobre.†

'Clima' suggests the uncertain weather of economic crisis when what the poet asks for is the sureness and eternity of 'cielo'. In these poems, he sees hunger and suffering around him, growing more rapidly than human ability to deal with it. In 'Los nueve monstruos' [The Nine Monsters] the evil simply grows of its own accord as man loses control of a world he has made:

> crece el mal por razones que ignoramos
> y es una inundación con propios líquidos,
> con propio barro y propia nube sólida‡

In this poem, the world is turned literally upside down, nature is wrenched from its function and only suffering and pain are on the increase. But it is not simply the system that is to blame. The *Poemas humanos* are an ironic comment on human failure, on the grandiose design and the pitiful slavery of men who can never liberate themselves from their bodily appetites. In 'El alma que sufrió de su cuerpo'

---

* O how the sensation wrinkles so, o how a fixed idea has entered my nail.
† Execrable system, climate in the name of sky of bronchial tube and bankruptcy, the enormous amount of money it costs to be poor.
‡ evil grows for reasons which we do not know and it is a flooding in its own liquids with its own clay and its own solid cloud.

[The Soul which suffered of its Body], man weeps and drinks, bleeds and eats, because whatever mental or spiritual suffering he undergoes, his bodily needs must still be satisfied. Man is simply an unhappy monkey, 'Darwin's boy', 'cautivo en tu enorme libertad/arrastrado por tu hércules autónomo...' [captive in your enormous liberty, dragged by your autonomous Hercules]. But this struggle for life, incarnated in industrial society and in the city which is 'hecha de lobos abrazados' [made of embraced wolves], leads to the horror of hunger and unemployment, of lives lived in poverty within the wealth of the city.

> El parado, la ve yendo y viniendo
> monumental, llevando sus ayunos en la cabeza cóncava,
> en el pecho sus piojos purísimos,
> y abajo
> su pequeño sonido, el de su pelvis
> callado entre dos grandes decisiones,
> y abajo,
> más abajo
> un papelito, un clavo, una cerilla.*

In the shadow of the 'monumental' city, the unemployed man sits motionless, hungry, dirty, poised between 'two great decisions of birth and death'. Under his feet are the detritus of civilisation—the paper, the nail and the match—end products of an industrialisation which now seems to have come to a standstill.

In these circumstances, human life is reduced to utter nullity. In 'La rueda del hambriento' [The Hungry Man's Circle], the poet identifies himself with the hungry but as in *Trilce*, the hunger he feels extends beyond the physical, it is a hunger for meaning, for a sense of identity. In the poem, he begs for a stone on which to sit or 'bread' on which to sit. The stone symbolises faith and certainty, bread symbolises communion. But his passionate plea for 'algo, en fin, de beber, de comer, de vivir, de reposarse' [something, at last, to drink, eat, live and rest on] has no answer. He ends the poem tragically:

> Hallo una extraña forma, está muy rota
> y sucia mi camisa
> y ya no tengo nada, esto es horrendo.†

* The unemployed sees monumental (the city), coming and going, and carries his fastings in his concave head, and his very pure lice in his breast and below his small sound, that of his pelvis, silent between two great decisions and below, lower down, a little paper, a nail, a match.
† I find a strange form, my shirt is very torn and dirty and I have nothing left, it is horrible.

In some poems, this absolute lack of anything that makes life worth living is treated with a sort of wry humour.

> Habiendo atravesado
> quince años; después, quince, y, antes, quince,
> uno se siente, en realidad, tontillo,
> es natural, por lo demás, qué hacer!
> Y que dejar de hacer, que es lo peor!
> Sino vivir, sino llegar
> a ser lo que es uno entre millones,
> de panes, entre miles de vinos, entre cientos de bocas,
> entre el sol y su rayo que es de luna
> y entre la misa, el pan, el vino y mi alma.*

The poet is simply one among millions. Whereas the Christian Mass of bread and wine had once given individual life meaning he can now only resign himself to unimportance. In some poems, there is an unmistakable nostalgia for a lost dignity that Catholic faith had given man. 'Hoy es domingo,' he says, 'me viene a la cabeza la idea, al pecho el llanto' [Today is Sunday, the idea comes to my head, the lament to my heart]. On the other hand, if it were Monday:

> vendríame al corazón la idea,
> al seso, el llanto
> y a la garganta, una gana espantosa de ahogar
> lo que ahora siento,
> como un hombre que soy y que he sufrido.†

If 'Sunday' symbolises the lost faith, Monday brings him to realisation of the grey, anguished world of modern man, a world in which reason is impotent, in which the brain weeps.

The sense of approaching death gave the poems an added urgency. In 'Paris, Octubre 1936', he takes ironic leave of his 'gran situación' [great situation]:

> De todo esto yo soy el único que parte,
> De este banco me voy, de mis calzones,
> de mi gran situación, de mis acciones,

---

* Having gone through fifteen years and then fifteen and fifteen before, one feels, in reality, rather silly. It's natural besides, what can one do.
  And what can one stop doing which is worse, except live, except manage to be what one is among millions of loaves of bread, among thousands of bottles of wine and hundreds of mouths, midst the sun and its ray which is the moon and the mass, bread, wine and the soul.
† the idea would come to the heart, to the brain weeping and to the throat a terrible desire to stifle what I feel now as a man that I am and who has suffered.

de mi número hendido parte a parte,
de todo esto yo soy el único que parte.

De los Campos Elíseos o al dar vuelta
la extraña callejuela de la Luna,
mi defunción se va, parte mi cuna,
y, rodeada de gente, sola, suelta,
mi semejanza humana dase vuelta
y despacha sus sombras una a una.

Y me alejo de todo, porque todo
se queda para hacer la coartada;
mi zapato, su ojal, también su lodo,
y hasta el doblez del codo
de mi propia camisa abotonada.*

The Champs Elysées, the 'callejuela de la Luna', his shoes and his shirt have a permanency which he has not. Against these objective elements, he balances his own fragile identity made up of abstraction like his 'situation', his 'actions', his 'number', his 'shadows'. Thus in his collection Vallejo strips the individual of any identity. Life has no meaning except that conferred by death. 'En suma,' he declared, 'no poseo, para expresar mi vida sino mi muerte' [In short, I do not have anything to express my life except my death].

Poemas humanos present an even more tragic view of life than *Trilce*. In the latter, he had awoken to the consciousness of adult suffering, but in the former death was on him, bringing him the knowledge that there had really been nothing:

No es grato morir, señor, si en la vida nada se deja y si en la muerte nada es posible, sino sobre lo que pudo dejarse en la vida.†

España, aparta de mí este cáliz [*Spain, Take Thou this Chalice from me*], though written at the same time as *Poemas humanos*, has a more hopeful and prophetic tone, although Vallejo felt a deep sense of guilt at not

---

* Of all this I am the only one who is going away. From this bench, I go, from my pants, from my great situation, from my actions, from my number, split from side to side, from all this I am the only one to go away.

  From the Champs-Elysées and after going through the strange street of the Moon, my demise goes away, leaves with my cradle and surrounded by people, alone, loose, my human likeness turns round and finishes off its shadows one by one.

  And I go away from everything because everything is left behind as an alibi; my shoe, my button-hole, their dirt as well, and even the elbow lining of my own buttoned shirt.

† It is not nice to die, sir, if in life nothing is left and if in death nothing is possible except on that which could be left in life.

being able to participate more actively in the war. Yet death is still the main theme, perhaps a death that is more meaningful than that of workers dying of starvation—but death nevertheless:

> Miré el cadáver, su raudo orden visible
> y el desorden lentísimo de su alma;
> le vi sobrevivir; hubo en su boca
> la edad entrecortada de dos bocas.
> Le gritaron su número: pedazos.
> Le gritaron su amor; más le valiera!
> Le gritaron su bala: también muerta!
>
> Y su orden digestivo sosteníase
> y el desorden de su alma, atrás, en balde.
> Le dejaron y oyeron, y es entonces
> que el cadáver
> casi vivió en secreto, en un instante;
> más le auscultaron mentalmente y ¡fechas!*

Although this is included among poems of war, we recognise pre-occupations that have been there since *Los heraldos negros*. The physical order of the soldier's body is apparently intact, but the soul is in 'disorder'; his identity, his 'number' has disappeared and when they probe him mentally, there are only dates. Thus even civil war centres on the same problems of the significance of the human individual.

Vallejo's poetry is too complex to be analysed in a few pages, but the few examples quoted should give some idea of the way he invented new techniques to meet the needs of a poetry of modern man. But this is not cerebral poetry. In each poem, Vallejo's anguish is the powerful mainspring, 'su extraña y necesaria verdad' [its strange and necessary truth] as one critic has called it.[1]

Pablo Neruda

Neruda was born in 1904 in the town of Parral in southern Chile. His family name was Neftalí Reyes (he adopted the pen-name Pablo Neruda after he had begun to write) and his father was a train driver who, on the death of his wife, moved to the town of Temuco, a pioneer

---

* I looked at the corpse, at its swift visible order, and the very slow disorder of the soul; I saw him survive; in his mouth there was the confused age of two mouths. They shouted his number—pieces. They shouted his love; this was better. They shouted his bullet: still dead.

And his digestive order stayed intact and the disorder of his soul behind in vain. They left him and listened and it is then that the body almost lived in secret, in an instant; but they listened to his brain and—dates!

settlement in the remote south. The young Neruda grew up in a wilderness whose flora and fauna had never been mapped and classified. He lived in houses made from newly-felled logs and all his life the frontier has haunted him. But though he wrote some poems before leaving Temuco, it was the first impact of the city that provided the most powerful stimulus of creation. Far from the tightly-knit community in which he grew up, he faced loneliness and isolation that only love and poetry could overcome. Soon after his arrival in Santiago, he published *La canción de la fiesta* [*Fiesta Song*] (1921) and *Crepusculario* [*Of Twilight*] (1923) and the *Veinte poemas de amor y una canción desesperada* [*Twenty Poems of Love and a Desperate Song*] (1924) which was to become his most popular collection. From this point on, the story of his life and his poetry have been indivisible.

Neruda's poetry cannot be approached through 'influences' or by reference to European movements. Like Vallejo, he was well acquainted with the avant-garde, and critics have indicated the influence of Surrealism, of T. S. Eliot and of many other poets on his work. But whatever his reading of other poetry may have been, he had a strong personal statement to make for which he appropriated and developed new forms and techniques. He rejected intellectual generalisations, however. For him poetry was always intuition, 'physical absorption of the world':

en la casa de la poesía no permanece nada sino lo que fue escrito con sangre para ser escuchado por la sangre.*[1]

It follows that Neruda's poetry springs out of direct experience, much of it being autobiographical. The five-volume *Memorial de Isla Negra* (1964) is the story of his life in poetry, and parts of the *Canto general* (1950) takes the form of autobiographical confession. But quite apart from these direct statements, the main body of his verse directly reflects personal experience and immediate emotions. This does not mean, however, that his technique is simple. On the contrary, from *Veinte poemas*, he has built up each poem on a structure of personal associations which spread out ripples of imagery. The reader himself has the burden of linking the associations, of allowing their cumulative effect to pile up into a total experience. Neruda himself, speaking of *Residencia en la tierra*, likened his technique to a ritual. He declared of this collection:

* in the house of poetry nothing remains except that which was written with blood to be listened to with blood.

Es un montón de versos de gran monotonía, casi rituales, con misterio y dolores como los hacían los viejos poetas.*[1]

Through repetition, through waves of associations, he hopes to create a mood of receptivity in which logic and rational concatenations can be avoided. This perhaps explains why, when he began to write social poetry after joining the Communist Party in 1939, he was able to make the transition into writing a rhetorical poetry intended to be read aloud with great ease and effectiveness.

The first truly Nerudan collection of poetry was *Veinte poemas de amor*, a collection that presented an adolescent's vision of the world through love. In the solitude that Neruda felt after his arrival in the city, he could only project himself upon the beloved object, upon the woman whom he came to identify with nature and the natural, with a life force that was totally opposed to the deadness of urban living. Yet the woman is not always in perfect communion:

Tú, mujer, ¿qué eres allí, qué raya, qué varilla de ese abanico inmenso? Estabas lejos como ahora.†

But the woman *is* the objective world. 'Te pareces al mundo en tu actitud de entrega' [You are like the world in your attitude of surrender], he declares, but it is the natural world that manifests itself in her and is always associated with her. Thus he speaks of 'tus brazos de piedra' [your arms of stone] or likens her to an earth shell in which the earth sings and in sadness 'las hojas caían en el agua de tu alma' [the leaves fell on the water of your soul]. She is like a fish, her hands like grapes, 'tu boca de ciruela' [your mouth of plum]. Though intensely desired, the woman of *Veinte poemas*[2] is frequently distant, incommunicable: 'Tu presencia es ajena, extraña a mí como una cosa' [Your presence is alien, strange to me like a thing], or again he asks, 'Quién eres tú, quién eres?' [Who are you, who are you?]. And thus the poems perpetually oscillate between communion through love, or attempted communion, and the tragic solitude vividly expressed in 'Poema Siete' in which the poet desperately sends out signals as if shipwrecked; while the girl is likened to the threatening sea:

Sólo guardas tinieblas, hembra distante y mía/de tu mirada emerge a veces la costa del espanto/Inclinado en las tardes echo mis tristes redes a ese mar/que sacude tus ojos oceánicos.‡

---

* It is a pile of very monotonous verses, almost ritual, with mystery and suffering as the old poets used to compose.

† You, woman, what are you there, what groove, what stick of that immense fan? You were far away as you are now.

‡ You only have shadows, my distant woman, from your glance there sometimes

The *Veinte poemas* represent the universal longing for communion through love which every young person feels, and in Spanish America they were also the first really modern love poems, the first break with Modernist and Romantic cliché. But Neruda's next book, *Tentativa del hombre infinito* [*Tentative of infinite man*] (1926) was less successful. It is a transitional work in which the poet explores the new techniques of Surrealism.

In 1927, Neruda was sent to the East as consul. In Rangoon, Colombo, and later in Java, the isolation he had experienced in Santiago intensified. Here he was cut off from those who spoke Spanish, plunged into the midst of a civilisation that was strange and alien to him. He was not to waste his time however. In what were then British colonies, he read English literature, came across the poems of T. S. Eliot and of other English writers, and he composed the first volume of his *Residencia en la tierra* [*Residence on Earth*]. The fortunes of this collection were to be uneven. The first volume was published in 1933 after years of effort, and was reprinted with a second collection, also called *Residencia en la tierra* in 1935. In 1947, Neruda published *Tercera Residencia* [*Third Residence*] which marked a break with the style of earlier volumes and was a rejection of what he now considered to be an élite form of poetry.

The first two collections of *Residencia* included poems written between 1925 and 1935. Intense, visionary, even apocalyptic, it is hardly surprising that Neruda was later to reject these works as negative, for they do indeed present a terrifying vision of a world in perpetual erosion. The essence of the world, its unity, is its tendency to disintegrate and return to primal chaos. Few poems offer the possibility of any communion with others; instead the poet is completely alone 'entre materias desvencijadas' [among broken-down substances]. In 'Unidad', the law common to all phenomena is that of disintegration. 'Me rodea una misma cosa, un solo movimiento' [One single thing, one single movement surrounds me]. How can one categorise experience of such vertiginous flux, this 'movimiento sin tregua y un nombre confuso' [tireless movement and confused subject]? Only, Neruda believed, by creating the poetic analogue of flux, with the grammatical order in suspension and the images flowing restlessly one onto the other. In the following part of a poem, Neruda reaches out for a sense of his own identity, but his sole consciousness is of

emerges the coast of fear. Bending down in the afternoons, I throw my sad nets into that sea which your oceanic eyes shake.

time passing, destroying the present and offering him only pale visions of past selves:

> Así, pues, como una vigía tornado insensible y ciego,
> incrédulo y condenado a un doloroso acecho,
> frente a la pared en que cada día del tiempo se une,
> mis rostros diferentes se arriman y encadenan
> como grandes flores pálidas y pesadas
> tenazmente substituídas y difuntas.*

Grammatically, the poem is ambiguous. A verb like 'estoy' or 'me siento' seems wanting before 'como una vigia'; at the same time the omission of such a verb is significant, for it would suggest a state, something that halted or appeared to halt the implacable flow of time. Instead the poet suggests two contradictory ideas: that of the watchman ['vigia'] and the watch ['acecho'] and also the contradictory notion of blindness and insensitivity, thus representing the individual's uneasy alertness as he notes the days passing and at the same time his blindness and inability to know what will happen next. The present is non-existent, no more than a wall on which he sees his present self slip back into the past; the moments which had once been consecutive become indistinguishable. While there is clearly a link of association between the images—watchman suggests fortress or prison, hence the wall; in turn, this suggests a wall of execution and hence the flowers placed on a grave. At the same time, each image contributes to and enriches the others. The verse, too, begins with the tentative 'Así, pues' [So, then], to end on the definitive 'difuntas' [dead].

Critics have talked of *Residencia* as if the poetry, by denying established order, was itself mere chaos. But this is not so. The oneiric [dream] succession of images has its own order—but it is perhaps more like the order of waves beating on a shore than the order of a construction. For instance in 'El fantasma del buque de carga' [The Phantom of the Cargo Boat], a hasty first reading might give the impression of a metaphor whimsically expanded to hyperbolic proportions. The tired boat creaks across the sea in an interminable voyage, laden with a cargo of grey sacks which in the poet's fantasy are likened to grey animals with grey ears, their full shapes reminding him of pregnant women waiting outside a movie house. But greyness and patience are inseparable from the theme of the poem, for the one suggests monotony

---

* So, then, like a watchman now insensitive and blind, incredulous and condemned to a sorrowful watch, before a wall on which each day of time unites, my different faces draw near and link like great pale flowers, heavy, tenaciously substituted and dead.

the other waiting, and the boat is itself subject to the monotonous beat of the waves and its waiting is the expectation of an inevitable end. The poem advances through the dialectic of the passive boat and the destroying waves, the concrete solid objects which are being eroded and the 'phantom' time which proves stronger than they:

> los roperos, las verdes carpetas de las mesas,
> el color de las cortinas y del suelo,
> todo ha sufrido el lento vacío de sus manos
> y su respiración ha gastado las cosas.*

The objects are worn away, the water triumphs over time:

> Sin gastarse las aguas, sin costumbre ni tiempo,
> verdes de cantidad, eficaces y frías,
> tocan el negro estómago del buque y su materia
> lavan, sus costras rotas, sus arrugas de hierro,
> roen las aguas vivas la cáscara del buque
> traficando sus largas banderas de espuma
> y sus dientes de sal volando en gotas.†

Throughout this verse the visual and tactile elements, the coldness of the sea, the green waves, the 'flags' of foam, its 'teeth' of salt, also support another order of imagery, the cold probing of this monstrous element slowly laying bare the skeleton of the boat.

In *Residencia*, Neruda makes a distinction between the grey 'death' of material objects, vividly evoked in the sordidness of shabby boarding-houses and old furniture, and the death of organic things. So in 'Walking Around', manufactured objects take on a singularly pitiful aspect:

> Yo paseo con calma, con ojos, con zapatos,
> con furia, con olvido,
> paso, cruzo oficinas y tiendas de ortopedia,
> y patios donde hay ropas colgadas de un alambre:
> calzoncillos, toallas y camisas que lloran
> lentas lágrimas sucias.‡

---

* the wardrobes, green tablecloths, the colour of the curtain and the ground, all have suffered the slow emptying of your hands and your breath has wasted things.
† The waters do not waste away; they have no habits or time, they are green with quantity, effective and cold. They touch the black stomach of the boat and wash its substance, its broken crust, its iron wrinkles, the living waters gnaw the husk of the boat, trading their long flags of foam and their teeth of salt which flies in drops.
‡ I walk about calmly with eyes, with shoes, with anger, with forgetfulness. I walk about, go through offices and orthopaedic shops and yards in which there is washing hung from a wire—pants, towels and shirts which weep slow dirty tears.

Here, too, there is a visual image of dripping clothes which also has an emotional force, strengthened by previous references to the 'tiendas de ortopedia'. The accumulation of objects, 'towels and shirts', also reinforces the idea of everyday monotony suggested in the 'oficinas' of the previous line.

But from this law of monotony and sordidness, the things of nature do escape. They have at least the beauty of nature and the eternity that nature's constant renewal endows them with. Thus, in his poem to the 'Celery', he writes:

> entráis, en medio de la niebla hundida,
> hasta crecer en mí, hasta comunicarme
> la luz oscura y la rosa de la tierra.*

This 'dark light' which comes to the poet from the earth is the only suggestion in *Residencia* of any positive schemes of values.

Between writing the poems included in the first two volumes of *Residencia* and the *Tercera Residencia*, Neruda underwent the experience of the Spanish Civil War. He had returned to Chile and then to Europe in the early 1930s, and was appointed Consul to Barcelona in 1934. In Spain, he made friends with the Spanish Communist poet, Rafael Alberti, and edited his own avant-garde magazine, *Caballo verde para la poesía*, in which he made a characteristic defence of impure poetry which would communicate the noise and sweat of labour, and hatred as well as love. With the outbreak of the Civil War, he became actively involved in organising help for the Republican side, and this new commitment is reflected in the poems of the *Tercera Residencia* where he recognises his oneness with the whole of humanity:

> Yo de los hombres tengo la misma mano herida,
> yo sostengo la misma copa roja
> e igual asombro enfurecido.†

A whole section of this collection was published as 'España en el corazón' [Spain in the Heart] and gave the first examples of Neruda's public writing. They sustained a high note of indignation against the forces of reaction:

> Venid a ver la sangre por las calles,
> venid a ver

---

* you enter in the midst of sunken mist until you grow in me, until you communicate to me the dark light and rose of the earth.
† I have the same wounded hand of all men, I hold the same red cup and the same furious astonishment.

la sangre por las calles,
venid a ver la sangre
por las calles.*

The ritualistic repetition which had already been a feature of the poetry of *Residencia* here attains the force of incantation, and one of the poems culminates with a litany of names of cities:

Peñarrubia, Cedrillas,
Alcocer, Tamurejo,
Aguadulce, Pedrera,
Fuente, Palmera, Colmenar, Sepúlveda.

Not surprisingly, these were the first of his poems which he regularly read aloud to ordinary people.

Neruda joined the Communist Party, and during the 1940s became increasingly active in political life. He was elected Senator in Chile in 1944 and after delivering a speech bitterly denouncing the President, González Videla, he had to go into hiding and later into exile. But this was also a period of poetic creation and one that saw the composition of his major work, the *Canto general* (1950), which he had begun to write as early as 1938 on the death of his father. This poem was an attempt to break out of the hermetic style of *Residencia* and the 'élitism' of Spanish poetry and create a modern epic. His first plan was to compose a Chilean epic, but during the decade during which he was writing it, the original plan expanded and the final version covered the whole of the Americas.

The *Canto general* consists of fifteen sections. The first is a record of the flora and fauna of America. There follows a meditation on the Inca ruins of Macchu Picchu, and sections on the conquerors and oppressors of the Americans and on champions of the people such as Bartolomé de las Casas. The sixth section, 'América no invoco tu nombre en vano' [America I do not invoke your name in vain], presents a geographical panorama of the continent. From this, Neruda passes in the subsequent sections to Chile and its workers and peasants; Section Nine is entitled 'Qué despierta el leñador' [Let the wood-cutter awake] and is addressed to the United States, invoking the spirit of Lincoln and condemning imperialism. The later sections prove the poet's own origins, his country and the seascapes he loves and ends with a section called 'Yo soy' [I am], which is an affirmation of his life and beliefs and expression of gratitude to the Communist Party.

* Come and see the blood on the streets, come and see the blood on the streets, come and see the blood on the streets.

A poem of this length and scope must of necessity be uneven, and there are sections which deal with ephemeral political material. Yet such sections are more than counterbalanced by several magnificent flights, particularly those parts which invoke the flora and fauna of the continent, the Pacific Ocean and the ancient civilisations of America. Although *Canto general* was not intended for an élite audience and has in fact been read to meetings of ordinary people in many parts of the globe, the poetry is by no means simple. If we take the 'Alturas de Macchu Picchu' as an example, we find an exceedingly complex poetic structure in which the poet moves from a statement of his own solitude and alienation and gradually attains a new state of awareness of human solidarity. There are twelve sub-sections to this part of the poem, and these are grounded on an actual experience, that of visiting the Inca ruins which were discovered among remote Andean peaks and whose anonymous builders left no record of their civilisation except the stones themselves. The confrontation of the poet with an ancient civilisation recalls, at first reading, Heredia's meditation on the Aztecs in the 'Teocalli de Cholula'. But Neruda is much more involved than Heredia was. He himself and his own consciousness are inseparable from his exploration into the historical past. In the first section of the poem, the poet is conscious only of the inadequacy of his individuality in the rootless, meaningless life of the city:

> Del aire al aire, como una red vacía
> iba yo entre las calles y la atmósfera, llegando y despidiendo.*

Through the 'empty net' of the individual consciousness, time slips away; the recurrent 'otoño' [autumn] with its overtones of withering and age emphasises a feeling of failure, a sense of waste—also expressed in the seasonal image of the 'gastada primavera humana' [spent human spring]. To Stanza Six the poem is a descent, down into individual consciousness and the failure of any individual life to give the poet a sense of values or significance. 'El ser como el maíz se desgranaba en el inacabable/granero de los hechos perdidos' [The self like corn was seeded in the unending barn of lost events]. The search for the 'indestructible' in man leads him only to death: 'rodé muriendo de mi propria muerte' [I wandered about, dying of my own death]. But with Stanza Six the ascending movement of the section begins. He climbs up the mountainside and the stone steps of this 'alto arrecife

---

* From air to air, like an empty net, I walked between the streets and the atmosphere, arriving and saying farewell.

de la aurora humana'. The recurrent image in these later sections is that of the coral reef, the durable rock made from the myriads of small mortal organisms. The deaths that gave life to this monument of stone ('una vida de piedra después de tantas vidas' [a life of stone after many lives]) haunt the poet who, in Section Six breaks into a litany of praise to the:

> Aguila sideral, viña de bruma.
> Bastión perdido, cimitarra ciega.
> Cinturón estrellado, pan solemne.*

But the stones, the air that surrounds them, the past time to which they bear witness, seem to negate humanity. The poet can only guess at the frustrated lives upon which Macchu Picchu had been built, the human suffering that had gone to its making, and he asks, 'Macchu Picchu, pusiste piedras en la piedra, y en la base, harapo?' [Macchu Picchu, did you place stone upon stone and rags at the base?]. It is at this point that the two themes of the poem—the loneliness of the poet and the forgotten humanity who had built the fortress—converge. The poet first intuits certain human individuals, Juan Cortapiedras, Juan Comefrío, Juan Piesdescalzos, and then in the final section of the poem comes to the realisation that his task is to give life to these forgotten, anonymous beings, to restore them to their place in history. In this way, he as well as they finds a sense of identity:

> Dadme el silencio, el agua, la esperanza,
> Dadme la lucha, el hierro, los volcanes
> Apegadme los cuerpos como imanes.
> Acudid a mis venas y a mi boca.
> Hablad por mis palabras y mi sangre.†

These impressive closing lines illustrate the vast gulf that exists between Vallejo's poetic technique, which sought to break down the rhetoric of Spanish, and that of Neruda who deliberately uses rhetorical devices. His rhythms are those of the Church, those of prayer, litany and chant, and he reads his own poems in a chanting voice. The sonorous epithet, the rolling feminine word-ending, the use of alliteration, make this an auditory poetry whereas Vallejo's often used the support of visual devices.

Canto general represented Neruda's first real attempt to escape

---

* Sidereal eagle, vine of mist, lost bastion, blind scimitar, starry girdle, solemn bread.
† Give me silence, water, hope, give me struggle, iron, volcanoes, stick bodies to me like magnets, come to my veins and to my mouth. Speak through my words and blood.

from an élitist concept of poetry. Yet, before addressing himself to the task of creating a poetry that could be enjoyed by simple people, he published another collection of love poems. *Los versos del capitán* [*The Captain's Verses*] were published anonymously under a pseudonym in Italy and were addressed to the 'novia' [the bride] of the captain who was the supposed author. These are the intimate confessions of Neruda's love for Matilde Urrutia whom he later married. Nothing could be a greater contrast than the intimate love poems and *Las uvas y el viento* [*Grapes and the Wind*] (1954) published after a journey to Eastern Europe and China. Yet in both of the collections, there is a new simplicity, a joy in simple everyday things—the woman he loves washing handkerchiefs, the water flowing under the bridges of Prague —that anticipates the *Odas elementales* [*Elemental Odes*] (1954), the *Nuevas odas elementales* (1956) and the *Tercer libro de Odas* (1957). In all these short-lined poems, Neruda addresses himself to the most elemental aspects of human existence—to 'the couple', to 'time', to the sea, to wood and rain. They express his desire that art should become clearer and more accessible. 'Las artes van aclarándose', he had declared 'van dejando atrás la tortura y la agonía del individuo sofocado' [The arts are becoming more understandable, they are leaving behind the torment and agony of the stifled individual][1] and in a poem addressed to the book, he described the literature of the future as one which:

> vuelve
> a tener nieve o musgo
> para que las pisadas
> o los ojos
> vayan grabando
> huellas.*

In other words, the poem would once again be integral to human life. His vision here is a vision of the future, of a man who is no longer alienated but realises himself in work and activity. Neruda's poetry is here intended as a restoration of man's sense of joy in the elemental and the archetypal pattern. Thus, the ode to wood which reminds him of his childhood is also an ode to the new creative civilisation:

> y así nace y comienza
> a recorrer el mundo
> la madera,

* again has snow or moss so that the footsteps or the eyes may engrave their tracks.

hasta ser constructora silenciosa
hasta sufrir y proteger
construyendo
la vivienda
en donde cada dia
se encontrarán el hombre, la mujer
y la vida.*

However, simplicity may not necessarily be a virtue in poetry. Certainly there is a loss of allusiveness and ambiguity which enriches rather than detracts from poetic meaning. And in *Estravagario* (1958), the poet returned to a baroque style which he had never entirely abandoned even in the *Odas* and which seemed to come more naturally to him. Thus in 'No me hagan caso', he returns to the description of sea-life in a semi-comic style:

> Yo conozco todas las algas,
> los ojos blancos de la arena,
> las pequeñas mercaderías
> de las mareas en Otoño
> y ando como grueso pelicano
> levantando nidos mojados.†

Neruda's most recent collections include *Plenos Poderes* [*Full Powers*] (1962), the autobiographical *Memorial de Isla Negra* and *Cien Sonetos de Amor* [*One Hundred Love Sonnets*]. He has also made his debut as a playwright.[1]

Neruda is a major figure in Spanish–American literature. The quantity of his output at first sight may seem a guarantee of lack of depth, and he does indeed often lapse into facility but this is by no means always the rule. His poetry reaches the heights of the greatest. It is a worthy monument to a human and generous personality who has made a valiant attempt to overcome the more negative aspects of contemporary poetry.

Octavio Paz

Born in Mexico in 1914, Paz was the son of Zapata's representative in New York, and grew up in a family who had identified themselves with the cause of the Revolution. He founded his own literary maga-

---

* and so the wood is born and begins to go round the world, until it becomes a silent constructor, until it suffers and protects by constructing the house in which each day is to be found man, woman and life.
† I know all the algae, the white eyes of sand, the small merchandise of the autumn tides and I walk like a fat pelican lifting up wet nests.

zine, *Barandal*, in 1931, and for some years the writing of poetry and political and social commitment divided his attention. He helped to run a school in Yucatán in the 1930s and in 1937, during the Spanish Civil War, he attended the Writers' Congress in which both Vallejo and Neruda had taken part. But his literary influences were far-removed from any committed view of literature. First T. S. Eliot and then St Jean Perse and later the Surrealists and Indian religions made deep impressions on him. The magazine *Taller* which he founded in 1939 published translations of poems of Hölderlin, Rimbaud and Blake. These diverse influences have one thing in common—they are all visionary, deeply at war with modern society, and concerned with something that lies beyond the world of phenomena. And Paz developed a view of poetry from which he has deviated little and which follows in a direct line from the nineteenth-century visionaries and the Surrealists. In *El arco y la lira* [*The Bow and the Lyre*] and *Los signos en rotación* [*Signs in Rotation*] as well as in his essays on poets, he hypostatises poetry. Characteristic, for instance, is his description of the relation of poetry to society, which he sees as a perpetual conflict of opposites.

Condenados a una perpetua conjunción que se resuelve en instantánea discordia, los dos términos buscan una conversión mutua; poetizar la vida social, socializar la palabra poética. Transformación de la sociedad en comunidad creadora, en poema vivo; y del poema en vida social, en imagen encarnada.*[1]

His definition of poetry he puts in the form of a question:

El poema ¿no es ese espacio vibrante sobre el cual se proyecta un puñado de signos como un ideograma que fuese un surtidor de significaciones? Espacio, proyección, ideograma; estas tres palabras aluden a una operación que consiste en desplegar un lugar, un aquí, que reciba y sostenga una escritura: fragmentos que se reagrupan y buscan constituir una figura, un núcleo de significados.†[2]

The word 'fountain' is one that recurs in his poetry; if the poem is a fountain of meaning, a pattern in space, then it follows that Paz does not, unlike Neruda, believe it to be a 'song', a direct expression of his

* Condemned to perpetual conjunction which is immediately transformed into discord, the two terms seek a mutual dialogue. To make social life poetic, to make the poetic word social. The transformation of society into a creative community, into a living poem; and the poem into social life, into an incarnate image.

† Isn't the poem a vibrant space on which is projected a handful of signs like an ideogram which is a fountain of meanings? Space, projection, ideogram; these three words allude to an operation which consists in unfolding a place, a 'here' which receives and sustains a writing; fragments which regroup and try to constitute a figure, a nucleus of meanings.

own emotion. It does, however, represent the poet's need to transcend himself and his limitations:

Todo poema es apetito por negar la sucesión y fundar un reino perdurable. Si el hombre es trascendencia, ir más allá de sí, el poeta es el signo más puro de ese continuo transcenderse.*[1]

But the poet's tool is the word, and not only does he use words but they create him:

El lenguaje crea al poeta y sólo en la medida en que las palabras nacen y mueren y renacen en su interior, él a su vez es creador.†[2]

For Paz, the word has always had a magic power. In some of the early poems of *Bajo tu clara sombra* [*Below your Clear Shadow*] written between 1935 and 1939, he wrote:

> Nacían las palabras
> y eran como palomas y luceros.‡

He often wrote poems about words or about poetry itself. In 'Palabra', the word is seen as contained in contradictions:

> oscura y luminosa;
> herida y fuente: espejo:
> espejo y resplandor;
> resplandor y puñal
> vivo puñal amado
> ya no puñal, sí mano suave; fruto.§

Each word suggests an association which somehow contradicts or cancels the previously suggested associations and yet is implied in them. The progression is dialectic. Similarly in a prose poem, 'Hacia un poema' [Towards a poem], he thinks of words as clusters of associations, some of them contradictory:

Palabras, frases, sílabas, astros que giran alrededor de un centro fijo. Dos cuerpos, muchos seres que se encuentran en una palabra. El papel se cubre de letras indelebles, que nadie dijo, que nadie dictó, que han caído allí y arden y queman y se apagan. Así, pues, existe la poesía, el amor existe. Y si yo no existo, existes tú. ¶

* Every poem is a striving to negate succession and found a lasting realm. If man is transcendence, the going beyond himself, the poet is the purest sign of this continuous transcendence.
† Language creates the poet and only insofar as words are born and die and are reborn in him is he in his turn a creator.
‡ Words were born and they were like doves or fireflies.
§ dark and luminous; wound and fountain; mirror; mirror and brilliance; brilliance and dagger, living loved dagger, now no dagger but a gentle hand, a fruit.
¶ Words, phrases, syllables, stars which turn around a fixed centre. Two bodies, many beings which meet in a word. Paper is covered with indelible letters which nobody

Paz therefore constructs the poem on the basis of very general images—water, fire, air, earth, dreams, mirrors; words which contain the maximum in association, the maximum in layers of myth. There are patterns, too, of opening and shutting, of communion and isolation.

But though Paz has had a consistent view of poetry and his repertoire of words and images has remained remarkably consistent, too, there has been a change of direction. Early poems tended to be concerned with identity while his more recent works are each intended as an experience, a happening, in which poet and reader attain a sense of unity and completion. The technique, too, has developed from early short-lined, tightly-organised poems, to the long-lined poems of his middle period, and under Eastern influence to the brief, haiku-like poems that he is now writing. We can compare two poems from different periods, an early 'Espejo' [Mirror] and '¿No hay salida?' [Is there no way out?] from a later period. In 'Espejo', in a quest for a sense of identity, the words play ambiguously, perpetually suggesting contradictions:

Frente a los juegos fatuos del espejo
mi ser es pira y es ceniza
respira y es ceniza,
y ardo y me quemo y resplandezco y miento
un yo que empuña, muerto
una daga de humo que le finge
la evidencia de sangre de la herida,
y un yo, mi yo penúltimo,
que sólo pide olvido, sombra, nada,
final mentira que lo enciende y quema.

De una máscara a otra
hay siempre un yo penúltimo que pide.
Y me hundo en mí mismo y no me toco.*

Here words are indeed fountains, spraying meanings and suggestion into the air, suggesting a perpetual process of negation and creation.

spoke, nobody dictated, which have fallen there and burn, scorch and are put out. So then, poetry exists and love exists. And if I do not exist, you exist.
* In front of the delusive games of the mirror, my being is pyre and ash, it breathes and is ash ash I burn and burn myself and am brilliant and I feign an 'I' which grasps, though dead, at the dagger of smoke which imitates the proof of blood of the wound and one 'I', the penultimate 'I' which only asks for oblivion, shadow, nothingness, a final lie which burns and consumes it.
    From one mask to another there is always a penultimate 'I' which asks, and I sink into myself and do not touch myself.

Thus the mirrors play 'juegos fatuos' [delusive games], but since this is very close to the Spanish for will-o'-the-wisp ['fuego fatuo'] this suggests the image of pyre and ash. The Spanish for pyre is 'pira' which is very near to 'respira' [breathes] and so the poem is the dialect i.e. process in which words (like the self) contain the seeds of their own destruction, from which in turn comes a new creation. In '¿No hay salida?' [Is there no way out?] a similar theme is treated more meditatively:

Todo está lejos, no hay regreso, los muertos no están muertos, los vivos no están vivos,
hay un muro, un ojo que es un pozo, todo tira hacia abajo, pesa el cuerpo,
pesan los pensamientos, todos los años son este minuto desplomándose interminablemente,
aquel cuarto de hotel de San Francisco me salió al paso en Bangkok, hoy es ayer, mañana es ayer.
la realidad es una escalera que no sube ni baja, no nos movemos, hoy es hoy, siempre es hoy.
siempre el ruido de los trenes que despedazan cada noche a la noche,
el recurrir a las palabras melladas
la perforación de muro, las idas y venidas, la realidad cerrando puertas.
poniendo comas, la puntuación del tiempo, todo está lejos, los muros son enormes,
está a millas de distancia el vaso de agua, tardará mil años en recorrer mi cuarto.
qué sonido remoto tiene la palabra vida, no estoy aqui, no hay aquí, este cuarto está en otra parte,
aquí es ninguna parte, poco a poco me he ido cerrando y no encuentro salida que no dé a este instante,
este instante soy yo, salí de pronto de mí mismo, no tengo nombre ni rostro,
yo está aqui, echado a mis pies, mirándome, mirándose mirarme mirado.
Fuera, en los jardines que atrasó el verano, una cigarra se ensaña contra la noche.
¿Estoy o estuve aqui?*

* All is far, there is no return, the dead are not dead, the living are not alive. There is a wall, an eye which is a well, all pulls from below, the body is heavy. Thoughts are heavy, all years are this minute interminably falling down; that hotel room in San Francisco came out to meet me in Bangkok; today is yesterday, tomorrow is yesterday. Reality is a staircase which does not go up or down, we do not move, today is today, it is always today. There is always the noise of trains which scatter each night during the night, always the recourse to dented words, the perforation of the wall, the goings and comings, reality closing doors, putting commas, the punctuation of time, all is afar, the walls are also enormous. A glass of water is miles away, I shall take a thousand years to go across my room. What a remote sound the word 'life' has, I am not here, there is no 'here', this room is somewhere else. Here is nowhere, little by little I have been closing myself in and I can find no exit that does not give onto this moment. This moment is me, I suddenly went out of myself. I have neither name nor face. I is here, down at my feet, looking at myself, looking at each other, looking at me, looked at. Outside in the gardens made late by summer, a cicada is angry at the night. I am or I was here?

Here the poem is less effective than 'Espejos' since the poet states, rather than evokes, the illusory nature of reality. The few particularised elements, such as the hotel room and the gardens, are set in circles of increasing abstraction. There is thus a vast difference between Vallejo's lived poetic experience and Paz's abstract meditation.

One of Paz's most ambitious poems is 'Piedra de sol' [Sunstone] written in a circular pattern and having the same number of lines as there were days in the Aztec calendar year. Within this circular container, Paz sets into play seemingly contradictory aspects of experience which are really one; and the past selves which are really the same self:

> rostro de llamas, rostro devorado
> adolescente rostro perseguido
> años fantasmas días circulares
> que dan al mismo patio, al mismo muro
> arde el instante y son un solo rostro
> los sucesivos rostros de la llama
> todos los nombres son un solo nombre
> todos los rostros son un solo rostro
> todos los siglos son un solo instante
> y por todo los siglos de los siglos
> cierra el paso al futuro un par de ojos.*

This poem is the poetic answer to the tragic situation Paz had expounded in his essays on the Mexican character, *El laberinto de la soledad* [*The Labyrinth of Solitude*]. If poetry is a way of transcending solitude, a form of communion, then the poem itself becomes a ritual of communion. If Neruda's poems establish a rite in which the need for human solidarity is expressed, Paz's poems are also a rite, and there is a similar play of effects by repetition.

Though mainly concerned with an exploration of Mexican beliefs and myths, *El laberinto de la soledad* includes many of Paz's most persistent theories. An appendix on 'La dialéctica de la soledad' [The Dialectic of Solitude], for instance, propounds the view that communion and love are almost impossible in modern society, yet man must continually try to break out of his solitude and seek to establish communion; but how is he to do this? Work is no longer creative and he is alienated from society. Paz sees only myth as a possible agent through

---

* face of flames, devoured face, persecuted adolescent face, phantom years, circular days which look on the same yard, on the same wall, the moment burns and they are a single face, the successive faces of the flame. All numbers are one number. All faces are only one face. All centuries are a single moment and for all the centuries of centuries, a pair of eyes blocks the way to the future.

which man transcends subjectivity. Through Myth and through the Fiesta, 'el hombre rompe su soledad y vuelve a ser uno con la creación' [man break his solitude and again becomes one with creation]. And the poem, too, acts as a 'ceremonia ritual, una Fiesta'[1] and thus allows man to escape magically from the prison of time.

In some ways Paz is the Borges of poetry; he, too, seeks a language akin to the universality of philosophical language, a general language which subsumes in its broad concepts the variety and flux of the world. Of the three important Spanish–American poets of this age, Paz is the most abstract.

RECENT POETRY

What of more recent trends? Spanish–American poetry is extremely vigorous, and there is a wealth of experiment, ranging from various types of 'beat' poets to the experiments in social poetry that have been made in Peru, Cuba and elsewhere. There are distinguished poets of the older generation like Ricardo Molinari (Argentina, 1898–) who cannot readily be fitted into categories. However, two broad lines of development seem to emerge. In Mexico, poets are more conservative in their use of language. Jaime Sabines (1925–) and Marco Antonio Montes de Oca (1932–), José Emilio Pacheco (1939–)— to name only a few—are not primarily concerned with revolutionising language and technique. They generally work within the limits of the literary language, accepting a tradition of literary language. In this, they are very different from the poets of Chile, Peru and other countries of South America who have created 'anti-poetry'. Poets of this area are seeking new modes of expression through rejection of tradition. Nicanor Parra (1914-), for instance, uses a dead-pan journalese style in his *Poemas y anti-poemas* in which he expresses the anguish of man caught in the trap of exigencies. Thus he writes flatly:

> Esta situación se prolongó por más de cinco años
> Por temporadas vivíamos juntos en una pieza redonda
> Que pagábamos a medias en un barrio de lujo cerca del cementerio.*[2]

A younger Chilean poet, Enrique Lihn (1929–), also uses colloquial elements in his poem but he constructs these in a series of collages which put together elements of his daily life, snatches of conversation and memory. Lihn's poems destroy the illusion fostered for centuries

* This situation went on for more than five years. Some times we lived together in a round room which we had partly paid for. It was in a wealthy suburb near the cemetery.

that there is some division between 'inner' and 'outer' experience, between imagination and perception. Here, for instance, is the final section of his poem 'Barro' [Clay]:

No hay más extraño que uno. Es la apariencia de otro quien terminó por frecuentarnos,
por aceptar finalmente una invitación reiterada.
Me pareció ver a mi sombra cuando le abrí la puerta, justo en el momento en que íbamos a salir.
La función había comenzado. 'Adelante. Adelante'.
'Te estábamos esperando', dije yo y ella dijo: 'No reconozco a los ingratos' con un curioso temblor en la voz.*[1]

The experience here is not simply of the self but of the 'divided self', the shadow by which man recognises his alienated state.

A very different poet is the Peruvian, Carlos Germán Belli (1927–), whose ¡ Oh hada cibernética! often deliberately parodies traditional literary language and techniques, and yet, as much as Lihn's poetry, conveys a thoroughly modern sense of anguish:

¡ Oh Hada Cibernética!
cuándo asolarás de un soplo
las lonjas que me apresan,
y me liberes
para que yo pueda entonces
dedicarme a buscar una mujer
dulce como el azúcar
suave como la seda
y comérmela en pedacitos
y gritar después:
'¡ abajo la lonja de azúcar
abajo la lonja de seda!'†

The poet's search for communication and fulfilment is here presented in a grotesque light for relationship with the desired woman of sugar and silk can only end in his devouring her with self-justificatory cries. The almost classical balance of the language is belied by the savagery of the sentiments expressed.

The modern movement in Spanish–American poetry began with

* There is nothing stranger than oneself. It is the appearance of another who finally frequents us, accepting at last an oft-repeated invitation. I thought I saw my shadow when I opened the door just as we were about to go out. The performance had begun. 'Come in. Come in'. 'I was waiting for you', I said and she said: 'I don't have anything to do with ungrateful people', with a curious tremor in her voice.
† Oh Cybernetic Muse when will you destroy with one breath the straps that bind me and liberate me so that I may then devote myself to looking for a woman, sweet as sugar and soft as silk and to eating her in little pieces to cry afterwards: 'down with the sugar strap, down with the silk strap!'

the impact of Surrealism and the avant-garde, which acted as a liberation. Vallejo, Neruda and Octavio Paz have used similar techniques to those of European and North-American poetry but their development has been wholly original. Vallejo, in particular, carried on what was virtually an assault on Spanish grammar syntax and literary language. He destroyed mystifications about the self and presented the existential experience of man living in a society and among other men. The best of contemporary poets, though they do not directly imitate him, attempt to achieve an 'unmystified' understanding of man. Neruda, on the other hand, has had less direct effect on subsequent generations. Indeed it is strange that at a time when in England and North American recited poetry is gaining ground, in Latin America poets seems largely to have abandoned this.

A NOTE ON THE THEATRE

Little has been said about the theatre. The omission seems all the more extraordinary in that the theatre has had a long and vigorous history in Mexico, Argentina and in Peru. Foreign companies with international reputations frequently visit Spanish–American capitals, and there has always been a certain public, even though it is a small one, for the theatre. In these circumstances the absence of universal or major dramatists is extraordinary. In the early years of the century, when Florencio Sánchez brought the naturalist theatre to Spanish America, the dearth of a major theatrical tradition was perhaps understandable in that the techniques of naturalism and the 'problem' play were of fairly limited and local appeal. His was still a provincial drama. But with the avant-garde experiments of the '20s, a new theatre might have been expected, and indeed Roberto Arlt the Argentine novelist did devote himself to playwriting for some years and produced one or two Pirandello-like plays.[1] In Mexico, too, Rodolfo Usigli (1905–) under the influence of George Bernard Shaw, broke away from realism to write several political farces and *El gesticulador* (staged in 1947, written in 1937) which was a cutting analysis of the Mexican need for the political lie. It concerned a man who impersonated a revolutionary general he knew to be dead but who, even when he told the truth about himself, was not believed, since the Mexicans preferred myth to reality. Usigli also wrote a number of dramas of middle-class life, e.g. *Medio tono* [*Half tone*], and two historical plays, *La corona de sombra* [*The crown of shadow*] and *La corona de luz* [*The crown of light*]. Only in Puerto Rico, with the plays of René Márques has there been any other country with a 'national drama' of this type. Argentina's leading dramatist to date, Samuel Eichelbaum (1894–), has been concerned with moral rather than with national problems. A less committed, more experimental, theatre has developed in Chile thanks to the encouragement of two university groups—the Teatro Experimental de la Universidad de Chile which later became the Instituto de Teatro de la Universidad de Chile; and the Teatro Experimental de la Universidad Católica. To date, the most interesting modern Chilean dramatist has been Luis Heiremans (1928–).

In Cuba, where one might have expected a post-revolutionary drama to have developed, there has not yet developed a flourishing drama. The most notable dramatist is José Triana (1933–), one of the few to have his work performed outside Spanish America.

Noche de los Asesinos [Night of the Assassins] (1965) and *El parque de la fraternidad [Fraternity Park]* show the influence of contemporary European theatre. The problems raised in *Noche de los Asesinos* are, however, similar to those raised in the contemporary poetry and the novel. The two acts of the play centre on the family and on society. Three characters, Lalo, Cuca and Beba, act out family relationships. At the end of the first act their father and mother are 'killed'. The second act takes the form of the trial with the characters acting out the accusers and the accused and eventually re-enacting the murder of the parents. The play reflects both the conflict between spontaneity and order and the tragic progress of human relations in which freedom invariably gives way to the 'killing' of the other. Triana's choice of theme, his demonstration of the deadening effect of routine, of set patterns and reactions brings him close to the poets whose work has been considered in this chapter—César Vallejo, Neruda and Octavio Paz—all of whom have touched on this theme in their poetry. And we shall find in the next chapter that the attack on dead order was also an important feature of prose writing.

The contemporary theatre is naturally most flourishing in large urban centres such as Mexico and Buenos Aires. In the former, Emilio Carballido (1925–) and Sergio Magaña (1924–) are the most established contemporary dramatists. In Colombia, Venezuela and Ecuador, the liveliest movements have stemmed from university theatre groups. The failure of Latin America to provide a really outstanding dramatist of international stature is surprising until we remember that the popularity of the theatre has been rivalled by the cinema in much of Latin America.

10 THE CONTEMPORARY NOVEL AND SHORT STORY

In 1925, there appeared in the Argentine avant-garde magazine, *Proa*, a translation of Molly Bloom's monologue in the closing section of James Joyce's *Ulysses*, with a note by a young translator, Jorge Luis Borges. 'Soy el primero que ha arribado al libro de Joyce' [I am the first to have arrived at Joyce's book], he declared, with all the pride of a Columbus reaching new shores. His contemporaries, however, were slow to follow him. For many years, the rest of *Ulysses* remained untranslated. The transformation wrought by Hemingway on the short story, by Joyce, Virginia Woolf, Kafka, Gide, Huxley, Faulkner on the novel had comparatively little impact in the '20s, when most novelists were engaged in the exploration of Latin-American reality or in the pursuit of social justice. The '20s, in particular, were years of revolutionary hope and euphoria while the '30s was a period of reaction and retrenchment in many countries, with the accompanying evils of economic crisis. Certainly as the years of euphoria faded, as revolutionary hope after revolutionary hope failed, so did an increasing number of novelists turn away from active participation in political movements. More and more, the revolution they sought was in technique.

Other factors, too, were at work. Realism and naturalism have produced few good novels in Spanish America. Reality is too complex and bizarre, society too dispersed, for the Balzacian style to be successful. On the other hand, certain writers who had used fantasy and allowed the imagination free play came nearer to a true picture of society. Indeed, from Modernism onwards, there had been a tradition of 'fantastic' writing. Leopoldo Lugones, for instance, produced a collection of weird and amazing stories. Horacio Quiroga, who had served his apprenticeship in the Modernist movement, was directly influenced by Edgar Allan Poe in *Los perseguidos* [*The Persecuted Ones*] and throughout his life was fascinated by the macabre and the abnormal. Rafael Arévalo Martínez (1884–), a brilliant Guatemalan Modernist, published *El hombre que parecía un caballo* [*The Man who*

Looked like a Horse] in 1914. The story deals with a characteristically Modernist theme—the conflict between spiritual ideal and animal instincts—but it did so by making the central character symbolic. He takes on the appearance of a horse and at the end of the story gallops away. The technique was somewhat akin to expressionism in painting. Arévalo Martínez later wrote a number of political satires set in imaginary countries which were analogues for Spanish America. *Oficina de paz en Orolandia* [*Office of Peace in Orolandia*] dealt with an imaginary peace organisation; *El mundo de los maharachías* [*The World of the Maharachías*] (1938) described a civilisation of superior monkey-like creatures with sentient tails; and in *Viaje a Ipanda* [*Voyage to Ipanda*] (1939) his fantasy took a Swiftian turn.

If fantasy-literature had a flickering but persistent life, the same cannot be said for the psychological novel, of which there were few outstanding examples. An overwhelming interest in social and national problems tended to divert writers from the study of individual psychology—with one notable exception, that of the Chilean, Eduardo Barrios (1884–1963).

Barrios wrote a number of novels which can be considered as case histories. He was less interested in the typical than in the abnormal. Thus *El niño que enloqueció de amor* [*The Boy who Went Mad from Love*] (1915) analyses the growth of an obsession in a young boy to the point of madness. In *Un perdido* [*The Failure*] (1917), the 'case' is that of a social misfit. In this novel, Barrios does analyse society as well as the individual, but only in so far as this provides the scaffolding from which the protagonist, Lucho, tumbles. The novel shows us a young man who is without the aggressive *macho* [male] characteristic that society demands, and who falls down the social scale from his upper-middle-class origins to the *demi-monde* until he ends 'un perdido', a bohemian outcast from society. In *El hermano asno* [*Brother Ass*], religious mania is explored. The conflict here takes place outside society, within a monastery in which, side by side, live Fray Rufino, renowned for saintliness but tormented by temptation of the flesh, and the more worldly Fray Lázaro, the narrator who had come into the monastery to escape from the tragedy of an unhappy love affair. Whereas Lázaro overcomes temptation, Rufino succumbs, but after his death it is Lázaro who takes on his 'crime' so that Rufino's reputation for saintliness should not be tainted. Even in an apparently 'social' novel, *Gran Señor y Rajadiablos* [*Gentleman and Hell-raiser*] (1948), Barrios is mainly interested in the depiction of a character of a previous generation—a lusty landowner. And in a final novel, *Los hombres del hombre* [*The Men of the Man*] (1950), there was a thoroughly modern preoccupation with the many conflicting personalities within a single man.

Apart from Barrios's studies of individual relations, psychological obsessions have invariably been very closely related to social questions. Of the very few exceptions, one should perhaps mention *La amortajada* [*The Shrouded One*] (1938) by María Luisa Bombal (1910–   ) in which a dead woman is visited by many of her family and the people with whom she had had close relationships. For a moment they 'relive' in her memory, but with her burial and decomposition, her individuality and her hold on the living gradually disintegrate. Another notable exception is *El túnel* [*The Tunnel*] (1948) by the Argentine writer Ernesto Sábato, a novel which deals with a paranoid painter, Castel, in the grip of an obsession with a married woman. Unable to possess her as completely as he would like, he kills her.

With these few exceptions, the outstanding contemporary writers are not directly concerned with psychological analysis. The roots of the modern novel are to be found in society and in the writer's confrontation with national problems. But the technique is no longer realism. It is the purpose of this chapter to trace the development of the social and metaphysical fantasy in Spanish America in the works of Arlt and Borges; to consider two pioneers of 'realismo mágico'— Carpentier and Asturias; and finally to examine the outstanding contemporary writers of each country who are working in this tradition.

THE SOCIAL AND METAPHYSICAL FANTASY

Roberto Arlt and Jorge Luis Borges

Arévalo Martinez's stories showed that the writer could explore social problems and the human personality without recourse to the techniques of realism. The European avant-garde, meanwhile, had found a rich new source of material in the subconscious. They saw that, by allowing imagination free play, the writer could break through the barrier of preconceptions and perceive new truths. But it was in the Argentine that the use of fantasy was vastly extended by two major writers: Roberto Arlt who used fantasy as a weapon of social satire; and Jorge Luis Borges whose fantasies were concerned with the philosophical and metaphysical constructions that human beings put on experience.

Roberto Arlt (1900–42) was the first serious explorer in Spanish America of the urban complex and its nightmares. He himself was the son of an immigrant who had found the struggle for life hard in the 'promised land' of America. Thrown at an early age on to his own resources, Arlt was forced into a variety of jobs. He had an intelligence that was dazzled by scientific inventions, but these talents could not be developed for he left school at an early age. He finally found his way into journalism, was associated with a socialist realist school of writers, the 'Boedo group' (which was named after the street in which they met), and like them felt a strong sense of identification with the poor and a distrust of élitism in literature. Yet his own work could not be contained within the limits of realism. His first novel, *El juguete rabioso* [*The Angry Toy*] (1927) was, however, strongly reminiscent of Gorky whose writings the Boedo group greatly admired. This black account of poverty and delinquency, based on his own childhood and youth, was long in finding a publisher and totally failed to make an impression on an Argentine literary scene that was dominated by the fashion-conscious élite. Yet Arlt told a powerful story of boys in the slums whose poor home backgrounds offered no food for the imagination except for the lurid adventures of bandits, those legendary figures of the 'penny dreadfuls'. The boys grow up dreaming of crime as the weapon that will liberate them both from poverty and from spiritual starvation. Real life, on the other hand, is a constant chain of frustration. The protagonist, Silvio Astier, works first as a shop assistant, in which job he is pitilessly exploited and then having joined the army in order to find an outlet for this scientific curiosity, finds that intelligence is superfluous. He is demobilised and sent back to the slums. Only the ending mars the book. Arlt, whose personal experience formed the background of the story, did not know how to bring it to a close. He has his protagonist betray some criminal associates and thus redeem himself in the eyes of society. Even so, the redemption is sour. Silvio Astier can only become a part of society through treachery.

Arlt's two outstanding novels are *Los siete locos* [*The Seven Madmen*] (1929) and *Los lanzallamas* [*The Flame Throwers*] (1931)—these being two parts of a single narrative. Once again, the protagonist, Erdosaín, is based on Arlt himself, but this time the novelist breaks the bonds of realism and writes a fantasy which is a crushing condemnation of modern society. Erdosaín is an embezzler whose wife leaves him in desperation at her life of poverty and who is threatened with prosecution unless he repays the money he has taken from his firm. He falls in with a group of madmen who conceive the plan of kidnapping the rich Barsut and raising money from him to start chains of brothels. The money they make is to be devoted to the destruction of society. The plot is less important, however, than the fantastic gallery of characters such as the Astrologer, the Melancholy Pimp and the Gold-Seeker, whose madness is only the desperate reaction of men whom society has rejected and who live in a state of anguish which is inseparable from modern life:

Esta zona de angustia era la consecuencia del sufrimiento de los hombres. Y como una nube de gas venenoso se trasladaba pesadamente de un punto a otro, penetrando murallas y atravesando los edificios, sin perder su forma plana y horizontal...*

Escape into fantasy leaves man in a sorrier dilemma than before. Erdosaín has the purest ideals of love but invariably finds himself with prostitutes. The constant process of disillusionment leaves him in a state of total alienation:

El no era ya un organismo envasando sufrimientos, sino algo más inhumana... quizá eso...un monstruo enroscado en sí mismo en el negro vientre de la pieza. Cada capa de oscuridad que descendía de sus párpados era un tejido placentario que lo aislaba más y más del universo de los hombres. Hasta la conciencia de ser, en él no ocupaba más de un centimetro cuadrado de sensibilidad.†

These states of alienation are characteristic of *urban* man, of man caught in the iron net of capitalist society which has systematised exploitation, robbery and murder. The seven madmen, in their plot to destroy 'this implacable society', employ society's own weapons of murder, prostitution and robbery. Arlt's account of the mad fantasies of his characters is interspersed with reports of real contemporary events—war in China, strikes, etc. Reality, in fact, outstrips fantasy.

Arlt was a pioneer in a field which few European novelists had entered successfully, and he conveyed a personal and nightmarish vision of a world in which the city itself was the main enemy. His point of view was that of the anarchist who sees a return to a simpler rural

---

* This zone of anguish was the consequence of the suffering of men. And like a cloud of venomous gas it moved heavily from one point to another, penetrating walls, passing through buildings, without losing its flat and horizontal shape...

† He was no longer an organism containing sufferings, but something more inhuman... perhaps this...a monster coiled round itself in the black stomach of the room. Each layer of darkness which descended from his eyelids was a placenta-like web that isolated him more and more from the universe of men. Even the consciousness of being did not occupy in him more than a square centimetre of sensibility.

society as the only effective solution. So the Gold-Seeker believes that in the solitude of nature man regains the sense of his own identity:

Desafiando la soledad, los peligros, la tristeza, el sol, lo infinito de la llanura, uno se siente otro hombre... distinto del rebaño de esclavos que agoniza en la ciudad.*

Arlt wrote two other novels, *El amor brujo* [*Bewitched Love*] (1932) and *El jorobadito* [*The Little Hunchback*] (1933) and published a collection of short stories, *Aguafuertes porteñas* [*Buenos Aires Etchings*] (1933).

Arlt's contemporary, Jorge Luis Borges, seems to have little in common with him. Socially they were light-years apart. Borges was born into a cultivated family, was educated in Switzerland and after the 1914–18 war went to live in Spain, where he was associated with the Ultraist movement and where he published his first poems. On his return to Buenos Aires in 1921, he helped to found or contributed to a number of little magazines such as *Prisma* (1921–2), *Proa* (1922–3) and *Martín Fierro* and published collections of poems, *Fervor de Buenos Aires* (1923), *Luna de enfrente* (1925), and *Cuaderno San Martín* (1929), in which the Ultraist technique of using startling metaphor was applied to the city scenes of Buenos Aires. However, such scenes were usually the starting point of a poetic meditation on illusion and reality, on dream and consciousness—which were to become obsessive preoccupations. Thus though Arlt and Borges were apparently very different writers, they meet on this common ground of fantasy.

Borges, however, did not easily find the genre most suited to his genius. For many years, the essay was his chief vehicle; essays in which he examined odd, unorthodox religious or philosophical beliefs, marvelling at the Cabbala or the Gnostics, or as in his *Historia de la eternidad* [*History of Eternity*] (1936), exploring cyclical time theories. These essays were his first approach to the narrative, of which he was later to confess:

I know that the least perishable part of my literary production is the narrative, yet for many years I did not dare to write stories. I thought that the paradise of the tale was forbidden to me.[1]

And when he published his *Historia universal de la infamia* [*Universal History of Evil*] (1935), he described this as 'the irresponsible game of a timid man who did not have the drive to write stories and distracted himself by falsifying and apostasising the tales of others.[2] This collec-

---

* Defying solitude, dangers, sadness, the sun, the infinity of the plain, one feels oneself another man, different from the flock of slaves who agonise in the city.

tion was a hybrid between the essays and his *ficciones*. The heroes of
evil he described were obscure historical characters revivified in the
author's imagination. But it was not until *Ficciones* [*Fictions*] (1944)
and *El Aleph* (1949) that his own style matured.[1]

The 'fiction' may take the form of a detective story, a piece of
literary criticism or historical investigation, the description of an imaginary country or planet, or of an imaginary heresy or controversy.
The whole scaffolding of the story is raised on footnotes and quotations
which give the description a weird air of probability. The crazy
construction built on these facts seems at one and the same time fantastic and possible. We realise that men have actually held equally
weird theories, committed equally strange acts. Like Arlt's social
fantasies, Borges's metaphysics reflect the madness that is there in
reality.

Borges is not interested either in straightforward allegory, or in
psychological analysis. He presents his characters in a hypothetical
situation which often has an analogy with intellectual problems men
have set themselves. The stories are in the nature of computer pro-
grammes patterned on the way the human mind works, but by analogue rather than by imitation. For instance, one common theme of
Borges's stories is that of a man caught in a trap which he has himself
constructed unwittingly. Believing himself to be acting freely, he is, in
fact, constructing a cage in which he will eventually be caught. All
human beings tend to rationalise, to seek patterns and symmetry in
experience, though in fact the initial motivation may be completely
irrational. 'La muerte y la brújula' [Death and the Compass], one of
Borges's finest stories, follows this pattern. In it the detective Lönnrot,
a student of Jewish religion and a bibliophile, is faced with a series of
mysterious murders which he immediately realises form a determined
pattern. By studying the place in which they take place and the dates
on which they were committed, Lönnrot is able to calculate exactly
where and when a fourth murder will occur. Unwittingly he has constructed his own death-trap, for when he goes to the place of the fourth
murder at the appointed time, he finds himself facing his enemy
Schardach who has built this labyrinth of events for the sole purpose of
trapping him. Borges's controlled prose hides a nightmarish universe
in which repetition and symmetry give the appearance of richness and
variety to what is in reality a monotonous sterility. The very garden
and the disposition of the villa in which Lönnrot meets his death is
analogous to man's systematisation of experience:

...a una Diana glacial en un nicho lóbrego correspondía en un segundo nicho otra Diana; un balcón se reflejaba en otro balcón; dobles escalinatas se abrían en doble balaustrada. Un Hermes de dos caras proyectaba una sombra monstruosa.*

Inside the house, rooms are reflected endlessly in mirrors:

...se cansó de abrir o entreabrir ventanas que le revelaban, afuera, el mismo desolado jardín ... *La casa no es tan grande,* pensó. *La agrandan la penumbra, la simetría, los espejos, los muchos años, mi desconocimiento, la soledad.*†

How often do Borges's characters construct vast patterns out of the simple elements of experience! The quarrelling theologians of 'Los teólogos' [The Theologians] invent ingenious refutations of heresies, but are really only concerned with getting the better of one another. The Chinese protagonist of 'El jardín de los senderos que se bifurcan' [The Garden of Forking Paths] kills a man and is himself executed as a spy because he wants to prove himself the equal of the Germans. Out of the infinity of choices which a man is offered (and of which one symbol is the garden of forking paths), man chooses the one that leads to his own destruction.

Borges once stated that he wished to give poetry the kind of universality that philosophy used to have.[1] He achieves this by making theories and ideas concrete in the *ficciones.* The themes may be metaphysical or abstract, but the situations are nightmarishly close to reality. For instance, when he wishes to show that the reader 'creates' a work of literature as much as its author, he does so by evaluating the work of an imaginary author, Pierre Menard, 'author of the Quixote'. Menard is a man who has recreated the Quixote in exactly the words Cervantes used. He acts out in practice what each reader of Don Quixote actually does. Again, when Borges wishes to examine what man would be if he could not express his thoughts in general ideas, he invents an actual man, 'Funes el memorioso', who is incapable of thinking in general terms. He sees an uncategorised world in all its detail and variety. In 'El inmortal', Borges examines a human situation as if men were immortal. His protagonist drinks of a river that gives him immortality and comes across a colony of immortals for whom there is no pain, no suffering and death—hence, they live in a state of indifference and

---

* ...to one icy Diana in a murky niche there corresponded in a second niche another Diana; one balcony was reflected in another balcony; double staircases opened on double balustrades. A two-faced Hermes projected a monstrous shadow.

† ...he got tired of opening or half-opening windows that revealed outside the same desolate garden ... The house is not so big, he thought. It seems bigger because of the shade, the symmetry, the mirrors, the many years, my ignorance and the solitude.

inactivity. They feel no sense of moral responsibility, no curiosity, no ambition. The city they have built is labyrinthine and absurd, and the protagonist finally drinks thankfully of the river that will restore his death to him.

The *ficciones* can therefore be described as extended metaphors or analogies, Borges's favourites being those of the labyrinth and the book. Many stories are, indeed, based on a single extended metaphor. In 'La biblioteca de Babel' [The Library of Babel], the universe is a library which consists of an infinite number of hexagonal rooms, each containing an equal number of books, with an equal number of letters and lines. The men who inhabit these rooms spend their lives in constant search for meaning; some postulate a catalogue of catalogues, others seek to prove or disprove the infinity of the library, some proceed in their investigations scientifically, others become mystics. The reader may, or may not, apply such theories to his own universe and his own search for meaning. Even if he does not, the effect of the story is disturbing, suggesting as it does futility and lack of meaning behind an apparent order. In 'La lotería de Babilonia' [The Babylon Lottery], Borges reverses this theme, for now he investigates the role of chance in experience. He imagines a state run like a lottery with totally whimsical rewards and punishments meted out according to the numbers drawn. Notwithstanding the total irrationality of this state of affairs, the Babylonians still construct religions, theories and systems designed to rationalise their experience.

Borges's universe, then, could be completely nihilistic but for one factor—the factor of imagination. Without dreams, without philosophies, however bizarre, life would be very much poorer. How absurd, for instance, would sex seem were it not for the mysteries that surround it and which he describes in 'La secta del fénix' [The Sect of the Phoenix].

For Borges, dream and imagination can even influence the world of positive fact. In 'Tlön, Uqbar, Orbis Tertius', objects from an imaginary planet appear in our world and reverse human assumptions as to the nature of reality. And in 'Las ruinas circulares' [The Circular Ruins], he suggests that we are projections of the imaginations of others like the protagonist who dreams a son, only to find that he himself had been dreamed by someone else. The effect of these stories is to suggest the illusory nature of reality, which, in any case, has always a subjective element.

Borges is the one major Spanish writer to have broken away from the idea of literature as an instrument. He derives his aesthetic from Croce, and his stories are simply intended to give enjoyment just as he enjoyed writing them. In this way, both reader and author abstract themselves for a moment from the flux of time and the suffering that is inseparable from the individuation principle. But though they have no message, the stories convey a sense of total human isolation and nihilism.

Since publishing the two volumes of *ficciones*, Borges has written little, for he has been afflicted with increasing blindness. During the Perón regime, he was persecuted and humiliated. On the fall of Perón, he became Director of the National Library and published *El hacedor* [*The Maker*] (1960), a selection of poems and short prose passages written with characteristic irony—like the following brief meditation on his toenails.

Dóciles medias los halagan de día y zapatos de cuero claveteados los fortifican, pero los dedos de mi pie no quieren saberlo. No les interesa otra cosa que emitir uñas: láminas córneas, semitransparentes y elásticas, para defenderse ¿de quién? Brutos y desconfiados como ellos solos, no dejan un segundo de preparar ese tenue armamento...—Cuando yo esté guardado en la Recoleta,[1] en una caja de color ceniciento provista de flores secas y de talismanes, continuarán su terco trabajo, hasta que los modere la corrupción. Ellos, y la barba en mi cara.*

The gentle irony cannot conceal the pessimism behind this, his awareness of the meaningless physical growth of his toenails even after death.

Borges has often been accused of cosmopolitanism and of neglecting his own environment. He defends himself on the grounds that Argentina has no other tradition than that of Europe, and declares that the Argentine writer may deal with universal themes and does not necessarily have to confine himself to regionalism. His *ficciones* are a triumphant vindication of this view. He has driven a narrow but deep furrow in Spanish–American letters.

'REALISMO MÁGICO'

Though Borges had translated part of *Ulysses* in the '20s, it was not until the 1940s that writers began to experiment widely with new techniques and introduced the stream of consciousness, unusual time

---

* Docile socks comfort them by day and leather nailed shoes fortify them, but my toes do not want to know. They are only interested in growing nails, corneal plates, semi-transparent and flexible, in order to defend themselves. Who from? Crude and suspicious as they alone know how, they do not stop for one moment preparing this flimsy armament...When I am kept in the Recoleta in an ash-coloured house with dried flowers and talismans, they will continue their obstinate work until corruption moderates them. They and the beard on my face.

sequences, complex structures and other devices into the novel. In the '40s, a substantial group of writers published works which incorporated new techniques. Such writers, to mention the more important ones, included Miguel Angel Asturias (Guatemala), Alejo Carpentier (Cuba), Juan Rulfo, Agustín Yáñez and José Revueltas in Mexico; Leopoldo. Marechal, Eduardo Mallea and Ernesto Sábato (Argentina); Juan Carlos Onetti in Uruguay. These writers will be considered in detail in relation to their national literatures. Their work differs greatly from that of their predecessors of the '20s for there is a wealth of formal experiment, a display of imaginative powers and a command of language hitherto unprecedented in Spanish America. The discussion of influences no longer has much meaning in relation to their work. Certainly reading Dos Passos, Faulkner and other modern North-American writers may have suggested to them ways of approaching their writing, but for the first time we are faced with a generation of novelists who were preoccupied with authenticity and who were willing to experiment with new language and methods to express the truth as they saw it.[1] The 'creolist' writer often forced himself to write of regions and peoples who were almost as foreign to his experience as the peoples of Asia. The present generation have rejected preconceived ideas as to what the novel should be about and the way it should be written. Without confining themselves to autobiography, they tend to start with what is nearest to them—the boarding school in which they grew up, their native town, the experience of being a poet, the dictatorship that overshadowed their childhood. From these firm moorings, they allow the balloon of imagination to rise into the air. However, one 'influence' on contemporary prose should be emphasised. As in poetry, Surrealism had a liberating effect. Its emphasis on creativity, on freshness of language and on subconscious as well as conscious elements opened up new areas to the novelists. Moreover the 'order' established by a series of brutal dictatorships—that of Machado in Cuba, Trujillo in the Dominican Republic, Ubico in Guatemala— tended to increase the novelists' emphasis on spontaneity as a revolt against brutalising order. Magic, dream and fantasy were weapons against bureaucracy and injustice. Before discussing the novel in relation to different areas of Spanish America, a special word should be said about two creators of 'realismo mágico' [magic realism],[2] who exemplify the importance of considering Surrealism in any account of the modern novel. These writers are Miguel Angel Asturias of Guatemala and Alejo Carpentier of Cuba.

Miguel Angel Asturias (1899–)

Asturias, awarded the Nobel prize for literature in 1967, began writing in the '20s and at that time had undergone two important experiences for his career as a writer. The first was his childhood and adolescence spent under the stern dictatorship of Estrada Cabrera and the liberation felt when that dictator fell in 1921; the second was his contact with Maya scholars at the *Musée de l'Homme* in Paris and his study of Indian cultures. On the first, he drew for material when writing his novel *El Señor Presidente* (1946); his study of Maya civilisation was to bring him both new material and techniques. His first essay into literature was *Leyendas de Guatemala* [*Legends of Guatemala*] (1930), a retelling of traditional stories. Half fairy-tale, half poetry, the legend penetrated the 'inner history' of America—the myths which remained in people's minds and gave them a sense of national tradition. But more than this, the *Leyendas* were written in a lyrical Spanish that held something of the flavour of translations from the Quiché:

En la ciudad de Copán, el Rey pasea sus venados de piel de plata por los jardines de Palacio. Adorna el real hombro la enjoyada pluma de nahual. Lleva en el pecho conchas de embrujar, tejidas sobre hilos de oro.*

Asturias's understanding of the Indians through their myths enabled him to write the extraordinary and unique Indianist novel, *Hombres de maíz* [*Men of Maize*] which has been described elsewhere. In this and in his earlier *Leyendas*, myths are more than just pretty stories. They present a view of the world as powerful and pervasive in its effect on the Guatemalan as that of Christianity on the Western mind. But myth can be evil as well as good and creative. In his greatest novel, *El Señor Presidente* [*Mr President*] (1946), he shows us into the dreams and reactions of men and women living in the nightmare of a dictatorship. Though based on incidents of the Estrada Cabrera dictatorship, the novel has no precise time or locale. From the beginning, his description of the tolling bells over the city takes us into an arena in which forces of light battle with forces of darkness. He begins, 'Alumbra, lumbre de alumbre, Luzbel de piedralumbre' [Light up, light of alum, Lucifer of tinder], in a sentence that both imitates the bells and has meaning on a mythic plane. The battle has, however, been temporarily won by the forces of darkness, incarnated in 'El

---

* In the city of Copan, the King walks his silver-skinned does in the Palace gardens. The royal shoulder is adorned with a jewelled feather of *nahual*. He wears on his breast magic shells, woven upon golden thread.

L

Señor Presidente', an evil demiurge surrounded by a forest of listening ears, a network of telephone wires and with absolute control over every citizen. In his state, free will is treason, individualism spells death. Characters react like puppets, and when they believe they are free find that the President has them in a trap. Yet people do rebel and assert their individuality. They do so because ultimately feelings triumph over the vast dehumanised system. An idiot, taunted by a general who imitates his cry of 'Mother', strangles the general; a woman tries desperately to save her husband, a doctor, even though she knows that it will be hopeless; a beggar too stupid to prevaricate is killed for telling the truth when the President wants him to tell a lie. And finally there is Cara de Angel, the President's ruthless favourite, his Lucifer, who tries to act of his own accord because he is tired of being a slave to the President. Having helped a general persecuted by the President to run away, he then falls in love with the general's daughter, Camila, and marries her, an act that spells doom. He ends his life in solitary confinement, reduced to a physical wreck and men-tally broken by the false news that the President sends him of his wife's unfaithfulness.

The drama of the novel takes place less on the conscious surface of life, more in the subconscious. Since people cannot talk or tell the truth, only their dreams, memories and imaginings can offer a clue to the way they feel. The woman who rushes to the President's palace to save her husband knows deep down that her journey is useless; the carriage she is travelling in appears therefore to be at a standstill:

El vehículo no rodaba, ella sentía que no rodaba, ella sentía que no rodaba, que las ruedas giraban alrededor de los ejes dormidos sin avanzar, que siempre estaban en el mismo punto y necesitaba salvar a su marido...Sí, sí, sí, sí, sí—se le desató el pelo—salvarlo...*

The woman's obsession and frustrations are objectified in the carriage which, like a nightmare vehicle, never gets any nearer to its goal. Characters are constantly covered in filth and excrement like the poor persecuted idiot who finds himself

cubierto de papeles, cueros, trapos, esqueletos de paraguas, alas de sombreros de paja, trastos de peltre agujereados, fragmentos de porcelana, cajas de cartón, pastas de libros, vidrios rotos, zapatos de lenguas abarquilladas al sol...†

---

* The vehicle did not move, she felt that it was not moving, she felt that it was not moving, that the wheels turned on sleeping axles without going forwards, always on the same spot and she had to save her husband. Yes, yes, yes, yes, yes—her hair fell loose—save him.

† covered in papers, leather, rags, skeletons of umbrellas, brims of straw hats, tin plates

—the detritus of the city, from which he has fled in agony. Others find their fears personified in giant hands or watching eyes.

But like Arlt, Asturias seems to condemn modern civilisation; for with trains, telephones and a bureaucracy, the President's rule is made more efficient. Fear can do its work more swiftly, be more universal. Only outside the city do characters feel some sense of release. Nevertheless, the negative force of fear can be counterbalanced by love, individual dignity and human solidarity, which even a dictatorship cannot stamp out entirely. The 'Kyrie Eleison' which ends the novel perhaps holds out a note of hope.

El señor Presidente was original partly because the author dispensed with conventional plot-sequence and presented events in a series of cinematic incidents. This construction emphasised the actual isolation of the characters one from another in conditions of dictatorship.

Asturias attempted to use similar techniques in a trilogy of the banana plantations: *Viento fuerte* [*Strong Wind*] (1950); *El Papa verde* [*Green Pope*] (1954); and *Los ojos de los enterrados* [*The Eyes of the Buried*] (1960). The protagonist of the first novel is a North American who leads a revolt of small producers against the monopoly banana company. The second is the story of the monopoly company, and the third describes the organisation of the workers and a triumphant strike. Asturias also published *Weekend en Guatemala* in 1956 after the overthrow of the Arbenz Government by an invasion from Honduras. His most recent novel, *Mulata de tal* (1963), gave characters myth-names such as 'Brujo Bragueta' [Wizard Fly-button] which were intended as modern equivalents to the *Popol Vuh* myth characters, but here the myth-making is less successful than in *Hombres de maíz*. Asturias's weakness has been a tendency to make his modern myths too regional. But in his earlier novels he has undoubtedly acted as a major influence on modern fiction.

Alejo Carpentier (1904–)

Though less deeply rooted by birth in Spanish America than Asturias—he is of French Cuban extraction—Carpentier also gained insight into the people through their popular culture. He first of all studied music and wrote a history of Cuban music. His literary career began in the '20s when he wrote some Afro-Cuban poems, and after settling in Paris he published a novel, *Ecué-Yamba-O* (1933), in which he included

with holes in them, bits of pot; cardboard boxes, book backs, broken glass; shoes with tongues curled in the sun. . .

a documentary account of Negro life and beliefs in the Cuban countryside and La Habana, with the adventures of Menegildo, a country boy who drifts to the city and there meets his death. Thereafter, Carpentier wrote little for some time until in the 1940s, he published an interesting experiment with time—'Viaje a la semilla' [Journey to the Seed], a short story which starts in modern Cuba and goes back to before the conquest. Everything moves in reverse, people die before they are married and are married before they are born, until the reader is taken back to primeval times. The story was symptomatic of the way Carpentier was thinking at this time. The patchwork of Caribbean civilisation fascinated him, with its layers of races, its waves of conquerors, its many languages. Many of his subsequent works were to delve into origins.

Like Miguel Angel Asturias, Carpentier had spent years in the literary circles of Paris amongst Surrealists and others who sought to experience the 'marvellous' in the drab cities of northern Europe. He was to find their imagination poor compared to the reality of the Caribbean. After a visit to Haiti in 1943, he discovered the 'real maravilloso' [marvellous reality] that lay at his own doorstep, and which had informed the imagination of her peoples from the conquest onwards. '¿Qué es la historia de América toda sino una crónica de lo real-maravilloso?' [What is the whole history of America but a chronicle of the 'marvellous-real'?] he wrote.[1]

The visit to Haiti was a turning-point. In 1949 he published *El reino de este mundo* [*The Kingdom of this World*], a novel set in Haiti during the period of the French Revolution—a period which has always fascinated Carpentier. The prosperous and peaceful island governed by the French conceals under a placid surface the subversive dreams and myths of the Negro slaves. One of these, Mackandal, a one-armed slave, runs away into the mountains, discovers deadly poisonous mushrooms and sets about poisoning cattle, horses and men to prepare the way for the return to power of the Negro race. Though he is caught and burned to death, his legend lives on, and the moment the French Revolution is declared the slaves rise against their masters; the former cook Henri Christophe takes power, organising a kingdom that is a weird parody of eighteenth-century France:

Por la explanada de honor iban y venían, en gran tráfago, militares vestidos de blanco, jóvenes capitanes de bicornio, todos constelados de reflejos, sonándose el sable sobre los muslos. Una ventana abierta descubría el trabajo de una orquesta de baile, en pleno ensayo. A las ventanas del palacio asomábanse damas

coronadas de plumas, con el abundante pecho alzado por el talle demasiado alto
de los vestidos a la moda.*

The fall of the French overlords, the rise and fall of this new black
dictator, are narrated through the experiences of a house-slave, Ti
Noel, who is one of the forced labourers who builds Henri Christophe's fortress of Sans Souci, who witnesses his downfall and lives to
return to the ruined country estate on which he had lived as a slave
and to see it fall into the hands of a new mulatto ruling-class. But this
is not mere historical reconstruction. The problem of implanting
European systems on the exotic soil of the New World is a perennial
one, and one in which the nature of the place invariably triumphs over
the imported plant. And the author's insight into the mind of a slave
for whom the island is a place of wonder and terror is brilliantly
conveyed in a lyrical and imaginative prose style. Here, for instance,
is a passage in which Ti Noel find himself entering the territory governed by Henri Christophe.

...a la vuelta de un sendero, las plantas y los árboles parecieron secarse, haciéndose esqueletos de plantas y de árboles, sobre una tierra que, de roja y grumosa,
había pasado a ser como de polvo de sótano. Ya no se veían cementerios claros,
con sus pequeños sepulcros de yeso blanco, como templos clásicos del tamaño de
perreras. Aquí los muertos se enterraban a orillas del camino, en una llanura
callada y hostil, invadida por cactos y aromos. A veces, una cobija abandonada
sobre su cuatro horcones significaba una huída de los habitantes ante miasmas
malévolos. Todas las vegetaciones que ahí crecían tenían filos, dardos, púas y
leches para hacer daño. Los pocos hombres que Ti Noel se encontraba no respondían al saludo, siguiendo con los ojos pegados al suelo, como el hocico de sus
perros. De pronto el negro se detuvo, respirando hondamente. Un chivo, ahor-
cado, colgaba de un árbol vestido de espinas.†

To the Negro, the countryside has signs which a more sophisticated
person would not have seen.

* On the esplanade, there came and went in a great hustle soldiers dressed in white,
young captains in cocked hats, all starred with reflections, their sabres thwacking
against their thighs. An open window revealed the dance orchestra playing in full
rehearsal. There appeared at the palace windows ladies crowned with feathers, with
large breasts raised up by the too-high waists of their fashionable gowns.
† ...around the bend of the path, the plants and trees seemed to dry up, becoming
skeletons of plants and trees on an earth that was once red and clotted and had become
like basement dust. There were no longer bright cemeteries, with their little tombs of
white plaster like classical temples the size of dog kennels. Here the dead were buried
by the side of the road in a silent and hostile plain, invaded by cactus and myrrh.
Sometimes a hut abandoned upon its four forks, signified a flight of the inhabitant,
before evil vapours. All the vegetation which grew there had sharp edges, spikes,
thorns and harmful juices. The few men whom Ti Noel met did not reply to his greet-
ing, going on with their eyes to the ground like a dog's nose. Soon the Negro stopped
and breathed deeply. A goat had been hung in a thorn tree.

El reino de este mundo was followed by a novel set in the present, *Los pasos perdidos* [*The Lost Steps*] (1953), which dealt with the same fundamental theme as the earlier work, that of the co-existence of the primeval jungle and of a civilisation imposed by European conquerors. The narrator and protagonist, however, is the antithesis of Ti Noel. He is a sophisticated product of the modern age, a musician whose actress wife takes the curtain nightly in an interminably successful play; a man who has a French mistress and whose social life is lived among people for ever talking of the latest theories and searching for new experiences. He is given the chance to escape this society when sent on an expedition into the jungles of Orinoco in search of primitive musical instruments. What begins as a cheap holiday with his French mistress becomes a serious quest for his own 'lost steps'. Abandoning the French woman at the frontier of civilisation, he falls in love with a woman of the country, and with her joins a strange band of adventurers who are sailing upriver to find an area as yet untouched by man. Here they will start anew, living with the environment rather than in conflict with it. But the musician is forced to abandon the experiment. As an artist, he cannot retreat into the past; for him, the modern world, however alienated, is inescapable.

Once again a conflict between fertile, inventive and marvellous nature and a stale, monotonous, over-ordered society is at the core of the book: spontaneity versus intellect; creativity versus routine; the marvellous versus the drab. It is a conflict that cannot be resolved, perhaps, though the author suggests that in Latin America human constructions are fragile and tawdry. One of the finest passages of the book concerns a city in which an attempted revolution momentarily suspends the routine of daily life. Immediately the jungle begins to take over again. Insects appear from water pipes, the hotel is alive with their scurrying:

De las bocas de los grifos surgían antenas que avizoraban, desconfiadas, sin sacar el cuerpo que las movía. Los armarios se llenaban de ruidos casi imperceptibles, papel roído, madera rascada, y quien hubiera abierto una puerta, de súbito, habría promovido fugas de insectos todavía inhábiles en correr sobre maderas enceradas, que de un mal resbalón quedaban de patas arriba, haciéndose los muertos. Un pomo de poción azucarada, dejado sobre un velador, atraía una ascensión de hormigas rojas. Había alimañas debajo de las alfombras y arañas que miraban desde el ojo de las cerraduras.*

* From the taps came antennae which probed suspiciously without the body that moved them coming out. The cupboards were filled with scarcely perceptible noises, of gnawed papers, scratched wood, and if anyone had opened a door, there would have

For Carpentier, the jungle is never far off even in the most sophisticated corners of the continent.

Carpentier's next novel, *El acoso* [*The Hunt*] (1956), seemed atypical, being a political novel set in a period of dictatorship. A student of architecture has taken part in a terrorist movement, is caught, tortured and gives away his fellow conspirators. When released, he is condemned to death by his former companions who track him down. The entire action is compressed into the briefest period of time—the time it takes to perform Beethoven's Eroica Symphony, for the condemned man has taken refuge in a concert hall during the performance. Scenes from the past flash across his mind as he listens to the music and as the concert ends and the hall empties, he is killed.

But though the novel is set in the present, its theme is not so very different from that of *El reino de este mundo* and a later novel, *El siglo de las luces*. In all of these, the ambiguous consequences of revolutionary violence preoccupy the author. In *El acoso* violence breeds violent opposition which in turn breeds more violence. The Revolution eats its own children.

El siglo de las luces [*The Age of Enlightenment*] (1962) is Carpentier's most ambitious novel, and brings together all his preoccupations—the sense of wonder at the natural beauties and richness of the Caribbean; the violence of Revolution; the contrast between European civilisation and American barbarism. It is the only one of his novels to deal with the Caribbean as a whole, for the action, which spans the French revolutionary period, passes from Cuba to Guadalupe, from Haiti to Cayenne. At the opening of the novel, a Cuban merchant has just died, leaving a son and daughter, Carlos and Sofía, and a nephew, Esteban. The abrupt removal of paternal authority is the signal for a new life for the children; they explore the house, play practical jokes and fall under the influence of the mysterious Victor Hugues who introduces them to fashionable ideas of emancipation and freemasonry. The convent-educated Sofía is finally seduced by him during the course of a sea voyage they take to Haiti. But the first revolutionary uprisings are already taking place. Sofía and Carlos remain in Cuba while Esteban follows Victor Hugues to Europe and the Revolution. Hugues, an admirer of Robespierre, is sent out to Guadalupe to take

___

been a sudden flight of insects who were still unable to run with ease upon polished wood and which slipped and stayed with their legs in the air, pretending to be dead. A pot of sugary potion left upon a night table drew up a column of red ants. There were insects under the carpets and spiders which looked from the keyholes.

over the island and to convey there the first guillotine. Esteban accompanies him as secretary, witnesses the degeneration of this idealist who defends his ideals by bloodshed, and once his idols fall feels nothing but cynicism.

La revolución se desmorona. No tengo ya de qué agarrarme. No creo en nada.*

Esteban returns to Cuba and is arrested. Sofía who had married a rich merchant, and had been quickly widowed, takes his place by the side of Victor Hugues who is now in charge of Cayenne. But she too, is disillusioned, for she sees him become a tool to implement reaction. First the Church has its power restored, then slavery returns. She too, abandons him and returns to Cuba and thence to Spain. The book ends on the 2nd of May when an anti-French uprising against the Spaniards is met by a ferocious repression and reprisals. Sofía and Esteban disappear and only Carlos, the merchant, remains.

The central character of Carpentier's novel, Victor Hugues, was a historical personage who, Carpentier says, attracted him for his very ambivalence.[1] He incarnates the contradictions of a revolution which started with the highest of ideals and ended in sordid cynicism, and which in America at least seemed totally without relevance to the environment and its conditions. Thus when Victor Hugues becomes governor of French Guiana, he dreams only of subduing the environment, attempting to construct

un ambicioso remedo de parque real cuyas estatuas y rotondas serían sorbidas por la maleza en el primer descuido, sirviendo de muletas, de cabo, a las incontables vegetaciones entregadas a la perpetua tarea de desajustar las piedras, dividir las murallas, fracturar mausoleos y aniquilar lo construído.†

Once again, the ceaseless and fruitless conflict of man and nature comes to the fore.

But this novel is far richer than any of Carpentier's previous works. The penchant for a baroque style, already evident in *Los pasos perdidos*, now reaches a truly magnificent realisation, especially in passages where the subject matter allows him full scope. In one notable section, Esteban explores the sea life of the region and comes upon an ideal world, a world untouched by symmetry and geometry, unknown to literature, a world of pure creation:

* The revolution is collapsing. I no longer have anything to hold on to. I do not believe in anything.
† An ambitious copy of a royal park whose statues and pavilions would be swallowed up by the bush at the slightest neglect and would serve in the end as supports for the countless plants which were engaged on the perpetual task of displacing the stones, dividing the walls, splitting the mausoleums and fracturing the construction.

De la Mar sometida a ciclos lunares, tornadiza, abierta o furiosa, ovillada o destejida, por siempre ajena al módulo, el teorema y la ecuación, surgían esos sorprendentes carapachos, símbolos en cifras y proporciones de lo que precisamente faltaba a la Madre. Fijación de desarrollos lineales, volutas legisladas, arquitecturas cónicas de una maravillosa precisión, equilibrios de volúmenes, arabescos tangibles que intuían todos los barroquismos por venir...Meditaba acerca de la poma del erizo, la hélice del muergo, las estrias de la venera jacobita, asombrándose ante aquella Ciencia de las Formas desplegada durante tantísimo tiempo frente a una humanidad aún sin ojos para pensarla.

¿Qué habrá en torno mío que esté ya definido, inscrito, presente, y que aún no pueda entender? ¿Qué signo, qué mensaje, qué advertencia, en los rizos de la achicoria,[1] el alfabeto de los musgos, la geometría de la pomarrosa? Mirar un caracol. Uno solo. Tedéum.*

Nature is still rich and unknown. Carpentier's novels show the comparative poverty of human ideas set in the midst of this wealth.

Perhaps it is arbitrary to select Asturias and Carpentier to represent the new Spanish–American novel. Yet they do exemplify more completely than other writers the awareness of contemporary developments of novelistic technique fused with vital experience of Latin America. We shall now turn to some of the many writers of the continent who have followed similar paths over the last decades. The characteristics of this new writing are:

1 A concern for form and language which is involved in any choice of subject matter.
2 A concern for authenticity. The writer is now unwilling to deal with experiences which he himself has not lived.
3 Ambitious scope.

THE MODERN NOVEL IN ARGENTINA

In the country of Arlt and Borges, the modern novel already had an experimental tradition. The magazine *Sur*, founded in 1931, also contributed to the knowledge of modern European and North-American

---

* From the sea, subject to the lunar cycles, whimsical, open or wild, agitated or relaxed, for ever alien to measure, theorem and equation, there emerged these surprising carapaces, symbols in numbers and proportions of what the Mother lacked. Fixation of linear developments, ordered curves, conic architectures of a marvellous precision, equilibriums of volumes, tangible arabesques which were intuitions of all future baroque shapes. He meditated on the poem of the sea-urchin, the propeller of the clam, the rays of the scallop, and he was astonished before that Science of Forms developed over so many years in the presence of a humanity which still had not eyes to think of it.

What would there be around me that was already defined, inscribed, present, which could not yet be understood? What sign, what message, what warning in the curls of the *achicoria* in the alphabet of the mosses, in the geometry of the rose apple. To look at a shell. One alone. Te Deum.

writers. But it was hardly surprising that the novel should develop along rather different lines than in countries like Cuba or Central America, for despite the vast hinterland of pampa, Argentina was above all a country of city-dwellers, and writers usually lived in Buenos Aires. In this city of rootless immigrants, national and individual identity were both in question.

In 1948, there appeared a novel with the significant title, *Adán Buenosayres [Adam Buenosayres]*. The hero is Adam because he is without antecedents and therefore the composite character of the city of Buenos Aires. Written by Leopoldo Marechal who worked on this novel for well over a decade, the hero incarnated the problems and searchings of the city itself. Born in the provinces, Adán studies in Europe and returns to his own city a stranger, 'portador de un mensaje de frescura que no sabe manifestar aun' [conveyor of a note of freshness which he still did not know how to express]. He cherishes an ideal love for Solveig, but his wanderings take him into brothels and cafés. Like Dante, he descends to hell, where he finds prominent members of the city, particularly merchants and traders, undergoing eternal punishment. But the novel, though impressive, had not yet found a really new language and structure.

Eduardo Mallea

It was Eduardo Mallea who was really to pose the problem of identity in novel form. Son of a doctor from Bahía Blanca, Mallea (1903–) arrived in Buenos Aires in the early '20s, to suffer the shock and loneliness of life in a big city. Though he published his *Cuentos para una inglesa desesperada [Stories for a Desperate Englishwoman]* as early as 1926, he passed many years in spiritual anguish during which he wrote for magazines, worked as a journalist and pondered on the problem of Argentine identity. His long essay, 'Historia de una pasión argentina' [History of an Argentine Passion] (1937), relates his search for the 'real' Argentina beneath the appearances of Buenos Aires. Mallea's experience is a common one in Spanish America, where the writer (usually not drawn from the circles of the governing élite) feels himself an outsider. Mallea saw the problem in cultural terms. Unable to participate in broad national or social movements, he lays stress on 'authentic' existence, believing that a writer must simply bear witness to the truth of his experience and keep his perceptions attuned to the 'inner' country and not to an external world of commerce and government. The year before publishing 'La historia', he had brought out a second volume of stories, *La ciudad junto al río inmóvil* [*The City of the Motionless River*] (1936). In one of these stories, 'Sumersión', Mallea dealt strikingly with the isolation of the immigrant, Avesquín, who

fluctuaba como un leño, en el foso circundante de la metropóli, sin penetrarla, como un leño seco e inerte. No tenía comunión con nadie. . .*

Mallea's first novel was *Fiesta en noviembre* [*November Party*] (1938). November is spring-time in the Argentine, and the title has an ironic ring, for the theme is that of sterility, and of the vanity of most people's lives. As usual in Mallea's work, only the artist and the sensitive stand apart. The novel is simply the story of a dinner-party given by the wealthy Señora Rague, for a party of diplomats and business men. But two people are detached from the events that go on around them; the Rague daughter, Marta, who in the course of the evening slips out unobserved to visit a sister, Brenda, who has just had an abortion; the other is the painter, Lintas, a man who like Mallea believes that humanity is divided into the 'pure' and the 'impure'. Lintas and Marta leave the party together. They are among the pure and they can communicate. Yet even this communion has an element of strangeness, for Mallea interweaves into the main theme of the novel the description of the execution of an unknown poet, the symbol of the death of intellect which he felt was taking place in the country.

Marta and Lintas are typical of the characters who were to haunt Mallea's novels, anguished and searching for their true selves, more or less conscious according to their type and circumstance. Tregua, the protagonist of *La bahía del silencio* [*The Bay of Silence*] (1940) searches for years for spiritual peace, and for a long time cannot find it either in the Argentine or in Europe. The title 'The Bay of Silence' symbolises an area of inner peace and equilibrium, set aside from the stormy sea of life. It is an area of consciousness in which those who are failures in practical life can find inner peace.

Todos ellos, y usted misma han llegado a ese sitio que lame sin corroerlo el mar de la furia, de la persecución y de la adversidad. Todos ellos, y usted, quién sabe cuántos otros de este mundo, han llegado a esa bahía, a ese lugar de espera, a esa bahía donde concentra su silencio y donde su fruto se prepara sin miedo a la tormenta, el ciclón, el vil tiempo.†

* drifted like wood in the ditch round the metropolis, drifted without penetrating it, like a dry, inert piece of wood. He had no communion with anybody...
† All of them and you yourself have reached that place where the sea of fury, of persecution and adversity washes without corrosion. All of them and you and who knows how many more in this world have reached that bay, that place of waiting, that bay

In *Todo verdor perecerá* [*All Green Shall Perish*] (1941), Mallea transports his theme to the provinces and paints a picture of a farmer's wife condemned to live in a countryside she hates, unable to communicate with her husband, surrounded by sterile fields whose crops are doomed to fail either through drought or frost. Agata's frustration turns into a dull hatred of her husband whom she allows to die of pneumonia, deliberately letting cold air into his room during a storm. Agata moves to the town, where she has a brief affair with a lawyer, but as soon as this is over, she recognises a solitude that nothing in the world will ever fill:

Le asaltó otra vez la obsesión de que si dejara de vivir de repente, su soledad sería eterna; de que toda compañía se origina en este mundo, nada más que en este mundo, y que si uno no lleva de acá abajo la semilla, todo será eterno horror.*

In her immense solitude even the children turn against her, hounding her from the town in which she grew up.

But solitude is the fate of even the wealthy and successful of Mallea's novels, of even the married or those with families. In *Las Aguilas* (1943), Román Ricarte inherits a huge estate and then watches his wife dissipate the money in fashionable living, until he is only left with the country house, Las Aguilas. Román seems a mere spectator in a course of events which he is powerless to halt. A sequel to the novel, *La torre* [*The Tower*] (1951), describes how Roberto, Román's son, constructed the 'inner' edifice to replace the material tower which a previous generation had built.

El país verdadero, no el falso; el lento, el largo, el eterno, no el rápido, el confuso, el precipitado.†

So human solitude can only be overcome by those men and women who abstract themselves from the phenomenal world.

The process of inner discovery which is central to all Mallea's novels makes them slow-moving, even sluggish. Narrative rather than conversation moves the action along; action takes place within people rather than without. One has the impression of a mystic without a religion: an impression borne out by a novel, *Los enemigos del alma*

where silence is concentrated and where its fruit ripens without fear of storm or cyclone or bad weather.
* Once again she was attacked by the obsession that if she stopped living suddenly, she would be alone for ever; and that all friendship originates in this world, only in this world, and that if one does not take the seed with one, all will be eternal horror.
† The true country not the false one; the slow, long, eternal one, not the rapid, confused and hasty one.

[*The Enemies of the Soul*] (1950), in which he personifies the world, the flesh and the devil in the brother and two sisters of the Guillén family who 'agonise' in the family house on the outskirts of a town. As in Mallea's other novels, the three characters are caught inescapably in an iron destiny imposed by their own characters. The author summed up the novel as:

una tempestad maligna, un círculo de orgullosos, un golfo de espíritus suspendidos sin progresión, la aridez de los que se manejan sin alma.*[1]

The elder sister destroys herself, the house and the rest of the family in a fire, as the only way out of their living hell.

For Mallea, the subject is perpetually threatened by the objective world which is his real enemy. His novels have this consistent theme:

la necesidad que cada cual lleva en sí de integrarse a sí mismo, en un improbo y pensativo esfuerzo por alcanzar y constituir dramáticamente su forma humana completa, en medio de un mundo que tiende a disolverlo, disminuirlo y parcializarlo, acosándolo, aterrándolo y fragmentándolo.†[2]

His novels are too numerous to be discussed separately, but they include, besides those mentioned, *El retorno* (1946), *El vínculo* (1946), *Chávez* (1953), *La sala de espera* (1953), *Sinbad* (1957) and *El barco de hielo* (1967).

Ernesto Sábato

Like Mallea, Ernesto Sábato displays a high seriousness and intensity in his work. Born in 1911, he has had three careers—as a political militant, as a mathematician and as a novelist. His two novels, *El túnel* (1948) and *Sobre héroes y tumbas* [*On Heroes and Tombs*] (1961) seem to explore areas which neither politics nor science could teach, the area of 'metaphysical solitude' which is the subject matter of *El túnel*. He believes that the novel dramatises the agony of 'man in crisis'; at the same time it is an assertion of human values in a society of 'hombrescosas'. Its perennial themes are 'La soledad, el absurdo, la muerte, la esperanza y la desesperación' [Solitude, absurdity, death, hope and despair].

El túnel is little more than a *nouvelle*, the story of a painter, Castel,

* an evil storm, a circle of proud people, a gulf of spirits suspended without progression, the sterility of those who act without souls.
† the necessity that each man has inside himself to find himself in a laborious and thoughtful struggle to reach and dramatically reconstitute his complete human form in the midst of a world which tends to dissolve, diminish and separate it, pursuing, destroying and fragmenting it.

whose obsessive love for a married woman leads him to murder her out of frustration. Compact and intense, the novel takes us into the mind of a compulsive neurotic for whom existence is a nightmare. *Sobre héroes y tumbas*, in contrast, is complex and variegated, covering vast expanses of Argentina's past and present society. Here he attempts the 'total novel' of the Argentine. He has described the work as:

> ...el drama de seres que han nacido y sufrido en este país angustiado. Y a través de él, un fragmento de drama que desgarra al hombre en cualquier parte: su anhelo de absoluto y eternidad condenado como está a la frustración y a la muerte.*[1]

The novel opens with a brief newspaper report telling of a crime in which a man was killed by his own daughter, who had then set fire to the room in which she had committed the crime and had herself died in the flames. The father Fernando Olmos, the daughter Alejandra, are descendants of a family of nineteenth-century 'heroes', pioneers and eccentrics who had helped to create the Argentine and whose 'destinies' cross with those of the contemporary characters in inter-larded scenes. The main characters both of the past and the present are lonely, half-mad and obsessed people. One of the links between past and present is an aunt who all her life has kept the severed head of her father in her room, and who died a very old woman in 1932 still ob-sessed by a tragedy that had happened three-quarters of a century before. Another link-character in the book, the poor student Martín who falls in love with Alejandra after meeting her accidentally in a park, is never able to liberate himself from the obsessive love which makes him pursue her and pursue her memory even after her death. It is his searchings and enquirings which help the reader to reconstruct her life. Similarly Alejandra's uncle, the writer Bruno, nurses a life-long, frustrated love for Alejandra's mother. But the central character of the novel, the man who expresses to the nth degree the obsessions and paranoia of his native Argentina is the father, Fernando Olmos, whose life has been a series of violent, contradictory acts. He meddles with anarchism, hovers on the borderline of crime and, it is implied, consummates an incestuous love for his daughter, which precipitates the final crime. Of him, Bruno says:

> Los locos, como los genios se levantan, a menudo catastróficamente, sobre las limitaciones de su patria o de su tiempo, entrando en esa tierra de nadie, dis-

---

* ...the drama of beings who have been born and have suffered in this anguished country. And through this, a fragment of the drama which threatens man in any place; his
  desire for the absolute and the eternal when he is condemned to frustration and death.

paratada y mágica delirante y tumultuosa, que los buenos ciudadanos contemplan con sentimientos cambiantes. Y sin embargo, esos individuos excepcionales, esos hombres fuera de la ley y de la patria conservan, a mi parecer, muchos de los atributos de la tierra en que nacieron. Y de los hombres que hasta ayer fueron sus semejantes aunque como deformados por un monstruoso sistema de proyección hecho con lentes torcidas y con amplificadores desaforados.*

Fernando is a monster, but an Argentine monster who lives out the tragedy of a man lost in darkness without moral or religious or political beliefs. About a quarter of the book is taken up by his 'Informe sobre ciegos' in which he sets out a report based on his paranoiac belief that the world is manipulated by a secret society of blind men who are in the service of the powers of darkness. All Fernando's real life enters into this 'informe', but deformed by an obsession. He does not see the objective world, but only the world of his vision in which he descends into the sewers of Buenos Aires, is imprisoned in a room and has an interminable and monstrous union with the 'blind woman'. Few writers have entered so effectively into the mind of a madman while at the same time conveying that the madness takes on characteristics imposed by the environment. The Buenos Aires of violent politics, of secret anarchist societies, of many nationalities, does not need much discretion to enter into Fernando's mad dream. Here, for instance, is his vision of the street of Banks:

El silencio y la soledad tenían esa impresionante vigencia que tienen siempre de noche en el barrio de los Bancos. Barrio mucho más silencioso y solitario, de noche, que cualquier otro; probablemente por contraste, por el violento ajetreo de esas calles durante el día; por el ruido, la inerrable confusión, el apuro, la inmensa multitud que allí se agita durante las horas de Oficina. Pero también, casi con certeza, por la soledad sagrada que reina en esos lugares cuando el Dinero descansa... Y también por la obvia razón de que en esos barrios no hay alimentos, no hay nada que permita la vida permanente de seres humanos, o siquiera de ratas o cucarachas; por la extremada limpieza que existe en esos reductos de la nada, donde todo es simbólico y a lo más papeloso; y aun esos papeles, aunque podrían representar cierto alimento para polillas y otros bichos pequeños, son guardados en formidables recintos de acero, invulnerables a cualquier raza de seres vivientes.†

---

* Madmen like geniuses often emerge catastrophically out of the limitations of their country or their time. They enter that no-man's land, absurd, magical, delirious and tumultuous, which good citizens contemplate with mixed feelings. And yet, those exceptional individuals, those men outside law and fatherland preserve, I believe, many of the attributes of the land of their birth and of the men who were, till yesterday, like themselves, although they see them as if deformed by a monstrous system of projection under distorting lenses with grotesque magnifications.

† There was that impressive silence and solitude that the banking quarter always has at night. It is a much more solitary and silent quarter by night than any other; probably by contrast with the violent bustle of these streets during the day and with the noise,

Sábato's nightmare vision has much in common with that of Arlt and also with those of Cortázar, probably the Spanish–American writer who has done most to revolutionise the technique of the novel.

Julio Cortázar

Born in 1914, Julio Cortázar has lived for many years in France, and can be considered an expatriate writer, unlike Mallea, Sábato and Borges who normally work and write in Buenos Aires. All Cortázar's early work was in short story form. He published *Bestiario* [*Bestiary*] in 1951, and this was followed by *Final del juego* [*End of the Game*] (1956) and *Las armas secretas* [*Secret Arms*] (1959). The stories do not present such obvious technical innovations as his novels, but even in the earliest collection, there is evidence of a bizarre and original imagination. The title story of *Bestiario*, for instance, is about a girl who goes to stay with her country relatives, around whose house a mysterious and ferocious tiger roams. The tiger perhaps symbolises the uncontrollable in human nature, but it is the little girl who knowingly allows the tiger to escape and maul a member of the family she hates. This introduction of a fantastic element into an otherwise realistic story is a common element in many of Cortázar's tales. But in his *Historias de cronopios y de famas* [*History of Cronopios and Famas*] (1962) he invents two types of personnage—the 'cronopios' who are intuitive, life-loving 'desordenados y tibios' [disorderly and warm] and the 'famas' who are conventional and utilitarian and cannot communicate with the 'cronopios'. Invention and fantasy are two important elements in Cortázar's work, methods of overcoming alienation, of restoring freedom of creation.

Cortázar's major works are his two novels, *Los premios* [*The Prizes*] (1960) and *Rayuela* [*Hopscotch*] (1963), both of which are 'open' novels, where there is an infinity of possible readings. At the end of *Los premios*, the author warns his readers against 'interpretations'. His work must simply be enjoyed:

> ...no me movieron intenciones alegóricas y mucho menos éticas. Si hacia el final algún personaje alcanza a entreverse a sí mismo, mientras algún otro recae

> the unmistakable confusion, the hurry, the immense crowd which stirs there during office hours. But also, always solitary, because of the sacred solitude that reigns in those places where Money rests...And also because of the obvious reasons that in those quarters there is no food, nothing that would permit the permanent life of human beings or even of rats or cockroaches; because of the extreme cleanliness that exists in these redoubts of nothingness in which all is symbolic or at most papery; and even those papers, though they could afford some food for moths and other small insects, are kept in formidable steel rooms, invulnerable to any race of living creatures.

blandamente en lo que el orden bien establecido lo insta a ser, son esos los juegos dialécticos cotidianos que cualquiera pueda contemplar a su alrededor o en el espejo del baño, sin pensar por ello en darles trascendencia.*

Los premios is the story of a group of characters from Buenos Aires— a wealthy industrialist, a proof-reader, a middle-class family—who have all been given a free cruise as a prize. The cruise is a mystery cruise and the passengers have no idea of their destination. As the hour of departure draws near, the ship's activities grow more and more strange, and the first night's voyage takes them only to a suburb of Buenos Aires. Rigorous rules debar the passengers from using certain parts of the boat and they find that no communication is possible with the crew. As the days pass, the passengers divide into two camps; those who accept the system and those who refuse to accept and try to explore beyond the forbidden limits. When one of the latter is killed, the passengers are taken back to Buenos Aires and are reintegrated into its life without difficulty. Acceptance or defiance of rules makes no difference at the end. Only one character, Persio, a proof-reader whose life is lived immediately and without imposed structures, seems to escape from the absurdity of the rest. Though Cortázar forbids interpretation in the novel, he still loads the dice a certain way.

For Cortázar the system is evil. People are irresistibly drawn to putting structures on experience, to creating routines and patterns. But structures divide and alienate people. Only by accepting freedom do human beings live.

In *Rayuela* he went further than in *Los premios* in creating a fluid novel structure which would restore the reader's as well as the characters' freedom. The novel can be read either in numerical sequence or, as the author suggests, in the order 73–1–2–116–3–84—or indeed in any one. If we follow the ordinary sequence, the characters are bound in time, and we have a story of an uprooted Argentine student, Horacio Oliveira, who lives with a girl called Maga in Paris and then after his return to Buenos Aires still feels haunted by her presence. Neither in France nor in Buenos Aires does he fit into society. But if we follow the author's suggested sequence, we have a different novel, one in which patterns are timeless, in which there is simultaneity of action. There is a totally free relationship between readers and characters.

* ...I was not moved by any allegorical intentions and still less by ethical considerations. If towards the end, some person manages to see something of himself, while some other softly falls back on what the established order wishes him to be, these are the daily dialectical games that anyone may contemplate around him, or in the bathroom mirror without for that reason, attaching any importance to it.

Morelli, a character whose writings are included in the second part of the novel, suggests that this is a way of involving the reader:

Por lo que me toca, me pregunto si alguna vez conseguiré hacer sentir que el verdadero y único personaje que me interesa es el lector, en la medida en que algo de lo que escribo debería contribuir a mutarlo, a desplazarlo, a extrañarlo, a enajenarlo.*

and he goes on to suggest that all systematic construction of characters and situations should be cut away. 'Método: la ironía, la autocrítica incesante, la incongruencia, la imaginación al servicio de nadie' [Method: irony, constant self-criticism, incongruity, free imagination].

There is thus not a plot, but patterns and events. One pattern is Oliveira's search for the spontaneity and freedom which Maga takes naturally. Another pattern is the attack on the conventional which extends even to the language. Oliveira, for instance, describes himself as 'Hespectador, hactivo. Había que hanalizar despacio el hasunto' [Honlooker, hactive. One ought to hanalyse the hattitude slowly] and boasts of using haitches the way some people use penicillin. He never makes dates with Maga because this would mean creating a structure. His counterpart in Buenos Aires is 'Traveler', a man who has never left the city and who works first in a circus and then in a mental home. In the second part of the novel, Oliveira has returned to Buenos Aires and lives near his friend, Traveler and his wife Tala, the Buenos Aires equivalent of Maga. Cortázar is not interested in psychological analysis nor in any element of verisimilitude in the relations of these four. Nor can his method be described as symbolism. Instead, he places the three people in situations which are intended as confrontations with the reader. In the following passage, for instance, Oliveira has wanted to borrow tea from his friend and in order to pass the tea from one house to another, they have constructed a bridge of planks across two floors of the apartment house. Tala balances precariously on the planks and meets Oliveira half-way. This apparently absurd incident includes situations, decisions, geographies, metaphysics, linguistic problems,— and even the tensions of tragedy:

Oliveira se echó de bruces en la ventana, y le tendió el brazo. Talita no tenía más que avanzar medio metro para tocar su mano.
'Es un perfecto caballero,' dijo Traveler. 'Se ve que ha leído el consejero social del profesor Maidana. Lo que se llama un conde. No te pierdas eso, Talita.'

* For my part, I wonder if I will some time manage to convey the impression that the true and only character that interests me is the reader, in that something of what I write ought to contribute to changing him, to displacing him, to puzzling and alienating him.

'Es la congelación,' dijo Oliveira. 'Descansá un poco, Talita, y franqueá el trecho remanente. No le hagas caso, ya se sabe que la nieve hace delirar antes del sueño inapelable.'

Pero Talita se había enderezado lentamente, y apoyándose en las dos manos trasladó su trasero veinte centimetros más atrás. Otro apoyo, y otros veinte centímetros. Oliveira, siempre con la mano tendida, parecía el pasajero de un barco que empieza a alejarse lentamente del muelle.*

The scene represents a kind of modern duel. Traveler's irony wins over Oliveira's fantasy (he insists that it is freezing although there is a heat wave). But the fact that the scene takes place many feet above the street in the most precarious of positions adds both to its intensity and to its absurdity. It is like the daring act of a trapeze artist—trivial in itself and yet given a certain significance by the risk involved.

The 'plank' scene is also characteristic of the anti-social or rather extra-social ambience of the novel. Characters are always marginal to society—bohemian students, tramps, circus performers, mental home patients—these are the only human beings apart from the central characters. Few characters work or have any routine. Yet Maga alone *lives* freedom without wasting her time in talk. She is in touch with 'lo perdido, lo extrañado' [the lost, the estranged].

For Cortázar as for Sábato, the novel is concerned with the crisis of modern man, and it must make the reader exercise the creativity which is one way of overcoming alienation.

The Modern Argentinian novel is more than Sábato, Cortázar and Mallea, though this study has, of necessity, been confined to these. Their preoccupation with solitude and alienation is remarkably consistent, though their methods of expressing this are radically opposed.

URUGUAY

For sociological reasons, few novels were written in Uruguay until recently. The absence of publishing facilities, the small market, induced writers to channel their efforts into the short story. And in the '20s and

---

* Oliveira threw himself face downwards at the window and stretched out his arm to her. Talita had only to advance half a yard to touch his hand.

'He's a perfect gentleman', said Traveler. 'You can see that he has read the etiquette book by Professor Maidana. How to address a count. Don't miss this Talita.'

'It's the frost,' said Oliveira. 'Rest a little, Talita and then cross the rest. Don't take any notice of him—you know that snow makes men delirious before they fall into the last sleep.'

But Talita had slowly straightened herself up and, resting herself on her two hands, she shifted her behind twenty centimetres backwards. Another grip and another twenty centimetres. Oliveira with his hand still stretched looked like a passenger on a boat which is beginning to move slowly away from the quayside.

'30s, writers such as Felisberto Hernández and Francisco Espínola adopted this form, the one outstanding novelist being the regional novelist, Enrique Amorim.

In 1939, however, there appeared *El pozo* [*The Well*] by Juan Carlos Onetti (1909–   ) who for many years abandoned his native country to live and work in Buenos Aires. *El pozo* not only signalled a major new talent but laid the foundation stones of Onetti's city of visions, which was to be inhabited by a race of bitter and suffering human beings for whom the entry into adult life was little short of a disaster. *El pozo* is narrated by a man of forty suffering from a disgust that embraces almost the whole of humanity. 'La poca gente que conozco...' he says, 'es indigna de que el sol toque en la cara' [The few people that I know are unworthy of having the sun touch their faces]. An extreme case of isolation, the man lives in squalor, separated from his wife, having only occasional contact with prostitutes, or the men he meets casually. The isolation is heightened by his feeling that Uruguay has not even a tradition that the individual can use as a support. 'Detrás de nosotros no hay nada', the narrator says. 'Un gaucho, dos gauchos, treinta y tres gauchos' [Behind us, there is nothing. One gaucho, two gauchos, thirty-three gauchos]. Laconic in his despair, he sees adult life as an impurity into which men inevitably fall after the first wonder of childhood. *Tierra de nadie* [*No man's land*] (1941) was the first novel of his to be set in Buenos Aires. In a number of brief scenes and conversations, the author presents the thoughts, meetings, love-affairs and occasional crimes of a group of people who meet in the city, often casually, who begin and end relationships and are, in general, condemned to the sordid and incomplete life that the city offers. The ending of the novel is characteristic of the author's view of life. The author, Aránzuru, sits by the river:

Invisible, a sus espaldas, estaba la ciudad con su aire sucio y las altas casas, con el ir y venir de las gentes, saludos, muertes, manos y rostros, juegos. Ya era la noche y la ciudad zumbaba bajo las luces, con sus hombres, sus sombreros, niños, pañuelos, escaparates, pasos, pasos como la sangre, como granizo, pasos como una corriente sin destino.*

The city is the only unity that binds the novel together.

Onetti now embarked on the writing of a series of novels and short

* Invisible, behind his back, was the city with its dirty air, its high buildings with the coming and going of people, greetings, deaths, hands and faces, games. It was already night and the city buzzed below the lights, with its men, its hats, boys, handkerchiefs, shopwindows, footsteps, footsteps like blood, like hail, footsteps like a current without a destination.

stories which dwelt on the sordidness of adult life: *Para esta noche* [*For this Night*] (1943); *La vida breve* [*The Short Life*] (1950); *Un sueño realizado y otros cuentos* [*A Dream Realised and Other Stories*]; *Los adioses* [*The Goodbyes*] (1954); *Una tumba sin nombre* [*A Nameless Grave*] (1959); *La cara de la desgracia* [*The Face of Shame*] (1960); *Jacob y el otro* [*Jacob and the Other*] (short stories, 1961); *El astillero* [*The Shipyard*] (1961); *El infierno tan temido* [*Hell so Feared*] (short stories, 1962); *Tan triste como ella* [*As Sad as Her*] (1963); *Juntacadáveres* (1965).

Of these, *El astillero* and *Juntacadáveres* deserve special mention since they are both set in the imaginary town of Santa María and have the same character, Larsen, who had also appeared in *Tierra de nadie*. Though published later, *Juntacadáveres* takes place earlier in time. The title is the nickname of one of the characters who comes to Santa María to open a brothel. Despite official support, the project is defeated by the women of the town, and the prostitutes forced to leave. The narrator, the adolescent Jorge Malabia, is the mouthpiece for Onetti's exposure of the impurity of life. He sees Santa María as his own invention in a passage which is surely the voice of the author; and speaks of the task of creating a whole population who 'habiten, ensucien, conmuevan, sean felices y malgasten...' [live, dirty, move, are happy, and mis-spend...].

Y en el juego, tengo que darles cuerpos, necesidades de amor y dinero, ambiciones disímiles y coincidentes, una fe nunca examinada en la inmortalidad y en el merecimiento de la inmortalidad.*

The contingence of these fictional characters only underlines the contingency of man in real life.

El astillero is a bitter masterpiece. Old and tired, Larsen, who has spent a lifetime in dubious business deals, conceives one final, glorious plan to regain a fortune. He plans to marry the daughter of a shipyard owner, Petrus, and build up the yard which is at present idle. He finds himself courting an idiot, and although Petrus names him manager of the shipyard, there are no ships, no work, only a couple of clerks, Gálvez and Kuhn, who earn their living by selling off the machinery. Larsen's efforts to refloat his fortunes are doomed to failure, but he enters into a strange dying parody of a magnate, who goes to work, examines documents (now years old) and courts Petrus's daughter.

---

* And in the game, I have to give them bodies, necessities of love and money, dissimilar and coinciding ambitions, a faith in immortality and the deserts of immortality that they never question.

It is like a weird imitation of life, the shipyard offering a symbolic landscape of ruin and desolation:

Erguido, contonéandose con exageración, esquivó hierros de formas y nombres perdidos que descansaban aprisionados en un torbellino de alambres, y penetró en la sombra, en el distante frío, en la reticencia del galpón. Pasó revista a los casilleros, a los hilos de lluvia, a los nidos de polvo y telarañas, a las maquinarias rojinegras que continuaban simulando dignidad. Caminó sin ruido hasta el fondo del hangar y buscó con las nalgas hasta sentarse en el borde de una balsa para naufragio. ...Imaginó sonriendo una ruido de ratas que devoraban bulones, tuercas y llaves en los casilleros.*

Here Larsen realises that he has reached the bottom, the final disaster 'vieja, fría, verdosa' [old, cold, and greenish].

Few modern Spanish–American writers achieve such an intense bitterness as Onetti, or express so persistently futility and decay. As Larsen finally faces defeat and sails away (to die within a week of pneumonia), he feels that he can detect

el susurro del musgo creciendo en los montones de ladrillos y el del orín devorando el hierro.†

Onetti is the most prolific and the most ambitious of contemporary Uruguayan novelists but two other writers deserve mention— Mario Benedetti and Carlos Martínez Moreno.

Mario Benedetti

Mario Benedetti (1920–   ) is author of a volume of short stories, *Montevideanos* (1959) and of three novels, *Quíen de nosotros* [*Who Among Us*] (1953), *La tregua* [*The Truce*], (1960) and *Gracias por el fuego* [*Thanks for the Light*] (1964).

In *Montevideanos*, he had explored a territory that was still comparatively new in Spanish America, that of the ordinary lives and dramas of the people of the city, shopworkers, a football player, schoolboys and their ordinary relationships.

His acute ear for colloquial speech and his power of observation distinguish his writing. Of all Spanish–American writers he is one

---

* Erect, exaggeratedly strutting, he avoided pieces of hanging iron with shapes and names which rested imprisoned on a confusion of wires and penetrated into the shade, into the distant cold, into the reticence of the shed. He reviewed the desks, the threads of rain, the nets of dust and spider webs, the reddish-black machines which continued simulating dignity. He walked noiselessly to the end of the shed and with his buttocks, he slid along until he found somewhere to sit on the edge of a raft.
  Smiling he imagined a rat noise which devoured bolts, screws and keys in the desks.
† The whisper of growing moss in the piles of brick and the rust devouring the iron.

who comes closest to reproducing the surface texture of life, of recognising work-relationships and the subtle interplay of individual
ambition and social censureship which determine many people's
actions. One of the main themes of his short stories is the exposure
of people's real relationships which have been masked by social conventions. A boy on a park bench listens to his father's conversation with
a friend and the father's image as an honourable citizen tumbles to the
ground. A woman and her lover embrace in front of a 'blind' husband
in 'Los pocillos' [The Cups] and he suddenly indicates that he can tell
the colour of the cups into which she is pouring coffee. A crooked foot-
baller finds it impossible to play badly enough since his personal pride
refuses to allow him deliberately to miss passes and neglect chances.
He is beaten up and ends in hospital. Dignity and honour depend in
Benedetti's stories on the opinion of peers or superiors, but the strain
of conforming to this social image is often too much. *Montevideanos*
shows us the real tensions of modern life rather than those tensions
which have been traditional in literature. Of the novels, *La tregua* and
Gracias por el fuego are the most interesting. The first is in the form of a
diary written by a middle-aged office worker on the verge of retire-
ment, who late in life falls in love with an office girl, Laura Avellaneda
and has a secret affair with her before she suddenly and unexpectedly
dies. The skill of *La tregua* lies in the acute observation, particularly
in the tension between the love-affair which represents an island of escape in the routine of office and family relationships. Here, for instance,
is a description of office work in which inhuman routine cannot entirely
kill human sentiments:

Trabajé toda la tarde con Avellaneda. Búsqueda de diferencias. Lo más aburrido
que existe. Siete centésimos. Pero en realidad se componía de dos diferencias
contrarias: una de dieciocho centésimos y otra de veinticinco. La pobre todavía
no agarró bien la onda. En un trabajo de estricto automatismo como éste, ella
se cansa igual que en cualquier otro que la fuerce a pensar y a buscar soluciones
propias. Yo estoy tan hecho a este tipo de búsquedas, que a veces las prefiero a
otra clase de trabajo. Hoy, por ejemplo, mientras ella me cantaba los números
y yo tildaba la cinta de sumar, me ejercité en irle contando los lunares que tiene
en su antebrazo izquierdo.★

★ I worked all the afternoon with Avellaneda. A hunt for discrepancies. The most boring
work that exists. Seven cents. But the truth was that there were two opposite errors,
one of 18 cents and the other of twenty-five. The poor girl still wasn't on the beam. In a
strictly automatic job like this she gets tired as she would in any other that makes her
think and seek her own solutions. I am so used to this type of investigation that sometimes I prefer it to any other type of work. Today, for example, while she sang out
the figures and I ticked the adding tape, I amused myself by counting the moles she has
on her left forearm.

Gracias por el fuego represents a break with this office world and a progress to more ambitious themes. It is the portrait of a financial magnate who controls most of Uruguay, seen through the eyes of a son who hates him but is finally unable to kill him and who can only commit suicide. The novel is thus concerned with a national theme. The father, an unscrupulous authoritarian who wins his way by guile and bribery rather than by overt violence, symbolises the weaknesses Benedetti sees in Uruguayan society.

Martínez Moreno

Carlos Martínez Moreno, born in 1917, has worked most of his life as a lawyer. Both his short stories and his novels are concerned with the analysis of national problems through concrete personal situations. His first collection of stories was *Los días por vivir* [*The Days Left to Live*] (1960); then *Cordelia* (1961) and *Los aborígenes* [*The Aborigines*] (1964). His novels include *El paredón* [*The Wall*] (1963), *La otra mitad* [*The Other Half*] (1967) and *En las primeras luces* [*At First Light*] (1967). In most of Martínez Moreno's stories and novels there is a framework of violence which contains or is contrasted with the often banal lives of the characters. In *El paredón*, for instance, Julio Calodoro goes on a visit to Cuba, recently liberated by Fidel Castro. The enthusiasm and violence of Cuba calls into question the legalistic and sterile Uruguayan political scene. In *La otra mitad* a woman is murdered and her husband commits suicide. The deaths shock, above all, the woman's lover; he reflects on their idyllic love affair in which there had been little warning of coming tragedy. In *En las primeras luces* a man is locked in the garden of a house in which he has fallen asleep. He tries to climb over the wall, fatally injures himself and bleeds slowly to death, brooding over the childhood he had spent in the house and his relations with his successful and unscrupulous cousin who now owns it.

Uruguayan writers are absorbed by legalism and the lack of extremes in their country; they see these as threats as great as those presented by violence elsewhere.

PARAGUAY

Paraguay's outstanding novelist and writer is Augusto Roa Bastos (1917–   ), who for many years has lived in Argentina, to which he escaped after political persecution. His two major works are *El trueno entre las hojas* [*Thunder in the Leaves*] (1953) and *Hijo de hombre* [*Son of Man*] (1959), both of which bear some similarities in style to the 'realismo mágico' of Asturias and Carpentier. Coming from a country which has been culturally isolated both from the rest of Spanish America and from Europe, he shows a remarkable sophistication of technique. His main theme is the freedom of spirit which characterises the human individual, and the social exploitation and oppressions which he meets; but these themes are not developed in a traditional social-protest framework. Instead, the writer creates his own symbolic world, using the myths and legends of his native country. In some of the stories for instance, 'Los carpincheros', nomadic gypsy hunters, symbolise a freedom which the factory and sugar workers are deprived of. Rivers and railways become symbols of escape, factories and prisons are microcosms of the country at large. Yet the stories are also lyrical even at moments of violence. In 'El trueno entre los hojas', the blind ex-prisoner and ex-strike leader sits by the river listening to the passing of the 'carpincheros' on St John's Eve:

Solano se aproximaba al borde de la barranca para sentirlos pasar. Los saludaba con el acordeón y ellos le respondían con sus gritos. Y cuando entre los fuegos el ojo de su corazón la veía pasar a ella, una extraña exaltación lo poseía. Dejaba de tocar y los ojos sin vida echaban su rocío. En cada gota se apagaban paisajes y brillaba el recuerdo con el color del fuego.
La última vez que se acercó, resbaló en la arena de la barranca y cayó al remanso donde guardaba su balsa, donde lavaba su ropa harapienta, de donde sacaba el agua para beber.
De allí lo sacaron los carpincheros que estuvieron toda la noche sondando el agua con sus botadores y sus arpones, al resplandor de las hogueras.*

The San Juan fires are a tradition that goes back to pagan times to the era of nature religions. They therefore symbolise a natural form of life against that of the factory which is burned down (again fire playing a symbolic role) in the course of the story.

In *Hijo de hombre*, the theme is once again repression and exploitation, but again Roa Bastos uses techniques which give the resistance the force of a national myth. The action of the novel covers a period

---

* Solano moved near to the edge of the ravine to hear them pass. He greeted them with his accordion and they replied with shouts. And when the eyes of his heart perceived them pass among the fires, a strange exaltation possessed him. He stopped playing and his lifeless eyes gave forth a dew. In each drop, landscapes were drowned and shone in memory with the colour of fire.
The last time that he drew near, he slipped on the sand of the ravine and fell in the pool where the raft was moored, where his ragged clothes were washed and from which he took his drinking water.
The *carpincheros* took him out after they had spent the night plumbing the water with their poles and harpoons in the light of the bonfires.

of nearly a hundred years. The events do not develop chronologically. Instead, the novel is divided into a number of related episodes, the link being either the characters involved or the place. Each episode centres around violence or rebellion. A leper carves a figure of Christ which the villagers of Itapé wish to put in the church. The priest opposes this, and defiantly they place the Christ on a hill overlooking the village and each year they parade it in the Good Friday procession as a 'victim who must be revenged rather than as a God who wished to die for men'. A mysterious doctor arrives in a village, cures patients, but is found cutting open the images of saints to look for gold. A plantation worker and his wife, Casiano Jara, escape from the plantations miraculously, and go to live in a railway carriage near Sapukai, a village in which a train-load of rebels had once been blown up by a munitions train that the government had sent against him. The railway carriage becomes a legendary symbol of resistance to the peasants, who believe that it travels the country on wheels of fire. In this carriage, their son Cristobal Jara organises yet another rising which is crushed, though he himself miraculously escapes when the lepers invade the village where he is hiding. Another section of the novel centres on the Chaco war in which Jara is killed by a soldier of his army who has gone mad with hunger and thirst. At the end of the novel, the returned soldiers from the Chaco war continue their violent struggle. A police chief is murdered, the man who had killed Jara is found shot. Struggle and bloodshed seem unending.

But as in the stories, Roa Bastos treats his theme with lyricism and imagination. Here, for instance, is the arrival of a young boy in Asunción, the same boy who will later go mad with thirst in the Chaco:

Vimos las casas altas, las calles empedradas, los carruajes tirados por caballos, los tranvías cuarteados por yuntas de mulitas de un solo color, que avanzaban entre los gritos de los mayorales.

Enfrente había una plaza llena de árboles. De trecho en trecho, algunas canillas de riego escupían chorritos de agua. Dejé a Damiana en la balaustrada y me metí corriendo entre los canteros. Lleno de sed, me agaché a beber junto a una de las canillas. En un momento, boca abajo contra el cielo, entreví algo inesperado que me hizo atragantar el chorrito. En un rincón, entre plantas, una mujer alta y blanca, de pie sobre un escalinata, comía pájaros sin moverse. Bajaban y se metían ellos mismos chillando alegremente en la boca rota. Se me antojó sentir el chasquido de los huesitos.*

* We saw the high buildings, the paved streets, the horse-drawn carriages, the trams drawn by yokes of mules of the same colour which advanced to the shouts of the drivers.
  In front there was a tree-filled square. At intervals irrigation drains spat out little

Roa Bastos's 'magic realism' reveals another world than that of official Paraguay which exists in the novel only as a negation of humanity and human values. The statue, the woman who 'crunches' the birds that fly into her mouth, becomes a monstrous symbol of these negative forces. On the other hand, the vital forces in the novel are all outside society. The man who carves the statue of Christ is a leper, and the leper colony later figures in the novel as a symbol of those who are beyond the reach of social organisation or organised religion. Except in the absurd Chaco war in the final part of the novel, the main characters are fugitives from society or justice. Normal daily work and routine are never shown; it is as if they had become impossible in a country dedicated to oppression.

THE ANDEAN REPUBLICS

The Peruvian novel is at present dominated by two totally different writers, Mario Vargas Llosa (1936–) and José María Arguedas (1911–).[1] The first is a highly sophisticated writer who has successfully introduced new techniques into the novel. The second believes that true Peruvian culture must draw on Indian civilisation and attitudes and has attempted to create a literary language which translates the spirit of Quechua.

Mario Vargas Llosa's first novel, *La ciudad y los perros* [*The City and the Dogs*] (1963), was based on his personal experience as a pupil in a military school, but the scope of the novel takes it far beyond autobiographical confession. The school is a microcosm. The pupils act out the relationships, the loyalties and the betrayals that are present in the world outside. The title of the book is itself significant. The city is Lima, whose cinemas, brothels and girls, and whose sea-shore lie beyond the walls of the school. Inside are the 'perros', the first-year students, momentarily isolated from the world they know and forced to stand up to the ritual bullying of the older students. They form a secret society to defend themselves, and the core of this society— Jaguar, Boa, but particularly Jaguar—convert this society into a circle which organises gambling, cheating at examinations and smuggling drink into the school. The school, whose discipline is intended to

streams of water. I left Damiana by the balustrade and went running among the channels. In an instant, face downwards, against the sky, I glimpsed something unexpected which made me swallow the water. In a corner, among some plants, a tall white woman standing on a stairway was eating birds motionlessly. They themselves came down and went into her mouth of their own accord, chirping merrily in her broken mouth. I thought I heard the crunching of their little bones.

inculcate 'obedience, work and courage', breeds a sub-society in which the strongest and most fearless becomes leader, in which work can be evaded by cheating and in which courage is often mere bullying. Interleaved with this sombre picture of the school are scenes in the city where pupils on their day off meet their girl-friends or visit their parents. But there too, even in these relationships apparent loyalty and obedience conceals betrayal and cowardice. What exists in a heightened form within the school also pervades society outside the school.

The events of the novel concern the theft of examination questions organised by the Jaguar, a fearsome character, an orphan whose chief quality is courage, and whose primitive moral code is based on the idea of loyalty to one's friends. Though cruel, he has sprung from a cruel environment and his code makes sense. He has a kind of *macho*[1] dignity and is disgusted with the coward and the weak. Jaguar forces Cava, a fellow-pupil, to steal the examination questions, but Cava is denounced in turn by 'The Slave', a weak misfit in the college who turns informer in order to get a Sunday leave to see his girl-friend. The Slave is mysteriously killed on manœuvres and Alberto turns betrayer and accuses Jaguar of the murder. But the circle of betrayals is almost infinite. Alberto himself had been taking out the Slave's girl-friend without his knowledge and so had also been involved in betrayal. However, Vargas Llosa makes no explicit moral judgment.

The novel plunges deep into the problems of growing up in Peru, where all values are distorted. In the school are pupils from all over the country, ready to be moulded to the requirements of that society. Vargas Llosa examines how, given these conditions, an individual cannot formulate an inner-directed moral code, or attain a broader sense of humanity. The sources of corruption are multiple. Rewards go to the betrayers, and not to those like Jaguar who have a simple sense of justice. At the same time simple judgments are discouraged. The Jaguar comes to repent of having baited the Slave, because he realises when he himself is accused of being an informer and ostracised that loyalty to the group only has force so long as one feels identified with it. The Slave had neither accepted the values of the school nor those of the group and therefore 'betrayal' did not apply to him.

In *La ciudad y los perros*, everything conspires to encourage in the boys the development of those false values of *machismo* which pervade Peruvian society. Only the truly fearless Jaguar who has no need for false *macho* values is able to change and become more human. The rest are condemned.

The prose of the novel matches the subject matter. The action is presented through the stream of consciousness of the different cadets interspersed with objective description. There is no lyricism. The verb becomes all important, as in the following passage which describes the manœuvres:

Antes que cesara el sonido metálico, el capitán Garrido vió que la primera fila de ataque, dividida en tres cuerpos, salía impulsada en un movimiento simultáneo: los tres grupos se abrían en abanico, avanzaban a toda velocidad desplegándose adelante y hacia los lados, igual a un pavo real que yergue su poderoso plumaje. Precedidos de los brigadieres, los cadetes corrían doblados sobre sí mismos, la mano derecha aferrada al fusil, que colgaba perpendicular, el cañón apuntando al cielo de través, la culata a pocos centímetros del suelo. Luego escuchó un segundo silbato, menos largo pero más agudo que el primero y más lejano—porque el teniente Gamboa también corría, de medio lado, para controlar los detalles de la progresión—, y al instante la línea, como pulverizada por una ráfaga invisible, desaparecía entre las hierbas: el capitán pensó en los soldados de latón de las tómbolas cuando el perdigón los derriba.*

The final phrase in which the captain sees the cadets as toy soldiers in a fairground sets the tone of the book. Society and its institutions are a denial of other people's humanity—at least as these are constituted in modern Peru. The cadets will go on being manipulated for the rest of their lives unless, like the Jaguar, they can assert their own individuality.

A short novel, *Los cachorros* [*The Puppies*] (1967) also dealt with the *macho* complex in Peru. A schoolboy, Cuéllar, a keen member of the football team, is bitten by a dog and castrated. During adolescence, his impotence is of little importance, as he can compensate in sports and group activities, but inevitably he must leave school and enter an adult world in which fast sports cars and car-racing cannot compensate for his lack of masculinity. The story is no case history. The castration is in a sense symbolic, and as in *La ciudad y los perros* externally-imposed and distorted values threaten the individual's sense of his dignity and worth.

* Before the metallic sound stopped, Captain Garrido saw the first line of attack, divided into three parts, advance in a single movement. The three groups opened out into a fan, and advanced at top speed opening out in front and at the sides like a peacock lifting up its powerful plumage. Preceded by the sergeant majors, the cadets ran, doubled over, their right hands grasping their rifles which stuck out with their barrels pointing behind and their butts a few inches from the ground. Then he heard a second whistle, less long but shriller than the first and further away—because Lieutenant Gamboa was also running to one side to supervise the details of the attack—and at once, the line, as if blown away by an invisible blast disappeared among the grass. The captain thought of tin soldiers in the fairground when the shot brings them down.

Vargas Llosa's most ambitious novel is *La casa verde* [*The Green House*] (1966) in which he broke away from the environment of Lima. The two poles which magnetise the events of the novel are the jungle village of Santa María Nieves in Marañón and the town of Piura surrounded by its arid plain. Each section of the novel is divided into a number of sub-sections which centre on a different character, or group of characters. There is a community of missionary nuns living on the edge of the jungle; there is Bonifacia, a novice who marries an army Sergeant and who, when the Sergeant is arrested, ends in a brothel. There is a pilot, Nieves. There is the adventurer, Fuschía, who had come from Brazil and is engaged on an interminable flight. There is the harpist Anselmo from the town of Piura and the group of 'inconquistables', the underdogs from one of the poor districts of the town. The author does not take the lives of these characters and interweave them in a chronological sequence. Different moments from their lives are described and placed within the structure of the book in non-sequential order in a way that effectively breaks the reader's tendency to look for patterns of development or identity with one character.

But despite the new environment, the theme is very close to that of *La ciudad y los perros*. It is the story of corruption and the story of civilisation. Bonifacia, the 'Selvática' [the woman from the jungle], is a pivotal figure in this novel of a primitive world which is exploited by the Church, then by the army and finally by commercialism in the brothel. She is a symbol of this jungle region, and to the end of the novel retains a fierce loyalty to her origins. She is the eternal victim, the counterpart of the adventurer, Fuschía, an escaped prisoner, a Japanese from Brazil whose dream has been to make riches out of the jungle. His life has been a series of betrayals until he finds that he has leprosy and is left to die in a leper colony. Fuschía knows that business is dirty, but he knows too that his own small-scale smuggling is as nothing compared with the large-scale exploitation carried on by government officials and their accomplices. But there are other poles of opposites—the missionary community imposing purity and chastity among the Indians is counterbalanced by the brothel, the antithesis of purity. This is the 'casa verde' of Piura constructed by Don Anselmo who then seduces a blind girl and, when she dies in childbirth has her secretly buried. The 'casa verde' is burned to the ground by an angry crowd, but Anselmo reappears as a harpist whose daughter in her turn comes to own a brothel.

As in *La ciudad y los perros* where a discipline of obedience and hard work breeds disobedience and cheating, so in *La casa verde*, the excessive puritanism of the mission has its counterpart in the open sexuality of the brothel.

The technique of *La casa verde* is highly complex. The usual frontier-lines between narrative and conversation, between present and past, actuality and flashback are broken down. Here, for instance, in the following passage, narrative flows into conversation, past into present:

El Teniente deja de hacer adiós cuando la embarcación es sólo una lucecita blanca sobre el río. Los guardias se echan las maletas al hombro, suben el embarcadero, en la Plaza de Santa María de Nieva se detienen y el Sargento señala las colinas: entre las dunas boscosas reverberan unos muros blancos, unas calaminas, ésa era la Misión, mi Teniente, la cuestecilla pedregosa estaba vacía, a eso le decían la Residencia, ahí vivían las monjitas, mi Teniente, y a la izquierda la capilla. Silhuetas indígenas circulan por el pueblo, los techos de las cabañas son de fibras y parecen capuchones.*

The passage illustrates how Vargas Llosa's style reflects the dialectic between external reality and the individual consciousness that is the theme of his novels.

José María Arguedas

The work of José María Arguedas has already been mentioned in connection with Indianist writing. His two major novels, *Los ríos profundos* and *Todas las sangres*, however, extend beyond the scope of Indianism. The modern Peruvian, he believes, is alienated. His culture, his psychological attitudes, his way of life are unreal, lacking in authenticity. Only through Indian music and song does he occasionally perceive the existence of totally different and more authentic values.

...en el fondo sienten bien ese arte indígena. Y ese arte los conmueve porque es la expresión más justa de sus propios sentimientos.†[1]

He believes that on the day when the Peruvian landowners overcome their egoism and allow the free development of the Indian and his culture a great art will arise with a 'definitivo valor universal'. His

---

* The Lieutenant stops waving goodbye when the boat is simply a small white light on the river. The guards throw the cases on their shoulders, climb up the quay and stop in the square of Santa María de Nieva and the Sergeant points to the hills; amongst the wooded dunes, shimmer white walls, and zinc, that was the Mission, Lieutenant, the little rocky hill was empty, this was called the Residence, there lived the nuns, Lieutenant, and the chapel was on the right. Indian silhouettes moved through the village, the roofs of the huts were of fibre and looked like hoods.

† ...in their depths they feel this Indian art; and that art moves them because it is the exact expression of their own feelings.

novels all show this conflict of races in all its crippling intensity. Ernesto, the protagonist of *Los ríos profundos* walks through the streets of Cuzco and finds that the Inca stones seem to boil with compressed life:

Era estático el muro, pero hervía por todas sus líneas y la superficie era cambiante.*

In contrast, the landowning relative, 'El Viejo', whom he goes to se e is repellantly mean, avaricious, living a death in life. The true and the false Peru exist side by side. Ernesto is sent to a Catholic boarding school in a hill town inhabited by *cholos* and surrounded by Indian communes and lands on which there are Indian workers. Again, he lives the conflict between two ways of life, the hypocritical life-denying code of the school and that evoked by his Indian top, the 'zumballya' which evokes the magic world of nature from which the Catholic community is separated. The school itself becomes a metaphor for the alienation of modern Peru. It is a place cut off from real life and upholds values which ultimately damage the boys. Like the Castilian conquerors, the school works on the ideology that nature must be suppressed, overcome; but suppression is not easy. Nature reasserts itself as when Ernesto, saying his rosary, evokes the image of

Apu k'arwarasu, Dios regional de mi aldea nativa. Tiene tres cumbres nevadas que se levantan sobre una cadena de montañas de rocas negras. Le rodean varios lagos en que viven garzas de plumaje rosado.†

And the sickness which invades the town and causes the closure of the school is itself like a vengeance of nature. In *Todas las sangres*, the purely cultural conflict of the earlier novel expands to include an economic and social conflict. Two rival brothers, Fermín and Bruno, have inherited lands, Indians and mines. Fermín is the progressive one:

Anhelo un Perú como Inglaterra: Bruno quiere una républica de indios, manejada por señores caritativos.‡

If Bruno's patriarchal administration is inadequate, Fermín's exploitation of the mines leads to disaster, for he sells out to a monopoly company. The Indians taught by Rendón Willka, an educated Indian, stand out against the demands of the company and are defeated by the

---

* The wall was static, but all its lines boiled and the surface was shining.
† Apu K'arwarasu, regional god of my native village. It has three snowy peaks which rise upon a chain of black, rocky mountains. Around it are several lakes on which live herons of rosy plumage.
‡ I would like a Peru like England. Bruno wants a republic of Indians governed by charitable gentlemen.

troops that are sent against them. All the varied labour-relations which exist between landowner, Indian and mestizo are covered in the novel in all their complexity. Outstanding is the portrayal of Rendón Willka as perhaps the first example in literature of an Indian character presented with the same complexity as a European or white Spanish American. However, perhaps the most remarkable aspect of the novel is the style, which even in straight narrative seems to conserve something of the rhythm and syntax of Quechua.

La voz oscura de los caracoles repercutía en las montañas, alcanzaba al sol y hacía vibrar las ramas del pisonay, que hizo caer el suelo ya enrojecido, varias de sus flores, pesadas, color de sangre.*

But whereas in earlier novels Arguedas had used many Quechua phrases, particularly in conversation, in *Todas las sangres*, he uses a kind of pidgin Spanish in which the Indians address their superiors. So Rendón Willka, replying to an engineer who has tried to bribe him:

'Tú borracho, patrón . . . Yo sano. Yo ganando plata con trabajo no más; otra plata es maldición de Dios; hace crecer gusano feo en el tuétano, en la sangre también.'†

Willka knows perfectly well how to speak Spanish but deliberately uses this kind of language as a sort of sly self-defense. The Indians' natural form of communication, that in which they express their own thoughts, is the song, and these are given by Arguedas in Quechua with Spanish translations. Arguedas thus breaks radically with traditional Spanish. Whether his style is valid for novels that deal with themes other than the Indian is, however, doubtful. Interesting and original the novels are, but they may well represent a last ditch stand as far as incorporating Quechua into a literary language is concerned.

COLOMBIA

The 'new world' of Gabriel García Márquez

Torn for many years by a bloody civil war, Colombia produced novels obsessed by the subject of 'la violencia'. Recently, however, a novelist has emerged who has fused all the elements of Colombian

---

* The dark voice of the conch shells reverberated in the mountains, reached the sun and made the boughs of pisonay vibrate and made several of its heavy blood-coloured flowers fall to the ground.

† 'You drunk, boss. . .I sober. I getting money just by work; other money is curse of God; it makes the ugly worm grow in the marrow, in the blood, too.'

life and written a novel of genius. Gabriel García Márquez was born in 1928 and first published *La hojarasca* [*Chaff*] (1955) which in retrospect appears to be the first sketch of his masterpiece, *Cien años de soledad*. In this first novel appeared elements which were to recur in nearly all his later work—a lonely town, cut off from the rest of civilisation, bitter political feuds that deaths and marriages cannot heal, the outsider who becomes the object of suspicion and hatred. The novel simply presents the reminiscences of three people, the only ones to attend the funeral of a so-called doctor who had earned the hatred of the community by refusing to attend the wounded after a political battle. The grandfather, his daughter and grandson, by walking behind the coffin of the ostracised man, assert a dignity and humanity that the town would deny. The theme was to recur in many of the stories of *Los funerales de la Mamá grande* [*The funeral of the Great Mother*] (1962) in which insignificant people stand up in solitary defiance against the weight of social censure. A woman whose son has been shot as a thief goes to see his grave, insisting that he had been a good man; she braves the hostile curiosity of the whole town to do this. In another story, a dentist deliberately extracts the corrupt mayor's tooth without an anaesthetic; while in 'La prodigiosa tarde de Baltasar' [Baltasar's Glorious Afternoon], a carpenter who makes bird-cages refuses to take pay from the town's richest man and gives away a free bird-cage in an act of generosity of which the other is incapable. Again and again in García Márquez's stories, a lonely, proud individual asserts a sense of dignity despite a society in which brutality and corruption triumph.

In the same year as the publication of *Los funerales*, García Márquez also published *La mala hora* [*The Evil Hour*] (1962), on the subject of a small town whose inhabitants are whipped to frenzy by a series of anonymous posters which publicise their misdeeds. But the most important work of this period was the intense, short novel, *El coronel no tiene quien le escriba* [*No-one Writes to the Colonel*] (1961), in which the theme of isolation is incarnated in the tragi-comic character of the Colonel who is the first in a line of great García Márquez eccentrics. Sixty years before the opening of the novel, the Colonel had fought in a civil war. According to a fifteen-year-old law, he was entitled to a pension for which he anxiously waits. But the pension never arrives, his only son has been shot and his sole remaining possession is a fighting cock which he cannot afford to feed. The story ends with the Colonel defiantly refusing to sell the cock though he and his wife face starvation. The intensity springs from the Colonel's larger-than-life character. As soon as García Márquez turned his back on realism, his novels attained real originality. Note, for instance, how the following passage extends a realistic situation to the edge of comedy.

The Colonel is with his wife:

Trató de explicar algo pero lo venció el sueño. Ella siguió hablando sordamente hasta cuando se dió cuenta de que su esposo dormía. Entonces salió del mosquitero y se paseó por la sala en tinieblas. Allí siguió hablando. El coronel la llamó en la madrugada.

Ella apareció en la puerta, espectral, iluminada desde abajo por la lámpara casi extinguida. La apagó antes de entrar al mosquitero. Pero siguió hablando.*

The slight distortion of reality when the wife goes on and on talking as the Colonel sleeps expresses desperation and at the same time conveys a slightly absurd and humorous effect. It was this technique which was to inform every line of *Cien años de soledad* [*A Hundred Years of Solitude*] (1967), one of the finest Spanish–American novels.

Cien años de soledad is the story of the rise and fall of the community of Macondo and of the family of Buendía. Macondo had been founded by Ursula and José Arcadio Buendía, who were in flight from their own guilt; for they were first cousins haunted by the ghost of a man José Arcadio had killed. They founded Macondo as far as possible from the sea coast from which they came, and in a region of impenetrable swamp and jungle. Here they give birth to a line of eccentric Aurelianos and José Arcadios, introvert dreamers and impulsive men of action; and to a line of extraordinary women—the tormented, sensual virgin Amaranta, the beautiful Remedios, who has no sense of shame and refuses to wear clothes. Remote from the rest of civilisation, the Buendías behave as if the Christian moral code had never existed. The male members of the family fall in love with their aunts or even their grandmothers; and one Aureliano Buendía marries an eleven-year-old girl who has only just stopped wetting her bed and who has to be lifted up to kiss the wedding guests.

In these early years Macondo is in a state of primal innocence. Nobody is older than thirty. There are no deaths. Aureliano Buendía spends his time proving that the world is round, unaware that this

---

* He tried to explain something but sleep overcame him. She went on talking softly until she realised that her husband was asleep. Then she emerged from under the mosquito net and walked about the shadowy room. There she went on talking. The colonel called her at dawn.

She appeared at the door, like a spectre, lit up from below from the almost extinguished light of the lamp. She put it out before getting in under the mosquito net. But she went on talking.

discovery has already been made. But Macondo, though isolated, is not completely cut off from outside influence. Foreign inventions—the magnet, the manufacture of ice, false teeth—appear in the town, thanks to a tribe of gypsies who have discovered a secret route across the marshes. This intermittent contact with other civilisations, is similar to the contact that Colombia and Latin America have had with Europe. Everything that happens in Macondo is a fantasy reflection of what has happened in Latin America, but the symbolism and analogies are never obtruded. The Buendía family are far too fascinating.

One of the themes of *Cien años de soledad* is the wonder and strangeness of a continent in which the fantastic is the normative. The odder the event, the nearer we feel to the reality of Latin America. Thus, when José Arcadio tries to leave Macondo he has to cut his way through a jungle of golden salamanders and bleeding lilies. And instead of finding a route to the sea, he comes across the petrified hull of a landlocked Spanish galleon marvellously trapped by the wilderness:

Ligeramente volteado a estribor, de su arboladura intacta colgaban las piltrafas escuálidas del velamen, entre jarcias adornadas de orquídeas. El casco, cubierto con una tersa coraza de rémora petrificada y musgo tierno, estaba firmemente enclavado en un suelo de piedras.*

Macondo's isolation is broken down by external forces—by civil war, by the railways and the banana plantation, which draw the inhabitants into politics and strife without changing their eccentric individuality. But 'progress' does not last. A four-year rainstorm restores Macondo to its primal chaos. And the birth of a child with a pig's tail—fruit of an incestuous union between Amaranta Ursula and her nephew—brings the family to an end.

Cien años de soledad is the novel that finally persuades us of the inadequacy of realism in dealing with the Spanish–American environment. From the very first line, the violence and the strange are juxtaposed:

Muchos años después, frente al pelotón de fusilamiento, el coronel Aureliano Buendía había de recordar aquella tarde remota en que su padre lo llevó a conocer el hielo.†

---

* It was slightly heeled over to starboard and from its intact masts there hung the scanty remains of the sail amongst rigging that was decorated with orchids. The hulk covered with a thick shell of petrified remora and tender moss, was firmly anchored in a stony soil.
† Many years later, before the firing-squad, Colonel Aureliano Buendía was to recall that remote afternoon on which his father took him to see ice for the first time.

The effect of the juxtaposition of the tragic and the trivial is finally comic, and comic exaggeration is the keystone of the style. In one extraordinary passage, after a José Arcadio Buendía has been killed by his wife, his blood shows an uncanny knowledge of the streets of Macondo and the road to the family house:

Un hilo de sangre salió por debajo de la puerta, atravesó la sala, salió a la calle, siguió en un curso directo por los andenes disparejos, descendió escalinatas y subió pretiles, pasó de largo por la Calle de los Turcos, dobló una esquina a la derecha y otra a la izquierda, volteó en ángulo recto frente a la casa de los Buendía, pasó por debajo de la puerta cerrada, atravesó la sala de visitas pegado a las paredes para no manchar los tapices, siguió por la otra sala, eludió en una curva amplia le mesa del comedor, avanzó por el corredor de las begonias y pasó sin ser visto por debajo de la silla de Amaranta que daba una lección de aritmética a Aureliano José, y se metió por el granero y apareció en la cocina donde Ursula se disponía a partir treinta y seis huevos para el pan.*

The accumulation of precise detail around an impossible event has a Rabelaisian quality. The technique recurs frequently. For instance, after a carnival fight over rival beauty queens, the dead are detailed precisely as 'nine clowns, four Columbines, seventeen playing card kings, one devil, three musicians, two French knights and three Japanese Empresses...'. Another humorous device is the externalising of the attributes of the Buendías in natural phenomena; the beautiful Remedios has a special odour which drives men mad; clouds of butterflies follow Meme Buendía. And Macondo itself is visited by a series of strange plagues—a plague of insomnia, of dead birds, the four-year rainstorm.

The novel reminds us that in a continent conquered by men who had absorbed the novels of chivalry and were haunted by tales of El Dorado, a continent in which nature has almost invariably triumphed over man, the marvellous must have a place in literature.

MEXICO

The post-revolutionary novel in Mexico was, until the 1940s, very much tied to the technique of realism. Two writers, José Revueltas

---

* A trickle of blood came out from under the door, crossed the living room and went out into the street. It followed a direct course along the uneven pavements, went down steps and up railings, passed by the Turk's Street, turned once to the right and then to the left, made a sharp turn before the Buendía's house, passed underneath the closed door, crossed the drawing-room, keeping close to the walls so as not to stain the carpets, went through the other room, avoided the ample curve of the dining table, advanced along the corridor with the begonias and passed unseen under the chair of Amaranta who was giving an arithmetic lesson to Aureliano José and then, entering the barn, it appeared in the kitchen where Ursula was about to break thirty-six eggs for the bread.

(1914–   ) and Agustín Yáñez (1904–   ) then published novels which dealt with traditional revolutionary themes in a totally new way. In *El luto humano* [*Human Mourning*] (1943), José Revueltas used a stream of consciousness technique in a story of a peasant community, and in *Al filo del agua* [*On the Eve of the Rain*], Agustín Yáñez described a remote town on the eve of the revolutionary storm using multiple viewpoint, stream of consciousness and symbolism. The two outstanding contemporary novelists, Juan Rulfo (1918–   ) and Carlos Fuentes (1929–   ), have absorbed the new techniques to create totally new styles of writing.

Juan Rulfo

A volume of short stories, *El llano en llamas* [*The Plain in Flames*], published in 1953, distinguished Rulfo as a writer of unusual brevity and economy. As against the baroque style of nearly all contemporary writers, his stories with their short sentences, their deliberate shying away from emotionally-loaded words, their concentration on behaviour rather than states of consciousness, seem to place him in quite a different category from the rest of his contemporaries. Yet what marks his work off from the social-protest novel is his refusal to involve the reader in judgments on events and characters. This attitude arises from Rulfo's view of human beings and their situation; for the world he moves in is one in which environment still dominates human beings. In the story 'Talpa', for instance, an adulterous couple drag the woman's husband on a pilgrimage knowing that he will die. They are guilty of his murder, and are haunted by their guilt when they return from the pilgrimage. But neither the sin nor the guilt are consciously conceived. They are a prey to forces which they do not understand. The revolutionaries of 'El llano en llamas' feel a savage glee as their leader takes to the hills, the glee of the peasant freed momentarily from his crippling routine; but his 'crimes' are seen as the irresponsible acts of a child. In 'Es que somos muy pobres' [It's Just that We are Very Poor] a girl stoically accepts the fate of being a prostitute as the last family possessions are lost in a flood. In Juan Rulfo's world, people do not make choices; their paths are laid out for them. Juan Rulfo's break with realism is also apparent in his tendency to eschew the normative, to choose the extraordinary rather than the ordinary case. But his outstanding work, and one of the outstanding works of Spanish–American literature, is his novel *Pedro Páramo* (1955) in which he left behind all compromise with realism and entered a world of magic and dream. On the surface, this is the story of a young landowner who inherits a farm loaded with debt, makes a good marriage and ends as the most powerful man in the country with a band of revolutionaries in his pay. But for the reader, Pedro Páramo is never alive. He is dead from the first pages of the book and so are all the people he had bullied or loved. The narration is in the form of a search. Juan Preciado has been told by his mother to go and look for his father Pedro Páramo in Comala. The mule-driver who take him declares 'we are all sons of Pedro Páramo' as he leaves Juan in the village where nothing is left but the sound of the voices of the dead on the air. Doña Eduviges, Damiana who had lived in Páramo's house, Dorotea a mad woman who had procured women for Páramo's son, all these appear as living people to Preciado. They talk to him and then float off into some drama of the past, still chasing some illusion they had held in life and which they can never convert into reality. Preciado himself dies without discovering his father, suffocated by these airy voices. And Páramo is present only in the memory of the dead. The whole of the first part of the novel has an uncanny, eerie quality as the illusory characters strain their ears for sounds from another world. Thus Doña Eduviges, when told that Preciado's mother is dead, comments:

Entonces, ésa fue la causa de que su voz la oyera tan débil, como si hubiera tenido que atravesar una distancia muy larga para llegar hasta aquí.*

A deep-rooted Mexican belief in the 'life' of the dead is thus imaginatively transposed. Their real as opposed to their stereotyped attitudes are given voice. Like the old woman, Dorotea, who has never really believed in the soul's heaven and is glad that her soul wanders the earth while her body remains buried in her native village.

Allá hallarás mi querencia. El lugar que yo quise. Donde los sueños me enflaquecieron. Mi pueblo, levantado sobre la llanura. Lleno de árboles y de hojas, como una alcancía donde hemos guardado nuestros recuerdos.†

But what distinguishes these dead characters is their incommunicability. They had all once lived in the same village. They had loved, hated and hurt one another, but in death as in life they remain locked in their illusions. Damiana, once Pedro's mistress, for instance, eter-

---

* Then that was why her voice was so weak, as if it had to cross a very great distance to reach here.

† There you will find my home. The place I loved. Where dreams made me thin. The village rising on a plain. Full of trees and leaves like a box in which we have stored up our memories.

nally waits for his return; Dorotea, though dead, still ponders on the frustration of her motherhood, just as in life she had nursed her imaginary baby. And Pedro Páramo all his life had been hopelessly in love with a miner's daughter, Susana, a woman who remained faithful to the memory of her first husband, Florencio, even after she was married to Páramo. Pedro Páramo and Susana lived for love, but not love for each other. But the illusions are destructive. When Susana dies, Pedro Páramo spends his years gazing at the road to the cemetery and allowing his land to fall into ruin.

Desde entonces la tierra se quedó baldía y como en ruinas. Daba pena verla llenándose de achaques con tanta plaga que la invadió en cuanto la dejaron sola. ...Y todo por las ideas de Don Pedro, por sus pleitos de alma.*

The potentially fertile lands are in ruin when he dies.

Pedro Páramo can, of course, be taken as a symbolic figure, the figure of the Mexico of landowners and *caciques*. His death occurs in the 1920s when the post-revolutionary governments began to destroy the foundations of the old social structures that still persisted after the Revolution. But though the protagonist is a landowner, this is not a novel about economic exploitation. The author plunges deeper into the myths that Mexicans really live by. Thus Pedro Páramo is the *macho*, a vigorous exploiter, who nevertheless cherishes the illusion of communion with Susana whom he never comes to know. Dorotea nurses the motherhood illusion of all Mexican women. Miguel Páramo represents another aspect of the *macho* myth, but the stallion he rides, the symbol of his masculinity, finally kills him. Only the myths live on when the men and women are dead.

In a poetic form, the novel expresses the inner solitude and inability to communicate which the poet and essayist, Octavio Paz, sees as one of the main characteristics of his countrymen. As Susana's father exclaims: '¿Que hemos hecho? ¿Por qué se nos ha podrido el alma?' [What have we done? Why has our soul rotted?]

Carlos Fuentes

'¿Qué hemos hecho?' could well have described the theme of Fuentes's novels and short stories. The son of a Mexican diplomat, brought up abroad, he began his writing career with a volume of short stories, *Los días enmascarados* [*The Masked Days*] (1953) and a novel, *La región*

* From that moment, the earth remained fallow and as if in ruins. It was terrible to see it overrun with such infirmities and so many scourges which invaded it as soon as it was left alone. And all because of the ideas of Don Pedro, for the conflicts of his soul.

más transparente [*The Clearer Region*] (1958) which sprang out of the confrontation of a restless, cosmopolitan mind with a country that was half-primitive, which had institutionalised its myths and was out of touch with its own reality. The city is symbolised by Ixta Cienfuegos who visits slums and society parties, listens to confessions and self-justifications. The protagonists are the inhabitants of this brash post-revolutionary city; the plutocrat of peasant origin, Federico Robles; the aristocratic Ovando family who had lost their lands in the Revolution but are now on their way back to prominence; Rodrigo Pola, the poor student who marries a wealthy heiress; Norma, daughter of a new-rich trader, who is never quite accepted by fashionable society. There are also the humbler members of society—the wetbacks,[1] taxi-drivers and prostitutes. But it is the middle class that Fuentes is most interested in. They are the new men, the leaders who have betrayed the Revolution, and whose selfish ambitions are no more laudable than those of the landed aristocracy they have replaced. Those members of the middle class like Federico Robles who seem more capable of salvation cannot maintain themselves in its orbit. Robles goes bankrupt and leaves the city.

La región is quite evidently influenced by the writings of a generation of essayists, beginning with Samuel Ramos (1897–1959) and Alfonso Reyes (1889–1959) and including the poet, Octavio Paz, whose *El laberinto de la soledad* [*Labyrinth of Solitude*] (1950) was a study of the Mexican character and myths. The characters in *La región* have betrayed the Revolution because they have converted the heroes of the fighting into totems, because their institutionalised myths hide reality and stifle an authentic national life. However, the technique of Fuentes in this novel has not yet succeeded in matching the subject matter. His second novel, *Las buenas conciencias* [*The Good Consciences*] (1959) was more conventional in approach, a biography of the adolescence and youth of Jaime Ceballos, one of the characters who in the early novel had made a wealthy marriage as a step into the ruling élite. The novel is an analysis of the way an idealistic boy of middle-class provincial family, at first in revolt against the false values of his elders, becomes himself one of the corrupt. The theme of Revolution betrayed was most effectively dealt with in *La muerte de Artemio Cruz* [*The Death of Artemio Cruz*] (1962). Artemio, born an illegitimate outcast, is given a chance to rise by the Revolution. Embittered by the death of a woman he loves, he becomes a hard-bitten, ruthless schemer who marries a wealthy woman and comes to own business, newspapers and politicians.

He moves confidently in a world of his own making. But at the beginning of the novel, Artemio lies in hospital, his body no longer controlled by his will, his death imminent. What we learn of him and his past will be through the last thoughts of a dying man and through the reflections of the family and business associates at his bed-side. Artemio Cruz's stream of consciousness is divided into two: the 'yo' which cannot relinquish the ego interest in business and labour disputes, and the deeper consciousness which addresses Artemio as 'tu', which recognises that he has lived a false life and speaks of the 'tantos momentos de mera gesticulación' [many moments of mere gesturing]. It is this part of his personality which registers the process of pain and discomfort and the breakdown of his body and which in the last moments before death tries to recover the sense of authenticity and truth which the ego has denied. The deeper self recognises Artemio's failing as the basic failing of the Mexican—his need to violate in order to affirm himself. It is this self which acknowledges that, if Artemio Cruz has survived through the hazardous revolutionary and post-revolutionary years, it is not out of real valour.

...sobrevivirás, no por ser el más fuerte, sino por el azar oscuro de un universo cada vez más frío, en el que sólo sobrevivirán los organismos que sepan conservar la temperatura de su cuerpo frente a los cambios de medio, los que concentren esa masa nerviosa frontal y pueden predecir el peligro, buscar el alimento, organizar su movimiento y dirigir su nado en el océano redondo proliferante, atestado de los orígenes.*

In choosing to 'survive', Artemio has killed the men he might have been and follows the path dictated by 'interés' [interest], 'miedo' [fear], 'orgullo' [pride]. This division is emphasised by the structure of the book (the dialogue between the 'yo' and the 'tu' of Artemio) and the obvious division between what he is and what he might have been. The objective reality is described in a third-person narrative which records the milestones of his life, in which each personal triumph of the ego has meant the sacrifice of a friend, a companion or a relation. In his last delirium, he returns to the early innocence of his orphaned childhood.

In *La muerte de Artemio Cruz*, Fuentes finally attained a technique

* ...you will survive not because you are the strongest but because of the obscure chance of a Universe which is growing colder and in which there will only survive those organisms which know how to preserve their body temperature in changes of environment, those who concentrate that nervous frontal mass and can foretell danger, seek food, organise their movement and direct their swimming in the round proliferating ocean crammed with origins.

that really allowed him to penetrate more deeply into the human personality. By splitting the 'yo' and the 'tu', the interplay of ego and superego was dramatised. In *Cambio de piel* [*Change of Skin*] (1967), Fuentes presents the reader with an infinitely more ambitious project—nothing less than a map of the Mexican unconscious mind. He himself once described the themes of the novel as

la historia de los sentimientos privados, viejos y nostálgicamente acariciados, con los que queremos justificar nuestra vida y la pasión de un mundo que los niega.*[1]

In all his novels, he had been concerned with defining the limits of personal responsibility, but in this one, he does so by constructing a complex model and then destroying it before our very eyes in order to emphasise that this is merely a construct. Originally entitled *El sueño* [*The Dream*], the novel has a narrator who creates the 'dream', and the four main characters are perhaps figments of his imagination which represent the world as it appears to him. The main central section of the work is the story of a car-ride between Mexico City and Vera Cruz. In the car, there are four people—Javier; his wife, a North-American Jewess called Elizabeth; his mistress, Isabel; and Elizabeth's lover, a Sudetan German called Franz. As this is a dream the car speeds towards Vera Cruz, but the four characters never get further than the town of Cholula and the hotel room where they make love and quarrel. A third dimension is added by the voyeur-narrator who addresses the two women characters as 'tu'. Between them, the four characters represent innumerable conflicts and tensions. There are the racial tensions of the Jewess Elizabeth bearing her racial memories of oppression; there are the national conflicts of the Mexican faced with the challenge of the North American and the European; there are the generational conflicts between the three older members of the party and Isabel, the student; there are the sexual rivalries and attractions; there are conflicts between the ideal and myth world that each character holds onto and the 'real' world, between society symbolised in its enduring monuments—the Aztec pyramid, the Catholic church, the Nazi crematorium, the lunatic asylum and the individual. Above all, the novel poses the question of where the individual ends and the social begins, and of what constitutes an 'individual' when even their myths are social. But Fuentes also writes an 'open' novel. The relations of the four characters are only part of the story and the whole of the end

---

* the history of private feelings which are ancient and nostalgically caressed, those with which we would justify our lives and passion in a world that denies them.

of the work is concerned with 'exposing' his own characters and his own method, of insisting that the novel is a 'personal happening', a 'lie' through which Fuentes—and the reader—can escape the stranglehold of 'la vie quotidienne'. This is a novel that synthesises the whole of Mexican consciousness. In the following passage, the four people walk through Cholula; as they walk, the novelist cuts back to the distant past to remind us of events of the conquest that had taken place on the ground on which they walked and in a single paragraph of description, the whole society is seen at a single glance.

Caminaron sin hablar, cansados, contagiados por la vida muerta de este pueblo, acentuada por el intento falso de bullicio que venía del altoparlante con su twist repetido una y otra vez, en honor de la señorita Lucila Hernández, en honor de la simpática Dolores Padilla, en honor de la bella Iris Alonso; en la bicicletería del portal, tres jóvenes con el torso desnudo engrasaban, hacían girar las ruedas, canjeaban albures y sonreían idiotamente cuando pasaron Franz e Isabel, Javier y Elizabeth. Los olores del azufre emanaban de esos baños donde una mujer, en el umbral, mostraba sus caderas floreadas mientras azotaba con la palma abierta a un niño que se negaba a entrar y en el registro de electores un pintor pasaba la brocha sobre la fachada, borrando poco a poco la propaganda electoral antigua, la CROM con Adolfo López Mateos, y la reciente, la CROM con Gustavo Díaz Ordaz[1] y el salón de billares *El 10 de Mayo* estaba vacío, detrás de sus puertas de batientes, debajo de un aviso: 'se prohibe jugar a los menores de edad' y un viejo con chaleco desabotonado y camisa a rayas sin cuello frotaba lentamente el gis sobre la punta del taco y bostezaba, mostrando los huecos negros de su dentadura y una mujer se mecía en un sillón de bejuco frente al consultorio médico que ocupaba la esquina y se anunciaba con letras plateadas sobre fondo negro, enfermedades de niños, de la piel y venéreo-sifilis, análisis de sangre, orina, esputo, materiales fecales... *

* They walked without speaking, tired and affected by the dead life of this town which was increased by the factitious effort to create bustling life which came from the loudspeakers with the repeated twists in honour of Miss Lucila Hernández, in honour of charming Dolores Padilla, in honour of beautiful Iris Alonso; in the bicycle shop in the arcade, three young men with their chests bare, greased and spun the wheels, exchanging bets and smiling idiotically when Franz, Isabel, Javier and Elizabeth went past. The smell of sulphur came from those baths, where a woman standing in the doorway showed her flowered thighs as she beat a child with her open hand because it was refusing to go in, and on the electoral registry building, a painter painted over the front and little by little erased the old electoral posters, the CROM with Adolfo López Mateos and the recent CROM with Gustavo Díaz Ordaz. And the billiard saloon, 'The Tenth of May', was empty; behind its swing doors, a notice, 'Those under 21 not allowed to play', and an old man with his waistcoat unbuttoned and wearing a striped shirt without a collar slowly rubbed chalk on the end of the cue and yawned, showing the black cavities in his teeth; and a woman rocked herself on a cane chair in front of the doctor's surgery on the corner where, in silver letters over a black background, there was a notice that read 'Children's diseases, skin and venereal diseases, blood, urine, sputum and foecal analysis'...

This horizontal glance that takes in everything at one moment, gives way to a vertical sounding in which different historical periods appear simultaneously in the consciousness of the characters. The language too breaks the back of Spanish rhetoric, using the imported words of a North-American culture while the characters are absorbing classical antiquity; as in the following extract where Franz is questioning Elizabeth about her stay in Greece.

'No había luz electrica. ¿Qué hacían en la noche?'
    'We played footsie, Mr. District Attorney. Oye, así no vamos a ningun lado. Este es un momento muy lírico, muy poético y tú quieres hacer investarios, tú.'
    'Mar armado con las armas de Troya.'
    'Pop. Lit. ¿No estas aburrida, Dragona?'*

Fuentes tries to cut through the notion of what we think our consciousness ought to be in order to present us with what it actually is. But this is also a particularly Mexican consciousness. The four characters speed through the countryside, past huts and scenery that remind them of films, locked in their own preoccupations and conflicts, interested only in the pre-Columbian ruins because these, like a labyrinth, lead them back to the self. It is a consciousness turned in on itself, which fails to act on the outside world, tragically isolated.

Fuentes has two other published works, *Zona Sagrada* (1967) a novel which presents the personal vision of a young man haunted by the myth-like personality of his mother, a famous film star, and a volume of short stories, *Cantar de ciegos* (1964).[1]

SUMMARY

This chapter offers only a brief survey of the contemporary Spanish–American novel. Nothing has been said of the talented generation of 1950 in Chile which includes José Donoso, Enrique Lafourcade and Jorge Edwards, nor of the modern Cuban novel represented by Guillermo Cabrera Infante (1929–), Severo Sarduy (1937–), who has enjoyed a *succès d'estime* in Paris, and Lezama Lima, author of the outstanding novel *Paradiso* (1966), which attempts to show the formation of a poetic consciousness. In Ecuador, there has been a continuation of the 'magic realism' (which the Guayaquil school had anticipated)—notably by Adalberto Ortiz (1914–) in his novel *Juyungo* (1943).

* 'There was no electric light. What did you do at night?'
    'We played footsie, Mr District Attorney. Listen. We're not going anywhere. This is a very poetic, a very poetic moment and you are asking for inventories.'
    'A sea armed with the arms of Troy.'
    'Pop. Lit. Aren't you bored, dragon?'

And in Venezuela, Miguel Otero Silva (1908–　) has written two outstanding novels, *Casas muertas* [*Dead Houses*] (1955) and *Oficina número uno* [*Office Number One*] (1961) which depict the decline of the old rural Venezuela and the rise of a nation whose life centres on the oil-field; while Salvador Garmendia (1928–　) has written stories and novels which are intensified visions of the sordid. His three main novels are *Los pequeños seres* (1959), *La mala vida* (1968) and *Los habitantes* (1968).

With the modern novel, Spanish–American literature has reached maturity. Never have there been so many writers who have mastered personal styles, nor so many novels which experiment freely without imitating the European or North-American novel. The last two decades have witnessed an intense technical exploration as varied and lively as that going on anywhere in the world. More novelists than ever before have found a public outside their own continent, while within Spanish America there is a growing reading public whose interest is primarily in the native product. This interest has given the writer a new sense of responsibility. Up to the present, he has worked in isolation, an outsider from society, often an exile. The contemporary writer may still choose to live outside his own country but he has an ever-increasing public within it. The possible results of this entirely new situation are still to be seen. Whatever the future holds, contemporary Spanish–American literature is in a flourishing state and perhaps the time is not far distant when we in Europe will go a-begging.

CONCLUSION

The sixteenth-century discoverers were astonished to find that the inhabitants of the New World looked very much like themselves. They found none of the monstrous shapes, square heads and green hair which some of their contemporaries had imagined. But this very similarity of the Indians increased the conquerors' horror and surprise at the weird customs and practices they encountered. A sixteenth-century engraving which shows the Indians of Puerto Rico experimenting on a Spaniard to see if he is mortal illustrates the mutual incomprehension of these two societies. The Indians expected the Spaniards to have supernatural powers and found to their disappointment that they were ordinary men. The Spaniards expected men who looked like themselves to behave in the same way and to play according to the rules of the game.

Something of this mutual misunderstanding has continued to dog the relationship of Latin America to the rest of the world. Latin Americans have often expected miracles of Europe and have been disappointed to find her fallible; while for Europeans the exotic dream of America often turns out to be a distorting mirror in which they see their own grotesque reflection. To avoid falling into such sterile attitudes, we must destroy our preconceived frameworks and start from the phenomenon itself. And we must go back to the most basic and obvious fact of all, the fact that Latin America is part of the 'under-developed' world and that it is so because it has formerly been a colony of Spain and economically dependent on Europe.

Although at first sight economic dependence may seem alien to literary culture, the two cannot be altogether separated. An 'under-developed' country is not only economically under-developed but has fewer schools, poorer universities, more limited publishing facilities. This cultural dependence, glaring during the colonial period, did not break down with independence. Spanish–American writers then found themselves free of Spain but with no national tradition in which to work, no university facilities or higher education. They were therefore either self-educated, training themselves by reading imported French, English, German or Spanish literature or by travelling abroad. Contrast this situation with that of the European writer of the period, who would normally be educated in a European school, read his own literature and thus gain a firm foothold on his own culture before venturing into the field of foreign literature. His own literature gave him a vantage point for viewing other cultures. The Latin American, on the other hand, found himself viewing his own culture from the vantage point of Europe. Moreover, his literary education, while it acquainted him with many aspects of human experience, did not give him any sense of what it meant to be a Peruvian or a Chilean or an Argentinian.

The writer's distance from his own society was aggravated by the fact that culturally he had outstripped his fellow countrymen. The high level of illiteracy was like a raised drawbridge which shut him out from communication. When Einstein discovered the theory of relativity he did not have to start teaching mathematics in order to explain what he meant. There were plenty of people able to understand his theory and share his excitement. But the Spanish–American writer who discovered new literary marvels had no-one to share them with. Before he could even talk to his fellow-countrymen about Romanticism and Naturalism, they had to be taught to read and write. Throughout the nineteenth century writers were engaged in a desperate struggle to match their literary sophistication with their crude environment. Not surprisingly they often felt happier among their literary peers in Europe and some became exiles either out of choice or necessity. José María Heredia, José Martí, Darío, Alberto Blest Gana—these are only a few who lived for a long period of their adult life outside Latin America.

Paradoxically, the difficulties and disadvantages of the nineteenth-century writer did not stop him from feeling that he had an important part to play in his country's future. Indeed the gap between his culture and that of his fellow-nationals encouraged him to try to bring his superior knowledge to bear on social and political problems. In the absence of an educated ruling élite, he had to be prophet, critic and architect of the new society. Hence literature and politics were closely linked in his mind, and the link was strengthened by the fact that his main forums of discussion were the cafés, the bookshops and the literary clubs. Political blueprints and novels and poems were alike the fruit of these meetings and associations of intellectuals. Thus, the Cuban literary circle which met in the home of Domingo Delmonte was as dedicated to the cause of freedom as it was to the creation of a Cuban literature. In the Argentine, writers and intellectuals founded the *Asociación de Mayo* whose aim was to combat the dictatorship of Rosas and whose programme was political, social and cultural. In Chile, a *Sociedad Literaria*, founded in 1842, had the aim of creating a sense of national pride through literature. In Peru, Manuel González Prada founded a literary circle in 1886 in order to reform and regenerate his country after its humiliating defeat by Chile. It is obvious that the literature written by members of these groups must have a political bias. Indeed, throughout the nineteenth century it was generally assumed that literature should civilise, educate or even serve as an instrument of reform. Much writing, therefore, was overtly political. Novels attacked Spanish colonial rule (those of Fernández de Lizardi, for example) or they exposed the evils of slavery or dictatorship. Some writing was exemplary. The poems of Olmedo and of Andrés Bello, for instance, set up ideals to guide the citizens of the new republics. Many novels were written with the intention of teaching people episodes from national history. And even literature which described the landscape or national types and customs did so in order to stress national originality and hence to help achieve spiritual emancipation from Europe. The weaknesses of much nineteenth-century literature arises from this confusion of function. Sometimes a polemical essay like *Facundo* is more successful than polemic disguised in novel form. Novels such as *Amalia* or *Cecilia Valdés* often waver between the demands of literature and the demands of polemic. But if writers were bold in attacking political abuses through literature, they were timid in their approach to the Spanish language whose conventions and vocabulary they accepted despite the fact that literary Spanish was often far removed from the language spoken in America. Indeed, far from breaking new ground some writers of the period used a deliberately archaic style in order to give a 'classical' cast to their ideas. Montalvo is a good example of a man who chose to write in a prose style which has the quality and cadences of seventeenth-century Castilian. Only in a few isolated cases was there a successful attempt to wed new themes to new language and form. *Martín Fierro* achieved a successful blend of folk tradition, regional languages and familiar outlaw story; and Ricardo Palma, in his *Tradiciones peruanas* also broke through Spanish academic tradition and boldly created a language to suit his theme. But in general, before José Martí and the Modernists came onto the scene, there was little appreciation of the need to revitalise the language.

For this reason alone, Modernism marks a decisive turning point in the history of Spanish–American literature.

The Modernists were not, of course, interested in regional peculiarities of language. What they wanted above all was to identify Spanish America with the most advanced literary culture—that of France—and to break out of the provincialism which dependence on Spain had implied. In one respect the Modernist 'revolt' merely reflects a shifting of relationships. From satellites of Spain, the Spanish–American republics became satellites of France and North America. Nevertheless, the stress that the Modernists placed on language and style was of paramount importance, though its first effect was to separate Spanish–American literature into two strands—that which cultivated style and that which cultivated commitment. Between the previous Modernist writing of an Enrique Larreta and the rough outraged prose of a Baldomero Lillo there was a gulf that is not entirely explicable by their different educations. The committed writer tended to think of the Modernist or post-Modernist as decadent—too much interested in aesthetic problems and too little in the problems of his society. With the '20s and the active engagement of many writers in the political struggle these differences were accentuated. Roughness, documentary truth, realism, were assumed to be marks of a greater sincerity, a higher regard for the sufferings of the poor. Ricardo Güiraldes was exceptional in his preoccupation both with style and with the expression of national values in literature.

The Latin–American avant-garde of the '20s, therefore, often tended to be either on the defensive or to be extremely aggressive, depending on the environment. In Mexico where an upsurge of cultural nationalism followed the Revolution, the avant-garde was on the defensive. In Buenos Aires the young writers of *Proa* and *Martín Fierro* were very much on the attack. And in the final analysis, it was the avant-garde rather than the social realists who achieved the most dramatic and worthwhile results.

Dada and Surrealism and other European movements rejected preconceived patterns and forms, destroyed literary establishments, refused to recognise fixed grammatical structures or 'classical' moulds. The influence of these movements was therefore to liberate Latin Americans from the last vestiges of the bonds of Spanish rhetoric. The liberation was first achieved in poetry, especially in the poetry of Cesar Vallejo who can be said to have thrown a bomb onto literary Castilian. His work was not merely destructive. Using a totally new vocabulary of colloquialism, scientific language, invented words, new metaphors, he reconstructed a fresh poetry, a poetry of 'third world' man, orphaned and lost in a universe he did not create. He was the first poet to succeed in decolonising the Latin–American imagination. Experiment was slower to be introduced into the novel and prose writing. But here too it was the avant-garde rather than the documentary realists who made the most creative contribution. Borges, Roberto Arlt, and later Asturias and Carpentier opened the doors of fantasy. Their stories and novels revealed how poor and arid realism and naturalism had become in a Latin–American context. After all, these were styles developed to express the textures and tragedies of middle-class quotidian life at a moment when money and money values were replacing Christian-based morality. The European bourgeois novel was concerned with the norm, the typical. Latin–American writers, on the other hand, were constantly faced with the odd, the extraordinary, the monstrous, seldom with anything that matched this European middle-class norm; and it was only by devising and inventing literary forms which could encompass these weird mutations that they could achieve a verisimilitude of their own. The linguistic virtuosity of a Cortázar, the fantasy of a García Márquez, the superimposition of different strands of time and different geographical locations in Vargas Llosa, bring us nearer to the experience of Latin America than did the realist and naturalist novels of an earlier period.

At the outset of this study, the difficulty of generalising about Spanish-speaking America was emphasised. Yet the term, 'Spanish America' or 'Latin America' appears on almost every page. Many critics believe that there is no more justification for talking of Spanish–American literature than for talking of European literature. Yet, although broad generalisations concerning the whole continent are sometimes inaccurate, it is equally misleading to consider each country as a separate entity. Europeans speak many different languages, whereas Spanish America has a single language, a fact which makes it easier for writers from one country to influence or be influenced by those of another. The Spanish–American countries are neither entirely united nor entirely separate. And this is further complicated by the fact that there are regional constellations—the Plate region, the Andean republics, the Caribbean—which have special characteristics not evident elsewhere. Even in colonial times, the Spanish Empire was an overall unity which contained regional variations. The Viceroyalties of Mexico and Peru, in particular, were like two separate solar systems, with Lima as the more conservative and Hispanic pole, and Mexico as the more avant-garde extreme. In the nineteenth century, national differences were emphasised and exaggerated as the new countries strove to affirm their separate identities, often resorting to war, aggression or chauvinistic shows of force to create patriotic sentiment. This nationalism is reflected in literature. Yet even at the height of nationalism, the writers of the continent maintained contact, exchanged ideas, and were often animated by a sense of solidarity with 'Latin America' which transcended narrow nationalisms. Of necessity, the writers of this period were indefatigable travellers: Sarmiento spent years in Chile and died in Paraguay; Echeverría found refuge in Montevideo; Hostos travelled the length and breadth of America and the Caribbean; Martí lived in the United States, Venezuela and Guatemala; Heredia in the United States and Mexico; Darío in Chile and the Argentine. The common Spanish language made it easy for writers to live, work and write in other countries. With Rodó, the supranational ideal assumed even greater importance and writers consciously began to promote the intellectual unity of the continent. The foundation of the *América* publishing house by Blanco Fombona, the foundation of the *Mundial* magazine in Paris are but two examples of the practical interpretation of this ideal. In recent years this unity has been pursued on a political plane, but more interesting from a literary point of view is the fact that post-revolutionary governments in Mexico, Guatemala, and more recently in Cuba, have also tended to emphasize the cultural unity of the continent. Vasconcelos attracted writers and artists from all over America. Guatemala in the late '40s became the meeting point for writers from Central America. Cuba holds yearly gatherings for writers and intellectuals and offers prizes for the novel, poetry, the essay and drama.

A practical development which has helped to break down the barriers between nations is the emergence of Buenos Aires and Mexico as two major publishing centres. This is a surprisingly recent development, particularly in Mexico. Up to the Second World War, commercial publishing throughout Spanish America was on a very small scale and often confined to a tiny national market. The Second World War blocked sources of outside supply and helped the growth of publishing ventures on more than a national scale. For the first time, writers who have their books published in their own continent stand a good chance of being widely read. They are no longer obliged to seek publication in

France, the United States or Spain, although Barcelona has emerged as an important publishing centre for Latin-American literature. The improvement in the standard of writing, the development of large-scale commercial publishing, the emergence of a literate middle class in certain areas means that it is possible to earn a living by writing, although those who are fortunate enough to do so remain few in number.

There is no doubt that the arid, sterile and unfavourable environment in which many nineteenth-century writers lived and worked has now been transformed. When we look back at the tragedy of a Hostos, of an Asunción Silva or an Echeverría, we can only be amazed that they wrote at all. Latin America remains under-developed, a prey to exploitation; there are still authoritarian regimes which practise censorship. Yet as far as literature is concerned, one cannot help being optimistic. Step by step over the last two centuries writers have slowly freed their imaginations from the heritage of colonialism. Latin America may be economically backward, but no-one can now say this of her literature.

NOTES

INTRODUCTION

Page 2

1 Bernal Díaz del Castillo, *Historia verdadera de la conquista de la Nueva España*
Porrúa, Mexico, 1960), p. 428.

Page 3

1 *Libro de Chilam Balam de Chumayel*, ed. Antonio Mediz Bolio (ediciones de la
Universidad Nacional Autónoma, Mexico, 1941), p. 26.
2 *Ibid.* p. 25.

Page 4

1 *Poma de Ayala*, 'Las primeras edades del Perú', an interpretative study by
Julio C. Tello (publicaciones del museo de antropología, Lima, 1939), p. 28.
2 *Creole*: refers to Spanish Americans of European descent but born in America.

Page 5

1 *Mestizo*: refers to Spanish Americans of part Spanish, part Indian descent.

Page 7

1 Quoted by Miguel Léon-Portilla, *Las literaturas precolombinas de México*,
(Pormaca, Peru, Mexico, 1964), p. 88.
2 *Ibid.* p. 30.

Page 10

1 Bernal Díaz del Castillo, *Historia verdadera de la conquista de la Nueva España*,
pp. 171–2.

Page 11

1 *Ibid.* p. 149.
2 *Parte primera de la Crónica del Perú* (Seville, 1553).

Page 13

1 Letter of Bartolomé de las Casas printed as Appendix IV to Antonio María
Fabié, *Vida y escritos de Don Fray Bartolomé de las Casas, obispo de Chiapa* (Madrid,
1879), II, 52.

Page 15

1 *Obras del Padre José de Acosta: Estudio preliminar y edición del P. Francisco
Mateos* (Madrid, 1954), p. 38.

Page 16

1 *Ibid.* p. 26.

Page 18

1 Irving, A. Leonard, *Books of the Brave*, p. 81.
2 I. A. Leonard, *Baroque Times in Old Mexico*, chapter VI.

Page 19

1 *Infortunios de Alonzo Ramírez, descríbelos D. Carlos de Sigüenza y Góngora*, Collection of rare and curious books dealing with America (Madrid, 1902), XX, 73.

Page 20

1 Quoted in Leonard, *Baroque Times*, p. 150, and untranslatable.

Page 21

1 Quoted *ibid.* p. 209.

Page 23

1 *Ibid.* pp. 188–9.

CHAPTER I

Page 28

1 Mariano Picón Salas, *A Cultural History of Spanish America*, pp. 159–60.

Page 29

1 M. Bataillon summarises the evidence for the authorship in the introduction to *Carrió de la Vandera: 'Lazarillo de ciegos caminantes'* (Travaux et mémoires de l'Institut de Hautes Etudes de l'Amérique Latine, no. 8, Paris, 1962).

Page 40

1 García Moreno was a scholar and this generalisation cannot apply to him.

Page 43

1 Parts of Pablo Neruda's *Canto general*, written in the 1940s, could properly be considered as the most recent examples of this tradition.

CHAPTER 2

Page 46

1 These groups are mentioned by Marguerite C. Suárez-Murias in *La novela romántica en Hispanoamérica* (New York, 1963).
2 Quoted *ibid.* pp. 64–5.

Page 47

1 *Dogma socialista y otras páginas políticas* (Angel Estrada y Cia, Buenos Aires, 1958), p. 92.

Page 48

1 Revolution here refers to the Independence.

Page 49

1 First published in *Rimas* (1837).

Page 50

1 E. Martínez Estrada, *Muerte y transfiguración de Martín Fierro*, 2nd ed. (2 vols. Fondo de cultura económica, Mexico, Buenos Aires, 1958), II, 129.

2 *Chiripá:* leather apron which passes between the legs and which is worn by the gaucho.

3 *Achuradora:* woman who extracts the entrails from a dead animal.

Page 51

1 The 'unitarios' or supporters of a centralised Argentina were the opponents of Rosas, who was a Federalist.

Page 52

1 *Dogma socialista*, p. 93.

Page 55

1 See, for example, Martínez Estrada, *Radiografía de la Pampa* (2 vols. Losada, Buenos Aires, 1942).

Page 56

1 Quoted by Suárez-Murias, *La novela romántica*, p. 76.

Page 57

1 *Mashorca* [literally 'more hanging'] was the nickname given to the Rosas police.

Page 58

1 Lavalle was the defeated enemy of Rosas.

Page 59

1 Written in 1839 and published, with alterations, in 1880.

2 An 1817 treaty had set up a tribunal (the Mixed Arbitration Tribunal), composed of Spaniards and Englishmen, designed to deal with infractions of the abolition of slave trading.

Page 61

1 Mentioned by J. A. Portuondo, *Bosquejo histórico de las letras cubanas* (Havana, 1960).

2 As such, he appears as a character in *Prim*, one of the *Episodios nacionales* by the Spanish novelist Galdós.

Page 63

1 Club in which talks and discussions were held.

2 Quoted by Suárez-Murias, *La novela romántica*, pp. 88–9, from a speech by the President of the *Ateneo*.

Page 64

1 From the introduction to *Lanza y Sable*.
2 From a letter quoted in the prologue by Emir Rodríguez Monegal to *Nativa* (Biblioteca Artigas, Montevideo, 1964).

Page 65

1 See the prologue by Emir Rodríguez Monegal to *Nativa*, for an extensive consideration of this point.

Page 67

1 *Costumbrismo:* refers to a type of literature which concentrates on the description of manners.

Page 68

1 'El desastre del 13' refers to the defeat of Peru by Chile and the Chilean occupation of Lima in January 1881.
2 *Cartas inéditas de don Ricardo Palma*, Introduccíon y notas de Rubén Vargas Ugarte S.J. (Lima, 1964), p. 13.

Page 69

1 *Ibid.* p. 41.

Page 70

1 From 'Un predicador de lujo', *Tradiciones peruanas completas* (Aguilar, Madrid, 1964), pp. 789–90.

Page 71

1 'Poesía épica y poesía lírica', from *La literatura nacional*, I, 277–8.

Page 72

1 Quoted by Suárez-Murias, *La novela romántica*, p. 191.
2 *Zarco* means 'blue-eyed' and is the nickname of the villain.

CHAPTER 3

Page 75

1 No-one has dealt with the background to *Martín Fierro* better than E. Martínez Estrada in *Muerte y transfiguración de Martín Fierro*.

Page 76

1 Introduction to *Santos Vega* (Paris, 1872).
2 See *Poesía gauchesca*, anthology compiled by Jorge Luis Borges and Adolfo Bioy Casares (2 vols. Fondo de cultura económica, Mexico, Buenos Aires, 1955), II, 358.

Page 77

1 Quoted by Martínez Estrada, *Muerte y transfiguración*, II, 209.
2 J. L. Borges, *El Gaucho Martín Fierro* (Diamante, London, 1964), p. 23.

Page 78

1 The editions and the reception of critics are discussed by Martínez Estrada, *Muerte y transfiguración*, I, 414–53.
2 Included in *Poesía gauchesca*, comp. Borges and Casares, II, 576.

Page 80

1 Martínez Estrada, *Muerte y transfiguración*, I, 188–200.
2 *Hacienda* is used here in its original meaning of cattle.

Page 81

1 Included in *Poesía gauchesca*, comp. Borges and Casares, II, 633.

CHAPTER 4

Page 92

1 Adolfo Prieto, *Literatura autobiográfica argentina*, 2nd ed. (Jorge Alvarez, Buenos Aires, 1966), p. 148.

Page 93

1 *Ibid.*

Page 94

1 Leopoldo Zea, *The Latin American Mind* (University of Oklahoma Press, 1963).

Page 98

1 Included in *Páginas libres* (Paris, 1894), p. 72.

Page 99

1 *Páginas libres*, p. 154.
2 *Ibid.* p. 22.
3 *Ibid.* p. 243.

Page 100

1 'Pántum sin rima', from *Minúsculas*.

Page 101

1 From *Grafitos* (Paris, 1937).
2 *Chonta:* a kind of palm.
3 In *Baladas peruanas* (Santiago, 1935).

Page 102

1 *Leyendas y recortes* (Lima, 1893), p. 164.

Page 104

1 *Obras completas* (26 vols. Editorial Nacional de Cuba, 1966), XX, 324.
2 *Ibid.* XX, 459.

Page 105

1 'Mi raza', *Patria* (New York, 1893); *Obras completas*, II, 298–300.
2 *Obras completas*, XV, 8.
3 *Ibid.* XV, 367.
4 From 'Odio del mar', *Versos libres*.

Page 107

1 *Ibid.* XVI, 131.

Page 109

1 *Ibid.* XVI, 105.
2 *Obras completas*, XVI, 85.

Page 112

1 *Albarico:* type of palm.
2 *Obras completas*, VIII, 216–17.

Page 114

1 *Sociedad de la Igualdad:* a progressive society which attacked the government of Montt.

Page 118

1 From his essay, 'Nuestra America', *Obras completas*.

CHAPTER 5
Page 119
1 Rubén Darío *Obras completas* (5 vols. Aguado, Madrid, 1950–5), II, 21.

Page 120

1 Quoted by John M. Fein, *Modernismo in Chilean Literature* (Duke University Press, Durham, N.C., 1965).

Page 122

1 From 'Victor Hugo', included in *Poesías de la primera época (1876–91)* and in *Poesías completas* (3rd ed. Porrúa, Mexico, 1952).

Page 123

1 *El Modernismo. Notas de un curso*, ed. R. Gullón and E. Fernández Méndez (Madrid, 1962).
2 Quoted in his 'Sobre el concepto del modernismo', *España en América* (Estudios de la Universidad de Puerto Rico, 1955), p. 176.
3 'Después del Carnaval', *Obras completas* IV, 772.

Page 125

1 *Obras completas*, IV, 875.

Page 126

1 Reprinted in the prologue to Silva, *Poesías completas* (Aguilar, Madrid, 1952), and originally written as a preface to the first edition.

Page 129

1 See note, *Poesías completas*, p. 196.

Page 130

1 'Crepúsculo', *ibid*. pp. 45–7.

Page 135

1 Gutiérrez Nájera, *Cuentos completas* (F.C.E., Mexico, 1958), pp. 131–4.

Page 144

1 'El Sátiro y el Centauro', *Obras completas*, IV, 78–81.

CHAPTER 6

Page 163

1 Quoted by Fein, *Modernismo in Chilean Literature*, p. 116.

Page 167

1 From *Alma América*, first published in 1906, and included in *Obras completas* (Mexico, 1954).
2 *Criollista* from *criollo*.

Page 168

1 Antonio de Undurraga, *Pezoa Véliz* (Santiago, 1951), pp. 188–9.

Page 176

1 *Caciquismo*: domination by a *cacique* [boss].

Page 181

1 See Augusto d'Halmar, *Memorias de un tolstoyano*; also, Fernando Alegría, *Las fronteras del realismo: literatura chilena del siglo XX* (Zig-Zag, Santiago, 1962).

Page 185

1 *Ladino*: Spanish-speaking inhabitant with Indian blood in his veins.

Page 187

1 *Letras y letrados de Hispano-America* (Paris, 1908), pp. 61–2.

Page 188

1 *Obras completas* (Epesa, Madrid, 1952), p. xxx.

Page 191

1 *Gringo:* in the Argentine refers to a foreigner, particularly to an Italian.

CHAPTER 7

Page 202

1 *Mezcal:* a liquor made from cactus.

Page 212

1 *Totumo, merecure:* trees native to the high plains of Venezuela.
2 *Talisayo:* Indian cock.
3 *Paraulata:* type of bird.
4 *Guirirí:* type of wild duck.
5 *Corocora:* type of coco palm.

Page 213

1 *Machismo:* from *macho,* manly or virile, is deep-rooted in Latin-American attitudes. Apart from the obvious sexual connotations, the word implies a violent imposition of one's own will over all rivals.

Page 214

1 *Sarrapia:* tree whose seed is used for snuff and which is also valuable as timber.

Page 222

1 The *Decálogo* is included in the Crisol selection of Quiroga's stories— *Cuentos escogidos* (3rd ed. Aguilar, 1962).

Page 223

1 *Chiripá:* leather apron, worn by the gaucho. It passes between the legs and acts as a protection for clothes when riding.
2 *Tosca:* pool formed in limestone.

Page 224

1 *Obras completas* (Emecé, Buenos Aires, 1962), p. 27.
2 *Ibid.* pp. 742–3.

Page 227

1 *Tero:* long-legged white bird (*Vanellus cayenensis*).

CHAPTER 8

Page 231

1 I have dealt with this in more detail in *The Modern Culture of Latin America* (Pall Mall, 1967).

Page 232

1 From *El montuvio ecuatoriano* (Imán, Buenos Aires, 1937), p. 60.

Page 233

1 *Gamonal:* like *cacique*, it means boss or overlord.

Page 239

1 Ecuadorian money unit.

Page 243

1 *Chicha:* fermented maize drink.

Page 244

1 *Yaya:* 'grandfather'.

Page 245

1 *Mashca:* flour of toasted grain; *cuchipapa:* type of potato.

CHAPTER 9

Page 261

1 Gloria Videla, *El Ultraísmo* (Gredos, Madrid, 1963).

Page 262

1 See Videla, *ibid*.

Page 266

1 From an appendix included in 'Muerte sin fin' (Imprenta-Universitaria, Mexico, 1952).

Page 270

1 The title is an invention.

Page 271

1 Quoted by Fernández Retamar in his introduction to Vallejo's *Poesías completas* (Casa de las Americas, La Habana, 1965), pp. xiv–xv.

Page 275

1 *Trilce*, p. xv.

Page 279

1 Fernández Retamar, in his introduction to Vallejo's *Poesías completas*, p. xvi.

Page 280

1 Quoted by Emir Rodríguez Monegal, *El viajero inmóvil* (Buenos Aires, 1966), p. 90; and included originally as an editorial in the third number of Neruda's magazine, *Caballo verde para la poesía*.

Page 281

1 Rodríguez Monegal, *El viajero inmóvil*, p. 65.
2 The relation between the poems and Neruda's experience is dealt with by Rodríguez Monegal, *ibid.*

Page 289

1 Quoted by Rodríguez Monegal, *ibid.* p. 155.

Page 290

1 *Fulgor y muerte de Joaquín Murieta* [*Brilliance and Death of Joaquín Murieta*] was first produced in Santiago in 1967.

Page 291

1 *Los signos en rotación* (Sur, Buenos Aires, 1965).
2 *Ibid.*

Page 292

1 *El arco y la lira* (Fondo de cultura económica, Mexico, 1956), p. 264.
2 *Los signos en rotación.*

Page 296

1 *El laberinto de la soledad* (3rd ed. Fondo de cultura económica, Mexico, 1959), p. 164.
2 From 'La víbora' in *Poemas y anti-poemas.*

Page 297

1 From *La pieza oscura, 1955–62* (Editorial Universitaria, Santiago, 1963).

Page 298

1 See Raúl H. Castagnino, *El teatro de Roberto Arlt* (La Plata, 1964).

CHAPTER 10

Page 305

1 See Ana María Barranechea, *Borges, the Labyrinth Maker* (New York University Press, 1965), p. 152.
2 *Historia universal de la infamia* (Emecé, Losada, Buenos Aires), Introduction, p. 10.

Page 306

1 The stories in these collections were written over a period of years, from 1938 onwards.

Page 307

1 G. S. Fraser, *News from South America* (London, 1949), p. 175.

374 *Notes*

Page 309

1 La Recoleta: cemetery of Buenos Aires.

Page 310

1 I have dealt with their emphasis on 'authenticity' in my book, *The Modern Culture of Latin America.*
2 This term has recently been coined to categorise novels which use myth and legend.

Page 314

1 From a prologue to the edition published for the Festival de Libro Cubano (Lima, Peru, no date), p. 12.

Page 318

1 See epilogue to the novel.

Page 319

1 *Achicoria:* plant native to Cuba.

Page 323

1 Preface to novel (2nd ed. 1958).
2 *Notas de un novelista* (Emecé, Buenos Aires, 1954), p. 77.

Page 324

1 *El escritor y sus fantasmas* (2nd ed. Aguilar, Buenos Aires, 1964), p. 17. He is referring especially to the 'Informe sobre ciegos'.

Page 337

1 Also discussed in Chapter 8.

Page 338

1 The terms *macho* and *machismo* are defined in note to page 213.

Page 341

1 See introduction to *Canto Kechwa* (Lima, 1938).

Page 351

1 Wetbacks: Mexicans who illegally crossed to the United States to work, usually by swimming the Río Grande.

Page 353

1 *Confrontaciones: los narradores ante el público* (Joaquín Mortiz, Mexico, 1966), pp. 137–55.

Page 354

1 Adolfo López Mateos and Gustavo Díaz Ordaz: two former Mexican Presidents.

Page 355

1 Fuentes has also written the Jamesian story, *Aura* (Era, Mexico, 1962).

READING LISTS

The following books, listed under the titles of the relevant chapters, are readily available in bookshops or libraries. Details of works or editions not so available are given in the Notes to the text (pp. 364–74).

INTRODUCTION

General Background

Durand, J. *La transformación social del conquistador.* 2 vols. Porrúa y Obregón, Mexico, 1953.

Hanke, Lewis. *The Spanish Struggle for Justice in the Conquest of America.* University of Philadelphia Press, 1949.

Herring, Hubert. *A History of Latin America from the Beginnings to the Present.* 2nd ed. Knopf, New York, 1963.

Kirkpatrick, F. A. *Los conquistadores españoles.* 7th ed. Espasa-Calpe (Austral), Buenos Aires, 1960.

Lazo, Raimundo. *Historia de la literatura hispanoamericana.* Vol. 1, 1492–1780. Porrúa, Mexico, 1965.

Leonard, Irving A. *Baroque Times in Old Mexico.* University of Michigan Press, Ann Arbor, 1959.

—— *Books of the Brave.* Harvard University Press, Cambridge, Mass., 1949. 2nd ed. Gordian Press Inc., New York, 1964.

Moses, Bernard. *The Establishment of Spanish Rule in America.* Cooper Square, New York, 1965.

Nicholson, Irene. *Firefly in the Night A Study of Ancient Mexican Poetry and Symbolism.* Faber and Faber, London, 1959.

Parry, J. H. *The Spanish Seaborne Empire.* Hutchinson, London, 1966.

Pendle, George. *A History of Latin America.* Penguin Books, London, 1963.

Pfandl, Ludwig. *Sor Juana Inés de la Cruz, La Décima Musa de México.* Instituto de Investigaciones Estéticas, Mexico, 1963.

Picón Salas, Mariano. *A Cultural History of Spanish America from Conquest to Independence.* University of California Press, Berkeley and Los Angeles, 1962.

Texts

Pre-Columbian and post-conquest Indian literatures

Asturias, Miguel Angel (ed.). *Poesía precolombina.* Fabril, Buenos Aires, 1960.

Garibay, Angel M. *La literatura de los Aztecas.* Joaquín Mortiz, Mexico, 1964.

León-Portilla, Miguel. *The Broken Spears, The Aztec Account of the Conquest of Mexico.* Constable, London, 1962.

—— *Las literaturas precolombinas de México.* Pormaca, Peru, Mexico, 1964.

Libro de Chilam Balam de Chumayel. Ed. Antonio Mediz Bolio. Ediciones de la Universidad Nacional Autónoma, Mexico, 1911.

Poma de Ayala, 'Las primeras edades del Perú'. An interpretative study by Julio C. Tello. Museo de Antropología, Lima, 1939.

Popol Vuh. Ed. A. Recinos. 2nd ed. Fondo de cultura económica, Mexico, 1953.

Rabinal Achi. Adaptación de José Antonio Villacorta. Editorial Noval, Buenos Aires, 1944.

Sahagún, Bernardino de. *Historia de las Cosas de Nueva España.* 4 vols. Porrúa, Mexico, 1956.

Hispanic

Acosta, Padre José de. *Obras: Estudio preliminar y edición del P. Francisco Mateos.* Madrid, 1954.

Cabeza de Vaca, Alvar Núñez. *Naufragios y comentarios.* 4th ed. Espasa-Calpe (Austral), 1957.

Cieza de León, Pedro de. *Parte primera de la Chronica del Peru.* Seville, 1553.

Colón, Cristobal. *Diario de Colón; Libro de la primera navegación y descubrimiento de las Indias.* Ed. Carlos Sanza. Madrid, 1962.

Cortés, Hernán. *Cartas de Relación.* Preface by Manuel Alcalá. Porrúa, Mexico, 1960.

De las Casas, Bartolomé. *Tratados.* Fonde de cultura económica, Mexico, 1966.

Díaz del Castillo, Bernal. *Historia verdadera de la conquista de la Nueva España.* Porrúa, Mexico, 1960.

Ercilla, Alonso de. *La Araucana.* Editorial del Pacífico, Santiago, 1956.

Garcilaso de la Vega, 'El Inca'. *Comentarios Reales.* 6th ed. Espasa-Calpe (Austral), 1961.

González de Eslava. *Coloquios espirituales y sacramentales.* 2 vols. Porrúa, Mexico, 1958.

Juana Inés de la Cruz, Sor. *Obras completas.* 4 vols. Fondo de cultura económica, Mexico, 1962.

―― *Antología.* Ed. Elías L. Rivers. Biblioteca Anaya, Salamanca, Madrid, Barcelona, 1965.

· Núñez de Pineda y Bascuñán, Francisco. *Cautiverio feliz y razón de las guerras dilatadas de Chile.* Preface by D. Barros Atana. Colección de historiadores de Chile, Santiago, 1863.

Rodríguez Freile, J. *El carnero de Bogotá.* Bogotá, 1884.

Sigüenza y Góngora, Carlos de. *Infortunios de Alonso Ramírez.* Included in the anthology, *La novela de Mexico Colonial,* ed. Antonio Castro Leal. Mexico, 1965.

I: INDEPENDENCE AND LITERARY EMANCIPATION

General Background

Humphreys, R. A. and Lynch, J. *The Origins of Latin American Revolutions, 1808–1826.* Knopf, New York, 1966.

Robertson, William Spence. *Rise of the Spanish–American Republics.* Collier, London, 1961.

Whitaker, A. P. (ed.) *Latin America and the Enlightenment.* 2nd ed. Great Seal Books, Cornell University Press, Ithaca, New York, 1961.

Texts

Bello, Andrés. *El pensamiento vivo de Andrés Bello.* Ed. G. Arciniegas. Losada, Buenos Aires, 1946.
—— *Antología poética.* Angel Estrada y Cia, Buenos Aires, 1952.
Bolívar, Simón. *Obras completas.* 2 vols. Lex, La Habana, 1947.
Carrió de la Vandera, Alonso. *Lazarillo de ciegos caminantes.* 2nd ed. Espasa-Calpe (Austral), Buenos Aires, 1947. *Ibid.*, ed. and with introduction by M. Bataillon. Travaux et mémoires de l'Institut de Hautes Etudes de l'Amérique Latine, no. 8, Paris, 1962.
Fernández de Lizardi, José Joaquín. *Don Catrín de la Fachenda.* Editorial cultura, Mexico, 1944.
—— *El Periquillo Sarniento.* 4th ed. Porrúa, Mexico, 1962.
Heredia, José María de. *Poesías completas.* 2 vols. La Habana, 1940.
Olmedo, José Joaquín de. *Poesías completas.* F.C.E., Mexico, 1947.
Santa Cruz y Espejo, Francisco Eugenio de. *El nuevo Luciano de Quito, 1779.* Clásicos Ecuatorianos, Quito, 1944.

2: LITERATURE AND NATIONALISM
General Background

Alegría, Fernando. *Historia de la novela hispanoamericana.* 3rd ed. Ediciones de Andrea (Manuales Studium), 1966.
Anderson Imbert, Enrique. *Historia de la literatura hispanoamericana.* Vol. 1. Fondo de cultura económica, Mexico, 1961.
Brushwood, J. S. *The Romantic Novel in Mexico.* University of Missouri Studies, Columbia, Missouri, 1954.
Portuondo, J. A. *Bosquejo histórico de las letras cubanas.* Havana, 1960.
Suárez-Murias, Marguerite C. *La novela romántica en Hispanoamérica.* New York, 1963.

Texts

Acevedo Díaz, Eduardo. *Ismael.* Prologue by Roberto de Ibáñez. Ministerio de Instrucción Pública, Montevideo, 1953.
—— *Nativa.* Prologue by E. Rodríguez Monegal. Biblioteca Artigas, Montevideo, 1964.
—— *Grito de gloria.* Ministerio de Instrucción Pública y Provisión social, Montevideo, 1964.
—— *Lanza y sable.* Ministerio de Instrucción Pública y Provisión social, Montevideo, 1965.
Altamirano, Ignacio Manuel. *El Zarco. La navidad en las montañas.* Porrúa, Mexico, 1960.
—— *Clemencia y La navidad en las montañas.* Porrúa, Mexico, 1964.
Echeverría, Esteban. *Dogma socialista y otras páginas políticas.* Angel Estrada y Cia, Buenos Aires, 1958.
—— *La cautiva y El matadero.* 7th ed. Sopena, Buenos Aires, 1962.
Mármol, José. *Amalia.* Estrada, Buenos Aires, 1944.
Palma, Ricardo. *Tradiciones peruanas completas.* Aguilar, Madrid, 1964.
—— *Cartas inéditas de don Ricardo Palma.* Introducción y notas de Rubén Vargas Ugarte S. J. Lima, 1964.
Sarmiento, D. *Facundo: Civilización y barbarie.* Espasa-Calpe, Buenos Aires, 1958.

3: LITERATURE AND AMERICAN EXPERIENCE
General Background

Alegría, Fernando. *Historia de la novela hispanoamericana.* 3rd ed. Ediciones de Andrea (Manuales Studium), Mexico, 1966.

Borges, J. L. *El Gaucho Martín Fierro.* Diamante, London, 1964.

Cometta Manzoni, Aida. *El indio en la poesía de América española.* Joaquín Torres, Buenos Aires, 1939.

Martínez Estrada, E. *Muerte y transfiguración de Martín Fierro.* 2 vols. 2nd ed. Fondo de cultura económica, Mexico, Buenos Aires, 1958.

Meléndez, Concha. *La novela indianista en Hispanoamérica (1832–89).* Ediciones de la Universidad de Puerto Rico, Rio Piedras, 1961.

Suárez-Murias, Marguerite C. *La novela romántica en Hispanoamérica.* New York, 1963.

Anthologies

Borges, Jorge Luis, and Bioy Casares, Adolfo (compilers). *Antología Poesía gauchesca.* 2 vols. Fondo de cultura económica, Mexico, Buenos Aires, 1955. (This includes all the major gauchesque works.)

Menéndez y Pelayo, M. *Antología de poetas hispanoamericanos.* Madrid, 1893–5.

Texts

Galván, Manuel de Jesús. *Enriquillo.* Las Américas, New York, 1964.

González, Joaquín, V. *Mis montañas.* Ed. G. Ara. 7th ed. Editorial Kapeluse, Buenos Aires, 1965.

Hernández, José. *Martín Fierro.* 8th ed. Losada, Buenos Aires, 1953.

Isaacs, Jorge María. *Obras completas I.* Ediciones Academicas, Medellín, 1966.

Mansilla, Lucio V. *Una excursión a los indios ranqueles.* Prologue by C. A. Leumann. 3rd ed. Espasa-Calpe (Austral), Buenos Aires, 1948.

Mera, Juan León de. *Cumandá.* Espasa-Calpe (Austral), Buenos Aires, 1961.

4: TO CHANGE SOCIETY
General Background

Castro, Raúl Silva. *Alberto Blest Gana.* Santiago, 1955.

Prieto, Adolfo. *Literatura autobiográfica argentina.* 2nd ed. Jorge Alvarez, Buenos Aires, 1966.

Zea, Leopoldo. *The Latin American Mind.* University of Oklahoma Press, 1963.

Texts

Blest Gana, Alberto. *Martín Rivas.* Zig-Zag, Santiago, 1956.

—— *Durante la Reconquista.* Zig-Zag, Santiago, 1960.

—— *Los transplantados.* Zig-Zag, Santiago, 1961.

—— *El ideal de un calavera.* Zig-Zag, Santiago, 1964.

Cambaceres, Eugenio. *Obras completas.* Santa Fé, Argentina, 1956.

González Prada, Manuel. *Minúsculas.* Lima, 1900.

—— *Exóticas.* Lima, 1911.

—— *Páginas libres.* Paris, 1894.

—— *Baladas peruanas.* Santiago, 1935.

—— *Grafitos.* Paris, 1937.

—— *Propaganda y ataque.* New ed. Buenos Aires, 1939.

Martí, José. *Obras completas*. 26 vols. Editorial Nacional de Cuba, 1966.
Matto de Turner, Clorinda. *Aves sin nido*. Buenos Aires, 1889.
—— *Leyendas y recortes*. Lima, 1893.
Montalvo, Juan. *Los siete tratados*. Garnier, Paris, 1912.
—— *Capítulos que se le olviadaron a Cervantes*. Garnier, Paris, 1921.

5: MODERNISM
General Background

Fein, John M. *Modernismo in Chilean Literature*. Duke University Press, Durham, N.C., 1965.
Gullón, Ricardo. *Direcciones del modernismo*. Gredos, Madrid, 1963.
Henríquez Ureña, Max. *Breve historia del modernismo*. 2nd ed. Fondo de cultura económica, Mexico, 1962.
Onís, Federico de. *España en América*. Estudio de la Universidad de Puerto Rico, 1955.
Salinas, Pedro. *La poesía de Rubén Darío*. 2nd ed. Losada, Buenos Aires, 1958.

Texts

Agustini, Delmira. *Poesías completas*. 3rd ed. Losada, Buenos Aires, 1962.
Casal, Julián del. *Poesías completas*. Ministerio de Educación, Havana, 1945.
Darío, Rubén. *Obras completas*. 5 vols. Aguado, Madrid, 1950–5.
—— *Obras poéticas completas*. 10th ed. Aguilar, Madrid, 1967.
Díaz Mirón, Salvador. *Poesías completas*. 3rd ed. Porrúa, Mexico, 1952.
González Martínez, Enrique. *Antología poética*. 3rd ed. Espasa-Calpe (Austral), Buenos Aires and Mexico, 1944.
Gutiérrez Nájera, Manuel. *Poesías completas*. 2 vols. Porrúa, Mexico, 1953.
—— *Cuentos completos*. Fondo de cultura económica, Mexico, 1958.
Herrera y Reissig, Julio. *Poesías completas*. 3rd ed. Losada, Buenos Aires, 1958.
Jaimes Freyre, Ricardo. *Poesías completas*. Claridad, Buenos Aires, 1944.
Larreta, Enrique. *La gloria de don Ramiro*. In *Obras completas*, Plenitude, Madrid, 1958.
Nervo, Amado. *Obras completas*. 5 vols. Aguilar, Madrid, 1950–5.
Palma, Clemente. *Cuentos malévolos*. Barcelona, 1904.
Silva, José Asunción. *Poesías completas*. Aguilar, Madrid, 1952.

6: THE REDISCOVERY OF THE NEW WORLD
General Background

Alegría, Fernando. *Las fronteras del realismo: literatura chilena del siglo XX*. Zig-Zag, Santiago, 1962.
Franco, J. *The Modern Culture of Latin America*. Pall Mall, London, 1967.

Texts

Arguedas, Alcides. *Pueblo enfermo* and *Raza de bronce*. Included in *Obras completas*. 2 vols. Aguilar, Mexico, 1959.
Blanco Fombona, Rufino. *Obras selectas*. Ed. Gabaldón Márquez. Ediciones Edime, Madrid and Caracas, 1958.
Carrasquilla, Tomás. *Obras completas*. Epesa, Madrid, 1952.

Chocano, José Santos. *Obras completas.* Aguilar, Mexico, 1954.

Fernández Moreno, Baldomero. *Antología.* 6th ed. Espasa-Calpe (Austral), Buenos Aires, 1954.

Gálvez, Manuel. *Obras escogidas.* Aguilar, Madrid, 1949.

Gamboa, Federico. *Obras completas.* Fondo de cultura económica, Mexico, 1965.

García Calderón, Ventura. *La venganza del cóndor.* Mundo Latino, Madrid, 1924.

Gerchunoff, Albert. *Los gauchos judíos.* Biblioteca de escritores argentinos, Buenos Aires, 1936.

Latorre, Mariano. *Sus mejores cuentos.* 3rd ed. Nascimento, Santiago, 1962.

Lillo, Baldomero. *Sub sole.* 3rd ed. Nascimento, Santiago, 1943.

—— *Sub terra.* 5th ed. Nascimento, Santiago, 1956.

López Velarde, Ramón. *Poesías completas y el minutero.* Porrúa, Mexico, 1957.

Lugones, Leopoldo. *Obras poéticas completas.* 3rd ed. Aguilar, Madrid, 1959.

Martínez, Luis. *A la costa.* 2nd ed. Casa de la Cultura Ecuatoriana, Quito. 1959.

Payró, Roberto. *Pago chico.* 5th ed. Losada, Buenos Aires, 1943.

—— *Divertidas aventuras del nieto de Juan Moreira.* Losada, Buenos Aires, 1957.

—— *El casamiento de Laucha.* 5th ed. Losada, Buenos Aires, 1961.

Pezoa Véliz, Carlos. *Antología.* Zig-Zag, Santiago, 1957.

Reyles, Carlos. *Beba.* Dornaleche y Reyes impresore, Montevideo, 1894.

—— *El embrujo de Sevilla.* Espasa-Calpe (Austral), Buenos Aires, 1944.

—— *El terruño.* Losada, Buenos Aires, 1945.

Valdelomar, Abraham. *Los hijos del sol.* Editorial Enforion, Ciudad de los Reyes del Peru, 1921.

Viana, Javier de. *Campo.* Ediciones de la Banda Oriental. Montevideo, 1966.

7: REGIONALISM IN THE NOVEL AND SHORT STORY
General Background

Alegría, Fernando. *Historia de la novela hispanoamericana.* 3rd ed. Ediciones de Andrea (Manuales Studium), Mexico, 1966.

Brushwood, J. S. *Mexico in its Novel.* Austin, Texas, 1966.

Dunham, Lowell. *Rómulo Gallegos, vida y obra.* Ediciones de Andrea (Manuales Studium), Mexico, 1957.

Previtali, Giovanni. *Ricardo Güiraldes and 'Don Segundo Sombra'.* Hispanic Institute, New York, 1963.

Rodríguez Monegal, Emir. *Narradores de esta América.* Alfa, Montevideo (n.d.).

Texts

Amorim, Enrique. *El caballo y su sombra.* Losada, Buenos Aires, 1945.

—— *El paisano Aguilar.* Siglo Veinte, Buenos Aires, 1946.

—— *La desembocadura.* Losada, Buenos Aires, 1958.

Azuela, Mariano. *Obras completas.* Introduction by Francisco Monterde. 3 vols. Mexico, 1958–60.

Gallegos, Rómulo. *Obras completas.* 2 vols. Aguilar, Madrid, 1958.

Güiraldes, Ricardo. *Obras completas.* Emecé, Buenos Aires, 1962.

Guzmán, Martín Luis. *El águila y la serpiente.* In *Obras completas de Martín Luis Guzmán.* 2 vols. Mexico, 1961.

Lynch, Benito. *El romance de un gaucho.* Kraft, Buenos Aires, 1961.

—— *El inglés de los güesos.* Troquel, Lumen, Buenos Aires, 1966.

Quiroga, Horacio. *Cuentos escogidos.* Colección Crisol, with prologue by Guillermo de Torre. 3rd ed. Aguilar, 1962.
Rivera, Eustacio. *La vorágine.* 6th ed. Losado, Buenos Aires, 1957.
Romero, José Rubén. *Obras completas.* Mexico, 1957.
Vasconcelos, José. *Obras completas.* 4 vols. Mexico, 1957-61.

8: REALISM AND THE NOVEL
General Background
Alegría, Fernando. *Las fronteras del realismo: literatura chilena del siglo XX.* Zig-Zag, Santiago, 1962.
Cometta Manzoni, Aida. *El indio en la novela de América.* Editorial Futuro, Buenos Aires, 1960.
Rojas, Angel F. *La novela ecuatoriana.* Fondo de cultura económica, Mexico and Buenos Aires, 1948.

Texts
Aguilera Malta, Demetrio, Gallegos Lara, Joaquín, and Gil Gilbert, Enrique. *Los que se van...* 2nd ed. Casa de la Cultura Ecuatoriana, Quito, 1955.
Aguilera Malta, Demetrio. *Don Goyo.* Cenit, Madrid, 1933.
—— *La isla virgen.* Casa de la Cultura Ecuatoriana, Quito, 1954.
Alegría, Ciro. *El mundo es ancho y ajeno.* 20th ed. Losada, Buenos Aires, 1961.
Arguedas, José María. *Yawar Fiesta.* Populibros Peruanos (n.d.).
—— *Los ríos profundos.* Losada, Buenos Aires, 1958.
—— *Todas las sangres.* Losada, Buenos Aires, 1964.
Asturias, Miguel Angel. *Leyendas de Guatemala* and *Hombres de maíz.* Included in Vol. 1 of *Obras escogidas.* 2nd ed. Aguilar, Madrid, 1964.
Castellanos, Rosario. *Balún Canán.* Fondo de cultura económica, Mexico, 1957.
—— *Oficio de tinieblas.* Joaquín Mortíz, Mexico, 1962.
Cuadra, José de la. *El montuvio ecuatoriano.* Imán, Buenos Aires, 1937.
—— *Obras completas.* Casa de la Cultura Ecuatoriana, Quito, 1958.
Gil Gilbert, Enrique. *Nuestro pan.* Librería Vera, Guayaquil, 1942.
Icaza, Jorge. *Cholos.* 2nd ed. Atahualpa, Quito, 1939.
—— *En las calles.* Losada, Buenos Aires, 1944.
—— *Huasipungo.* 2nd ed. Losada, Buenos Aires, 1953.
Pozas, Ricardo. *Juan Pérez Jolote.* 5th ed. Fondo de cultura económica, Mexico, 1965.
Rojas, Manuel. *Obras completas.* Zig-Zag, Santiago, 1961.

9: THE AVANTE-GARDE IN POETRY
General Background
Abril, Xavier. *Vallejo, Ensayo de aproximación crítica.* Buenos Aires, 1958.
Dauster, Frank N. *Ensayos sobre poesía mexicano.* Mexico, 1963.
—— *Historia del teatro hispanoamericano, siglos XIX y XX.* Ediciones de Andreas (Manuales Studium), Mexico, 1966.
Fernández Moreno, César. *La realidad y los papeles.* Aguilar, Madrid, 1961.
Knapp Jones, Willis. *Behind Spanish American Footlights.* University of Texas Press, Austin, London, 1966.

Monguió, Luis. *César Vallejo (1892–1938), Vida y obra—bibliografía—antología.* Hispanic Institute, New York, 1952.

Rodríguez Monegal, E. *El viajero inmóvil.* Buenos Aires, 1966.

Solórzano, Carlos. *Teatro latinoamericano del siglo XX.* Editorial Nueva Visión, Buenos Aires, 1961.

Videla, Gloria. *El ultraísmo.* Gredos, Madrid, 1963.

Xirau, Ramón. *Octavio Paz: el sentido de la palabra.* Joaquín Mortiz, Mexico, 1970.

Anthologies

Paz, Octavio. *Poesía en movimiento, siglo veintiuno.* Mexico, 1966.

Pellegrini, Aldo. *Antología de la poesía viva latinoamericana.* Seix Barral, Barcelona, 1966.

Solórzano, Carlos. *El teatro hispanoamericano contemporáneo.* 2 vols. Fondo de cultura económica, Mexico and Buenos Aires, 1964.

Texts

Neruda, Pablo. *Obras completas.* 2nd ed. Losada, Buenos Aires, 1962.

—— *Obras completas.* 3rd ed. 2 vols. Buenos Aires, 1967.

Paz, Octavio. *El arco y la lira.* Fondo de cultura económica, Mexico, 1956.

—— *Libertad bajo palabra.* Fondo de cultura económica, Mexico, 1960.

—— *El laberinto de la soledad.* 3rd ed. Fondo de cultura económica, Mexico, 1963.

—— *Los signos en rotación.* Sur, Buenos Aires, 1965.

—— *Corriente alterna.* Mexico, 1966.

—— *Ladera este.* Mexico, 1969.

—— *Salamandra.* Mexico, 1966.

Triana, José. *La noche de los asesinos.* La Habana, 1965.

Vallejo, César. *Poesías completas.* Introduction by Fernández Retamar. Casa de las Americas, La Habana, 1965.

—— *Obra poética completa.* Moncloa, Lima, 1968.

10: THE CONTEMPORARY NOVEL AND SHORT STORY

General Background

Alegría, Fernando. *Historia de la novela hispanoamericana.* 3rd ed. Ediciones de Andrea (Manuales Studium), Mexico, 1966.

Harss, L. *Los nuestros.* Sudamericana, Buenos Aires, 1966.

Lafforgue (ed.) *Nueva novela latinoamericana.* I. Buenos Aires, 1969.

Loveluck, J. *La novela hispanoamericana.* Santiago de Chile, 1966.

Ortega, Julio. *La contemplación y la fiesta.* Lima, 1968.

Anthology

Alegría, Fernando. *Novelistas contemporáneos hispanoamericanos.* Heath, Boston, 1964.

Texts

Arévalo Martínez, Rafael. *El hombre que parecía un caballo.* Edición Universitaria, Guatemala, 1951.

Arguedas, José María. *Los ríos profundos.* Losada, Buenos Aires, 1958.

—— *Todas las sangres.* Losada, Buenos Aires, 1964.

Arlt, Roberto. *Novelas completas y cuentos.* Fabril, Buenos Aires, 1963.

Asturias, Miguel Angel. *Obras escogidas.* 3 vols. Aguilar, Madrid, 1955.

Barrios, Eduardo. *Obras completas.* 2 vols. Zig-Zag, Santiago, 1962.

Benedetti, Mario. *La tregua.* Alfa, Montevideo, 1963.
—— *Gracias por el fuego.* Alfa, Montevideo, 1964.
—— *Montevideanos.* Alfa, Montevideo, 1964.
Bombal, Maria. *La amortajada.* 3rd ed. Nascimento, Santiago, 1962.
Borges, Jorge Luis. *Obras completas.* 3 vols. Emecé, Buenos Aires, 1966.
Cabrera Infante, Guillermo. *Tres tristes tigres.* Seix Barral, Barcelona, 1967.
Carpentier, Alejo. *El siglo de las luces.* Ediapsa, Mexico, 1952.
—— *El acoso.* Losada, Buenos Aires, 1956.
—— *El reino de este mundo.* Organizaciñon Continental de los Festivales del Libro,
    Lima, 1958.
—— *Guerra del tiempo.* Ediapsa, Mexico, 1958.
—— *Los pasos perdidos.* Compañía General de Ediciones, Mexico, 1959.
Cortázar, Julio. *Las armas secretas.* Sudamericana, Buenos Aires, 1959.
—— *Rayuela.* Sudamericana, Buenos Aires, 1963.
—— *Final del juego.* 2nd ed. Sudamericana, Buenos Aires, 1964.
—— *Los premios.* 3rd ed. Sudamericana, Buenos Aires, 1965.
—— *Todos los fuegos son fuego.* Sudamericana, Buenos Aires, 1966.
Fuentes, Carlos. *Las buenas conciencias.* 3rd ed. Fondo de cultura económica,
    Mexico, 1961.
—— *La muerte de Artemio Cruz.* Fondo de cultura económica, Mexico, 1962.
—— *La región más transparente.* 4th ed. Fondo de cultura económica, Mexico, 1965.
—— *Cantar de ciegos.* 3rd ed. Joaquín Mortiz, Mexico, 1967.
—— *Cambio de piel.* Joaquín Mortiz, Mexico, 1967.
—— *Zona sagrada.* Siglo veintiuno, Mexico, 1967.
García Márquez, Gabriel. *La hojarasca.* 1st ed. Bogotá (n.d.). Later ed. Montevideo,
    1965.
—— *La mala hora.* Esso, Columbiana, 1962.
—— *Los funerales de la Mamá Grande.* Jalapa, Mexico, 1962.
—— *El coronel no tiene quien le escriba.* 2nd ed. Era, Mexico, 1963.
—— *Cien años de soledad.* Sudamericana, Buenos Aires, 1967.
Lezama Lima, José. *Paradiso.* Contemporáneos, La Habana, 1966.
Mallea, Eduardo. *Notas de un novelista.* Emecé, Buenos Aires, 1954.
—— *Obras completas.* 2 vols. Emecé, Buenos Aires, 1961.
Marechal, Leopoldo. *Adán Buenosayres.* 3rd ed. Sudamericana, Buenos Aires, 1966.
Onetti, Juan Carlos. *El astillero.* Compañía General Fabril Editora, Buenos Aires,
    1961.
—— *Juntacadáveres.* Montevideo, 1965.
—— *El pozo* (1939). Ara, Montevideo, 1965.
—— *Tierra de nadie* (1941). Ediciones de la Banda Oriental, Montevideo, 1965.
Revueltas, José. *El luto humano.* Editorial Mexico, Mexico, 1943.
Roa Bastos, Augusto. *El trueno entre las hojas.* Losada, Buenos Aires, 1961.
—— *Hijo de hombre.* 2nd ed. Losada, Buenos Aires, 1965.
Rulfo, Juan. *Pedro Páramo.* 4th ed. Fondo de cultura económica, Mexico, 1963.
Sábato, Ernesto. *Sobre héroes y tumbas.* 3rd ed. Fabril, Buenos Aires, 1964.
—— *El escritor y sus fantasmas.* 2nd ed. Aguilar, Buenos Aires, 1964.
—— *El túnel.* 2nd ed. Sudamericana, 1967.
Vargas Llosa, Mario. *La ciudad y los perros.* Seix Barral, Barcelona, 1963.
—— *La casa verde.* Seix Barral, Barcelona, 1966.
—— *Los cachorros.* Lumen, Barcelona, 1967.
—— *Conversación en la catedral.* 2 vols. Barcelona, 1969.

INDEX OF AUTHORS

NOTE. Country of origin and dates are given for Spanish–American authors only: asterisked entries denote politicians as opposed to authors.